Assignment: Trouble

ASSIGNMENT: TROUBLE

Foreign Correspondent at Large

Cornell W. Acheson

VANTAGE PRESS
New York / Washington / Atlanta
Los Angeles / Chicago

FIRST EDITION

All rights reserved, including the right of
reproduction in whole or in part in any form.

Copyright © 1984 by Cornell W. Acheson

Published by Vantage Press, Inc.
516 West 34th Street, New York, New York 10001

Manufactured in the United States of America
ISBN: 533-05983-6

Library of Congress Catalog Card No.: 83-90973

To Floyd Henson, Peter, and Ria

Contents

Acknowledgments ix
Introduction xi

I.	Dubious Beginnings	1
II.	Novice into the Deep End	5
III.	To War in a Taxi	19
IV.	Wages of Folly	31
V.	Battle at Rachel's Tomb	37
VI.	All-Points Coverage	47
VII.	Leaving Bleeding Jerusalem	55
VIII.	Overseas Assignment, Fulltime	69
IX.	"Tourism" in Algeria	79
X.	Lull in Cyprus	89
XI.	A Fruitless Garden	99
XII.	Greece, an Unrefreshing Pause	103
XIII.	Pungent Antiquity!	111
XIV.	Through the Back of Beyond	123
XV.	From "How-to" to "What"	135
XVI.	Deadly Mountain Warfare	139
XVII.	Boneyards, Battlefields and Crypts	149
XVIII.	Colonialism's "Terminal" Spasm	155
XIX.	"Characters" and Cobras	165
XX.	"He Who Beats"	175
XXI.	Losers, Good and Bad	183
XXII.	Slave Pits and Palaces	193
XXIII.	Politicians as "Messiahs"	201
XXIV.	Success Story or Silly Season	213
XXV.	Orthodoxy and Animism	225
XXVI.	Uproar, Mayhem and Genteel Spirits	239
XXVII.	"Stay in Your Car!"	249
XXVIII.	"Shark!"	263

XXIX.	Typewriter to Tractor	273
XXX.	Domestic Wildlife	285
XXXI.	Back to the Typewriter	293
XXXII.	On the Air	301
XXXIII.	Led Astray by a Machine	309
XXXIV.	Back on the Air	315
XXXV.	The Devil's Work	321
XXXVI.	Twilight of an Empire	329
XXXVII.	Bloody Ending	339
	Epilogue	347
	Index	349

Acknowledgments

Legions of newspapermen and -women contributed to this chronicle, none of them consciously but all of them crucially, among them, as an elite cadre whose members guided and goaded me as I accumulated its substance and without whom it wouldn't exist: Wendell Phillippi, Fremont Power, Dick Tucker, Gene Pulliam, Jr., Bill Wildhack, all the *Indianapolis News* staff, Morley and Phyllis Cassidy, the *Philadelphia Bulletin* staff, John Stewart, the *Pathfinder News Magazine* staff, Jock Calder from Reuters, Carter Davidson, Jim Pringle, Max Boyd from the Associated Press, Bob Hecox from *Paramount News,* Carl Gossett, Farnsworth Fowle, the *New York Times* staff, Frank Scherschel from *Life,* and many other "old pros."

Many are dead now, as are some of the publications for which they worked. For me they aren't. Some of them are named in this work. All of them are there.

There too are two special "civilians" who propped me up: Lillian Close, born in the dusty distance of South Africa's Free State, whose cultured tastefulness, unlimited skills as a secretary and devotion as a friend served me so well for a decade and more, and Georgia Ruff, without whose experience, talent, and boundless patience my manuscript would have died a-borning.

In addition, grateful acknowledgments are also due to the *Indianapolis News,* the *Tucson Citizen* (formerly the *Tucson Daily Citizen*), and the *Dallas Morning News* for permission to quote from previously printed columns. Acknowledgments are also due the following publications and radio stations, all of which are now, unfortunately, defunct: *Pathfinder News Magazine; Smart Set; Philadelphia Bulletin; New York Herald Tribune; Blackwoods Magazine;* radio station WILZ in St. Petersburg, Florida; Rhodesia Broadcasting Corporation; and the Rhodesia Television Corporation. The author also wishes to extend his thanks to a number of his colleagues for the use of certain personal correspondence.

"Duke" Acheson
Huffman, Texas

Introduction

One of the earliest intimations I had that life would have its stirring moments took the form of a threat to cut my throat.

I was age nine. Skipping homeward after happy moments at a flyblown ice cream emporium on the outskirts of Philadelphia, I had darted off the bustle of Lancaster Pike and into the shadowed calm of a side street.

Here in the genteel hush of Main Line affluence autumn leaves dusted the tarmacadam surface of the lane. On either side, behind ranks of giant oaks, brick and graystone homes loomed beyond velvet lawns, and in the rear livery stables hunched together near tennis courts. Here and there white iron furniture congregated in courtly clumps.

All very stolid, aloof and tranquil. And safe.

At a point where the sight and sound of the pike dropped away and the silence was palpable, that first lesson in what life could be like took place.

With scarcely a sound, out of the rhododendrons and honeysuckle lunged a juvenile in blue overall and green knit cap, a glittering knife in one hand and, quite suddenly, me in the other.

"Listen, boy," he hissed. "Gimme yo' money or ah'm gonna cut yo' froat."

Unworldly as I was, I got the message. And my reflexes were lightning quick. In a flash what I had, he got. Promising he'd "come git" me if I "tol' de cops," he belted me across the ear and lumbered off into the shrubbery. With all my ready money. Fourteen cents.

I made the mile home in what I recall was a straight line and shrieked the details to my father, who promptly "tol' de cops." Who, thank goodness, did nothing.

At that early stage fear moved in with the other accumulating furniture of my mind and grew as later on I invited a few wars and other bizarre excitements to contribute to it. News reporting became my trade; Africa, principally, my "beat." Beginning in the late nineteen-fifties, that continent's people thrashed out from under colonial rule and into the vagaries of independence. It was an exciting period and a violent one.

Early on, I made Rhodesia the home base from which I "covered" much of the continent. As it turned out, few countries in Africa would be a happy choice for a white man to settle. Rhodesia was no exception. By the time the mid-nineteen-seventies arrived, I had had enough of a gory civil war in which rebellious blacks were slowly beating the ruling whites into handing the country over to African control, and I picked up my option to return, with my family and accumulated chattels, to the United States.

If a black man first taught me life could be frightening, and more black men later crushed my hope for a muted old age in a distant land, that's unhappy coincidence. Not a message.

Between these two events there was to be a lot of journalism with here and there what the English might call a "spot of bother." And that's what this account is really all about.

Assignment: Trouble

CHAPTER I

Dubious Beginnings

My career as a newsman began in 1946, when I became a cub reporter for the *Indianapolis News*, in default of work I'd prepared for with the State Department in Washington. I went into World War Two equipped with a science degree in foreign service from Georgetown University. I was demobbed two years later with a lot of brutally practical experience in "foreign service" to go with the degree. And no State Department job.

Sure-footed in English composition, lightly seasoned in journalism as editor of a college paper, and overflowing with misplaced optimism I opted for newspapering. Back home in Indiana with my wife and youngster, I discovered that just to begin I needed all the help I could get. And found the man who had all I needed.

My then father-in-law, Donald Jameson, a man of many parts, all of them unique, knew Mickey McCarty in upper-echelon management at the *Indianapolis News*. At "Pappy" Jameson's request he foisted me onto Herb Hill, managing editor, who hired me at thirty five dollars a week.

I spent the early months tapping out miles of obituaries and social notes and was otherwise glued to the city desk answering phones and rewriting trivial snippets from the competition papers. Sympathetic veterans coached me in our few quiet hours, and I grew in the craft, steadily and painfully. My first "outside" assignment served to underscore just how painfully.

Police radio reported a child had fallen out a window above a busy street, plummeted three stories, and survived. That was all, and I was sent to flesh out the rest of it. I got the address wrong and arrived after competition reporters had been and gone, taking with them all the snapshots of the year-old babe. In the trade, a picture with a tale like this one is 50 percent of the story. Furthermore, the distraught mother refused to talk to any more reporters and I had to interview children who'd been playing in the street at the time.

They saw "this kid," they said, crawling along the windowsill, and when they'd shouted at him to go back, he'd simply thrown himself, giggling, out into space. Thinking quickly, this gaggle of urchins, age six to ten, had clustered together and "caught the kid like a flyball" just before he disintegrated on the sidewalk. So they said. So I did too, quoting "neighbors" as my source. It made a most unusual story on the front page, even without the picture. But when the other papers came out, my career nearly ended prematurely.

The child, it turned out, had indeed fallen the three stories, headed for certain death, but no juvenile heroes had rushed to catch him in flight. He'd landed, bottom up, in a trashcan, had been temporarily transfigured by gooey debris and permanently marked by a cut across the bridge of his nose inflicted by the raw edge of a Heinz tomato soup can.

"Sure was wedged into that can," the mother had told the other reporters. "Had to wear it for I don't know how long afore we figured out how to git it off 'thout takin' his face with it."

There was some measured discussion at the *News* about which was the more acceptable story, with my few supporters insisting the running catch took the honors. But Hill insisted truth took precedence over invention and told me pointedly that I'd do well to recognize the difference.

I sharpened my discrimination, and, while I rarely got a story as exhilarating as the human "flyball," I certainly covered a gamut of the day's events.

I exposed unsafe conditions at the municipal dog pound, was in on the collapse of the City Parks Department potting shed, and pilloried the State Highway Department for a miscalculation that resulted in its trying to build a roadway through the lounge of a downtown retirement home. Fraudulent rat exterminators I attacked with the same vigor as I did purveyors of fake psychiatric cures and medical quacks dispensing vinegar for diabetes.

The time came when, as I produced features praising weight-lifting as therapy, Pinkerton detectives and the obstetrical skills of a taxi driver caught short on the run to the hospital, I began to think seriously of more significant fare. My salary had improved, along with my typing and an eye for an honest witness, and I'd been at it for two years, about six after my entrance to Georgetown aiming at diplomatic employment abroad. Admittedly, a world war and a State Department unready for me had frustrated my peacetime overseas designs up to then, but the time for a decision had, I felt, arrived.

In the Near East the conflict that was to stretch to decades of sporadic warfare between Jew and Arab was just beginning; the British Empire had begun disintegrating with Indian independence and the threatened end of its League of Nations' mandate in Palestine. There was also a war against the communists not far away in the mountains of Greece. Either of these trouble spots could be a likely place to start my foreign adventures.

I asked Herb Hill to give me a crack at it. We had, I argued, only the wire services to cover the area—no man of our own. I was temporarily "in funds" and could pay fares and some expenses if he'd keep me on the domestic payroll. Luckily, Herb, a small, pale leprechaun of a man with silver hair, was keenly interested in news from abroad. He raised his eyebrows, pursed his lips, coughed delicately, and said "yes."

A month later, April 21, 1948, I left for Egypt on an overseas assignment that was, one way and another, to last for thirty years.

CHAPTER II

Novice into the Deep End

The flight to Cairo from New York's Idlewild Airport was in a TWA piston-engined plane, and a fitful journey it was. Loaded with drunken roughnecks headed back for the Near East oilfields after a long leave in the States, the plane hosted a flying brawl through Gander, in Newfoundland, to Shannon, Ireland, where a pause to correct engine troubles kept us on the ground twenty-four hours. We got as far as Geneva, were grounded again, this time for two days, and arrived in the Egyptian capital three days overdue.

Egypt's major airport in those days was a wartime British leftover, a scattering of paint-peeling off-white buildings squatting in the desert heat. The British army had, as a homey touch, planted gardens and edged them with bricks stuck diagonally into the ground like rows of pointed teeth. Now, most of the teeth had been broken off and the plants were gone, replaced by assorted rubbish and clumps of flies that hummed and pulsated in the heat. Altogether a poor welcome.

Native officials matched the dreary state of decay. The immigration man I got wore a crumpled khaki uniform and a sour expression. He gazed at the visa in my passport, upside down, for a moment with no comment and then went away to return with a small, sweaty, potato-shaped officer in dirty whites, who shouted at me in excellent English.

Was I a Jew? He bellowed the question, and the room suddenly fell silent. At that time Washington's pro-Jewish political posture had, it seemed, resulted in the United States press being branded as anti-Arab. American reporters were routinely suspected as propagandists for the Jewish cause or, worse, as spies. And on that morning of our arrival the atmosphere in the room was heavy with hostility. Arab armies, in the preceding few days, had been battered into a rout all over the Sinai desert by a far smaller Jewish force. An American newsman had described a vast junkyard of smoking Egyptian equipment and a battleground littered with boots discarded by Arab soldiers who ran faster barefooted.

I knew nothing of this defeat as I stood there, the sweat trickling down my back, but it didn't take great sensitivity to detect a touchiness that could get me shipped out on the next plane or tossed into jail. I became the soul of courtesy and patience.

I wasn't a Jew, I told him; I was a Christian, and, anyway, I was there as an observer. Nothing more. Apparently he wasn't ready to call me a liar publicly and, controversy in that sultry sinkhole was avoided as a matter of course. After an intimidating period of thumbing slowly through largely empty pages of the passport and whispering to his cohort, he threw it on the counter and went away. It was stamped and handed back to me, and I was told to go to customs, down the passage in another building.

An hour later, the contents of my Val-Pac and musette bag having been dumped out on the counter, pawed over, and discussed by an assortment of officials, I fell, cursing, into a taxi and damning bureaucracy as a worldwide scourge—customs in particular.

Indeed, over the years, if I had anything to declare or not, I approached customs with loathing, dreading the upcoming ordeal as a humiliating, calculated insult. I learned to list every single item whether it was declarable or not, its country of origin and its value in lire, drachmas, kwachas or whatever. Usually, the officer, confronted with this labored show of honesty, and horrified at the thought of the assessing and calculating time he'd be forced to spend, hurriedly scratched his hieroglyphs on the luggage and waved me on.

It's advisable to head such a list with neutral and exotic articles such as "bronze slave anklets," "Okapi tail hairs," "fly whisk woven," "bones (witch doctors', for throwing)," and the like. Then the Russian mink laprobes and opium-pipe kit, packed near the bottom, are not likely to be noticed.

Only once have I tried smuggling, and, as I look back, the decision did seem entirely justified at the time.

Official customs clearance was scheduled to take place at a remote desert outpost in the upper reaches of the Sahara desert at the town of Oujda on the Algerian/Moroccan border. Since "Oujda" is scarcely a household word, I may be forgiven for expecting only a cursory check.

As my notes of the time reveal, the approach to the town was on a ribbon of blacktop laid across "sandy wastes" and straight as an arrow down the center of a wide valley. On either side, the desert swept away in shallow waves toward the mountains, purplish profiles pasted against a lemon sky. The land was empty of life but for a few goats idly chewing the insulation from telephone lines that had long since blown off poles improvised from dead trees.

The oven-hot wind scorching up the plain had battered the tired old Citroen with clouds of sand and flying bits of Saharan flora. The speed dropped to a crawl, and for several hours the vehicle groaned along, occasionally darting ahead like a scared hare when a large dune blocked the rush of air. Utter desolation. Hardly a locale where officials would be stationed at all, much less the painstaking martinets I encountered.

Admittedly, I had asked for trouble. I had neglected to get a "trip tique," an international certificate of ownership for the car, I had no international driver's license, and my exit permit had been improperly completed in Algiers. Each of these problems had to be solved in turn following protracted, shouted conversations over that goat-chewed line to Algiers. Hot, anxious hours passed, a punishment I might have accepted as only my just deserts but for mounting apprehension about one tricky omission in my declaration.

During the wait, customs had surprisingly agreed to accept an oral statement supplementing written formalities and had merely glanced through the car windows at dust-coated belongings. What I hadn't declared, however, was one French MAB 7.6 mm "pistolet." I had a permit for Algerian territory covering the gun, 100 rounds of ammunition, and three extra magazines but foreigners caught carrying arms across north African boundaries in the years after the war were summarily jailed by officials tired of being repeatedly shot up by "illegals" on the run.

I didn't really expect to end up in prison, but I knew if I declared the weapon it would automatically be confiscated. This was the beginning of a trip that would take me thousands of miles through an unfriendly African continent, and laughable as this popgun might have been, it did afford some comfort. So I'd dropped it, loaded, into the side pocket of my bush jacket, confident I wouldn't actually be frisked. The rest of the ammunition and magazines I cached in the baggage, given only a cursory onceover. This lifted part of my apprehension but did nothing for the weight in my side pocket.

A real bush jacket has patch pockets, square pouches hanging loosely against the side of the garment. They're a godsend as catchalls, and mine already bulged with odds and ends. The small, flat weapon did little to increase the bulk, but, as I paced the still heat of the tin shack, it grew heavier at every step.

The space allotted passengers was a narrow corridor between a bank of windows and the long counter running the length of the room. Behind this was an office full of angry voices, a property room stacked with confiscated contraband, and a small, empty cell with barred windows. There was no place to sit.

At the end of the first anguished hour the corridor had become far too narrow for me and my swollen side pocket. Twice I'd spun around eagerly to answer a question and slammed the pocket against the boarding, miraculously without comment from the officials. Once, when a relief man entered the shack, I turned quickly in greeting and caught him a numbing blow in the midriff. Apparently, jittery, sweating travelers must have thumped him regularly, for other than a fleeting grimace of pain he gave no sign he had noticed.

By the time I was released, having deposited a fortune in francs as ransom, and climbed back into the Citroen, I felt old and wrinkled. Never once since then have I knowingly breached customs regulations. I say "knowingly," because, more than once, having had my exhaustive listing officially vetted, I have been chilled by the post-customs discovery that my wife, or others in my family, has a handbag or pockets full of forbidden plant seeds, illegal currency, and undeclared jewelry, and that, in fact, one whole suitcase, unbeknownst to me, has been literally stuffed with items, all forbidden or dutiable.

Official techniques for torturing travellers vary the world over, of course. American customs men, for example, suffer from incipient mistrust and chronic exhaustion. They always demand that at least one bag be opened, usually the one it took half a hotel staff to help you close. The contents leap out at the official who paws through them with weary indifference. Finally, disappointed, he abandons a heap of belongings that somehow have quadrupled in bulk, disfigures the bag with indelible chalk, and moves listlessly on to the next victim.

In England a brisk, smartly uniformed inspector who could easily pass for an admiral of the fleet holds up a card with five thousand words on it. Somewhere in this interminable text, it recounts what you must declare and the penalties if you don't: the rack, transportation to distant colonies, and the like. To get halfway down the card, you must be a speed reader with 20/20 vision, because he doesn't really hold it up; he fans himself briefly with it, puts it down, and starts mumbling questions. His speech is soft and beautifully modulated, and you can't understand a word he says. This has you leaning forward, off balance, muttering "What?" "How's that?" and "I beg your pardon?" until all poise is shattered and you'd cheerfully admit to any crime he suggests. Fortunately, this uneven contest has been abandoned by the British. There's even a "green route" for those with nothing to declare, and, although it's watched over by a rank of uniformed guards crouched like vultures ready to spot-check anyone overdoing nonchalance, it is a civilized show of faith in mankind's best impulses.

The Frenchman wears a rumpled, navy-blue costume, scuffed open-toed brown sandals over white socks and is crisply hostile, the standard

French approach to all foreigners. Since you probably don't speak his language fluently he has branded you a half-wit at the outset so anything you say or do will be used against you. He may ask you to open something but he rarely stoops to stirring things around inside it, preferring to watch you do it while he raises his eyes to Heaven, tosses his palms upward, says, "Ah, mon Dieu!" or "Pouff!" and otherwise displays a practiced Gallic contempt.

I do, however, recall with a soft sigh a remarkable transit through Le Bourget, when French customs and immigration were on strike.

I'd arrived from Rome in an Alitalia tri-motored Fokker aircraft, an antique with one of the engines in the nose and a much-patched canvas skin. It wasn't long after the war, and the Italians were—let's face it—a bit slow getting back on their feet. At Rome airport it had lumbered down the bumpy runway and flapped into the air, just short of collision with a battered anti-aircraft tower, for a flight fraught with unorthodoxy.

All the stewardesses seemed to be models, modelling. No uniforms. Their voluptuous Mediterranean figures had been cunningly draped with exotic materials, the better to enhance each bump and grind in their movement down the aisle. The passengers, all males, were a study in mass lechery. The young captain, apparently deciding this was too good to be left to the customers, exited the business end of the plane and joined in, ordering a huge lunch washed down with an alarming amount of red wine. After nearly an hour of shameless indiscipline, he lunged to his feet and, pinching a bottom here and there, stumbled off toward the pointed end. Although his junior co-pilot had meanwhile done the best he could, it was a bit short of expert. We overshot Le Bourget by miles, and, after weaving our way back in a maze of ruptured traffic patterns, hurtled in to leap-frog down what turned out to be the wrong runway, narrowly avoided a parked plane, and came to a screeching halt that filled the cabin with flying personal possessions, crockery, glassware, and stewardesses.

Adding to the impromptu nature of this off-the-cuff landing was the complete absence of ground personnel. Back in the 1940s the airport management, not each individual airline, was chiefly responsible for staffing travel bays. On this morning and at the last minute, the striking customs and immigration officials had been joined by airport personnel. This left the captain, visibly unsteady on his feet, and the crew from cockpit and cabin, to disembark the paying customers. With the help of some of the more seasoned travelers, he managed to wrestle open an exit door and fold steps down to the ground, but he and the co-pilot suffered multiple contusions when the baggage porte exploded open prematurely, hurling luggage all over the concrete apron.

But our reward awaited. No immigration, no customs. No porters either, yet what I had to carry in those days I handled easily. All the usual obstacles to a gracious arrival removed, we had walked serenely through to waiting cabs.

But on that sweltering morning in Cairo, the Le Bourget triumph was months away. The taxi into which I'd fallen, cursing, hissed and smoked, its horn constantly bleating, and got me into the city where I paid the driver far too much and stumbled into the cooling luxury of Shepheard's Hotel.

In a room as spacious as a squash court, the decor antiseptic white with Persian carpeting backdropping clumps of bulky oak furniture, I flopped onto an ornate iron fourposter, the linen lightly rustled by the breeze from a wooden fan whomping lazily overhead and started my first overseas assignment with first things first. Five hours' sleep.

Later that afternoon, refreshed by the rest and a romp in a bath resembling a huge marble tureen on bronze cats' feet, and wearing a pinkish seersucker suit ever after referred to by my English colleagues as my "ice cream suit," I descended to the "long bar."

Off the cavernous main lounge, the area traditionally was reserved for "gentlemen only," the mahogany bar itself rubbed to a rich leathern sheen by generations of male elbows. The furnishings were grim with seriously antique and spectacularly uncomfortable chairs clustered round knee-high tables resembling large bronze cymbals resting on carved wooden legs. The ladies rarely braved this austerity but took their drinks in the lounge where grotesquely overstuffed furniture provided slightly less painful sitting.

The bar was empty when I entered, but for the European barman in black mess jacket and dusky Arab waiters in white duck and red fezzes. And a moustached, graying man in shirt sleeves who, viewed from a distance, might have been a faintly seedy David Niven.

I swung onto a bar stool, ordered a drink, and began worrying in earnest. I had to find an office with Egyptians in it who could, and would, accredit me as a visiting American newsman, which, in turn would permit me to arrange for a subsequent trip to Jerusalem. I had ten days and not the faintest idea where to start. I called for another drink.

"Have this with me," David Niven invited in disappointing American and signalled the barman by pointing at our glasses.

"Just arrived?" He peered at me through a haze of swirling tobacco smoke.

Yes, I had, I said with lazy boredom as if "just arriving" at places like Cairo was the height of tedium after years of world travel.

"First assignment overseas?"

So much for acting.

I admitted it. What's more, I broke down and told him I hadn't a clue about my next move except that I knew one had to be made and soon.

David Niven, whose real name doesn't matter, was correspondent in the Near East for the *New York Times*. He'd been ousted from Palestine, he said, by the British authorities, serving out the last days of the Mandate in a bloody, three-way war with Jewish terrorist groups and Arab irregulars. The reason: an affair with a Jewish girl suspected of being a spy for the underground. The affair was to lead to marriage and a return to life in the States, but for now he had agreed to leave Palestine with the understanding she would be granted an exit permit to join him. That had been a lifetime ago, he said, and she was still in Jerusalem.

Having cut sharply across my queries with this bitter bit of personal history, apparently more to get it off his chest than identify himself, he fell silent for a moment.

And then he said: "Go see Max Boyd. Associated Press. He's leaving for Jerusalem sometime soon. If anyone can help you, he can."

The next day I did, and Max could. But first I had to get a temporary Egyptian accreditation and, somewhat daunting, exit papers to leave the country for Palestine, a move viewed by the authorities with distinct hostility. Why send another American newsman into Palestine to beef up the bias favoring the Jewish cause? Getting the papers wouldn't be easy, but it was up to me to try before Max could be of any help. And he told me where to go.

Before boarding the plane in New York, I had gone the route taken by travelers bound for the world's distant outbacks and equipped myself with a lightweight minimum including khaki bush jackets and trousers. These, with a pair of English hiking boots, became my "uniform" for the ensuing few months. The "ice cream suit" I saved for grand occasions.

During almost a week following my first talk with Max, I put at least thirty miles on the boots. Cairene taxidrivers charged exorbitant rates for sightseeing trips they made out of the shortest haul, and joining the swarm of humanity blanketing the bell-clanging streetcars involved a risk I wasn't prepared to take. So, I walked. From Shepheard's to the American embassy, to the American University in Cairo, and to numerous Egyptian government buildings. And back again. Repeatedly.

Actually, I enjoyed the trips afoot; marveled at the wonder of so diverse and noisy a population, apparently all 1.5 million on the streets at once. I learned to turn away the currency black marketeers buying dollars at a premium and the vagabonds who whispered up, hoarsely hawking stolen jewelry, watches, fountain pens, and bogus artifacts from the tombs of the pharaohs.

En route to the embassy I had to traverse Khan el Khalili, the municipal market, a pungently perfumed agglomeration of stands and barrows, of carpets and canvas stretched out in the dust, all displaying an assortment of merchandise from fly-blown cows' feet to tinkling temple bells. On one trip I had barely left the market when the cheerful rabble became a murderous mob. For reasons I never learned, they pulled a Jew and his wife, visitors from Philadelphia, out of their stalled taxi and literally tore them apart. How they identified the couple as Jewish, and what sparked off the violence, remains a mystery. When I retraced my steps, returning to the market about an hour later, the bloody remains were concealed under hessian sheeting and guarded by police. All around this pathetic heap, the din of the market had picked up its normal pitch, business carrying on, oblivious.

Aside from this unhappy episode, my walks around Cairo were pleasant, uneventful, and professionally fruitless. At the end of three days, my only document was a card, with photograph, from the American University in Cairo, stating, in Arabic, that I was a "Christian member of the Episcopal Church." Unfortunately, the snapshot, taken of me in khakis with my hair crew cut and my facial features more than normally distorted by shadows, made me look markedly semitic. I've kept it as a memento only, never daring to produce it to back up my bona fides. Desert Arabs, who lightheartedly dismembered any passing Jew, would have found this photograph all the excuse they needed.

I'd gone to the university to do some study on Near East history while I awaited action on my exit visa application, and this card had been pressed on me by an agitated, Einstein-looking professor who somehow managed to be, at once, sympathetic and disapproving. He was bitterly opposed to the founding of the Jewish state, lectured me on the merits of the Arab cause and crushed my already pulpy morale by insisting that if I made it to Jerusalem by whatever means it would be a miracle. And then he gave me that unfortunate identification, which could have doomed me to fulfill his prophecy.

The embassy validated my U.S. passport for travel to Palestine, dispensed bland comment on the situation there, and were, all in all, most correct. Later, crawling around in the dust near the U.S. Consulate in Jerusalem, where Thomas Wasson, Consulate General, had just been shot by an Arab sniper, I thought back to these moments with the brittle, neatly pressed young diplomat holding forth in carefully noncommittal phrases. It wasn't a satisfying memory.

I had three days left on my Egyptian visa when I returned to the Associated Press office and Max Boyd with nothing to show for my efforts but a church membership card. Max was not impressed. But neither was he surprised. Tall and slender, fair and balding, soft of speech, Max was vastly experienced. He listened without comment to my hysterical accounting of the week's frustrations, mainly in the corridors of Egyptian bureaucratic power, advised me to relax, and made a phone call.

Now, this in itself, the phone call, was a testing experience and a pretty neat trick if you could complete it. Attempting phone calls in most foreign countries is, and has long been, one of life's most baffling experiences. In Cairo, in 1948, each try was an experiment.

The occupying British, preferring the tried-and-true messenger with forked stick, had only grudgingly bowed to the demands of the century and installed the system in about 1914. And having made this mind-boggling concession to modernity, they left it at that. By 1948, with scores of improvised additions made under the stress of World War Two, the contrivance was a cruel joke. Nonetheless and probably because he was calling the number of a high official in the Department of Information, Max did, in time, get through and arrange an appointment for me.

The building housing the Information offices was a barracks-like brick structure, its gloomy precincts surrounded by a makeshift security fence abutting the street. It and other similar bureaucratic bailiwicks were part of the Arab League caserne on the edge of Cairo's downtown.

I threaded my way through a break in the barbed wire under the rifles of a squad of soldiers to a sally port, where a Samson-sized Egyptian sergeant frisked me with embarrassing thoroughness. This indelicate operation completed and responding to my request to see Max's contact, he made a phone call I could almost feel oozing its way into the inner depths of the headquarters, like mud through a pipe. After an interminable wait and a lengthier conversation, he slammed down the receiver and ordered me to accompany a corporal guide.

Immediately inside the main doorway to the left was a small cell marked by the sour odor and bruised aspect of a police interrogation room. An effort had been made to soften the atmosphere with a worn rug, the ubiquitous brass-cymbal tea table covered with Arab League publicity pamphlets, an upholstered couch stuffed with lumps, and some spartan wooden chairs.

The corporal ushered me in and closed the door. After an hour I had methodically checked out my surroundings several times, noting that the clerestory windows were barred and the only door was locked from the outside. I was certainly here on sufferance.

And what would this official of towering authority be like, and on whose whim hung the success or failure of my first adult journalism? I knew from experience that King Farouk and his favorites, wielding a heavy hand, still governed the country as a private fiefdom.

One evening I'd seen the king with some of his more adhesive lackeys sweep into a Heliopolis nightclub, ease his bulk down at a central table, and take command. Everything halted, including music and floorshow, while his wants were catered to. When satisfied, he imperiously waved a hand. As though a cine film, stopped in midframe, had started again, the scene came to life.

The "big band" playing for dancing was excellent, pounding out the Glenn Miller, Dorsey, and Goodman favorites of the day. Until, that is, a deafening screech issued from the king's general presence and the club music ran down like a tired calliope. The king, it developed, was displeased with the swinging rendition and had ordered an aide to turn up a portable radio under the table. About this time, thoroughly miffed by this running display of infantile boorishness, we rose as a group from our table and prepared to leave. This too, might have displeased the king it seemed, for we were ordered by several of the royal party's musclemen to remain until His Royal Highness decided to leave, two fun-filled hours later.

Farouk in appearance resembled a large, pale bowling ball in a double-breasted dark pinstripe with a maroon fez on top. This and a small smudge of moustache made him an easy caricature. I never saw him in anything but this parody of Western dress. But many of his hangers-on wore traditional flowing robes, gallibeahs, djellabahs and, on their heads, the Kafiah, a linen cloth held in place by a beaded ring of black camel's hair. Some even wore great, curved scimitars and daggers, and his bodyguards, staring everyone down the way security men do, had openly sported Webley .45s in leather holsters. All very warlike and forbidding.

Sitting in my cell I wondered if Max's friend, about whom Max had told me nothing, would be robed and accoutered in similar fashion. Perhaps an ebony spade beard, a nutbrown visage, clouded and ominous with piercing black eyes.

"For God's sake! Acheson! What the hell are you doing here?"

Thus spake Zaki Saad el Din, arrayed in navy-blue blazer, gray flannel trousers, and dark-brown–suede shoes, the very model of an English gentleman and handsome as Omar Sharif. He had backed through the brass-studded mahogany portal, talking to someone in the outer lobby, turned, and stopped dead when he saw me.

"Zaki!" I shrieked in turn, struggling out of the depths of the couch. "It can't be! Never occurred to me. But, of course, Cairo!" I was babbling, and he burst out laughing, embraced me warmly, and then stepped back, suddenly brisk and businesslike.

"But this is nonsense," he said, abruptly starting for the door. "Come. We'll go to my office. I'll cancel all my appointments."

And we were off down corridors echoing the slap of guards' rifles snapped to present arms and the sound of heels crashing together; even the swish of much bowing and backing off by civilian trespassers whispered round us. It was most impressive, and I lapped it up.

Our association had begun in October, 1943, in, of all places, the barracks of the U.S. Army's Military Police Training Battalions, Fort Custer, Michigan. Both of us were preparing for army roles in, first, "Civil Affairs" as the Allies invaded German-conquered country and, subsequently, as "Military Government" in occupied Germany. Battalion personnel were, largely, draftees chosen for professions appropriate to the work, lawyers, civil engineers, police and firemen, municipal executives, hospital administrators, and the like. The pot into which we'd all been thrown had been the Combat Military Police with later graduation to a specialized corps.

Zaki Saad and I had qualified on vaguely similar grounds; foreign-language aptitude, university education, and, allegedly, some intellectual skills flexible enough to adapt to the peculiar demands of war-torn civilian communities. Many of the men were volunteers; not a few came with medical waivers for ailments, including age, that might have otherwise kept them out. It was a pretty impressive lot.

Zaki Saad had his own special standing. Related to Nahas Pasha, a high-ranking Egyptian both in family and in Cairo's ruling hierarchy, he had graduated from university levels in the United States and received a special dispensation to attend the MP School at Battle Creek. When I'd gone off to the war in Europe, he'd returned to his homeland and a job in, I think, wartime intelligence. Later, that war over, he had had a few years' varied experience in Cairo's bureaucratic battlefield and finally touched down, comfortably, in the public liaison job.

"Been in this job about a year now," he said as he ushered me into an office that was the nearest one could come to an executive suite in the caserne and motioned me to a chair. We had a few whiskeys, reminisced a bit, and then got down to my business.

Within a few hours I had all the documents I needed attesting to my status as a journalist of irreproachable standing. Within a few more hours I had also acquired the beginning of the most spectacular hangover in a long career of competitive boozing, a perilous state I maintained full bore well into the following day.

This meant I took it with me to Max's.

"Successful?" Max raised his eyebrows.

Knowing he'd heard about my reunion with Zaki Saad I smiled wanly and said nothing.

"Nearly imprisoned for bawdy behavior in public places and now," he looked me up and down with as near as Max would let himself get to outright glee, "on the brink of death."

No comment.

"But," he rolled a sheet into his typewriter, "you've been successful and are now free to come and go, officially free. You'll leave with us for Jerusalem in the morning. Tomorrow, April thirtieth. Four o'clock. By taxi."

"There *is* no cheaper way," Max shrugged when I complained that hundreds of miles by cab was more than I had bargained for. "The only way the trains go these days is up. In chunks. Sabotage daily. Coastwise shipping is the same except it goes down, and the airlines have quit flying into Tel Aviv or anywhere else. It's too dangerous."

My share of the fare, he said, would be $150, and we'd meet on the street near the Associated Press office at 3:30 A.M. If I was late, he added not unkindly, I'd be left behind. There would be a long day ahead and we must leave on schedule.

Back at Shepheard's I slept most of the day away, packed, paid my account for an early-morning departure, and, settling in a quiet corner of the front veranda, watched the city light up around me in the gathering darkness and pondered what the future held. So far I'd been lucky and the view from where I sat was exciting. Just how basic were my handicaps as a new boy I would only discover later. But my struggle for official acceptance in Cairo had given me a hint.

Unless a newsman is accredited to an internationally known journal with editorial clout, his arrival in an unfamiliar trouble spot can be a jarring experience. In attempts to collect the reams of documents that are vital if he's to get where the news is, he finds he's been sent to the rear of the line, where he waits. And waits.

My sole accreditation then and on later assignments for several publications was legitimate and entirely acceptable but fell rather short of dazzling. I would eventually collect a cubit or two of stature as a result of brief flashes of notability, yet over the years each new assignment would find me battling to establish credibility.

The *Indianapolis News* is a paper not without some standing in the United States and at one time was a tower of editorial excellence and power. But, overseas, claiming staff status on the *News* was like announcing you could play the Jew's harp: nice but less than crucial.

One of the other publications for which I was a stringer and subsequently bureau chief in Germany was in the same league. A magazine with a format not unlike *Time* but with an almost exclusively rural readership, it had considerable stateside circulation with instant recognition in the American prairies and even in some veteran journalistic circles. But in far-flung outposts, the title, *Pathfinder News Magazine,* produced total indifference.

Although resenting being labelled an inconsequential hick, I chose a cheerful show of patience in preference to storming indignation. This meant I usually had to wait two or three days for press indentity cards most of my colleagues got in a matter of hours. This humility often paid off later in confidences not entrusted to others but more often left me at the post while seasoned competitors rolled up a tidy lead in a gamut from decent accommodation to official "private briefings."

The effect on me was predictable. I would be forced, each time, into an orgy of recklessness just to catch up: bumming rides with bomb-toting terrorists, night patrols behind enemy lines. Like that. Luckily this lack of good sense came naturally.

On the veranda at Shepheard's the waiter broke into my reverie and I found that the night had grown softer, sweetened by the scent from bowers of potted flowers and hushed as traffic noises faded away toward the fringes of the city.

I paid up and made my way through the shadowed caverns of the lounge and hallways, the lamps dimmed for the night, to the ornate iron cage that passed for an elevator.

Shepheard's, which I would not see again, was a very special place. Oriental carpets were everywhere laid on floors and hanging on walls. The light reflected off the brass fittings and turned carpets to gold, and the bronze lanterns hanging on chains from high overhead seemed to change shape as they twisted in the warm currents stirred by the fans. A few servants in white gowns, maroon cummerbunds, and red fezes padded about, bowing and making small coughing noises.

All this lush colonial opulence, a constant reminder to the natives of their inferior status, contributed to the sense of outrage that crystalized in the Gamal Abdul Nasser "revolution" of 1952 and blew Shepheard's away forever. As a monument to foreign domination and a traditional alien refuge, it was burned to the ground at the height of the frenzy directed at the European. King Farouk went too, hounded out by Nasser and his military clique, to a sanctuary in Italy, where he fattened and died in March, 1965.

The next day a dim early dawn allowed only a flickering last glimpse of Shepheard's, as at 3:00 A.M., I hurtled off the veranda steps into a cab for the meeting with Max and the others. But the lush luxury I'd enjoyed during that brief stay I'd not forget.

CHAPTER III

To War in a Taxi

I arrived at the prearranged meeting place at just after three o'clock and could make out others in the pale glow of the streetlight. What I took to be our taxi was at the curbside, panting metallically, a 1937 Dodge four-door sedan looking painfully decrepit for what I had understood would be a rough trip over difficult terrain. It appeared to have been black once but now was grayish, sandblasted, and rusty. The dark little man in a black suit talking to Max obviously was the bandit who was getting five hundred dollars for this two hundred–mile jaunt. In the event, it was a fee that turned out to be cheap at the price.

"Greetings," Max glanced at my luggage. "Right on time. Put the Val-Pac and musette bag on the roof rack and hold onto your typewriter," and he turned back to the perusal of a map spread out on the Dodge's hood, ignoring a new arrival who rounded the corner at a trot. The newcomer was dark, his battered good looks taut and pale, a man of average height and square build. He held a camera in one hand and, after dropping his suitcase, held out the other in greeting.

"Jim Pringle," he said, and the Irish hung in the air. "Come to die with us, eh? Good to have your company," and he climbed into the free front seat of the car, Speed Graphic in his lap, and slammed the door. When I'd settled in the back, he glanced over his shoulder.

"Only been out o' that hellhole a week," he said. "Been there four months before that. A bed o' roses it isn't," and he fell silent. I learned later that Pringle was the man the A.P. sent on the dirty assignments. This, plus bad luck, had made his recent stay in Jerusalem tougher than usual.

Playing soccer in the hotel corridor with the child of Carter Davidson, A.P. bureau chief in the Holy Land, he'd characteristically let fly with a tremendous kick, missed the ball, hit the wall, and broken two toes. For weeks he'd hobbled around, his foot in a cast. At one time he was forced to crawl backward down a main street in front of an advancing Jewish patrol, fire from Arab snipers behind him chipping bits out of the macadam. He lost most of the cast but he got the pictures. His one week leave in Cairo hadn't made up for months of that sort of risk.

Max slid in beside me, the driver crashed into gear, and we lurched off through the silent streets.

"Here's the drill," Max said. "We head for the Suez Canal and cross it near Ismaillia. We ferry over. From there we head north to the old caravan route and keep on it to the Palestine border post at Auja, some distance inside the frontier. And then Beersheba, Hebron, Bethlehem, and Jerusalem. It'll be slow going—bad road—patrols. Won't get there until midafternoon."

"Aye," Pringle snorted, " 'twill be a good day's work if we get halfway." He swung around to look wryly at Max. "With all thim murderin' wogs on the prowl."

Max shrugged, "We'll make it all right," and the driver, in butchered English, assured us he was a "Christian-Arab," as if this would solve any problems.

"But when stop," he said, turning to look back at Max, "I talk. You, nobody, not talking. Okay?"

Boyd readily agreed, and the driver faced forward again just in time to avoid a head-on collision with the only other moving car on the darkened street.

By now the city was waking, and its human substance seemed to well up and ooze from all its ancient pores and flow around us as we rattled over the cobbles, a uniquely Cairene stench floating up in the gathering warmth. The road across the delta was roughly black-topped all the way to Ismaillia although this was of little advantage since the way was so jammed with donkey, camel, bicycle and pedestrian traffic we'd have maimed them by the score at anything over twenty miles an hour.

We got to the ferry before noon. I remember little about boarding except that there was a clot of human beings, livestock and vehicles from prams to pantechnicons moving off against a swarm struggling to embark; a shrieking shambles. Somehow the two managed to sieve through each other and we rolled onto the wooden planking behind an aged lorry and a bunch of heavily laden camels just as the ferry slid out from shore.

When the car came to a halt we shoved open the doors against the crush and got out for a stretch. I managed to ease my way forward through the crowd and along a border of ankle-high railway ties edging the platform toward the only open space I could see. What I didn't see was why it was open space.

No sooner had I stepped into it when a large, dirty, white camel, wearing a muzzle like a mean dog, shifted sharply over against me and, before I could heed the shout of its owner, lashed its encumbered snout around and belted me backwards over the ties and into the water.

I surfaced, gagging, jammed against the hull by the current but sliding aft with alarming speed. Just short of disappearing into the boiling yellow wake, I seized a length of loose rope and, with the help of passengers shouting with laughter and hugely enjoying this break in the routine, clawed my way back aboard.

It was over so quickly that Boyd and Pringle only moved to join the rescuers as I was heaved unceremoniously onto the filthy deck. Max pulled me, sodden and breathless, to my feet, gently concerned about my health. Pringle, unsympathetic, merely eyed me scornfully and turned away shaking his head.

A dip in the Nile, especially where it is an open sewer, is a pretty disgusting experience. That, plus the bruising the beast inflicted on my shoulder and the gooey mess to which the dunking had reduced my hard-won official papers, confirmed my low opinion of camels in general. It was years before I had my revenge and was able to vent my spleen in a piece I wrote for "Information Plus," a radio column-of-the-air broadcast first in the States and later on Radio Rhodesia and the South African broadcasting system. It went, roughly, like this:

> Not so long ago the Philadelphia Zoo reported an unusual incident: a camel had been browbeaten by, of all things, a chicken, a run-of-the-mill Rhode Island Red.
>
> Before the chicken's arrival this big freak had lumbered about the cage, chewing its cud and viewing his private world with sad contempt. Then the bird arrived, built a nest in his bed of thorns, and drove him into terrified residence in a far corner of the billet. With one vicious kick he could have strained her through the wire netting. But he did nothing. Just cowered there. Sulking.
>
> Concerned, the zookeepers removed the hen and her new family, and the camel returned to its gloomy routine, its ego bruised beyond recovery.
>
> Now, I like this story. Any time a camel gets its comeuppance, I'm delighted. Take that snooty expression. As if he knows something that no one else does. The more infuriating because, in fact, he does.
>
> According to the story, Mohammed the Prophet frequently rode the desert alone during the time he was receiving his revelations from God. He'd already compiled his Five Pillars of Islam when,

one day, as he stopped near a waterhole, God revealed a sixth. For reasons of his own, Mohammed decided that five was enough, and he swore the camel, who'd been listening, to eternal secrecy. The camel agreed, took the oath, and ever since this ungainly hulk has plodded through the centuries with that nauseating, supercilious look on his face.

I included a bit about being propelled into the smelly Nile and then:

> Another time I was doing a story in the wastes of Algeria and Bou Saada, an age-old way stop on the caravan route across the Sahara from the East into Morocco. Here the inhabitants milled about exhibiting fits of primitive enterprise, such as operating a bordello of classic dimensions and impressive personnel. Yet, even with that to remember, what sticks, burning, in my memory was my first ride on a camel.
> At a "garage du chameau," a camel garage, a score of the animals lay about like mounds of softly groaning rubbish. The so-called saddles were grimy slabs of cotton waste, into which the rider settled gingerly while the beast remained prone. When it rose, it was in a series of fore-and-aft jerks that whipsawed me first around its prickly neck, then back onto its motheaten rump, and so on, until, thank God, it stood still, the ground left far below me. And when it moved it was torture.
> It walks with an exaggerated retching motion. In no time my knees were raw from trying to keep aloft, and I was certain that if I'd fallen off I'd have been trampled or chewed to a pulp. I was utterly intimidated and the things had their complete way with me.
> Today, however, I know better. If one must associate with camels, one has only to keep a chicken handy for protection.

By the time we docked near Chalet of the Khedive, a grubby adobe village, the khaki bush jacket and trousers that were to be my uniform of the next few months had dried and hardened to an evil-smelling crust. In the confines of the taxi, in desert heat, this enriched the atmosphere beyond description. Indeed, so weighty was the aura that I was surprised I got no groans of protest from my hosts. The reason soon became apparent. My war-wise comrades had other things on their minds.

After we'd left Ismaillia, a deserted, onetime British garrison town, all the more dead for the scraggly, wounded flowerbeds bordering the empty billets, we rattled northward for about an hour before arriving at a place called El Kantara, a calloused cluster of life next to the canal.

From this point, eastward into the Sinai wastes, the ancient caravan route had tied West and East together for centuries. From 5,000 B.C., it had provided an avenue of conquest for Egyptians and Assyrians (in opposite directions), Romans, the hordes of Islam, the Crusaders on foray for fun and profit, the Ottomans, the French, and the British. And, in between, marauding Bedouin tribesmen regularly raided the rich camel trains transporting frankincense and myrrh, olive oil, black slaves and white ones. Certainly these attractions were reason enough for all the activity over this unprepossessing bit of grime, but the principal reason, of course, was that it was a main track connecting widely separated marketplaces—Europe and the Far East. For us it was the only passable overland route from the Egyptian border to Jerusalem.

We angled right just south of El Kantara and then straight east along the old way, the Mediterranean some forty miles off to our left. The Bedouins still roamed the area. Their enthusiasm for plunder had been dampened only slightly over the years by the presence of roving British patrols, and Max and Pringle, who'd had experience with the Arab brigands, were edgy.

Even the patrols had become sporadic at best. The anticipated end of the mandate in Palestine and preparations for withdrawal of United Kingdom forces had reduced policing of the area. In any event, the Bedouins had, predictably, joined the Arab side in the mounting conflict and operated as irregulars. Casual plunder was common practice, but now they had a cause, outriders for Islam against the Jews. And the British.

Except for the heat and the wild ride over the rolling, pot-holed surface, the trip had proceeded uneventfully until about an hour out of El Kantara. Zooming over the blind crest of a hillock, the old Dodge plunged down the other side and came to a jarring halt in the outer edge of an errant sand dune that had wandered across the highway. Only by swinging hard left into the scrub had the driver avoided a deeper burial.

As it was, we were stuck fast, the rear wheels up to the axle in a foot of silt. We'd have to heave out of this and, somehow, circle around the end of the dune and back onto the tar surface, not a happy prospect with the thermometer over the 100 mark.

It was while we were excavating that they appeared.

Max, sweat-soaked and weary, had straightened up to ease his aching back when, with comic swiftness, he was back in place digging like a prairie dog.

"We have visitors, girls," he gasped.

The "Christian Arab" driver, who'd already seen them but had remained silent, hissed, "No talk, okay?" He dropped the tire iron he was using and walked around to the front of the vehicle. Pringle and I, after quick glances at the top of the dune, carried on digging.

There were five of them visible, shapeless ghosts on horseback, dirty gray burnooses gathered at the waist by wide bands, from which protruded daggers and assorted small arms. Three of them had ancient flintlocks angled across their backs, and the two horsemen who sidled, sliding, down the dune toward us, held newer, bolt-action weapons ready across the saddle. As they halted at a cautious distance on the other side of the roadway, we all stopped work and watched the cabdriver approach them, chattering "Salaams" and a babble of what we presumed was reassurance.

The riders remained silent and immobile, staring fixedly over the driver's head at the three of us. Only when the cabbie, comically out of place in his dark Western "business suit," stepped off the tar in their direction did they deign to notice him, swinging gunbarrels in his direction and slamming rounds into breeches with a crack that stopped our breathing. And his. Suddenly it was deathly still, the only sound the snap of the Dodge's overheated engine block. I glanced at Pringle and reckoned that if I was as pale as he was, I must be chalk white. Max was standing next to me, his face flushed from the digging, but his expression relaxed. With his arms lightly folded across his chest he was a model of easy composure.

After a suitably ominous pause, the rider nearest our driver swung down off his mount, slung his rifle, and beckoned us forward. We joined the cabbie on the roadway and waited.

I don't remember the details of the next few minutes. I do recall handing over my passport to the man, a hawk-faced ancient whose ferocious mien was enhanced by a personal aroma compounded of horse sweat, wood smoke, and spoiled meat. He went laboriously through the motions of checking the papers, returning them to the driver. Mine, he inexplicably tossed to the ground, where I left them until he'd remounted.

"Give money," the driver demanded turning to us, and we shelled out what we had in Egyptian pounds, about one hundred dollars' worth. The leader leaned from his saddle, snatched the wad in his grubby hand, and stuffed it deep into the festering recesses of his robe.

Abruptly his venomous deadpan gave way to laughing conversation with the driver, and he motioned two of the obviously junior members of the band down from the horizon to help us push the car back on the highway. That done, they mounted, and the gang wheeled up the slope and were gone.

We'd spoken not a word, as instructed, and even now as we ducked back into the car, chitchat was limited to "Wow!" and "Phew!" and "Holy Shit!" We had been on our way ten minutes in a state of mute shock before Max asked the chauffeur how we'd got off so easily.

"Don't know," the man shrugged. "Only want money. These not bad men," he added, implying that any deeds short of murder were virtuous.

When I said they could have fooled me, he laughed and explained they had nothing better to do so had become scouts for the Egyptian army assigned to the area along the Palestine frontier. The men signed on, he said, for a few days' rations and quit when they felt like it.

"We're lucky," he beamed into the rearview mirror. "They say English police near here so they hurry."

The rest of the trip was without further incident. At the border post, the British authorities processed us routinely, only briefly puzzled by my wrinkled documents now dried to parchment in the heat. Some anxious moments did enliven things from Beersheba to Hebron, when we passed the smoking hulks of burned-out military and civilian vehicles at a point where the road slid through a narrow defile in the hills. Heavy fire from guns and small arms from the flanking high ground had torn up the route only a short time before. We could only hope they'd stopped for the day.

Our luck held and in the late afternoon we entered Jerusalem through the eucalyptus and pine grove of the German colony, past the main railway station on our right and out onto a dismayingly naked stretch. Normally this was a pretty busy pitch with Jews and Arabs shooting at each other and the British shooting at both of them. This afternoon, however, it was relatively quiet. Someone did potshot our way, dusting up the ground around us and sending one slug clanging off the left front fender, but whoever it was only played at it. We rattled safely off the plain and into a barren roundabout near the David Building, a five-story structure standing alone on the left, and stopped next to an Irish Fusiliers roadblock at the bottom of King George V Avenue.

The troops manning the post were surprised we'd made it by way of Beersheba and Hebron, since no one else had, either way, for several days. We squatted within the circle of sandbags and cobblestones for a few moments after our papers had been checked while Max responded to queries about conditions along the route. Around us the men maintained an uneasy watch.

"Bloody balmy, that's wot you are," one of them snorted. "Through all them fockin' passes! Bloody mad."

Max completed his briefing and, once more back in the Dodge, we took off up the avenue, passing the low skeletons of small buildings on both sides, skidded hard right into a narrow street and screeched to a halt in front of a yellowish shoebox-shaped building.

"The Pantiles Hotel! Your front-line home away from home," Pringle announced in ringing tones before he piled out hauling kit with him. We paid the driver in a mishmash of dollar travelers checks, and English and Palestine pounds. He counted it with deliberate care, dumped the rest of our luggage on the sidewalk, and without a word of thanks or farewell he slid back into the vehicle and disappeared in a cloud of stinking smoke. We never saw him again.

While the others carried their clobber up the tile steps and into the lobby, I stepped out into the empty street and had a look around.

The Pantiles Hotel stood in an area surrounded by mostly grass-grown heaps of rubble and the craters of onetime basements. Beyond a barren lot across the street was the concrete wreckage of Yemin Moshe, a Jewish quarter hammered to remnants by Arab artillery fire from the Old City wall, plainly visible in the near distance.

These ancient ramparts, remnants of those that encompassed Solomon's Jerusalem two thousand years earlier, loomed high above the floor of the Valley of Hinnom, separating the old town from the accretions that passed for growth and change in parts of the New City. It occurred to me fleetingly that shells missing Yemin Moshe targets might easily whistle over and alter the front elevation of the Pantiles, but the hotel seemed largely intact and with luck would remain so. In ragged formation on the same side as the Pantiles were derelict buildings, their windows broken and gaping, stuccoed exteriors pockmarked by bullets and shrapnel. Barely visible at the top of a shallow rise was the ruined section of the King David Hotel. North of that, barely seen over the roof of our hotel, was the top of the YMCA tower, a Jerusalem landmark that more closely resembled the minaret from which the muezzin calls the Muslim faithful to prayer than the "steeple" of a Christian monument. Perhaps, in the ecumenical "City of God," this was an appropriate mix, even if the ostensible ecumenicists were busily butchering each other in large batches.

Later, when I grew more familiar with the area, I learned that not far from the rear of the Pantiles was the American Consulate General. Across Mamillah Road from the consulate was Mamillah Cemetery, last resting place for the Muslim community, and around both were the once posh suburbs, now battered and mostly deserted. Farther north at the top of King George Avenue the New City began, occupied exclusively by the Jews and an ugly jumble of nouveau notions about progressive architecture, a painful contrast to the comfortable huddle of the "old" community.

Certainly, the Pantiles was in a war zone. Only the hotel appeared to have a planned profile, all the other structures having had great bites taken out of them. Much of the King David had been blown up by Jewish terrorists a few months earlier. Zeroing in on the British officers' mess, a time bomb in a trashcan had obliterated one section, killing ninety-one and wounding scores of others. Newsmen billeted in the Pantiles, I learned later, had rushed up to help in rescue work, many of them pulling what was left of friends from the debris.

However new and rousing all this might be for me, it was old and sad for many of the men I'd be working with. Some had been posted there long before the Palestine killing had begun in earnest and were old hands at sorting out the dead from the dying, an exercise that, however often one did it, never came naturally.

The troubles, of course, had begun decades before the King David slaughter, troubles seeded, first, by Britain's Balfour Declaration of November, 1917, establishing, in principle, a Jewish National Home in Palestine. In 1920 the League of Nations took the second step by an April resolution assigning a postwar mandate over the area to Great Britain and League approval of that mandate by council in July of 1922.

The Arabs, variously employed during the Great War by both sides, with time out for foraging on their own account, took a dim view of this cavalier disposition of much of their native land. The year following the council action, Palestinian Arabs rioted, briefly and without effect, throughout the country. From that time, until the depressed period of the thirties produced protest against all authority, Arab rage simmered just below the surface.

For the Jews, the "National Home" was not a happy one. A sense of unease grew during the three decades after Versailles. Resentment of the mandatory power (whose officials often openly sympathized with the Arabs) daily produced violent protest. The "Holocaust" of World War II gave a new impetus to Theodor Herzl's Zionist dream of a Jewish Homeland. Thousands of Jews had worn the blue and white shoulder patch of the Jewish Brigade Group (Hatikvah Yehudit Lochemet) and fought with valor as part of the British Eighth Army in Italy. Not only had Herzl's aspirations become demands after the incredible massacre of millions of their race, but they, the Jews, had fought for that dream, not in silent suffering but actively, on a battleground in Italy.

And "come home" they had. By the thousands, legally and circumventing the immigration procedures. And at "home," things got worse. And worse. And to the bitterness of the twenties and thirties, the broken promises and crushed hopes, was added a new dimension, a kind of murderous anger. And Palestine became a running sore, stinking with hatreds.

It was really jolly. As any copper with the Palestine Police Force, the official British unit, serving there from 1923 to the end of the Mandate, in 1948, would relate.

From 1936 to 1939 Arabs got in murderous licks at Jewish settlements in widespread "disturbances." Added to the mass murder of the Nazi concentration camps, this produced a Jewish paranoia even more pronounced. They began collecting weapons (and there were plenty to be had). The Arabs followed suit. The government reacted with arms searches that were less than amiable. Resentment on all sides swelled into a slow burn and in 1944 found its outlets.

Two terrorist organizations were, by then, well established, the Irgun Zvai Leumi (National Military Organization), numbering several thousand (it claimed responsibility for the King David bombing) and the Stern Gang, a "few hundred" fanatics. Both stemmed from extremist wings of the militant Zionism spawned in pre-war Poland; both translated to Palestine and with one aim: destroy the mandate authority and establish an independent Israel.

The Stern Gang, fathered in Poland by Isaac Stern in 1937, joined the Polish forces resisting the Nazis. Many were subsequently captured by the Russians and later released. Once free, they found their way to Palestine and in time were assembled under Stern once more as a secret terrorist society. Its sole purpose was to drive the British out of the country, the assassination of military and government personnel being its avowed instrument. In one of the most gruesome episodes of this underground warfare, a squad of British soldiers was captured and the men hanged, their bodies booby-trapped so that many of their comrades, cutting them down, were also killed or mutilated. Stern himself was killed by Palestine Police in a skirmish in 1942.

One of the leaders of the Irgun was Menachem Begin, who was to become Prime Minister of Israel in 1977. Taxed with the unsavory record of the Irgun, Begin and numerous Israeli apologists heatedly reject the "terrorist" label. Indeed, Irgun forces did frequently operate openly, wearing identifying armbands when they fought alongside the Haganah in sporadic clashes with the Arabs. They also demanded they be treated as prisoners of war when taken by the authorities. But attacking the agencies of the mandate was a no-holds-barred operation and resulted in the deaths at the King David, scarcely testimony to a regard for the rules of land warfare.

That Begin, once a wanted criminal, should have become Prime Minister, surprised few. In the post-war years personal records attesting to imprisonment and "dead or alive" posters were invaluable credentials for politicians aspiring to posts in the former colonial territories, Begin,

Kwame Nkrumah of the Gold Coast, Kenyatta of Kenya and India's Nehru to name a few. Their acceptance by the rest of the world was the result of war-weariness, ignorance, a willingness in some quarters to let bygones be bygones and a sense that a new era was dawning, an era of righteousness that must atone for what were seen as the evils of the past.

In the van of the anti-colonial movement, subtly prodded forward by the Soviet Union, was the United States. The venue for its first active espousal of this cause was the U.N. General Assembly's 1948 Paris meeting at the Place de Trocadero, across the Seine River from the Eiffel Tower. Butt of America's indignation in the fall of Forty-eight was Holland, being humiliated and otherwise intimidated out of its East Indian possessions.

A seasoned observer of man's follies and certainly no colonialist, Theodore H. White was to observe in his *Search of History* that "The target of United States morality at the session was Holland; we were getting the Dutch out of the East Indies at the same time as, in those days, we were busily urging all white empires out of everywhere."

This crusade against the status quo failed to provide much in the way of replacement leadership, political or economic, for the newly independent. As a result, millions the world over were condemned to periods of chaotic irresolution and anarchy.

Britain, as the largest empire and bearing the lion's share of approbrium, was unable to fight back. With her human and material substance drained away in two world wars in forty years, she no longer could dispose the energies that had thrust her out over a major portion of the globe. The courage, imagination, arrogance, and missionary zeal that had produced the most expansive and workable empire in history had largely run away in the sands.

This was a great pity. My mature conviction characterizes the British Empire as a "good thing."

Contrary to the view that the West is responsible for all the miseries the Third World suffers, it should be patently obvious that, had it been possible *not* to have colonialism, that Third World would be even more wretched than it is. Much of its substance was drawn off by Western countries, true enough. And this exploitation did leave behind vacuums in the matter and the mind of the now-developing areas. Yet, the contact alone introduced primitive peoples to a world they could not, in any case, long avoid, and at the very least, began to educate them in its vagaries. In any event, argument about it is fatuous. Colonialism was inevitable. And inevitably it carried with it man's basic baggage of good as well as evil.

CHAPTER IV

Wages of Folly

The afternoon I arrived in Jerusalem in that spring of 1948, just as the United Nations readied for its Trocadero meeting, Britain's Palestine mandate was coming to an end, and the country was readying to take off on its own. The prospect was as grim as the Pantiles' surroundings. The hotel stood, starkly vulnerable, in a bald spot on the forward positions of the Jewish-held area.

"Couldn't have picked a better place to watch the war," I said to Pringle, who'd silently joined me at the curb down the steps from the front door. Small-arms fire broke out somewhere near the Phosphate Building, and he took my elbow and guided me toward the hotel entrance.

"Aye, 'tis indeed," he said, "and about this time every evenin' the fightin' picks up. We can watch it from the inside. That way we keep holes out of the hide, as they say, and anyway, that's where the whiskey is."

Inside, the hotel had the look and feel of an empty storehouse. It echoed. There were no visible furnishings, no carpets on the red granolithic flooring, no pictures on the walls, and the doors leading into rooms off the main corridor all gaped open. There was a second story that I assumed was the same. Above that, on the flat roof I'd noticed from outside, was the water tank and housing for the stairway opening and another brick hut for central electrical fittings. The interior decor featured plastered concrete painted pink and dirty white. All very dreary but easy to maintain cheaply.

The Arab management having prudently decamped with most of the fittings when the battle moved into the neighborhood, the place was now a press billet with Carter Davidson, Associated Press bureau chief in Jerusalem, stuck with the job of concierge/manager. The refugee owners had left it to the press to maintain a "guest list" and a record of food and drink consumed. Within ten days of my "registration" we were reduced to beer (a cellarful), matzoth and marmalade and whatever anyone could buy or scrounge in the New City. Everywhere tea and coffee were short; so was sugar. We could wash clothing only at mealtimes. Power cutoffs in our area were erratic but usually occurred between meals and from about 8:00 P.M. until 7:00 A.M. Soap was scarce. Nonetheless, through friends in the army and police and resident good Samaritans, the hotel "guests" got along well enough.

"I put your stuff in that front room," Pringle said as we entered the building and gestured down the dimly lit hallway. "You can bunk there until the shootin' gets too close. When that happens, move into the hallway. I'd put you in the back, but all those rooms are taken. Check in with Davidson when you can. Right there," and he pointed to a door near the front entrance with "Office" on the lintel. "Should be back soon" and then he was gone, up the stairs to what I supposed was his sleeping accommodation. Max had simply disappeared.

Alone in the apparently empty building, I walked down the hall to the door Pringle'd indicated. Inside the gloom my Val-Pac and musette bag were shadowy lumps on the floor, and there were two beds, a straight-backed wooden chair, and a deal table. Otherwise the room was bare. Most of the glass in the windows was gone.

No lights, Pringle had said, were allowed in front rooms even when the power was on, so I fumbled what I needed for the night out of my bags, dragged them into a corner and flopped down on the bed nearest the window, close to the wall and some protection from occasional flying bits. After seventeen anxious hours, I was punch drunk and lay there listening to the mounting racket outside and wondering how the hell I'd come to this pretty pass.

Certainly I hadn't started out in this direction. Born October 5, 1918, at Doctor's Hospital, New York City, I was an addition to a substantial and affluent clan. The Acheson family was large and lent consequence by the patriarch, Dr. Edward Goodrich Acheson, who had exploited his native energies and genius to rise from humble Scots/Irish beginnings in western Pennsylvania to be the prime mover in his own industrial empire.

With the former Margaret Maher, of New York's Borough of Brooklyn, then a country village innocent of the grisly distinctions to which it became heir, he produced nine children, later settling them and many of his grandchildren on farmland acreage off Lundy's Lane, some ten miles into Canada from Niagara Falls.

Meanwhile, anticipating what became a social norm in the mid-1900s, my parents, Delite Cornelia Nannette and John Huyler Acheson, were divorced in 1921. The reasons for their break largely remained their private concern.

My mother and I moved to the New York Park Avenue apartment of a befuddled widow of my maternal grandfather, Cornell Woolley, a well-to-do textile merchant for whom I'd been named.

Mother and child soon vacated these gloomy digs for Philadelphia and the Monte Vista Apartments (things were frightfully Spanish in the twenties) located in what was an acceptable, even enviable, part of the city's western fringes. Today it is labelled a ghetto.

The stay there was not without its moments.

My mother, engaged in unfamiliar employment as a file clerk in a bank, got in the way of an electric safe-deposit drawer and had her leg broken. I was threatened with a juvenile police record when the driver of an ice truck caught me stealing from his parked vehicle. And gangsters with masks on leaped from a black touring car and threatened to shoot my nursemaid, Lillian, as she walked me home from kindergarten. They left one man with a huge gun pointed at my quivering guardian while they set about their dirty work: robbing the deliveryman in a nearby, horse-drawn milk wagon. Dangerous living.

Delite, an intelligent and attractive woman, soon was remarried to a brilliant young stockbroker, Henry Clay Fox, Jr., a native Philadelphian. They were married at the Park Avenue address, and I officiated in some fringe capacity. I remembered only that I did it in a gray woolen knickerbocker (plus-four style) suit, the buckles fastened above the knees (below was for grownups). Streaming perspiration, my hair plastered to my skull, I recall heat, sweet smells, and large, dark-clothed people in forbidding Edwardian surroundings. That was 1927. My new father I would love without reserve as a gracious, caring, and truly remarkable man.

There were private schools and a year and a half at Wesleyan University in Middletown, Connecticut. Halfway through the second year there, John Huyler died. I took it very hard and, somehow academically crippled, elected not to return for the second semester. Instead I went to work as a broker's clerk at Philadelphia's Moyer & Company, the banker's firm in which my stepfather was a partner. I held the job for two years and at night studied accounting and commercial law at the Wharton School of Business and Finance at the University of Pennsylvania.

In 1940 I married Patricia Jameson. Radiant, shapely, and sharply intelligent (I'd met her one summer when I was in the cavalry at Culver Military Academy and she was vacationing nearby), "Trish" was loving and loyal and saw me through the confusing years it took to leave Philadelphia and return to finish college at Georgetown. She watched me leave for the war in the autumn of 1943 and took our year-old son, John

Huyler II to Indianapolis and her family's Central Avenue home for "the duration."

For a time between graduation from Georgetown and army induction, I'd worked as an analyst with the government Board of Economic Warfare. Housed in temporary buildings scattered about Washington's mall, the staff of the board was heavily weighted with far-left radicals. It provided me a rarified intellectual atmosphere and I collected some useful cynicism about public service. At the same time I never stopped pressing for military duty. Classified A-1 and awaiting call-up, I knew my near-blindness without glasses condemned me to be a uniformed clerk. To avoid this I provided the draft board with a medical certification attesting to a mechanical, not disease, disability. This suggested my sight would not deteriorate at a speed that should worry the military.

My hope was to be attached to the newly formed army G-5 Section, Civil Affairs/Military Government. The G-5 teams were assigned to combat units and were dropped off to supervise the care, control, and rehabilitation of civil communities overrun in the fighting. For someone educated in "Foreign Service," with French as a foreign language, trained at the Board of Economic Warfare (B.E.W.) in the economic life of Europe, I should have been a "natural" for G-5. As it turned out I was classed a naval rating, and assigned shore duty in Norfolk, Virginia. A friendly brigadier in the right place got me transferred to the Military Police Training Depot, Fort Custer, Michigan. For those who lasted the course as an M.P., including judo, bayonet drill, and twenty-mile marches and had a college degree, there was promotion to Civil Affairs/Military Government training. I made it.

Almost two weeks aboard the U.S. Coast Guard vessel *Billy Mitchell* got me into the Firth of Clyde in Scotland and most of the way toward the European Theater of Operations. From Scotland my unit went southward through the Irish Sea to Liverpool on a coaster normally doing duty as a cattle boat. In fact, as we filed aboard, it had just disembarked what must have been enough beef on the hoof to feed the entire British army for a year.

Below decks it was ripe. My shallow bunk was six inches above the deck and a sloshing bilge that slapped against the planking of this improvised bier repeatedly splashed a meaty spray of liquid cowdung the length of my prostrate form. Enemy planes were said to have homed in on the aromatic cloud that hovered over the Liverpool docks as we debouched onto the quay.

The skills so hard won at Georgetown, the B.E.W., and Fort Custer would be largely overlooked. I was lofted from private to staff sergeant, at which eminence I spent most of the war surviving. I typed imaginative reports of the wonders of military aid to civilian populations, drove a jeep on such dubious sallies as the transport of long woolen underwear through a storm of enemy mortar and machine-gun fire to totally uncaring French civilians. And dug foxholes. Three feet wide and eighteen inches deep from St. Lô on the Cotentin Peninsula to the town of Bar Le Duc in eastern France, four hundred forty-nine kilometers.

When the war ended, and immeasurably enriched by this military career, I offered my talents to the *Indianapolis News*.

In the event, it turned out to be a calling for which I was reasonably suited. Yet, the demands it made on me as a learner were severe. Unsure of myself, I'd overworked long hours, made the job paramount, and hid my inadequacies behind an unbecoming and phony worldliness that included the earnest, if passing, delusion that I had special social gifts. Within two years, this pose, with the pecadillos that went with it, had pulled my marriage apart.

And all that, I concluded, rolling off the bunk in that Jerusalem bedroom, was quite enough to explain, "how the hell I'd come to this pretty pass."

CHAPTER V

Battle at Rachel's Tomb

Almost two weeks to the day after we'd arrived from Cairo, the British mandate ended, May 14, 1948. The city, its tensions ticking louder as the day had drawn near, went off with a roar. My story to the *Indianapolis News* went in part like this:

> At 11:15 A.M. May 14 the last British soldier left his post in the New City. At that moment heavily armed Jewish Haganah troops streamed down King George Avenue and occupied the positions just below the Pantiles Hotel, where the foreign press is billeted.
> Elsewhere in the New City Jewish forces, Irgun Zvei Leumi, Haganah, and units of the Stern Gang, moved into place around Barclays Bank, the post office, the Italian Hospital, and near Damascus Gate. An Irgun squad crept toward the Palestine Police Training Depot at Sheik Jarrah.
> Arab reinforcements moved into positions facing the strongest Jewish encroachment and swung around from Sheik Jarrah to the Talpiyot section to the south, thus straddling the road we'd traveled from Bethlehem.
> At about 12:15 P.M., heavy firing broke out near Jaffa Gate, Yemin Moshe, and the German Quarter, northeast of Talpiyot. Near the center of Jerusalem the Jews fought an inch-by-inch battle toward Damascus Gate.
> The war was on in earnest. . . .

Actually there'd been quite a lot of sniper practice for days. Gunnery exercises with an aged French .75 firing from the Old City wall, had been sporadic, with shells dropping here and there around the Pantiles. A small mortar bomb landed on the hotel roof and, perforating the water tank, reduced us to bucketing water in from an abandoned house nearby.

As the fourteenth neared, the correspondents had moved out of front rooms into the hallways to sleep and set up an impromptu newsroom, using a telephone leading out of Carter's office. Movement about the place was on all fours below windowsill level or on the run.

The front vestibule, with its heavy oaken portal, was one of the few safe areas, and on the way to talk to Davidson I rose to my feet and approached his door. Just as I reached it, there was a popping sound followed by a tinkling glass, a series of "thunking" noises, and then the whirr of something metallic being stirred in a bowl. And then Carter appeared, his chunky frame filling the doorway, his normallly placid expression altered to dead-white astonishment.

A .303 bullet had shattered the window near his desk (the popping sound and tinkling glass), had ricocheted around the four walls at about head height and finished up whistling about in the corner washbasin. The slug was still hot when we picked it out of the bowl.

"That damned thing nearly went through my right ear," he protested, and so it had, missing his head by inches as he sat at his desk.

As if the routine at the Pantiles wasn't fraught enough, we undertook frequent visits to Jewish Agency press briefings uptown in the New City. To get there, we piled into an aged convertible, the property of the Associated Press, reaching the car without attracting too much attention by slipping out the rear of the building. In the run for the town center we first cruised slowly along a narrow sanitary lane, reserved normally for rubbish collections, to halt behind garden walls where the alley met King George Avenue. After a moment's revving the antique engine until it threatened to fly off in all directions, Davidson would throw the vehicle forward into the avenue, swing hard right up the hill, screech around a "rond point" about halfway to the top, and in an exposed area between a cemetery and open ground, dash the last few hundred yards to the Haganah roadblock. All agreed Carter's driving was far more hair-raising than the risk we'd be blown up, although on one occasion we did experience a near thing that couldn't be blamed on Davidson.

About eight of us had climbed aboard for the trip back down to the Pantiles after a particularly bibulous briefing, a special tipple prompted by a more than normally arid news fare about "consolidating previous gains." I sat in the back seat. Pringle perched on the folded supports of the collapsed convertible top, his legs dangling down over the left rear wheel. Others were jammed in around me or sat like birds on a rail along the back of the seat. I put my arm across Pringle's lap and gripped the roof hinge in a try at keeping him from bouncing off.

With Carter at the wheel, we cleared the roadblock and had gone about twenty yards, picking up speed, when the world exploded.

The open area of Mamillah cemetery was on our left between us and the Arab-held Old City walls, and we certainly made an inviting target. We were aware the Legion pumped shells at this stretch of road as a harassment to traffic because they'd had a crack at us once before.

When the shell exploded, our first reaction was that they'd landed on target. Pringle threw himself violently backward across my lap, clutching his crotch and making dramatic Irish noises about the demise of his sexual career. The car careened, rocking wildly, across King George, until Carter righted it and to our shrieks of encouragement aimed for the "rond point," his foot flat on the floor.

I don't recall exactly who we all were that day. Those who took turns chancing the exploit included Jock Calder, Reuters; Bob ("Pepper") Martin, *New York Post;* Farnie Fowle and Dana Adams Schmidt, both the *New York Times;* Bob Hecox, *Paramount News;* Carl Gossett, *New York Times* photographer; Jim McClure, *Pathe News;* and Al Noderer, *Chicago Tribune.* And Pringle, Ken Bilbey, *New York Herald-Tribune,* and Davidson. Most of the contingent was in the car. And all of us miraculously made it into the lane behind the Pantiles not much the worse for the experience.

We later learned that the shell had hit midway up a metal light pole just as we'd passed, and the shower of fragments had been shrapnel and bits of the stanchion. The back of my wrist, where it had lain across Pringle's lap, was neatly if only slightly, sliced open, a near-miss that the Irishman insisted justified his panic. After that, although we continued to make the trip when we could, we staggered the schedule to confuse the gunners' planning and had no more trouble—from that .75 at least.

We quickly learned to accept the Pantiles' recurring hazards, largely because covering the real stories of the city's torment was proving so stimulating. Not that a bullet past one's ear during a morning shave was ignored. It just was placed in its proper spot on the scale of cold-sweat producers.

Prime obstacle to full coverage of the quickening war was, as usual, the bureaucracy set up ostensibly to keep the press informed and out of harm's way. Before the Mandate ended I was granted a Palestine Information Office pass, No. 1622, good from January 1, 1948, to June 30, 1948, in English, Hebrew and Arabic, and I added it to my Cairo American University document. After the Mandate ended, we all got periodic laissez-passes from the Jewish Agency.

The Arabs, whom we seemed always to visit in a zigzag dead run or crawling on our hands and knees beneath a hail of miscellaneous metal junk, were not well enough organized as a single headquarters to issue formal accreditation. They simply played each developing situation by ear, and if we had to dodge overly zealous and underalerted guards and other shooters to make contact with them, that was simply in the nature of the job.

Luckily for me, Carl Gossett, Davidson, Frank Scherschel of *Life,* Calder, and others seasoned in the techniques of circumventing press regulations and with a host of contacts in high places, took me under their wings. When first I arrived in Palestine, every story I covered was thanks to these men, Al Noderer, Martin, Hecox and the rest. Admittedly, as noted earlier, *Indianapolis News* "airmailers" scarcely loomed tall as competition for the likes of *Life* or Reuters, but Scherschel and the others spent time wet-nursing a neophyte that they might have used more fruitfully on their own stories.

Occasionally I did have a chance to return the favors.

With Mandate's end only a few days away, a Jewish strongpoint at a kibbutz south of the city, Ramat Rahel, "Rachel's Tomb," was high on the list of Arab priorities. With Ramat Rahel in their hands, they'd hold a tactical advantage on the road southward to the Negev Desert and have one more trump card in any dealings with the United Nations, scheduled to assume ceasefire responsibilities in Palestine June 10. After a year of bloody battles that saw "Rachel's Tomb" pass back and forth between the Jews and, variously, Arab Legion and Bedouin irregulars, it was back in the Haganah's hands again. The Jews intended to hold it at all costs and, with a major assault by the Arabs imminent, Davidson wanted the story covered for the Associated Press. He was otherwise committed, awaiting a Jewish offensive against a portion of the Old City during which it was thought the attackers would use, for the first time, a "secret weapon" they called "Davidka," a homemade rocket dubbed the "Little David." Carter wanted to be there if they did.

Reckoning I owed much to Carter, I volunteered to do the Ramat Rahel story for the A.P. The more important Old City story would be exhaustively covered by the wire services, and, anyway, the embattled village was more the kind of feature I'd learned to settle for. If the kubbutz held out, there'd be no problem. If it looked as if it wouldn't, I'd have to make a break for it. It was risky either way, but my offer had been easier to make after I'd learned that Pringle would be assigned the Ramat Rahel pictures. My escort was further strengthened when Bob Hecox, battlewise (he was even then recovering from leg wounds suffered in a set-to in Haifa) and vastly experienced, had asked at the last minute to go along.

Carter took the three of us in the old convertible. Following a circuitous route, circumventing Jewish and Arab positions, we arrived at a spot beyond the city limits. There he dropped us off on the side of a dirt road leading up the hill to the settlement. We were to call him when the job was done, and he'd come pick us up "wherever you are." It was late afternoon and Davidson's source had said our access would remain open only until nightfall, when the Arabs were expected to begin taking up positions around the hill. They were already in place on the far side, and sporadic fire could be heard as we panted up the path to the top. There Haganah sentries, alerted by radio, were expecting us.

In peacetime Ramat Rahel had been a prosperous colony of several hundred families, their livelihood coming from truck gardening, a dairy, and a small furniture factory. Vegetable plots and orchards and standard barnyard livestock fed the inhabitants, and a large bakery provided not only for the kibbutz but for much of the outlying district, Jews and Arabs alike. It had been a flourishing, happy community, gaily gardened in a floral flood of color, a veritable jewel in the sun, where the area's inhabitants had gathered for fairs and dances, special educational classes in animal husbandry, and other ventures.

When we clambered over the encircling outer wall, the place had been reduced to a stinking ruin. Only one building had anything resembling a roof. Once doubling as town hall and community meetingplace, it now served as a soldiers' mess, dormitory, and, in the greater protection of the basement, as a first-aid station. Now, sole inhabitants of the settlement were the Haganah.

Dead cows and sheep, bloated in the hot sun and acrawl with maggots, lay in moldering heaps. With the Arabs periodically drenching the hilltop with mortar bombs and maintaining a tattoo of sniper fire, there'd been no time to bury the remains. Trees and shrubbery were torn and ragged, and only the barest evidence of a once thriving village could be detected here and there beneath the blasted remnants.

Some two hundred yards to the southwest across a shallow, boulder-strewn valley was Mar Ilyas, a Greek Orthodox monastery, occupied now by Arab irregulars.

A young officer greeted us curtly and introduced the unit's doctor who'd be our guide, chosen because he spoke fluent English. Short, frail, and softspoken, he filled us in on the history of Ramat Rahel, gave us permission to wander the ruins alone at will, only pointing out areas where we might draw Arab fire and, if we were careless, stop some of it. When mortar bombs began whomping in at an increasing rate and it became too dark for pictures, we dumped our things in the cubicle we'd been assigned in the blockhouselike mess hall and joined the soldiers, most of them cleaning equipment.

Not a few had been with the Jewish Brigade Group and had seen wartime action before. Most, however, were teenagers from the kibbutzim, the communal collective farms. Some were from America—Chicago, Pittsburgh, and St. Paul, Minnesota—totalling perhaps half a dozen of some five hundred Americans fighting with the Haganah.

We ate a Spam stew, drank some South African brandy, and retired for a noisy, sleepless night. At first light we staggered out for scrambled powdered eggs, chunks of stale bread, and black British army "char," tea that'd dye your boots.

The day passed quickly. By noon Hecox and Pringle had finished collecting background pictures and I'd roamed the ruins interviewing everyone who spoke English or French. During the afternoon, things livened up a bit when the Arabs sailed a few shells our way and a probing attack on the south wall kept things hot for about half an hour.

"Tomorrow we'll catch it," the doctor said, as if to assure us that our trip had not been made for nothing. "They're expected to complete preparations tonight and will probably have a go tomorrow."

He was right. The next afternoon the mortaring started and increased in volume until by evening the settlement was shrouded in a thick pall of dust. Inside the aid station, men swathed in bloody sheeting lay, gray-faced, on the floor. The room shuddered constantly.

It was pointless to venture outside. Hecox had put his camera back in the case after a futile midafternoon try, when the three of us had crawled out on surrounding ramparts. Below us, the white-robed attackers swarmed convulsively around the base of the hill where the Jews managed to keep them pinned down. Ultimately the snap of incoming small-arms fire and an uncomfortably close shell that rattled the fillings in my teeth had sent us scrambling for the safety of the makeshift clinic.

"Too much for you?" a big, bearded Jew with bloodshot eyes in a dirty face snorted derisively.

Aware that my hands were shaking, that my face was ashen and that my voice, if I could summon it, would squeak and falter, I said nothing. (I have dreamed up some crushing replies in subsequent years but at that moment? Nothing.) The doctor came to my rescue.

"Leave him alone," he snapped at the man. "He'll get used to it, the way we all have. You'd look a bit sick too if you ever came out from behind that beard," and he poured me a large brandy.

The following day we had off with very little action. The "lull before more shit hits the fan," as the young Chicagoan put it, and the doctor agreed with him. The prospect was less than happy but in spite of a tendency to shake and grow faint at the slightest alarm, I stood ready to quake through another twenty-four hours if everyone else was. This time Hecox came to the rescue.

He had, he said, all the pictures he wanted and was anxious to get back to Jerusalem and send them off. Pringle concurred. There was little more I could do for Davidson, short of creeping, fatally wounded, from the final battle of Ramat Rahel to gargle out the account as my life blood burbled away into the sands of Zion. Convinced, however, that Davidson would not expect that much enthusiasm, I readily agreed with the Paramount man that it was time to "blow this dump." The young commander understood our need to get copy on the way and, glad to slough off the responsibility of keeping us alive, applauded our decision. After some short, sharp conversation in the aid station with his lieutenants and endless phone chatter with an apparently elusive command post in the Talpiyot sector, now become a battleground, he set out a timetable for our departure.

The escape plan was simple enough. Down the steep face of the hill on the back side away from the Arab positions at the Monastery of Mars Ilyas an ancient drainage ditch dropped to flat, open land and then, about three feet deep, crossed it for a distance of some two hundred yards. This would be enough to take us through the Arab perimeter. The area was a clear field of fire for both sides and for this reason remained unoccupied on all but the most fleeting basis. If we crouched low, we were told, we could make it in the darkness without being seen. Since I had come to spend more time on all fours than upright, cowering at full speed for a few hundred yards would be second nature.

A Haganah noncom, appropriately named David, with messages to carry, would guide us along the ditch into the Talpiyot section and, it was hoped, the newly established Jewish command post. The Arab force that had taken Talpiyot on the fourteenth still had it, it appeared, but were confidently expected to be routed out by the time we arrived. Which would be nice, especially since the Pringle-Hecox-Acheson party would arrive, stealthily on hands and knees, with a uniformed Jewish sergeant in the van.

Still, any misgivings we might have had were more than counterbalanced by the realization that the Arabs might overrun Ramat Rahel within the next few hours, butchering survivors willy nilly. We packed up and awaited nightfall.

When it came it was overcast, oven-hot, still, and black as a crypt. We were unable to find our way even through the familiar hilltop devastation and were forced to follow a pencil of light the guide dribbled along behind him. The doctor, ever conscious of his duty, shepherded us to the dropoff into the ditch, whispered a warm farewell and was gone.

Dead north from Ramat Rahel, in the vicinity of Yemin Moshe, the sky above the Old City flashed alight and the rumblings of the distant battle jarred the air with tiny blows against our eyes and eardrums. As the first Arab mortar bomb somersaulted in to crash down behind us, we slid off under the barbed wire concertina and scrabbled downward into the ditch.

Within seconds sweat, some hot some cold, had soaked through my bush jacket and the thighs of my trousers were drenched. I brought up the rear behind Pringle, and Hecox, with his clutch of clanking equipment, beetled along behind David. Silence, we'd been warned, was vital. The Arabs obviously knew of this aged watercourse and certainly would have secured it if the Jews, from the heights of Ramat Rahel, hadn't been able to draw a clear bead along its full length and sweep it sporadically with heavy machine gun fire. David obviously felt that the absence of these regular nighttime bursts plus the racket Hecox was making would alert every Arab from Galilee to the Sinai. After calling a halt and chewing us out in an angry whisper, he had apparently given up, consigning his soul to wherever it could go under the circumstances, and led the way at a good clip.

The bottom and sides of the trench were literally paved with slick, rounded boulders and landscaped with giant thistles. By the time we halted for a breather in a scoured-out bowl of the wadi, I'd been reduced to one large contusion stung to bleeding blisters by poison nettles. Yet, even in this tragic state, every nerve-end atwinge, I lay there appalled at the fireworks on the horizon. Flaming Jerusalem was flying off in all directions, great burning chunks of it arcing lazily into the air above the Vale of Kidron.

Still, this was scarcely novel for "The City of Peace," sacked fifteen times in the past six centuries. Today, of course, all of Palestine, as Israel, is a twentieth century marvel. Where we padded along goat trails, six-lane intercity boulevards sweep across the Judean hills, and the Jerusalem suburbs where we bellied along through those burning bushes rival affluent suburbs anywhere. Yet, it still is torn by terrorist bombs and someone has identified the "paradox" innate in Jerusalem's destiny as "never more powerfully the magnate of devotion, never more fatally the source of strife." Which quite neatly sums it up.

After what seemed an age under a steadily lowering ceiling of orange tracers that formed a crackling loose weave overhead and flares so revealing they seemed to pick out Hecox's bones through his shirt, it was suddenly very dark and quiet as we came out of the ditch into thick shrubbery. David rose to his feet, told us, out loud, to follow him closely and took off at a brisk walk through streets of a built-up ghost community that had to be Talpiyot. We'd gone only a few yards when, looming up around us out of the ground, were members of a Haganah patrol. The

Arabs had been driven out and Talpiyot was theirs. Almost.

I can't remember how it happened, but we joined the party and were pressed into service pushing a stalled Bedford five-ton truck. I'd hardly put a shoulder to it when, knocked to the ground by the soldier next to me, I watched, fascinated, as a bazooka shell roared up from behind us out of the blackness. Its flaming tail whooshed by within a few feet, and it hit a tree just in front of the Bedford, tearing the night into a corona of red and orange.

No one was more than scratched, and deafened, and eventually we made it to what I recall was a large, overstuffed room in a deserted mansion set deep in a grove of cypress. A luxurious, high-ceilinged library, furnished in ponderous Victorian discomfort, had been appropriated as temporary headquarters for the Haganah forces consolidating in the sector.

The telephone line to the Pantiles was intact, and I was able to reach Carter. He came out, the old convertible coughing its way through the smoke of the firelit night, and returned us to the Pantiles. I did my piece for the Associated Press and was able to follow it the next day with an account of the relief of the battered kibbutz. Palmach commando units had torn apart the flank of the attackers just as Arab forward units threatened to breach the inner defenses and the offensive collapsed.

Whatever had happened, I had paid back at least some of my debt to Carter. And, with so heavy an obligation, the repayment had been more than worth the risk.

CHAPTER VI

All-Points Coverage

In the ensuing few days the conflict tightened around the Pantiles. It limited our movement from the building, and if we did succeed in making it to the communications room of the American Consulate General, our sole cable facility, the allotment was twelve hundred words a day for a dozen correspondents. Twelve hundred words was scarcely enough for the average lead paragraph in one of Dana Adams Schmidt's *New York Times* stories. For me, sending airmailers by donkey through Jordan, it was no handicap, but the issue lacerated the already-jangling nerves of those who depended on it.

Food at the billet ran seriously short: sardines, matzoh, marmalade, and weak tea was a sumptuous meal. Some managed to do better, of course, but that was the fare for many of us. The only plentiful item was beer, crates of it. We were so short of water, we almost stooped to using Tuborg to shave in. Restaurants uptown in the New City were down to "brown soup," brussels sprouts, and leather mutton, hardly worth the risky run through sporadic whiffs of grape. A Franciscan monk who had regularly visited the Pantiles from the Old City beginning long before I arrived did appear with large loaves of doughy bread and a haunch of slightly overripe lamb.

One product the good father brought was news, tidbits about life in the Old City and tipoffs about impending Arab, and Jewish, action. Known to everyone, he moved without hindrance through the lines and no doubt was used by both sides to leak information. It was the Padre who told Carter and others about the expected use of "Davidka" in the attack on the Old City.

Most of the time we chased stories where we could, and the tighter things got the more we grasped at straws. An errant midnight shell through the wall of an apartment occupied by one of the correspondent's Jewish girl friends became story material because the girl was with Haganah intelligence, pretty weak justification at best.

There were, of course, stories well worth the scramble. One that Carl Gossett invited me along for involved the Red Cross duty to bury the dead on both sides. The dateline of the story I wrote for the *Indianapolis News* was the Katamon Quarter of the city:

> It has been five days since the Jewish Haganah forces recaptured Katamon. After a bitter twenty-four–hour battle both sides numbered scores of dead. Arabs not carried away by retreating units, have lain where they fell or were tossed into crude graves as a sanitary measure by the occupying Jews.
>
> Jean Courvoisier, one of four International Red Cross delegates stationed in Jerusalem, and three Jewish helpers were assigned the job of reclamation and burial.
>
> The first function of the Red Cross, identification, was messy, but the Arabs were readily distinguishable from other dead, and none were missed.
>
> From a rooftop, from a tangle of barbed wire and from the furrows of a family vegetable garden three khaki-clad bodies were recovered. Nine more were dragged from an ancient burial vault deep in the hillside near where the Greek Orthodox Monastery of St. Simeon is located.
>
> A British-imposed ceasefire in the area had been set to last forty-eight hours. By the time Courvoisier and his helpers arrived at St. Simeon, only thirty minutes of the truce remained. Already Arab sniper fire sang off the crude stone walls surrounding the monastery grounds, and after one particularly heavy fusillade Courvoisier, furious, leaped to the roof of the truck carrying the corpses and, waving a pitifully small Red Cross flag, shouted angrily at the distant marksmen as bullets thumped into the body of the vehicle.
>
> Courvoisier, at six feet three inches towering above the taciturn, bitter, little Jewish officer in charge at the monastery, demanded help recovering the bodies and got a flat refusal. Obviously the soldier hesitated to give an order his men might well ignore. Later he pitched in himself to help us pull the remains from the vault protesting that we should "leave well enough alone."
>
> It was no job for the faint-hearted or squeamish. Courvoisier has done this work in Italy and Germany and estimates he has buried some 2,000 war dead in the past decade. On one occasion a helper sickened and the big Swiss stripped off his jacket and dropped into the pit to tie the telephone line to the bodies and start them upward on their way out of the vault.

St. Simeon is fifty years old, new by Holy Land standards, but the ground here has been hallowed for centuries.

But not so's you'd notice it today.

During the Mandate we'd been able to cross battle lines by pre-arrangement with both sides and with a forceful assist from the British Public Relations Office. This gave us a unique opportunity to cover both sides of the conflict, but it did lay us open to charges, by Jews and Arabs, that we were spies for one side or the other. After a few nasty confrontations with Jewish authorities, it became such a chançy gamble that we abandoned it and selected one camp. Those of us at the Pantiles, to be inside Jewish lines once the Mandate did end, would have the choice made for us.

Anticipating these limitations, we had crammed in as much "dual" coverage as time and luck permitted. One such story involved a look at a roadblock at Bab El Wad on the Tel Aviv–to–Jerusalem roadway, one that was said to be preventing supplies from reaching the New City. First we went with the Jews.

The invitation from the Haganah was designed to prove to us that their only lifeline with the coast was actually cut. Since this, if true, could starve the city into submission, we accepted.

One squally morning, intermittently pouring with rain and steamy under the hot sun, Bilby, Davidson, Pringle, and I rattled out in the old convertible to a meeting with the Palmach squad that would be our escort.

The eight soldiers in the unit included three extremely tough and aggressive female precursors of the Women's Lib movement, one of them actually in charge. Displaying all the charm of a cornered panther, she snarled at us to do as we were told, beginning with keeping together to the rear of the patrol, and quickly took off through the scrubby highlands. After some fifteen minutes we were ordered to drop flat and crawl. This was less precaution, I was convinced, than calculated brutality. The sandy soil was matted with thistles and thorn bush and while this muscular shrew and her team were protected by heavy uniforms, we were sundered and slit, permanently engraved, within seconds.

Adding to this misery was the pop and ping of rifle fire overhead as we neared the lip of a shallow canyon. This had the effect of pushing us even harder into the nettles, and I'd just reached the stage when I'd have welcomed an Arab bullet between the eyes, when we rolled over the edge and down into the cover of a crude stone wall. The firing lessened and we worked our way down to the floor of the gorge, where a scattering of large boulders obstructed movement through a narrow section of the ravine. Two burned-out trucks and an overturned homemade armored car were testimony to the traffic problems but it hardly seemed the formidable obstacle the Jewish Agency had depicted.

To be able to say we'd done it, we left the patrol behind, its amazonian leader screaming Hebrew imprecations, and walked among the boulders and wrecked vehicles keeping a wary eye on the heights above us. The shooting had stopped, and we chose to walk out of the wadi (oasis) rather than repeat the drama of our early-morning creep through the heather.

In fact, we considered the entire operation, including the timorous skulk through the brambles, to have been laid on, an exaggeration to prove a point about the Arab strangulation of life in Jerusalem.

We did admit, however, that it was easier for us to wander about the area on foot, protected by our formidable guardians, than for a driver, vulnerable atop a bulldozer, to shift the blockage. It was also obvious that the Arab command, scarcely all untutored ruffians, had the subtlety to hold off during what was obviously a press visit. And that they could put the stopper back in the neck of the valley anytime they wanted. So long as they held the heights.

Knowing the Jews planned a major assault to clear these heights and anxious to see how the Arabs would cope with it, we determined to pay a visit to the opposition side.

A visit to Arab headquarters at Ramallah, some ten miles into the hill country north of Jerusalem, was arranged for us by the British. After an endless round of standard courtesies, cups of the sweet, muddy coffee, chat about American politics and even discussion about a visit to Wagnerian opera in Bayreuth, we were granted permission to join a contingent of Arab irregulars reinforcing others manning the ridges above the gorge. We would join the force the following morning. After a round of farewell formalities as fulsome as our welcome, we returned to the Pantiles and preparation for our trip to the Arab lines.

Normally such steps were relatively simple, requiring a minimum of secrecy to ensure we didn't inadvertently invite our competing colleagues. In this instance, however, we had to exercise extra precautions.

A *Newsweek Magazine* man, whose name doesn't deserve mention, had shadowed us the day before. This round, owlish little man, aware we hadn't piled into Carter's convertible for a drive in the country, had followed us out to the Bab El Wad road by car and then crept along behind us until we struck out into uncomfortable territory. There he backed off. Last seen by us, he was cringing behind the doorjamb of a ruined building, whence he shortly retired all the way back to the cable office. There, this cowardly, if admittedly sensible, maneuver permitted him to beat Davidson and Bilby by advance filing of copy consisting largely of guesswork. This was clever but it was fraud.

The next morning, each of us took off from the Pantiles, early, at different times and in different directions. On foot. Dumping him was easy, and we met at our car, parked on the Arab side of the crossover location the night before.

At Ramallah we met one Fawzi Bey el Kaouji, an Iraqi colonel leading the Bab el Wad action, and set up our visit to the frontlines. My *News* story dateline was the same as two days earlier:

> The Bedouin is noted for his fighting courage, his marksmanship with an antique rifle and his independence.
>
> For centuries he has eked out a bare existence in barren desert wastes. He is a tender of sheep, a wanderer and a freebooter of considerable skill. He appears to care little for anyone but his own. He will meticulously honor terms of a bargain and will cordially cut your throat if you fail to do the same.
>
> Today I accompanied a score of the men engaged in the fight for the narrow valley that is the lifeline from Tel Aviv to the New City of Jerusalem.
>
> The picture had changed since several of us went undeterred into the gorge two days ago. From an artillery position zeroed in on the blockaded roadway two miles distance, we observed Arab shells raining down on the area we'd visited.
>
> While we were being briefed by a Colonel Madi, Iraqi commander of the battery, two truckloads of Bedouins wound up the rocky incline. The only order, if that's the word, given to the men as they tumbled to the ground was "The Jews are over there; beyond that second hill."
>
> It was explained to me that any hint of a command could suggest a planned operation, rob the assault of the spontaneity favored by the Bedouin, and spoil his fun. Annoyed, he might simply pack up his gear and rifle and go home.
>
> Short and stocky, the ragged gallibeahs rendering them shapeless, and wound around with bandoleers of ammunition, they picked their way swiftly down the rocky slopes. It was hard going keeping up with them, and only when one of their number argued successfully for a pause to take stock were we able to catch up.
>
> In the distance, rifle and automatic-weapons fire rattled around the upland steeps, and overhead the shells from the covering battery cut the air with a hard, echoing crack.
>
> As we moved across the shallow valley floor toward the climb

upward to the hillcrest above the key highway, a messenger appeared running toward the line of advancing men. The Jews, he shouted, were now in command of Bab el Wad, a bit of news that, unaccountably, produced a chorus of cheers from his colleagues, who kept up the attack.

With the other newsmen I stopped and fell back short of the last slope, fearful that the Jews, if actually in command of the heights, might pick us off. Moving bodies looked all the same in the dust storm created by exploding shells. Nor could the Arabs behind us be counted on to know who we were. Or care.

In interviews we'd had back in Ramallah, it had been made clear that the Arab Command considers the battle for Bab el Wad the battle for Jerusalem.

One officer had a sharp reply when asked about civilian deaths: "So one hundred thousand Jews starve to death in the city," he shrugged. "They asked for it. When the British have left we will fight this thing out. Then either they will win or we will and it will be settled."

The Arabs lost the battle of Bab el Wad. And a lot more after that. But no one won them, either.

The Ramallah experience had been useful. We had listened, firsthand, to the Arab "case" for the first time, met Arab leaders as men with a cause no less passionately pursued than the homeland principle espoused by the Zionists. We were impressed by the case and its advocates, some of them graduates of Oxford and Cambridge, of Britain's military College at Sandhurst and the French Military academy at St. Cyr.

With more truth than tact, Pringle later remarked that, until Ramallah, the only Arabs he'd encountered "were dead or should have been." He was only being truthful when he said all he'd known had been a pretty sorry lot, lazy, sickly, half-blinded by traucoma, and so dirty that, in his colorful idiom, they "smelled like a mud flat."

Those we met in Ramallah and many others they represented had risen above the squalor of their beginnings or had been launched into life by influential and wealthy families. They were educated, thoughtful, and articulate. Yet within a few years, men of this type gave way to clever thugs like Yasir Arafat, Chairman of the Palestine Liberation Organization, an Arab leader motivated almost solely by consuming hatreds. In April, 1979, after Israel and Egypt, with the guidance of the American

President, had signed a treaty of peace, Arafat, charging Egypt with treason and America with duplicity, reportedly threatened to "chop off the hands" of the signatories.

This may be a common enough Near East remedy in law, but for the West it made a mockery of lofty P.L.O. rhetoric about "Justice."

CHAPTER VII

Leaving Bleeding Jerusalem

Back in Jerusalem British police and military readied for withdrawal. Tons of material had to be moved and a reasonably safe passage secured to coastal ports of embarkation at Haifa and at Egypt's Port Said. Adding to the difficulties of evacuation in the middle of a battle—and they were constantly attacked by Jewish and Arab forces—was a critical shortage of transport.

During the last days of the Mandate, many vehicles had been destroyed or hijacked and the government of Palestine, pressed to meet the May 14 deadline, decided it could not await replacements from Britain. The forces would have to make do with what they had, doubling occupancy and pushing the trucks into as many trips as they could stand before they collapsed. And it worked. At least most of the men and their equipment got to the P.O.E.'s. And others got out of Jerusalem to Allenby Barracks on the Bethlehem road, positions they could hold with ease until more transport could be sent back to collect them.

Yet, for one British batallion, ready to push off from their Jerusalem HQ on the eleventh of May, the lorries were counted and came up short.

The men had seen long service in Palestine as backup for the police and had suffered heavy casualties. The captain of one company told me he'd lost more than twenty men killed in one month, all shot on post duty and "all shot in the back."

"Aye, it's good to be leavin' this bloody country," he said, "but it's a pity we couldn't have had a proper dust-up with the gloves off before pullin' out."

What follows is taken from rather scrappy notes I've retained. As for names of individuals, Britain's Ministry of Defense, quite rightly, refuses to divulge information without "the written consent of the persons concerned or, if deceased, the written consent of the next of kin." I've not managed to trace any of them. Yet this is what I recall happened and identifies one of the men I remember made it happen.

By the night of May 12, much of the Battalion HQ and its records had been moved out of the city proper to Allenby Barracks. One company remained, billeted in the New City's western reaches not far from the top of King George V Avenue. The transport shortage threatened to force the unit into a "jitney move," the few available vehicles running back and forth to the assembly point. This would be a long and sloppy operation that, moreover, would break the company into small squads highly vulnerable to the kind of hit-and-run attacks that had shredded their ranks for months.

The commanding officer, I remember only as a large man with an "aluminium" hand substituting for one lost in World War Two. My notes do not identify him. Carl Gossett had taken me along to share an interview with him at what was left of Battalion HQ. He was dour to the point of being speechless but this I recorded:

> "I have no wish to 'jitney out,' " he said. "I have a better plan that might be just what's needed to pull the bastards into the open where we can have a right good 'go' at 'em."

When asked what this alternative was, he only shrugged, heaved to his feet and, after a perfunctory salute, left the room.

"Now, he'd be a bluidy fool ta tell ye that, now wouldna 'e?" His aide, a brick-built, ruddy-faced major with black hair on the back of his hands, walked us to the door. Whatever the plan, the only way out was down King George Avenue past the Pantiles.

The next morning, as dawn crept over the city in a silvery haze, we were waiting, crouched on the second-floor balcony off Jock Calder's room. We had a clear view the length of the thoroughfare, leftward to the roadblock at the bottom of the avenue, manned by one of the battalion units, and of the roadway beyond that bisected the barren lands stretching out toward the railway station and Allenby Barracks. Movement down King George past the roadblock and out into this open space could be an adventure. The taxi bringing us across it from Cairo had been hit, and things had livened up considerably since then. From the Jewish posts in Yemin Moshe and Arab positions on the Old City wall, it was a shooting gallery. Just the night before, as the batallion readied to move, the darkness had been stitched up by threads of tracer fire over the area and blasted by mortar and grenade explosions.

Now it was quiet, deathly so, as if the city lay exhausted. We'd waited silently in the dawn chill for perhaps half an hour before we heard them coming from up King George on our right, the steady clomp of hobnailed boots pounding out a measured beat to the skirl of the pipes.

Calder, a Highland Light Infantry major with World War Two service in the Levant, knelt beside me, his face very pale.

At first the heavy foliage concealed them from us, but at the roundabout near where our A.P. convertible had been hit by bits of the Arab .75, they came into view, two khaki-clad lines abreast on either side of the boulevard, in full battle dress, rifles swung by the breech to the slow rhythm of the step, the officers on the flanks of the columns.

Down the middle of the deserted street, centered on the khaki lines, his silver buckles gleaming in the patent-leather belting, his baton flashing high in the rising sun, strode a giant pipe major, his kilt swinging to the lilt of the pipes. What tune the pipers played, I don't recall but, in battle kit like the others and spotted at intervals the length of the company files, they belted out the eerie, martial melodies that chill the hardest hearts and swell the stunted runt to ten times his size. I nearly wept to watch them go.

Around the roadblock at the bottom, still his baton flashing, the pipes reaching for a higher, harder pitch, the pipe major stepped out into the open plain. To us, brought to our feet heedless of the danger, it seemed that all that part of Jerusalem held its breath, the tramp of the boots and the skirl of the pipes the only sound.

The column split around the circle and snaked out and down the berms on either side of the road, the roadblock detail abandoning the post to drop in at the end of the procession. In the center of the plain, the men appeared to us to hang in space, there in the shimmering distance, and then, quite suddenly, they were gone.

Only as the pipers, the last men in each file, faded into the leafy undergrowth bordering the German colony was there a response from the concealed marksmen, one shot, a petulant, angry crack of sound in the stillness. And then dead quiet again.

I remember standing on the balcony and scarcely breathing, only moving off with the others when a bullet tore the edge off the door frame and all hell broke loose in and around Yemin Moshe.

I think most of us felt that, after the gallant performance of the battallion and their "tin-fisted" C.O., Jerusalem without them might continue to be long on deeds of bravery but would have lost something vital in pageantry and panache.

After that the pace of the battle picked up, almost in our own backyard.

On May 21, 1948, at midday, near the entrance to the U.S. Consulate General on Mamillah Road, Herbert N. Walker, Chief Radioman, U.S.

Naval Communications Unit, was knocked off his feet by a hail of machine-gun bullets and fatally wounded.

At noon the next day, at almost the same spot, Thomas C. Wasson, the consul general, was shot. A sniper's bullet pierced his right shoulder and both lungs. Treated at Hadassah English Mission Hospital, where he'd been taken by the crew of a Haganah armored car, he died of shock early the following morning. A month earlier Wasson had been appointed by President Truman as the United States representative on the three-man United Nations Truce Commission for Palestine. Of his fifty-two years, Wasson had served twenty-four in the U.S. Foreign Service, most of them in high-risk posts.

Chief Petty Officer Walker died the same day.

We hadn't heard about Walker but knew of Wasson's shooting only minutes after it happened and ran through back streets to the alley next to the consulate building. At the point where the alley intersected Mamillah Road, we pulled up sharply. There was a smear of blackening blood in the dust. Several other consular employees had been shot at here during previous months, one of them seriously wounded.

We paused to plan the next move and then, employing a street-fighting technique picked up during World War Two, sprinted in a group down Mamillah Road and into the Consulate entrance. (If we'd gone one by one, the sniper, zeroing in on the corner of the consulate wall and waiting for the next to go, would have got at least one of us.) Inside the building, consulate employees huddled in shocked silence. After a short time we exited through a rear service entrance and returned to the Pantiles.

At 10:00 A.M., May 24, I covered last rites for the dead and filed a story for the *News,* some of which read:

> In the grounds of the Convent of the Holy Rosary banks of crude wooden benches accommodated the 50-odd persons attending. Near the archway leading into a small chapel, the flag-draped coffins rested on two wooden tables covered with white napery. The convent buildings formed a semi-circle around the improvised sanctuary.
>
> At 4:10 P.M., during what was described as a lull in the running battle for the city, an Anglican priest stepped forward from the shadow of the arch. Except for distant, staccato sounds of battle, the garden was quiet. A score of newsmen, American, British, and Jewish, members of the consular staff and representatives from the Belgian consulate and the United Nations rose and stood in silence. Wasson had been returning from a Truce Commission meeting at the French Consulate General when he was shot. Many of those who'd attended were present.

"Now is Christ risen from the dead and become the first fruits of them that slept" and in strangely calm and unworldly contrast to the noise of surrounding slaughter the service was intoned. Near the makeshift altar two bearded friars stood, dressed in the brown robes and skullcaps of the Franciscans and near them, heads bowed, was a cluster of sisters of the Rosary.

After the service, the body of the Consul General was placed for temporary interment in the chapel crypt, special permission received from the Latin Patriarch since Wasson was an Episcopalian.

The sailor was buried under olive trees in the convent garden. Both bodies are expected to be removed later to America.

As a contingent of navy men lowered the chief's body into the grave and grimly shoveled in the rocky soil, a shell whispered overhead and plunged with a roar into Mamillah Cemetery across the road.

I'd finished the story with something like "ashes to ashes on one side of Mamillah Road, dust to dust (visibly) on the other" but the *News* copy desk, in its delicacy, scrubbed it.

On May 14, final day of the Mandate, Thomas J. Gannon, a consular guard, had been shot in the back near St. Julien's Hotel in the New City, but on the day Wasson was hit he was reported recovering.

George J. Burns, a clerk-stenographer with the U.N. Truce Commission and a native of Brooklyn, New York, was wounded slightly in the Jerusalem fighting on the day of the Wasson-Walker funeral. We weren't able to find out readily where the incident took place and, I fear, didn't try very hard. By then the city's death toll, combatants and observers, was so high, we rarely counted those who, however badly shot up, managed to stay alive. Some we did, of course.

Jimmy Lide, a twenty-nine–year–old cipher clerk at the consulate, narrowly missed permanent crippling when, at the spot where Wasson was dropped, a bullet went through the fleshy part of his right leg just below the knee, knocking him flat. Luckily, as the *New York Times* noted, "It did not injure a nerve, the bone nor a major artery."

Lide, if he's still with us, would, I know, be distressed to learn that his employers at the State Department, at least the Department's Division of Public Liason, to whom I wrote four years and ten months after this harrowing near-miss, reported that "Our records show (very little on the young Marine and) nothing on James Lyde (Lide?)."

Who the snipers were, we never found out, although we'd have bet a case of Tuborg on the Arabs. Some of us went so far as to make this charge. It produced a barrage of denials and documentary obfuscation declaring that the direction of bullets was not from the Y.M.C.A. Tower, our choice for the Wasson sniper's position.

A State Department press release of June 4, 1948, states in part: "Officers of the Consulate General and others who have been fired upon at the same place where Mr. Wasson was wounded have never laid eyes on sniper (ibid) who has fired from complete concealment."

This suggests that the allegation Wasson had told his Jewish nurse at Hadassah Hospital that "The Arabs shot me, and I saw two of them" was not true. We weren't so sure.

It is true the Jewish Agency did protest to the United Nations only a few hours before Wasson was hit that the Arabs were using the Y.M.C.A. tower as a sniper's nest. It could have been possible for the Jews, acting as agents provocateurs, to have shot Wasson, or anyone handy, so they could blame it on the Arabs. This seems unlikely, even in the shoddy moral climate of Jerusalem in the spring of forty-eight.

As that spring of forty-eight gave way to summer, and our movement became increasingly circumscribed, many of us at the Pantiles were making plans to leave the city. We couldn't just pack up and take off, of course. We were tightly girdled by a perimeter of battle lines that shifted with the fortunes of war and anyway could not be expected to open up upon request and let us through.

Davidson, with several others, agreed to approach the International Red Cross for advice (although Carter was not planning to leave himself). Those of us wishing to be included in an evacuation plan signed a petition addressed to the local authorities. Meanwhile we continued our reporting efforts on a shortening rein under multiplying dangers.

The Pantiles was a wreck. All its front, south-facing windows were blown out, and the floors and stairwells were littered with bits of plaster and broken glass. For one three-day period we were literally trapped inside this dustbin, unable to move out through the hail of small-arms fire showered on the place. This precipitated a move by some into the center of the New City. Those of us without uptown friends or ready cash elected to stick it out. This disappointed the Haganah, anxious to move into the hotel as a front-line strongpoint, but they respected our "international" status nonetheless and left us alone.

The small American flag we'd pinned to a rake handle on the roof failed miserably as protective coloration. Rather it proved to be an aiming point for sniper determination of distance and windage and it waved in pitiful defiance for less than twenty-four hours. Snapped off by a sharpshooting rifleman the rake handle was replaced by the haft of a rubber "plumber's helper" jammed into the slats of a rooftop ventilator.

Even though we were able to survive in this battered bunker, the world outside, when we managed to visit it, had grown very unfriendly and unpredictable.

On May 14, more than a week before Wasson's death, the Acting High Commissioner for Palestine, Lt. Gen. Sir Alan Cunningham, had departed Government House for Kallandia Airport accompanied by a Lifeguard Regiment escort and leaving behind a Highland Light Infantry Regimental Honor Guard to lower the Union Jack as soon as it was known he'd officially left the country.

At exactly 8:30 A.M. the guard officer received word that the general had lifted into the air off the Airport runway, and he shouted his detail to attention. The piper, standing alone atop the tower where the flag stirred in the early morning breeze, heaved the pipes into the doleful "Lochaber No More." The colors eased down the staff until, just before they dropped below the parapet, the "Lochaber" dirge gave way to the even more soulful "Death of the Flag."

The guard detail, not particularly long on sentiment, piled raucously into waiting Jeeps and took off for Allenby Barracks, glad to be gone. As they pulled through the gate, a Red Cross flag jerked up the same flagpole, and Government House, the royal coat of arms still displayed above the main portal, became a hospital.

The ceremony over, Martin, an A.P. photographer driving his agency Jeep, the only press car left operational, and I had made for the Old City through the Vale of Kidron with the Jaffa Gate and entrance to that part of the Arab sector our first objective. Our intention was to record the reactions of the inhabitants to the news of the High Commissioner's departure and to learn what military movement might take place now that the British had gone. Our first taste of their "reactions" came as we stopped outside Jaffa Gate.

We had pulled up to park the vehicle and walk. In the dusty square before the great gate there was rather less of milling humanity than usual, but things still seemed amiable enough. But weren't.

Just as I stepped to the ground I heard the photographer protesting in high-pitched and quavering accents and turned to find him recoiling against the back of the seat, the six-inch barrel of a huge naval revolver stuffed up his nose. Holding this intimidating ordnance was a skinny, unshaven and thoroughly disreputable, teenage Arab in a filthy white shirt and black trousers three sizes too large for him belted in folds around his waist.

"Get out! I want Jeep," he shouted, and turned the gun on me.

Stunned by the sudden development, I simply stood there, open-mouthed. I recall that when I regained my senses I urged the driver to "tromp on it and get the hell out of here," a thoroughly stupid idea that could have produced three dead newsmen as well as a missing Jeep.

Martin's good sense, experience, and languid command of most situations saved us. He had quietly debussed from the back, taking the camera and a gadgetbag full of precious film and equipment with him, tapping me on the shoulder as he went, and motioning me to follow. I had done as he ordered; the photographer tumbled after us, and the wild man with the gun scrambled into the vehicle and left us standing in a cloud of dust.

We made the climb on foot up hillside pathways and steep cobbled streets back to the Pantiles, where Martin notified the Haganah by phone that someone unauthorized was jeeping about town as the "Associated Press." This quick action was as selfish as it was public spirited. If an A.P. Jeep was allowed through a Haganah roadblock on the strength of its ostensible press "credentials" and then blew up that part of town, news vehicles would thenceforth be suspect and reporters' freedoms even more circumscribed than they already were.

And the thugs tried just that, charging a Jewish checkpoint. Alerted by Martin's call the defenders blew away the attackers and our Jeep with one well-directed bazooka shell.

After the Jaffa Gate fiasco, movement for us became very chancy. Most of it, to Jewish Agency press conferences for example, was on foot. This left us unprotected and in at least one instance nearly got me pretty thoroughly subdivided.

Right next to the building housing the Jewish Agency, there was a popular ice cream bar, one we frequented for tea and cakes and the like, and normally crowded with young people, mostly off-duty military. I had just passed the entrance one noontime and turned into the doorway of the agency when the entire street was filled with brilliant light, a stunning roar, and, a fraction of a second later, a hurricane of glass and flying masonry.

A bomb had torn out the guts of the ice cream parlor and heaved it through the front of the shop onto the street. Blood was everywhere; torn human parts, powdered with a wet, red icing of blood and grit, had been blown in a wash across the street. I have no record of the casualties but the place usually was standing-room-only, with an occupancy of more than thirty, and the "body count" was high.

In the recess of the doorway I had escaped even the blast, but ever after that the walk uptown was recognized as more than faintly risky.

For the most part, however, there was a tedious sameness to each day. I sent so much copy out about "a city under siege," it would have had to be read backwards for variety. And getting any stories out at all had become well nigh impossible.

In the early days of my Jerusalem stay, departing journalists and businessmen and a few of the military who came by the Pantiles to say farewell would take my envelopes and mail them outside Palestine. Sometimes Arab refugees, stimulated by a fulsome greenback honorarium, agreed to mail my copy at the first "free" post office. I was lucky. Not one person to whom I entrusted this task ever let me down. All the copy got through to Indianapolis. This was a small miracle, considering the tortuous route it sometimes took by foot, horseback, truck, small plane and ship before it was put aboard a carrier for the States.

But with the post-Mandate war, the battle lines thickened, and the men who manned them were increasingly jumpy. Persons leaving the city didn't tell anyone their plans. They even began to avoid the Pantiles. We were known as a last port of call and were under constant surveillance by Jews and Arabs. Travelers simply slipped away, and my messenger service came to an end.

No word having been received from the Red Cross, some of us were prepared to try this disappearing act, conscious that our knowledge of the terrain was dangerous and that the only guides we might find would be extortionists. Yet, there were those among us who had to make a move, and we began collecting alternatives, most of them suicidal.

One plan would have had us arrange passage through a Haganah roadblock whence we would proceed, in file, into no-man's land behind a flag of truce. We'd haul our luggage and equipment in a two-wheeled scotch cart. I volunteered to carry the white flag with a face to match.

Later in the war, this was to be tried by an assortment of groups, but always under the protection of the United Nations, a patronage we didn't have. And whatever is said about that boondoggling babel on New York's East River, the United Nations staffers in the field were brave and highly qualified to do the often near-impossible tasks they were stuck with. We would have welcomed them as escorts.

But such U.N. field teams had not been set up in Jerusalem when we were contemplating our escape. They came with the subsequent cease-fire.

Nonetheless, we were prepared to ignore warnings that we'd finish up a disorderly queue of corpses and try our white-flag gambit when, unexpectedly, along came our colleagues with the Red Cross.

My story of what happened then is datelined "Amman, Jordan." It appeared in the *News* June 17, 1948, about ten days after we'd made the trek from Jerusalem.

The way from the chalk hills of Judea to the mountains of Jordan is tortuous, dusty and can be hot as Hell.

At least it was all these things when, with one overburdened donkey carrying our baggage, eight other correspondents, and I "escaped" from Jerusalem.

For fifteen days, virtually held suspended by the siege of the city, we had been unable to do much but attend the routine briefings of the Jewish Agency. Then the International Red Cross arranged a "ceasefire" to permit our movement through frontline sectors of the Haganah and Arab Legion lines and access to the outside world.

At midday we set out through the hills from the former Government House, now a Red Cross Hospital. Among the nine was Clare Hollingworth, (the *London Observer*), who, having suffered a leg injury when she tried to run through an oil drum during a mortar barrage the night before, got the only horse in the caravan. The term "horse" is used loosely, but it got Clare over some pretty terrible terrain.

The diminutive donkey slid down precipitous, slag-covered slopes under loads of typewriters, files and personal clobber that would have staggered a Percheron. For almost two hours in heat that mummified us, we stumbled round the southern edge of the Old City, parts of which were burning violently from an Arab attack that reduced the Jewish Quarter to near-surrender.

I plodded along behind the lead animal, prodded into astonishing feats of strength and agility by its driver, an extraordinary apparition.

He wore low, Oxford shoes, scuffed and split open, over brightly colored Argyle socks, the usual Arab gallibeah or nightshirtlike dress, his head protected from the sun by the traditional flowing kafiah. Over his shoulder, barrel-down, he carried a drumloaded Thompson submachine gun that he must have found rusting on a long-deserted battleground.

One of my jobs was to keep an eye on this brigand and collect anything he might slip off the load into the scrub for future reference. My gagging down the back of his neck as we struggled over the broken landscape must have unnerved him, for he suspended banditry, and nothing went missing.

We finally arrived near the foot of the Mount of Olives, near the southeast corner of the Old City walls. There we joined other correspondents, until then trapped inside Arab-held Jerusalem, and made for Amman in an aged Bedford with a raving lunatic at the wheel. Perhaps "high" on hashish, he played "chicken" with every oncoming Iraqi army and Arab Legion vehicle for the full hour it took to reach Amman. And this along a mountain track edged on one side by cliff, on the other by a sheer drop into an apparently bottomless canyon.

Once in Amman, the driver was forced to slow the pace and proceed with some care through the busy streets. In front of the Philadelphia Hotel we disembarked in a disorderly scramble and headed straight for the bar. After a generous sampling of well-nigh–forgotten delights, we hived off to write our stories.

I set up on a cocktail table in a corner, dumping my effects on the camp bed the management of the overcrowded hostel had assigned me between the billiard table and a cue rack.

I finished the story, paid the hotel concierge lavishly to post it, and, as nightime slipped over Amman, sauntered across the street and in among the ruins of the Roman amphitheater quarried out of the hillside. Built about 250 B.C. during the Ptolemy Philadelphus occupation of what had been ancient Rabbath Ammon in the time of King David, the open-air collosus had seated an audience of 6,000 in its heyday. With Ptolemy's ascension the city was rechristened Philadelphia and only retook its proper name 800 years later with the collapse of the Byzantine Empire.

Sprawling across hills and valleys, the city, most of its buildings constructed of shell-white limestone, quivers blindingly hot in the daytime and is luminescent in the moonlight. As I walked back to the hotel in the blackness, the moon was up, the town frothy white against the profiles of surrounding heights.

Although the bar was still crowded with regular clientele, they were outnumbered by journalists, soldiers, and itinerant merchants readying for bed. This uproarious process consisted of clearing sections of the room of furniture, selecting a likely looking bit of bedding and falling face down on it. If still able to find his feet, the guest pulled off his shoes and perhaps a few outer garments. Soon, "time gentlemen" having been called and the lights lowered, the cavernous old bistro echoed the stentorian discord of exhausted men asleep.

Even on the sagging canvas of my camp bed I had the best night in many weeks. During the latter part of the stay in Jerusalem there'd been a good chance that my stories might never reach their destination. No word had reached me from the *News*. I could have been thrashing about the Holy Land, digging up spectacular stuff and converting it to deathless prose only to have the copy used to start a campfire. At best. But that evening a sackful of mail, shortstopped at Arab Legion Headquarters in Amman for reasons not revealed, had been dumped on a billiard table in the bar. In the heap I'd found letters from my office acknowledging that all stories had been received and space found for the lot.

The following morning we awoke in a barroom litter and stale-booze atmosphere that would have sickened a coroner, but a walk in the crispness of 6:00 A.M. at an altitude of twenty-five hundred feet followed by a breakfast of lamb chops and real eggs, leavened bread, and English tea restored the most jaded among us. Arab coffee we avoided. We could manage it later in the day, but not in the early morning, especially a morning-after. Its principal characteristic is a granular silt that settles on the floor of the mouth near the base of the tongue and not only defies all effort to flush it away but continues to appear in dental crevices for days afterwards.

Later in the morning an Arab Legion officer put in a brief appearance for a curt announcement.

We had been permitted entry under arrangements made with the International Red Cross, he said, and were considered in transit to points outside the country. We would have until sundown to depart Jordan. His concluding "Any questions?" produced a babble of protest. Most of us had confidently expected to continue coverage of the war from Amman. If nothing else it would round out the picture, grossly onesided by dint of our entrapment in Jerusalem. But the Jordanians were adamant.

Two, Hecox and Fitzsimmons, Associated Press photographer, were expelled and later refused re-entry. No reasons given. Three, including Clare Hollingworth, elected to carry their case to higher authority and succeeded in extending their stay. And three of us, Martin, Bilby and I, chose to be in transit, it having been made clear there was no chance we'd be granted permission to remain. No reasons given.

I hadn't the foggiest idea how to exit this mountainous desolation. Not within a matter of hours. But Bilby made a plan. A twin-engined Rapide would take off from Amman airport as soon as we could get there, and well before sundown we were in the air headed for the Island of Cyprus.

It was an uneventful 260 crow-flight miles from Amman to the Cypriot capital of Nicosia. We flew over northern Palestine, a strip of Lebanon, and some 150 miles of Mediterranean, all of it in a northwesterly direction for an hour and a half and fifty dollars each, U.S. green. Our arrival had been anticipated by the British colonial administration, alerted from Amman, and its minions cleared us, granting short-term laissez-passes.

Within a few hours we'd booked into the Dome Hotel in Kyrenia, ancient northcoast port and for decades a tourist haven for Britain's empire civil servants. A peaceful community basking in the sun, and engaged in desultory fishing, it was an ideal spot to do nothing in comfort. For us it was a welcome end of the line. For a while at least.

My second-story room had a view of the little harbor, and its simple furnishings were opulent after the battered bivouac of the Pantiles and a share of the floor at the Philadelphia. I unpacked methodically for the first time since Shepheard's in Cairo, incredibly only just over a month earlier.

Another month, no less hectic, would disappear as suddenly as the last. I would fly to Haifa and the Palestine coastal area; go by boat, running illegal refugees and other contraband, to the Isle of Rhodes; and leapfrog, by air, Jeep, and muleback into the battle area of northern Greece before this baptism as a newsman overseas would end. But those stories fall naturally into place as part of a narrative that begins back in the City Room of the *News*.

CHAPTER VIII

Overseas Assignment, Fulltime

Wayne Guthrie walked slowly and deliberately toward me from the city desk precincts where he ruled supreme and dropped the weather story on my typewriter.

"Rewrite it but keep it simple," he demanded, nervously cracking his knuckles, adding, "Fair and Cooler until Friday, Weekend Skies Clouding Over . . . you know," and walking away turned back to me, "Quickly, time's running out."

I picked up the copy and stared fixedly at it, seeing nothing. Around me the predeadline rush produced the rattle and thunk and ringing bells of typewriters. Vacuum chutes that carried copy in little tubes to the composing room, inhaled sharply and rang their own bells. Reporters and copy-desk tyrants shouted four-letter expletives, telephones jangled, and over all hung an aroma compounded of tobacco smoke, ink, rubber cement, and bodies. It was, all of it, familiar and comfortable and should have quietly fueled my excitement as before. But it didn't.

Ever since I'd returned from the Near East a few months earlier, in late fall, I'd been out of it. Everyone else joined in the periodic agitation required to get an edition out as a matter of habit. My pulse scarcely upped a beat. Confronted with Guthrie's weather story, as with so much else, I found myself staring dumbly at the sheet of paper.

"Hey there, foreign correspondent man! Let's go! We're shorthanded. Let's make with some exotic doggerel about this boring Indiana weather."

Thus spoke Bob Hanika, city desk rewrite man, not noticeably impressed by "all this heroic Richard Harding Davis bullshit," as he put it.

Obediently, I shook myself awake and attacked the copy. Few things make for duller reworking than wire-service weather. But it's important. Few stories in the paper have a higher readership. So I tried.

Away down near the end of all the words about "fronts" and "high-pressure lows" I found what was for our part of the country the usual bit about a storm center forming up in the Canadian Rockies and "at last weather bureau reports headed for the American middle states." I decided out of pure cussedness to make it my lead, upgrading this normal and obscure highland flurry to a major, hovering cataclysm beating its way toward Indianapolis. When Guthrie saw it, he raised his eyebrows but let it go.

It certainly livened up the early afternoon edition. We hit the newsstands with the banner headline "Blizzard Coming" over my byline. The *Times,* our Hearst competitor, playing the same A.P. story with proper caution, ran a two-column center head calmly forecasting "Fair and Cooler."

Just after midnight, as the city slept and against all the odds, the *News's* imaginary snowstorm swept in from the north to dump traffic-snarling heaps all over Indianapolis.

This was the only time in memories alive then that one of the town's newspapers had beaten another on a weather story. Characteristically Guthrie only paused at my desk in one of his nervous rambles around the City Room, shook his head slowly, and passed on.

After that, however, my genius began to fray around the edges. The winter was, for me, devoted to plodding through off-street parking, smog-control, gambling dens, and obsolete buses, matters vital to the city but not designed to have me breathing hard. Came springtime, I couldn't control my urges any longer, left the paper, and went back overseas, this time as a stringer for the *News* and as a free-lance.

The difference between these two designations is subtle but significant. A stringer may be accredited to a home paper, can be assigned stories and is assured of at least that one outlet. The free-lancer farms out his copy wherever he thinks it'll be paid for, the term coming from the practice of the medieval freebooter knight who hired out his pike or lance to the highest bidder. I was also stringer for *Pathfinder Newsmagazine,* a bucolic *Time*-type publication, and wrote sporadically for the *Philadelphia Bulletin.* Morley Cassidy, a Near East colleague commissioned as editorial-page editor, bought all my submissions and gave me assignments for others. For the old *New York Herald Tribune* I also did editorial-page work, and sometimes the *Christian Science Monitor* took my copy. For the rest, I was for sale at a bargain rate.

First stop would be Great Britain, whence I would venture into middle Africa, in those days a strange and empty place seldom visited by the print or electronic media that was to scavenge it later. It was a very chancy venture, made all the more so by the lack of full accreditation.

When I previously had presented myself in Cairo and elsewhere as the *"Indianapolis News* correspondent," it may not have produced the fawning servility I'd have liked, but, compared to the reaction I got when I announced I was "representing several American publications on my own account," it had been truly prestigious. What I needed, I felt, was identity, not then a psychological buzzword but simply denoting credibility. Determined to begin establishing this before I left the States, I brazenly harvested a host of testimonials from friends.

Wendell Phillippi—*Indianapolis News* city editor replacing Wayne, who'd been relegated to writing a column, concluded a full page "to-whom-it-may-concern" with: "Mr. Acheson is a man of integrity. His freshness and imagination are great assets for writing, lecturing and reporting."

Dick Tucker, who had once covered the *News*'s labor beat and had since gone to the *Baltimore Evening Sun* (for which he was war correspondent in Korea, carrying out a wounded marine at Inchon), said I had "a quick sense of news, and energy and thoroughness in reporting and a talent for writing interestingly, accurately and comprehensively."

Don Underwood, the *News* Washington correspondent, allowed as how I was: "personable, intelligent, and informed" among numberless other virtues and the *News*'s highest authority, the publisher, Eugene S. Pulliam, Jr., said, shortly, that I was an "experienced and competent journalist."

This flood of accolades rushed to my head and rendered me insensible to all but the most extravagant praise for eight days. On the ninth I had a vaccination and "shots," five all at once, smallpox, typhoid, cholera, anti-tetanus, and yellow fever. When I awoke on the eleventh day, still agued and addlepated, I had been brought back to my normal entirely vincible self and judged these paeans for what they were, namely: the response of good friends intimidated by my overwhelming cheek. Among my most coveted testimonials, one I tucked away with private papers and never allowed to surface, came from Max Boyd: "To a Man Who Needs a Good Reporter: I'm glad to recommend Cornell W. 'Duke' Acheson, with whom I had the pleasure of working in the Middle East. 'Duke' has guts, energy, curiosity, and writing ability. He would be a worthwhile addition to any staff." It was dated November 30, 1948, Cairo.

My U.S. passport (No. 185093 and good for only two years at that time), and my World Health Organization record detailing my old and new knockout injections, were documents I still had from the Palestine war adventure. A booking for Britain on the steamship *Nieuw Amsterdam*, cabin number 60, June 10, 1949, was new, and so was my accommodation in the London home of Mrs. Norah Ellerie, 1, Sussex Place, Lancaster

Gate, a clean and commodious basement flat that easily housed me and the welter of luggage I'd accumulated since Jerusalem.

Mrs. Ellerie, a tiny, gray pillar of gossamer and lavender, spoke softly and gently oversaw a "family" boarding house. My friend from Wesleyan University (Connecticut) days, Gordon Taylor Sperry, a little round man from Ohio who brightened wherever he was, had served as a G.I. code clerk in London during World War Two and had lived at the *pension* run by this kindly Londoner. Concerned for me, he had demanded that I submit to her care at the beginning of this new, reckless enterprise, and I had happily agreed.

My married life had continued complicated, stricken with untoward indiscretions for which I unhappily must accept the blame. Those persons luckless enough to have been implicated then but fortunate subsequently to have set their own independent and rewarding courses are best absent from this narrative, at least for now. Thus will this chronicle be relieved of an embarrassing clumsiness and the professional substance of the work can "hang loose."

The time spent in Britain, some five weeks, found me pursuing a variety of stories in all directions, none so hard-earned as those collected during a fortnight's trip of 250 miles by bicycle. Renting a car was too costly, and walking around the island could have been tedious and would plainly overdo "getting down among the people." And this was to be my principal interest, to see at first hand why, three years after a war they'd won, Britain's people were so poor, so ill-fed and badly-clothed, so grayish and depressed in the sunniest summer since the Blitz. The bicycle seemed the only answer.

As this project advanced from a mere notion to actually tossing about for a wheeler I could borrow, I decided to do a story about a reporter doing a story by bicycle. For this I needed to know more about the machine. Hence, while Mrs. Ellerie's agents fanned out through the Paddington Station area in search of a bike for rent, I visited local libraries collecting background information about the thing. I found it variously described as "a lesser form of land transport," "a luxury for gilded youth," and, in an editorial in the *New York Herald Tribune* of 1895, as a discovery of "more importance to mankind than all the victories and defeats of Napoleon, with the First and Second Punic Wars thrown in." I was so impressed that I subsequently produced a radio story that went, in part:

> Although the first truly rideable bicycle appeared in 1839, there had been produced in Germany in 1816 a "dangerous and eccentric

toy," Baron von Drais von Sauerbronn's "hobby horse," two wheels connected by a rod. For some thirty-five years he had scootered happily about his forest estates on this excruciating device.

It's true that the velocipede, very similar to von Drais's two-wheeler, had been in use in 1770 and was of a design lifted from either an ancient Babylonian bas-relief or from sketches by Leonardo da Vinci. Britain also laid claim to its creation, documenting evidence showing the figure of a Cherub astride one in the stained glass window of a Buckinghamshire Parish Church of the sixteenth century. And the Chinese had one with bamboo wheels for which no date is given.

Still, it was von Drais's machine that became the "Dandy Horse" rage of Paris in the mid-nineteenth century, with hundreds of gay blades rushing about Montmartre sitting down.

The Scot Kirkpatrick MacMillan added pedals and, being a "high-spirited chap," raced stage coaches, rode down hills standing on the saddle, carried "pretty girls" on his shoulders and once was arrested for what was recorded as "furious driving."

It has come a long way since MacMillan, this fiendish machine, and today there are some 100 million crawling round the globe, some of them with ten speeds and comprised of as many as 1,042 parts.

The one I finally found was geared for one speed, with the Lord knows how many parts, and a crippled carrier over the rear wheel on which I loaded thirty pounds of clobber, including a typewriter. Most alarming of all, it was a "lady's" bike without center bar and equipped with a seat of exotic conformation. I had never analyzed the variance from a "gentleman's" seat, but it became obvious that the ladies' are assembled in quite a different way. Suffice it that after two days and some seventy miles I suffered localized spasms and an affliction that won't bear detailed description. At the close of the fifth day, however, my voice had returned downward, and dismounting was no longer painful. As I strode into the Hen and Chickens Pub on Sheffield's Green Castle Road at the end of the first week, not a man there would have suspected that a few days earlier I had been close to permanent neutering.

Actually having cycled fifty miles down farm roads off the main drag to talk to locals, I'd not only mastered the machine but toughened up considerably, which was just as well.

Not far from the midlands town of Bakewell I'd been pushing my lady's bike self-consciously through a crush of Sunday cyclists and hikers near the Duke of Devonshire's "Chatsworth" estate, when I turned off down a side lane. After a mile or so I encountered two knowledgeable-looking old-timers, fence-sitting in silence and watching the trickle of passers-by. I dismounted to question them as I had done so many others. These two, however, were different. Cloth caps down hard on grizzled heads and Sunday-clean in their collarless shirts, dark worsted waistcoats and wool trousers tucked into Wellington boots, they were openly hostile.

They made not a sign as I identified myself, and, when I asked in what I thought was a friendly manner if this wasn't some of the country famed for the breeding of the magnificent English Shire horses, they dropped their eyes to the ground where a huge fawny bull mastiff lay, his yellow eyes fixed on my Adam's apple, and said nothing. Then the older of the two, his face as folded and sagging as the mastiff's, raised his heavy blackthorn stick and pointed it at me.

" 'Tweren't fer Yank tractors doin' all t' plowin', 'twould be," he rumbled. "Thirty stud at Chatsworth afore the war; today there be four; won't be none soon."

I apologized but pointed out that Harry Ferguson, whose farm machines crawled over a large part of the globe, was a Briton. This rejoinder they took as bad manners, displayed by a mere lad and a Yank no less.

They made no move, eyeing me silently, but the dog, obviously sensing the interview was at an end, raised his bulk, some 200 pounds of it, and, with an indecent display of incisors, growled in my direction.

My credibility and manhood already handicapped by the lady's bicycle and further impaired by obvious misgivings as this monster gathered himself for goodness knew what outrage, I backed up to the narrow tarmac surface and prepared to return the way I'd come. No such luck. As if on some signal this maneater took up a position dead center the lane and faced my way. Fencing and dense hedgerows bordered the road on both sides, and there was no way round. My protests only met with continued silence from the men and mounting menace from the hound. Eventually, I gave in and, cringing inside, cycled off into the setting sun, clocking hours of additional mileage over hilly terrain before seeing Bakewell again.

Exhaustion and humiliation were penalty enough, but plans I'd enthusiastically made to include the Chatsworth tour that day had to be scrubbed, and this had been irksome to a degree.

An important part of the story of Britain's postwar poverty was the struggle of the country's embattled aristocracy to stay afloat financially. This struggle embraced measures to retain its expansive estate holdings. Chatsworth was a well-publicized example of how this might be done.

The Duke of Devonshire, Chatsworth's squire, had been among the first to open his estate to public view for a fee, income that would help him defray the costs of taxes and maintenance. The public, who know a bargain when they see one, flocked to the Derbyshire countryside and, for the equivalent of fifty cents apiece, bought an adventure down seemingly endless corridors of opulence.

More than one million visitors have crushed through those corridors since the summer of forty-nine, agog at the riches in furnishings and objets d'art, the galleries of priceless paintings and the splendor of the architecture and landscape acreage, grounds tended, even in Britain's most straitened years, by at least thirty gardeners. The sixty servants formerly employed in the inner manse had been replaced by eight wardens, the staff of the Chatsworth Company, Ltd., which managed the "display." The Duke and his family occupied rooms closed to the public and in that privacy totted up the change that had produced $23,000 in the first three months the properties had been on view.

Somewhere in this great house, I had learned, there hung a painting by John Singer Sargent titled *The Ladies Acheson*. It portrayed three dark-haired women, chosen for their great beauty and for their relationship to the Duke of Bedford, a cousin of Devonshire's. Painted in 1902, it was a classic garden scene of the era, the ladies positioned around a Grecian urn under spreading foliage. My relationship to these lasses had long been established, and my disappointment at not being able to see the picture, as well as Chatsworth itself, was both personal and professional.

As it was, I had to be satisfied to visit what was described as a "lesser house," that of the Fitzwilliams' Wentworth Woodhouse, not far away near Rotherham, an hour or so by bicycle from Sheffield.

Once one of Britain's largest private dwellings, it brooded majestically over surrounding parklands, its pillared facade sweeping along a frontage of 600 feet, and was, after all, a fair exchange as a second choice. Actually, in spite of its being emptied of its riches and now a hollow shell, its prideful days a memory, Wentworth Woodhouse was so impressive that, at a later date, I made it the subject of a radio script.

> Almost nothing in the history of architecture has matched Britain's stately homes for sheer bulk. They were built, most of them, from the 1500s onward, beginning in a time when the fruits of Queen Elizabeth I's canny commercial acumen were everywhere visible. Its peoples, a hardy, buccaneering lot, blessed with imagination unencumbered by scruple, literally stuffed the nation's coffers with the world's riches. Partly to display this and partly because it was expected of them, most successful entrepreneurs threw up these giant buildings as monuments to themselves and to the god Success. Rarely were they graceful.
>
> Depending on the era, they variously resembled French cha-

teaux, Genoese villas, Greek and Indian temples, and other reflections of doubtful taste imported from the four corners of the earth. Twenty thousand acres of encompassing grounds was not unusual. Entire Japanese gardens were reconstructed on the English moors, lakes dammed into being, rivers created—all very ostentatious, eccentric and competitive.

Succeeding generations bore the burden of upkeep by their own brand of freebooting. Ultimately they went into debt, or they sold up.

So it was with Wentworth Woodhouse. When I first saw it, its treasures, 2,000 separate pieces, were being auctioned off, and the main dwelling was being turned over to the local County Council, West Riding Educational Committee, as a school for women physical-education instructors. This rather tatty fate would have been unthinkable even a decade earlier, a blaspheme in earlier times.

The first Wentworth Woodhouse was built in 1215 by the first Earl Fitzwilliam. It was sacked and burned; was rebuilt; burned down again and renewed, oh, perhaps a dozen times over seven centuries.

Norman governors stopped there; Queen Elizabeth and entourage rested there in what must have been at least reasonable comfort in its 250 rooms. In later years the gardens teemed with herds of deer and Indian buffalo and Queen Victoria and George V were visitors.

After World War One, the seventh earl returned from soldiering in India to supervise the estate and, sadly, to watch helplesly as it fell on hard times. Much of his wealth had been drained away raising and equipping an infantry company to fight in 1914, a common practice among members of the established aristocracy. The Fitzwilliams, if not necessarily loved by the twentieth-century community around them, were, with reason, respected and even as their fortunes failed continued to be looked to for leadership.

The formal dissolution of the estate followed the death in 1948 of the eighth earl. The new owner, Eric Spencer, the ninth earl, and a character in his day, did not live at the Woodhouse but would oversee this crumbling away from a home in Oakham near Rutland, not far distant.

When I visited the Woodhouse, taxes were taking most of the $200,000 a year the Fitzwilliams would have devoted to its upkeep. As a private holding, it was doomed.

In fact, what was doomed to become accommodation for platoons of muscular females in sweatsuits thrashing about in a heady reek of wintergreen, cloves, and alcohol rub was not only a building where 12,000 panes of glass had once let in light over 90,000 square feet of exquisite carpeting and gaudy but magnificent antiquities; what was doomed as well was a habit of least five centuries of service to England.

It had been a dismal story and I was relieved when my research on the Woodhouse concluded. The unpretentious squalor of my own temporary home, the Hen and Chickens, with its flaking mustard-colored wallpaper, rationed bathwater, and hammocklike beds, made no demands on my imagination. If the "Hen" ever fell, it wouldn't have far to go, and this was somehow comforting.

So, too, was my association with Cathleen, the chatty waitress with whom I shared my reporting problems and minor triumphs. One evening she seemed distraught, her attention straying as I babbled on about the Fitzwilliams and their fate. Finally, I braked to a sudden halt and demanded to know what was bothering her, expecting a flood of intimate personal confidences.

"It's them bleedin' cigarettes," she snorted. "Can't you find anythin' else? You'll be drivin' me customers away!"

When I told her no self-respecting English tobacconist would sell a cycling Yank anything but Turkish Murads or the like, saving the scarce quality smokes for his regulars, she swore colorfully, told me to "put the bloody thing out," and left the dining room. When she returned, she put two Woodbines carefully on the table. Although these hard-to-get and costly pure Virginias did smell less moldy than the Turkish, they would, I knew, scorch my throat and lungs, and reduce me to paroxysms of coughing. Still, they were found only "under the counter" at about ten cents each, and represented for her a considerable sacrifice.

The hardships suffered by the British in 1949 were very bad. Lodging in the big cities, yet to be rebuilt after the bombings, was hard to come by. Some of the streets of Sheffield in July of that year still were clogged with heaps of rubble. Clothing was visibly threadbare, and in this once thriving commercial and industrial center food was in short supply. For Cathleen the food story was a favorite. Victuals of all kinds were scarce, she said, "and bloody pricey." As for meat: "Lor' luv yuh, mate!"

Halfway through the evening meal a few nights later, she abandoned the other diners and flumped down at my table. Her eyes were bright.

"Yuh know, the other night we was talkin' meat? How scarce it is? Well, I remembered a piece o'meat that'll fit right with your story, the one you're doin' about England's troubles. Down at Walker's butchery. Castle Hill Fish Market. 'E's been there donkey's years; sells the best meat in town when 'e's got it.

"Well, 'e's got a beef roast, I think it is, that's," she paused for effect, "a hundred years old!!" and she sat back triumphantly.

"Mind you," she leaned forward, grimacing, "it's pretty disgustin' lookin'. All deadlike. But then," she pushed her chair back, "you'd look pretty rum, too, if you was a hundred, now wouldn' yuh, hey?"

Mid-morning the next day I went along to Castle Hill and off to one side in the great echoing hall found one of the Walkers in rubber boots hosing down the floors, the white-marble display shelves and wooden chopping blocks already washed clean.

"We get the meat early and it goes," he said, explaining his early closing. "Used to be I'd spend the whole mornin' in the shop and part of the afternoon. Now," he shrugged, "I get what there is, still warm from slaughter, late in the day. It's on the counter first thing. Bloody awful! No seasonin', no 'angin' at all."

I told him I'd heard about one piece of meat he'd had " 'angin' " longer than any cut since the beginnings of butchery. He laughed and waved a huge wet hand toward a far corner of the shop.

"Lot of people know about that. Usually keep it there. That wooden hook. I'll get it. Just put it up," and in a moment he was back from the freezer with what appeared to be a small shrunken head, gray-brown, and faintly dusted with greenish mildew.

"A queer one, this," and he told me about it.

One spring morning in the year 1808, it was, just on a hundred forty-one years ago, during the troubles with Napoleon. A man pushed his way up to the counter in Charlie Sneezby's shop over in the old Fitzallan market on High Street, ordered a ten-pound beef roast, paid for it—four shillings and sixpence—"coupla quid today"—and asked Sneezby to hold it; said he'd collect it later in the day.

Long and short of it, he never came back. Still, he might have. And, after all, he'd paid for it. So it had to be kept for him. After a few days the roast was packed in ice and put in the cold room; later in the week it was lightly spiced and salted. Several months went by, and Sneezby pickled it in brine. And that's the way it remained, pickled hard and hanging on the wall hook in the shop for ninety-two years.

In 1900 the Fitzallan closed, and the Walkers bought out Sneezby's great-grandsons, moving the shop to Castle Hill. That pickled roast, weighing three pounds and its size reduced to a four-inch cube, went up on another hook, where I found it, pretty much unchanged, fifty years later.

CHAPTER IX

"Tourism" in Algeria

There aren't very many 140-year-old roasts of beef and Cathleen's Sneezby-Walker story was readily given space in the *Indianapolis News* and other outlets. And it was Cathleen's. I'd have missed it without her. It's this kind of source met in the chance encounter that, far more often than instructions from home, produces an interesting lead into a worthwhile story.

A few weeks after Cathleen, I'd left the British Isles and exchanged the likes of the Hen and Chickens for the Hotel Martinez in Algiers, a billet of similar no-star rating, a haunt catering to back-packers and other "Europe-on-Five-Dollars-a-Day" optimists. It was nonetheless adequate and boasted a friendly barman who hid out amid dense clusters of aspidistra, fern and banana plants, and presided over a meetingplace for the dispossessed and the on-the-make.

Here, in this dank atmosphere one evening, I followed up another chance encounter, this time with an Arab guide I'd met earlier in the day. He appeared a thoroughgoing Moslem, complete with flowing gallibeah, who shouldn't have accepted the whisky I offered him, but did. With a sigh of gratitude.

Our first meeting had taken place in the Kasbah, the storied native quarter that spills down the hills to the sea on the western edge of the city. One of the sulphurous drafts from a side alley had whipped the gossamer headdress from one of the female tourists he was guiding around this romantic sinkhole, and I'd recovered and returned it. We'd exchanged pleasantries, and for a time I'd joined the group.

Shepherding a gaggle of apprehensive Swiss visitors through the famed Kasbah has its drawbacks. The nervous ladies, huddled together in a protective hive, squealed with alarm as the ragged and blindingly smelly children ran shouting and giggling around them, and the men had drawn themselves tall and taut, aloof from the surroundings. Certainly they all had my sympathy. One of my stories to the *News* had read, in part:

> Charles Boyer as Pepi le Moko in the movie *Algiers* may have enticed jaded European females into his lair with "Come weez me to zee Kasbah," but I'll wager the silliest among them quailed at the first whiff of the quarter's special perfumes.
> The Kasbah is best described as an overpowering stench emanating from ancient, crumbling structures crouched along narrow cobbled byways and populated by pieces of people, fey degenerates with empty faces, albinos covered with rags against the burn of the sun, and fly-blown infants.
> And everything is wet. Slop buckets and dripping taps and stinking entrails oozing from butchers' hooks.
> Only the vegetables brightened the somber setting, and this is a delusion. The natural hues of green peppers, tomatoes and squash are heightened by the scruffy merchants who spit on them and polish off the saliva with a dirty shirttail.

Add to this the nature of the Swiss, game for a venturesome whirl among foreign primitives only so long as advanced planning has eliminated all unappetizing novelty, and the guide had his problems.

When I encountered him later that day, alone behind the aspidistra, he was slumped over the bar, eyes closed.

"May I offer you a drink," I said, adding hastily, "of some kind."

"What I really want," he looked at me blearily, "is a scotch on the rocks."

"I know," he shrugged off my surprise, "the Koran says Moslems do not drink alcohol; it is forbidden. This is a myth," and he told this tale.

One of Muhammed's uncles, he said, had come to Mecca to visit the Prophet, who at that time was compiling the account of revelations that was to become the Koran, the Moslem "Bible." The traveler tethered his camel outside the entrance to the dwelling, and soon afterwards a drunken mob debauched on the scene, butchered the camel, cooked and ate some of it, and scattered the bloody remains in the dust.

When Muhammed later saw his uncle to the door and found his relative's transport reduced to assorted cold cuts and offal, he was, as my companion put it, "shocked by the excess of the peasants," who lay about, covered with gore and surfeited to semiconsciousness.

Without so much as a by-your-leave, he abandoned his uncle, standing aghast on the threshold, threw himself down at his escritoire, and scratched off the prohibition.

"What he really meant, of course," my new acquaintance added, "was that intemperance is to be avoided," an interpretation I found to be rather too liberal under the circumstances, but let it go.

"Practice moderation, and the Koran is obeyed," he added and accepted another whisky.

This facile temporizing in fluent French contrasted markedly with his general appearance. He was short, dark-skinned, bucktoothed, pockmarked, and slight of build. Somehow, for all these handicaps, he carried himself with dignity and authority. I questioned him and soon had him telling me the story of his life. The whisky, even in moderation, loosened his tongue.

He had been born Amer Ben Said Ben Dokman, he said, one of six children, thirty-eight years ago in the Saharan town of Bou Saada, a terminus on the ancient caravan route across the desert from the East. His father, a noncommisioned officer in the French army, had been killed in France in 1915, as was one of his brothers. This drove his mother, Aischa, violently insane, and she was chained in a back room of their miserable hovel for years, he said, her demented wailing as familiar as the sigh of the ceaseless desert winds.

When he was old enough, he went with his family on a pilgrimage to the Grand Mosque of El Hamel, not far from Bou Saada. There, he said, his prayers brought about God's intervention, and the evil spell was broken. In less than a year Aischa was restored to a full and normal life.

In the meantime he eked out a living gathering and selling desert driftwood for cookfires. At age fifteen he got a dishwasher's job in Bou Saada's only hotel, the Sahara. He learned French, went to school as a protege of the French hotel proprietor, later became a guide in the Bou Saada district, and, praise Allah, was plucked off this dying vine by a Swiss travel agency enigmatically called Hotel Plan, and was now the company's head guide.

He joined his palms in prayer, made a little bow over his empty glass, and, this time, refused my offer of another drink.

He had just returned from the continent, he continued, with thirty-two Swiss visitors for his tenth Algerian tour. This followed a stay of several weeks in Europe, far removed, he said, "may God be praised," from his native village, spreadeagled on the blazing sands that flow through the valleys of the Atlas Mountain range.

"It means 'Father of Good Fortune,' Bou Saada," and he snorted. Still, he said, he owned a restaurant there and had a share in an aged bordello. Poor as the place might be, it was home. He was taking his new charges there for a glimpse of desert life within the next day or so. Would I like to go along?

Two mornings later, I slid into a seat behind Paul Girard, French driver of the motorcoach that would rattle its way eastward out of Algiers into the mountains of the Kabylie and then south toward the desert. Behind me, the Swiss chattered excitedly about the new adventure; the mood was festive; the early morning was cool; and it was good to get away from Algiers for a while.

In addition to being only slightly more livable outside the Kasbah than in it, the rest of Algiers suffered serious shortcomings, most of which were rooted in steadily accumulating garbage and a telephone, electrical and public works system that seemed improvised from minute to minute. While it was not without its old world charm, it did not wear too well, as I pointed out in a *News* story at the time:

> Algiers is a big (300,000), noisy and almost friendly city. Its public officials, including the police, are surprisingly cheerful and "muddle through" with genial resignation. Its hotel receptionists, however, are a special breed of misanthrope.
>
> On one of my visits to the city, I had searched vainly for a place to stay and succeeded only in being laughed out of five lobbies.
>
> *"Eh, bien* (shrieks of laughter), *vous faîtes la bête, monsieur"* (roughly: "Surely, you're joking!"). Some of the guests, it was said, were sleeping in the lounge.
>
> Finally a giant proprietress, sporting a neglected moustache and piratical earrings, who brooded over an establishment called the Martinez, gave me a room. She counted my pieces of luggage, evaluating them as she went, and shouted through registration and police formalities. The hotel register, here as in Europe, doubles as a sort of police blotter. This is practical, but it tends to cloud the welcome.
>
> The room was, well, interesting. Overlooking the railway goods yard, forever at peak shunting hours, it was equipped with a bed consisting of a slab of inflexible mattressing supported on a wire screen with feet at the corners. The shower, an unspeakable luxury in all but the poshest hotels, was a concrete box in a corner and proved to be a dirty trick. The nozzle had long since fallen off, and the rusty water battered the bather and sluiced down a goodly portion of the room at the same time. Clouds of flying insects droned in and out the screenless windows throughout the night, aerial cover for ground attacks by giant bedbugs.
>
> One of the less engaging things about Algiers are the hordes of newsboys, shoeshine urchins, beggars and the vendors of a range of trivia, all of it stolen. Dining at a sidewalk cafe, you can get your shoes shined constantly unless you sit on your feet, have a

variety of stuff from packets of contraceptives to plastic scarabs dumped on the table, and conversation is possible only at peak pitch.

If you go temporarily mad and swing at them with anything that's handy, they withdraw into jeering ranks practicing the English they learned from American soldiers during the war. This is very picturesque.

Perhaps, I speculated, staring out the window of the ancient bus as it steamed up the slopes of the Kabylie, Bou Saada's Oasis Hotel would be an improvement on the Martinez, and, with luck, all the children would be way out in the desert collecting driftwood.

One change became apparent as soon as we turned southward over the stony wastelands bordering the desert: the temperature. Much hotter. In the nineties and drier. The crisp and normally dewy-fresh Swiss began loosening garments, fanning themselves with Hotel Plan brochures that extolled the comforts of overland travel, and getting what they'd paid for: an African sojourn complete with thirst and prickly heat.

Bou Saada at 3:00 P.M. on a summer afternoon is a terrible mistake. Not unlike a Mexican village with a wide, dusty main street edged with thorn trees, the walls of flanking adobe dwellings eyeless in the shimmering heat, it resembles nothing so much as a cluster of mausoleums baking in the merciless sun. Out of sight in its hidden keeps and burrows there were, unbelievably, 18,000 souls who, when the heat abates, appear and coast aimlessly about the powdery thoroughfares or gather under the tin roofs of a scrofulous marketplace.

For the Swiss, exhausted from an eight-hour bus ride broken only briefly by a gritty luncheon stop, it was gruesome. Nor did the Hotel Oasis boost morale. The lobby was shady and cool but smelled like a wet dog, and in the upstairs bedrooms small electric fans screeched erratically in a losing effort to shift the dead air. It was an unpromising beginning.

At dinner that evening, the visitors, recoiling in distaste, wiped the gummy residue off flatware and plates and visibly winced at the wildlife scurrying restlessly about on the floor near the entrance to the kitchen.

Yet in spite of the scruffiness, the meal was a marked success. Beer, warm but excellent, the mutton-kebab with semolina, cloves, and cinnamon was tasty, and by nine o'clock the guests were sufficiently revived to move in a chattering group outside for a try at the town's nightlife. This was optimistic.

A virgin with a bag of gold could wander unmolested the width and breadth of King William's eleventh-century Britain. So he insisted and he probably was right. Things have changed everywhere for the worse. Today, in the unlikely event so unsullied and affluent a maiden existed and she chanced a walk around the block, she would be simultaneously deflowered and impoverished on the turn.

So it certainly could have been in Bou Saada's shadowy souk had the ladies not glued themselves together in a quivering clump, the males rung around them protectively. Fortunately, the procession down gloomy, reeking alleys ended after a few fleeting moments with entry through a large, weathered wooden door. Once inside, the group quickly relaxed in the warmly welcoming glow.

An aged, two-story caravanserai built around an open courtyard that appeared to be a branch of the municipal dump, this hostelry had served the cameleers and armed escorts of the desert trade for more than a thousand years. Prey to rowdy tribesmen, the place had repeatedly been sacked, rebuilt, and refurbished until, in the deceptive flickering light of pitch torches slanting outward from iron brackets on the pillars, it was a dilapidated but imposing pile.

The second story was, in fact, a wooden balcony that encircled the oval courtyard, open to the stars, and it accommodated a string of tiny cubicles devoted to a feverish pursuit of the world's oldest professional skills. Darkly handsome and scantily clad women, momentarily unemployed and catching their breath, leaned provocatively over the balustrade and eyed the milling newcomers.

On the ground floor under the balcony were the public rooms, entered through beaded curtains and used for cabarets, gaming, or more of the upstairs excitements. In our case it was a large, vaulted chamber, whitewashed and hung with oriental drapes and rugs, bronze oil lamps on the walls casting a wavering, golden illumination. On the wall facing the entrance was a musicians' "box," and tambours and pan-pipes and lutes struck up a deafening, thumping screech as we felt our way to leather poufs and cushions scattered about the stone slab flooring. Heavy clouds of incense nearly blinded us to the arrival of a troupe of Nautch dancers who floated in from a far corner.

It might have been the usual bump and grind with oriental overtones but wasn't. With odd ritual movements of hands and body and singularly personal overtures to each of the men, the girls produced a pretty compelling performance.

Indeed, one of the younger dancers, later identified as Josephine, easily overdid formal ceremonial. Fuller bodied and no newcomer to the craft, she was the prima performer when, the ladies having been politely removed to the outer courtyard, the girls, with nothing on but eye makeup and earrings, undulated around the room. And even though Josephine did deliver an earthier message than her colleagues, her beauty and skill transformed even that into something akin to art.

My escort for the evening had been a large, blonde lass we'll call Annelisa, from Munich. She'd joined the tour group as a hostess the night before we left Algiers and was good at the job. She spoke several languages, was pleasing to look at, patient, and muscular. On this visit to the bordello, she'd assumed command of a portion of the party and me, but had been forced to retire with the other females before the specialty number.

When the performance ended and the men struggled up off the poufs, there was a touch on my shoulder. Josephine, a diaphanous white wool shawl emphasizing her nakedness, glistening from her exertions, looked up at me and smiled.

"*Ça boum, m'sieur?*"

"Ah, oui. *Ça boum, mam'selle.*"

"Monsieur," she pouted prettily and took my arm. "Mon chou," she paused, "*tu veux,*" and her eyebrows lifted, "*faire le Zeeg Zeeg,*" and she moved against me. At which point I sensed Annelisa looming abaft my port quarter, a presence Josephine chose to ignore. Putting her small brown arms round my neck, pulling my face down to hers, she murmured intimate noises.

I don't know if it was the intimidation of the towering Brunhilde or my natural cowardice, but I chose the virtuous course. Craven that I am, I took Josephine's small hand in mine and babbled. I think I even said, "Not tonight, Josephine," and it's hard to sink any lower than that. And quite suddenly I was out in the courtyard, bundled along by Annelisa with the others, Josephine's ribald laughter and lewd observations ringing in my ears.

Even though this humiliation was easily to be matched by other graceless antics in my career as a cartoon Casanova, Josephine's damp beauty will continue to float before me long after all other dream fantasies have dimmed.

Back at the Oasis that night, Annelisa, her handsome face contorted with contempt, patted me on the head and sent me off to bed.

The next day the group visited the "Garage du Chameaux" for harrowing camel rides and pilgrimaged to the Grand Mosque of El Hamel. The morning following, the party returned to Algiers, where I left them, bidding Dokman a warm farewell over whiskies under the aspidistra and suffering a bone-crushing goodbye handshake from Annelisa.

There had been a lot of loose talk in Algiers about a rebel "maquis" operating in the Kabylie, a mountainous coastal province to the east, its aim being the independence of the colony of Algeria from France. It was rumored the gangs had shot up police installations, blown up bridges, and otherwise shattered the civil calm. By 1954 the same group would form part of the nucleus of a revolutionary force, the Front de Liberation Nationale (F.L.N.) bludgeoning the French into final retreat from the colony in 1962. But when I inquired about it in the summer of forty-nine, the government flatly denied its existence. This denial lost some credibility when the authorities followed it with a warning that continued prying into the matter could get me kicked out of the country.

Significant as the story was, looking into it further would have been fruitless. The few local contacts I'd made clammed up, intimidated by government, and the story withered away.

Unwilling to write off the trip, I motored on into the rugged wilderness of the Haute Kabylie to visit construction at the new Oued Agrouin hydroelectric and irrigation scheme. It was a formidable engineering feat, the French engineers, the world's best at this sort of thing, blasting huge caverns for miles through solid rock. After a few days splashing about dressed in wellington boots and oilskins hundreds of feet underground in a constantly soaking mist and struggling to master a stream of French technical jargon, I mailed off the story and headed back for Algiers. It was on this trip that I encountered the "Touring Hotel" in the port town of Bougie.

If Sheffield's Hen and Chickens had provided barely passable comforts and the Martinez and Oasis had been awful, accommodation at the Touring Hotel was the absolute bottom.

Bougie, seen from a distance, was a picturesque clutter of white stone and adobe buildings sprawling down a green hillside to the frothing fringe of the Mediterranean. Close up, it was another smelly kasbah.

It was late afternoon, and by the time I'd navigated the twisting, hilly streets searching fruitlessly for an empty room, the sun had dropped, and dusk had dirtied up the place even more. I had nearly abandoned hope when a tipsy postal clerk, weaving homeward after a pause at his favorite pub, cheerfully led me to the hotel entrance, "Le Touring" etched in flickering orange neon over the doorway.

Inside I was just turning away from reception where a rheumy-eyed relic had told me no rooms were free, when a hugely fat Arab in a too-tight, chalk-striped, black business suit bellied up beside me at the desk and clapped me on the shoulder.

"My dear sir," he boomed. "This idiot child of a camel has even fewer brains than manners," and with a flourish he slammed his key on the counter. "You shall have my room."

Waving away my protests, he said he'd stay with an acquaintance down the hall.

Before he'd arrived, I'd been conjuring up horrifying visions of what it must be like on the second floor of this fleabag and had actually accepted with relief the receptionist's curt dismissal. And then this meddlesome Samaritan had let his kindness run away with him.

My first impression was that my room had been abandoned years before, never to be visited again. In the pale smear of light from a fifteen-watt globe I could make out the bed with a bare mattress darkly stained and a grimy washbasin with a hissing tap. Grayish plaster walls, soiled and punctured, assorted rubbish strewn about the concrete flooring and a ragged rug completed the decor. The odor was pungent. There was obviously no profit in taking further inventory and, exhausted, I threw myself down on the poncho I'd tossed over the gruesome mattress and spent most of the night apprehensively listening to the wildlife scratch and pulsate about beneath me in the straw ticking. Outside in the alley the basso honking of a troubled donkey competed with screeching cats. Against this cacophonous background, fleets of bats wheeled in and out through the torn screening hanging over the alley window, revivifying the pungency with showers of guano and chittering ceaselessly. It was three days after I'd left Bougie before I was able to capture and execute the last flea, and longer for the bedbug bites to subside.

Nonetheless, as I pulled away, scratching, the next morning and took the coastal road for Algiers, I consoled myself that I'd hit the lowest I could get. Things couldn't be worse. In fact, hotels like Le Touring enhanced the glories of the great houses I'd visited, Shepheard's in Cairo, of course, and the Dome Hotel in Cyprus.

CHAPTER X

Lull in Cyprus

When we were expelled from Jordan in June of forty-eight, those of us who had booked into the Dome Hotel in Kyrenia had found it a welcome respite after Palestine. Our stay would have been painfully brief had it not been announced, shortly after our arrival, that a United Nations Near East peace conference would soon convene on the isle of Rhodes. This venue could be reached easily by flights from Cyprus via Athens, and, since we had to be somewhere in the interim, with relief we had chosen to wait in the seaside resort.

Kyrenia, the fishing village that was home to the Dome, has been there, dozing in the sun, since before the time of Christ. The hotel fronted on the sandy shoreline bordering the western arm of the tiny harbor. A hulking twelfth-century castle abutted the eastern curve and on the tranquil waters of the bay, a few aging motor trawlers and a host of fishermen's small sailboats rocked lazily in the warmth. Behind the hotel, on a bluff cresting the steep slopes of the Northern (Pentadactylos) Mountains, the ruined Crusader castle of St. Hilarion loomed gray and gloomy. Certainly for setting it was hard to beat the Dome. And although the interior of the hotel would never be mistaken for Claridge's in London, it was tidy and relaxed and very comforting.

The long bar faced a bank of windows overlooking the sea, and I recall only that this room and those leading off it were hushed and awash in underwater, blue-green reflections dancing on the walls. At night the atmosphere was sedate.

There was a reading room and a sepulchral salon where bridge was played by graying oldsters and a lounge with hideously overstuffed chairs and sofas and large paintings of heroic events like *Trafalgar* and *The Battle of the Nile*. The stillness was intimidating. The only break in the soft, well-modulated murmur was the teatime clink of spoons on saucers and the occasional pop of a potlid dropped shut.

It was gracious, privileged, and very British. If bloody mayhem was rampant in Greece and Palestine and incipient civil revolt threatened in half a dozen other nearby countries, these conditions were simply "unfortunate." Just as one didn't talk business "in club," so one avoided mixing social life and sordid reality. It was assumed that there were people in offices or in uniform someplace whose duty it was to handle such matters.

In 1948 Britain's empire was patently coming loose along the seams. The great Indian subcontinent had eased out from under the colonial wing the year previously. The Palestine mandate was being demolished, denying the British strategic position and influence and disconcerting rumblings were harbinger of troubles throughout the African colonies. For all this, many Britons seemed not to notice. They remained sublimely confident that the world would continue to recognize the United Kingdom's primacy. And anyway, if they seemed overly relaxed it must be remembered the Empire's glittering heights had been reached only after centuries of inspired endeavor and a bit of tranquil self-indulgence now was "no more than one's due."

Although I was willing to relax amid all this comforting rationalization and the perks that went with it at the Dome, there were those who loathed it. These were the wives of newsmen who were scattered across the Levant on assignments that were too threatful to permit them to take family along. The women reasoned, quite irrationally if understandably, that if the Empire hadn't started collapsing in such violent disorder they might still be at home in Keokuk. Or at least in some civilized posting like London. But here they were, shepherding young children in a strange place for God-only-knew how long and fearful that the next time they saw Father he'd be in a pine box. Or they worried he'd run off to Baghdad or somewhere with an oriental temptress or even just another bored wife from Keokuk.

There were, on the other hand, wives unencumbered by offspring or suspicions, who had a ball, especially those who had a fair complement of functioning brain cells as an aid. Some of them did dust off to Rome with newly won "friends," it's true, but for the most part they simply soaked up the plentiful wonders of Cyprus.

The island, which isn't the size of anyplace, really, unless it's Corsica, is a store of exciting historical memorabilia dating from 4,000 B.C. Aside from natural mineral wealth (copper = "Kyprios" = Cyprus) that had drawn miners, merchants and marauders since ancient times, its crossroads location had made it a major marketplace. From 1,400 B.C., it had been overrun sixteen different times by twelve different peoples.

Add to this the architectural and other cultural leavings abandoned in the launching of four Crusades during only two decades of the fourteenth century, and there were a lot of leftovers to gawk at, even discover. In the ruins of St. Hilarion, I unearthed a tiny piece of what was identified for me as ancient body armor.

For all this, the island wasn't unrelievedly a holiday idyll. Concentration camps ("collecting areas") run by the British for "illegals" caught making for Palestine were resented by the islanders, who were in sympathy with almost anything anti-colonial. Britain had, to all intents and purposes, administered Cyprus since 1878 even when it was still a Turkish possession; had annexed it formally in 1914 at the beginning of World War One; and had absorbed it as a crown colony in 1925.

Out in the countryside, animosities alive for centuries between islanders of Greek and Turkish background smoldered in the more than 600 small villages. In the towns this hostility, responsible even then for violence and the unrest that was to burst to the surface in bloody civil war during the mid-1950s, was already apparent. It was not entirely a happy land.

Still, for many of us, there was nothing unusual about tension, and we wandered the island oblivious and profiting much, often in most unusual circumstances.

Small curls of what I was told were octopus meat, dried and highly spiced, were delicacies at the Dome's long bar, and when I learned these slimy mollusks were caught in Kyrenia harbor, I wangled a place on a local diver's boat to watch the contest. From all I'd read, no self-respecting cephalopod gave up without a fight, and it could be interesting to peer cautiously over the gunwales while my host, Paul Passaportis, did the dirty work. Paul was in his mid-thirties, square built, and burnt mahogany by the sun, with a tumble of black hair over a broad, friendly face. He spoke softly and confidently in "school" English, stilted but fluent.

His craft was a small sailboat some fifteen feet long, all cockpit aft from the mast, stepped well forward near the bow, chunky and ungraceful, a working dory. Mid-afternoon of a hot cloudless day we coasted out to the mouth of the harbor in a light breeze and, where the sandy bottom flickered about fifteen feet down, dropped sail and drifted on the glassy surface.

Stuffing a short, wide-bladed knife into the waistband of a cotton loincloth, his only garment, he pointed down to what looked to me in the crystaline shimmering like clumps of seaweed or chunks of rock. Octopus, small ones.

"My size," he smiled.

"Sometimes," he continued, "these come up in nets but if you want only the octopus, and a good size one, you must fish only for them."

A "good-size" octopus or "squeed"—the terms squid and octopus seem to be interchangeable in the Mediterranean—when caught and flattened out on planking to dry will be two to four feet across to tips of the tentacles.

"I swim down over them," he said, "and I stab in the eyes. They make ink to hide but not much if you are quick; you watch," and blade in hand he went over the side.

His brown body, its shape distorted by the refraction as it dropped, wavered downward; there was a sudden commotion amid clouds of sand and gray mist, and seconds later he surfaced, tossing what looked like a lump of gray guts into the cockpit. The thing oozed a black slime from which the tentacles waved spasmodically, and centered in this glob was a small white beak, its biting equipment, snapping spasmodically. Altogether quite revolting.

Later Paul explained that the catch was gutted, the tentacles stretched out and nailed to any flat wooden surface like the door of a boatshed, and the thing allowed to dry in the sun. In time, cut up, the tentacles were marinated in vinegar and oil and spices for several days and then baked in a slow but very hot earthen oven.

"Squeed," as served in some restaurants, is a heap of little white rings, smothered in a savory sauce and if prepared properly easily lives up to its reputation as an epicure's delight.

But as far as I was concerned, the best place for the disgusting relics Paul was collecting around my feet was back on the bottom. Just as I'd made up my mind to escape over the side, Paul pulled himself into the cockpit, and we upped sail and slid back toward the wharf.

"You see these?" he turned his back to me. Diagonally up from hip to left shoulder, down his arm and, as he faced me again, across his stomach, were a series of ragged bluish scars, each about an inch in diameter.

He'd underestimated the size of the octopus, half concealed, he said, in a rock cavern on the bottom. When he stabbed it, the thing flapped seven arms out of the seaweed and enfolded him in gummy tendrils. The eighth one remained anchored to the rock and he had a frantic battle tearing it loose.

By the time he made it back to the surface, this gooey monster had glued itself all over him and he could barely stay afloat. Luckily he wasn't far from shore, he said, and managed to thrash himself and the wounded octopus up onto the beach. There he said he rolled around in the sand, loosening the suckers, until it released its grip. He got medical care for the bleeding holes in his hide and later flattened the thing out to find it measured six feet across, a big "squeed" for the Mediterranean.

The experience still sends cold chills all over me and later I made it the subject of a radio script:

> I wonder how many of us know what we're saying when we say something is moving at a "snail's pace." How fast *is* a snail's pace? Well, I've looked it up, and a snail's pace is, roughly, three hundred sixty one-thousandths of a mile per hour. That's twenty-three feet, ten inches a day. Flat out. No breaks. Now, related to snails, in the family called "mollusca," are octopus and squid, and they're really what I want to talk about.
>
> A squid has no backbone. In fact it's an assortment of ligaments and gristle stuck together in a highly flexible manner. The results are not appealing, and it's this dreadful appearance that has got him the reputation for smothering divers and embracing submarines. Actually, it seldom does either. The angriest squid in the oceans is more likely to take off in a cloud of black bubbles than come snarling into the attack. Which is just as well.
>
> It's carnivorous and can grow to a substantial size. The giant squid of the Pacific can have a body length of eight feet and an overall length, including its ten arms, of close to fifty-seven feet. Incidentally, only two of the ten arms are used to capture prey. The others are for steering, for supports and sometimes for defense. The squid's a voracious eater, has powerful jaws and tries very hard to live up to its nasty reputation.
>
> The octopus has been even more overrated as a man-eater. It slops around the depths pretty much minding its own business, but it's good to eat. So fishermen go after it, and, naturally, it fights back.

And here I told Paul's story of his struggle in Kyrenia harbor.

> In Pacific waters [to continue the radio script], one species can measure over thirty-two feet across, flattened out. All species use their arms much as a squid does, but since they haven't got the same strong jaws, they supplement the squeezing action they do have with a poisonous saliva that paralyzes their prey.

Paul's octopus, also, had a quite adequate biting beak as well as a sawlike bit of equipment for prying open clams and other shellfish.

Actually what an octopus prefers is to be left alone, like most people. It will even build a wall of boulders around itself and hide, which is more sad than savage.

In fact, the strenuous and risky labor to produce this protein as a pièce de résistance on a menu has long struck me as misdirected. Except for Kyrenia, where Paul's catch was processed into succulent bite-sized hors d'oeuvres and one restaurant I visited in Florence, where it was steeped in a delicious garlic sauce, I have seldom found it appetizing. For the most part, eating it can be rather like snapping one's way through a bowl of heavy-duty rubber bands.

There are any number of places on the island of Cyprus more inviting than Kyrenia during the hot, humid eighty-five–degree days of midsummer. Many footloose newspaper wives, traveling together with children in tow, took off on tours or headed for the mountains. One of many alternatives in the highlands was the Troödos range, where the peaks rear upward some 6,400 feet. There the temperatures average a cool, unhumid 70 in summer and chill 40s in winter, when it's not unusual to have a morning dip in Kyrenia's bay and a brisk afternoon slalom near the town of Troödos itself. The mountains were a favorite hangout for King Farouk and his entourage, all cordially despised but tolerated because of all their nice money.

I didn't have all that nice money but scraped together enough to hire an aged Vauxhall sedan with a man behind the wheel. He was no driver. What should have been an easy afternoon's run across the central plains and up into the cypress-shadowed quiet of the Troödos was a torment.

For him the car was a weapon. He shaved the elbows of plodding farmers, knocked pots and pans and other utensils from under the arm of one aged crone, sprayed produce around a village marketplace when we charged through a vegetable stand, and obliterated a goat. I had to buy the remains to restore the peace, and he insisted, over my vigorous protests, on taking the thing with us. This meant that we arrived at what was really a rather posh mountain aerie with a bleeding carcass draped over the left front fender.

He nearly ripped the rear door off unstable hinges playing the "compleat chauffeur," and, carrying my baggage, he led me into the hotel lobby in such exasperatingly good humor one would never have known we'd just traversed the Valley of Death.

He would, he shouted, return in two days' time. He always shouted. About everything. And in a trice he was gone, goat corpse and all.

Suddenly, in the lobby there was sweet, pine-smelling stillness. I closed my eyes and sighed with relief. When I opened them, a smiling, crisp little figure in a concierge's frock coat confronted me.

"I do apologize, monsieur," it said in dulcet tones, "for the driver's bad manners," and rolling his eyes ceiling-ward he tossed a deprecating hand at the departing car. "Santos is deaf. He hears little," he continued, "and shouts because," and he tittered tastefully, "he might say something he'd otherwise miss."

In the charge of this stand-up comic at the front desk was a hotel, English-owned and -operated and a copy of mountain hunting lodges the world over. It was extravagantly rustic with adzed beams and leather-framed horse brasses, bronze samovars and candle snuffers and those fox-hunting prints, "To the Craners of England." Bulbous leather easy chairs swallowed the unwary, and there was the usual mahogany-paneled "men's bar" echoing hearty laughter. In the carefully antiqued lounge, "the ladies" would, I guessed, chat softly around little tables, sip sweet sherry and toy with needlework and reputations. Most likely they'd be joined at some time by one of their more muscular numbers in riding habit who would stride in, slapping boot with crop, loudly shouting things like "Went ass over tit at the water again . . . Damme!" and laughing it off like the good sport she so obviously would be, bellowing at the same time for "a whisky."

After two days of walking briskly along mountain trails that meandered through the pine forest hush, I was ready to head back for Kyrenia and get set for the isle of Rhodes. The conference there would begin sometime in the following week. Santos, subdued by my flat demand we return directly to the north coast with a minimum of stunt driving, did not assault the pedestrian population again, although he did strain a rather magnificent black rooster through the radiator grill, and the left rear door fell off as we bounced around a sharp mountain turn. He retrieved it, and I had a breezy hour's ride with the door propped on the seat beside me.

We arrived without further mishap, and within a few hours I'd checked out of the Dome and was on my way to Limmasol and a bootleg boat passage to Rhodes. All my colleagues, anxious about my welfare it developed, were already there, awaiting the opening of the conference.

My trip to the Troödos had been designed in part as a display of how casually I had learned to take the pressures of work. When confusion was rampant, I'd yawned and gone on holiday.

I did manage to relax and enjoy the mountains but actually I was there because I hadn't anything else to do. Scheduled to go with my colleagues by plane to Athens, I had been left behind as a result of one of those foolish fortuities that may, from time to time, intrude upon the lives of even the most prudent among us. Which is one way of putting it.

Another way is that, with Noderer, Davidson, and other newsmen and wives, I had promoted a farewell evening jolly at a Kyrenia bistro, complete with Benny Goodman records on a wind-up Victrola, and at some time during the festivities had fallen off a cliff.

This was not as original as it may seem at first blush. The cliff began where the outdoor verandah ended, and in a solo terpsichorean frenzy I had neglected to note the boundary between the two.

The fall had been a mere twenty feet, some two stories, most of it through dense bougainvillea bush, and while lacerated here and there, I was only slightly spoiled. At the time, however, it seemed discreet to stay where I had landed and nap a bit rather than attempt the nearly vertical ascent back up through the shrubbery. My companions either didn't notice my dramatic departure or couldn't have cared less, for no search was conducted as far as I know.

When I awoke, it was to find the morning light feeling its way into a cave where I was neatly laid out on my back, head resting on a small boulder, arms folded across my chest. A chunky, very smelly black goat nuzzled me familiarly, and overhead the plane I should have been on snarled through the sky on its way to Athens, all the other newsmen who'd attended the previous night's soirée smugly aboard.

Later, back at the Dome, the receptionist, visibly flinching at my aroma and disarray but ever courteous, handed me a rude telegram just arrived from Athens: "Leave us leap up and greet the dawn with glad cry. . . . Noderer."

With no flights, scheduled or charter, available for connections to Rhodes for a week, I'd have to find a boat or miss the conference. It was then that, flaunting my nonchalance, I calmly holidayed in the Troödos.

Actually, I'd prevailed upon an anonymous representative of the *Cyprus Mail,* the island's only English-language newspaper, to try and get me a berth, and he'd succeeded even before I'd left for the mountains.

The voyage he'd set up for me certainly was furtive. The vessel would be moored alongside the mole in Limmasol. I was to say nothing to anyone about the trip—just show up dockside, get aboard, go below, settle somewhere, and wait. The trip would take two nights, cover about 270 nautical miles up the Turkish coast and the fee would be $150 U.S. cash. The boat would depart Cyprus's southern port near midnight, June 21, and, God willing, would arrive in Rhodes harbor some thirty hours later.

I arrived in Limmasol the night before, and, once settled into a whitewashed cell resembling a holding room at the morgue, I walked down the steep hill from this dosshouse to survey the harbor. It didn't take me long to find my boat, the only large pleasure launch with a Greek name.

The craft was forty-five feet fore and aft, an erstwhile rich-man's yacht converted to commercial use by clearing the decks for cargo and emptying much of the interior of creature comforts to provide storage space. It was wooden, clinker-built and hadn't seen paint for many voyages, leaving it a mildewed off-white and pale blue. It looked fast and rugged. There was no activity aboard.

The next evening at eight o'clock I carried my luggage up the gangway and, entering the first cabin door, went below. There was no one there. I sat on my Val-Pac and waited.

In about an hour, a rugged type in a peajacket appeared and, introducing himself as the captain, invited me into his quarters for a drink. He was a grizzled, square-built Englishman with a public-school accent. When he removed his jacket, he wore gray flannels, cream silk shirt, and cashmere cardigan, better suited to walking the Corgies than piloting questionable cargo. Still, my *Cyprus Mail* acquaintance had told me that transporting illicit cargo was the man's chosen calling, and whether or not he looked as if he matched his métier obviously had nothing to do with it.

The drink, in a corner of what had formerly been a billiard room, was a brusque formality. He pocketed my $150 without comment, told me he rarely carried passengers, and, payment or not, I was aboard on sufferance and thanks to my newspaper colleague. He introduced me to an officer as his first mate and radio officer, rose from the table, and abruptly left the cabin. I saw him only once more during the trip. The mate, a Greek who'd spent three World War Two years flying Royal Air Force bombers, took me to a cabin with porthole and spartan fittings, invited me to visit the radio shack anytime, and bowed out.

Apparently space on the upper deck aft, already chockablock with plywood chests battened down under canvas, began to fill up with human cargo after it got dark. I could hear the activity, voices hushed, and when I went topside about midnight to watch as we left harbor, I could see that perhaps a score of them had improvised shelter under the tarpaulins.

By the following noon we were beating along Turkish coastal waters through heavy seas, a treacherous passage at best and on this day whipped into a frenzy by high winds. Heavy rain hung around us like a curtain that hampered visibility but ripped open occasionally to reveal mountainous waves and billowing gray clouds rolling in from the northwest.

As I staggered forward to the radio shack, using lifelines hung along the bulkheads, the little vessel twisted and lunged through seas that kept the decks constantly awash. Aft, the "boat people" of this unhappy era huddled in soaking misery.

A story I wrote for the *News* went, in part, like this:

> The little Greek radioman planted his feet wide and leaned against the rail for support.
>
> "Everywhere there is war," he shouted, "why should the sea be peaceful?"
>
> He grimaced and looked upward at the rigging, snapping in the gale-strength winds.
>
> The small boat shuddered, the twin screws out of the water shaking the stern, and yawed violently. The door to the radio shack on the forward deck eased open slowly and then slammed shut.
>
> The man beside me pushed off from the rail, and I followed as he lurched along the lifelines. Inside the small cabin littered with apparatus, the sound of the storm was abruptly muffled as the door banged shut behind us. He slipped on a headset, handed me another, and we listened to an English voice report that his ship, a British frigate, was answering the distress call from a Jewish vessel under attack by, paradoxically, other Jewish forces. We followed the radio chatter avidly until, just as reports indicated the Jewish ship was under heavy fire from a shore battery, the transmission faded into static.

CHAPTER XI

A Fruitless Garden

By noon of our second day out of Limmasol, the sea had calmed, and by nightfall we could comfortably move about the craft and I spent a peaceful night. When I awoke, the Greek officer told me the captain wanted me in his cabin, on the trot. To reach his quarters I had to go on deck and was surprised to find them cleared, not a trace of the wretched human cargo that had suffered so during the storm; not a crate in sight, the deck planking hosed down and glistening.

"We land in about fifteen minutes, Mr. Acheson," the captain said. "Please leave the boat as soon as it docks."

I replied that, of course, I would do as he wished but, I added, "It occurred to me last evening that I have no visa or other papers permitting me to land on Greek soil."

"Such details are of no consequence," he said. "When we pull alongside, you disembark. Quickly." And possibly suspecting I'd argue about the documents, or even ask about disappearing deck cargo, he conducted me briskly to the door, bowed me out and shut it, firmly, behind me.

I did as I was told, fearfully, walking the interminable length of the concrete pier, past banks of warehouses still locked for the night, not a soul in sight, my hobnailed heels ringing echoes off the buildings. Convinced I'd be stopped by authorities at any moment, I was surprised to find myself out on the flamboyantly gardened boulevard leading to town. From there to the Hôtel des Roses, Rhodes's poshest and the scene of the conference, was a matter of minutes on foot through silent streets. The air was cool and softly perfumed as the sun began to warm the night's damp off the blooms, a rare moment of sweet calm.

One of my colleagues had booked me into his double room, banking on my ultimate arrival, and, after dumping my clobber in the sumptuous boudoir, I joined the others below in a mirrored salon overlooking the rose gardens.

Following some tasteless raillery about my penchant for flying, unassisted, off balconies, we got down to the matter of the peace conference.

It had convened the day before with the press excluded and Jewish and Arab delegations conducting leakproof meetings. The U.N. deputation was equally tight-lipped. Led by Count Folke Bernadotte, a stately Swedish aristocrat, it had studiously avoided newsman. Not without reason. Things had become very sticky.

The conference had been arranged to mediate differences between opponents during a brief moment of military stalemate when both sides were willing to cooperate in a U.N. ceasefire. By the time the conference opened, however, the situation had changed. Jews, the Arab targets having been outlawed by agreement, had taken to shooting at each other.

In fact, the communication the Greek radioman and I had chanced upon that stormy afternoon off the Turkish coast had logged a historic event in the life of what was to become the state of Israel. We didn't know it at the time but the battle we followed had taken place off the beaches of Tel Aviv and featured a future Prime Minister of the country, Menachim Begin, as leader of the Irgun Zvei Leumi in open revolt against the ad hoc Jewish government. Jew was fighting Jew for power. Details of this bloody free-for-all I collected in Rhodes.

Begin's Irgun had become increasingly at odds with the moderate policies of the Jewish leaders with whom the departing British had dealt and who formally conducted the war against the Arabs.

To strengthen its independence, the Irgun had procured a used U.S. Marine LST (landing ship, tank) and sailed from a port near Marseilles loaded with arms and about 800 volunteers from America and Europe.

The vessel was on the high seas headed for Palestine on June 11, the date when the Jewish representatives and the United Nations had signed an agreement prohibiting the import of war materiel during the period of truce. Ben-Gurion, head of the provisional government, had, however, secretly agreed to let the Irgun shipment, already en route, land at a secluded beach north of Tel Aviv.

Approaching Palestine waters, Begin, suspecting a double-cross by Ben-Gurion, radioed orders for all Irgun members, temporarily fighting alongside the Haganah as regular troops, to desert and come to the proposed landing place and unload the LST. The Irgun would now keep for themselves all the arms it had been previously agreed they would share with the Haganah.

Ben-Gurion got wind of the treachery and sent a brigade of crack troops to secure the arms and arrest the smugglers. A pitched battle ensued, and Begin, getting the worst of it, ordered the LST with its remaining cargo out to sea. A short time later, the boat was, by his order, beached at Tel Aviv. This constituted a defiant invitation to Ben-Gurion and the provisional government to openly declare war against other Jews.

Ben-Gurion didn't hesitate. Units of the Palmach, Haganah commandos, blew the ship, its cargo, and its volunteers out of the water. The Irgun as an independent fighting force, and disruptive of steps to establish a stable Jewish state, was crushed. Not long afterward the Stern Gang was also disbanded as an underground terrorist ring. Thus the Jews achieved a united front for the first time and a formidable leverage in dealing with the Arabs. And the U.N.

Not that this internecine Jewish warfare and subsequent solidarity really made much difference. The Rhodes conference had been from the beginning a nonstarter. Not even Bernadotte, clever and experienced as he was, would have been able to pull the extremes together. He held frequent, easygoing press conferences while perched on the back of a bar-lounge couch and, in a kind of desperation, he and his attractive American wife held chatty lobby sessions with newsmen and gave parties for everyone as part of a conciliatory effort.

It was no go. While we watched the count's efforts falter and fail, some of us tried to balance the gloom by writing stories about what a nice, appropriate venue the isle of Rhodes was for at least trying.

> Certainly this island is the right place to talk peace [I wrote for the *News*]. Nine times in its history it has been conquered, undergoing half a dozen sieges. If Jerusalem, today, suffers a deadly hail of lead and steel, Rhodes, long ago, suffered bombardments scarcely less lethal for being primitive.
>
> Lying in the ancient moats of the Old Walled City or half-buried in empty plots and piled in clusters about the city, "shells" of former times are found by the thousands.
>
> Rounded stone balls, from four to twenty-four inches in diameter and weighing up to 200 pounds, were catapulted into the city. Crashing into homes, creating bloody havoc in marketplaces, battering defenses, and careening down the narrow cobbled lanes, they spread as much terror as today's three-inch mortar does in the Holy City.
>
> But the island has known as much peacemaking as war. If there are no noticeable signs of hope for peace at the conference in the Hôtel des Roses—and there are none—then, perhaps, the spirit of past successful endeavor here may still influence present events.

Nothing worked. The conference broke up. Three months later, in September, 1948, in one of the war's cruelest blows, the count and his aide, Col. André Pierre Serrot, in Jerusalem pursuing "new initiatives," were killed in an ambush as their car edged through the rubble of the city's Katamon Quarter. Official announcements about reasons for the attack and those responsible were, like most "official" declarations, totally sterile.

> The ambush murder of unarmed men [I wrote for the *News*] is no new thing in Palestine, and dead neutrals are commonplace. Yet the slaughter of Bernadotte and Serrot is a mindless act.
> There can be little doubt a Jewish group was responsible. I have traveled the route the count took on his return from the former Government House outside the city many times. The Jews seized the section from the Arabs in a pitched twenty-four hour battle in early May and have had complete control there since that time.
> To the score of newsmen who associated with Bernadotte since he first took over the dangerous mediation job in early July, his murder is almost a personal affront. We liked him and, what's truly unusual, found him entirely credible.
> Called in on a task that had all the classic difficulties in any mediation, plus additional stresses of urgency and the flat refusal on both sides to give an inch, he had worked with uncommon energy and optimism.

None of us foresaw so violent a conclusion to the count's mission as his murder in Katamon, but there were few among us who hadn't expected his efforts to fail. The rush toward full-scale war had picked up too much momentum. Once started, it would last, in running campaigns and sporadic clashes, for more than thirty-five years.

For most of the newsmen at the Rhodes conference, it would be someone else's story. The majority had been on it long enough. It needed a fresh view. Even as the count had left Rhodes to return to the Palestine mainland, the press corps was breaking up, heading in assorted directions. Some of the men did return to Palestine to await replacements or to carry on for a while. Some of the rest of us took off to try another war.

CHAPTER XII

Greece, an Unrefreshing Pause

Although Rhodes was Greek territory and airport officials seldom checked international movement, our C-47 flight to Athens and the mainland was handled differently. There had been a clampdown on illicit traffic in arms, drugs, and human beings, mostly Jews, throughout the Levant, and an inspection of all documents had become routine.

My passport had been generously stamped by the Egyptian and Palestine governments (in English, Hebrew, and Arabic), and by Jordanian and Cypriot authorities. But no Greeks. I had, after all, simply jumped ship and booked in at the Hôtel des Roses. Officially, therefore, I couldn't really be in Rhodes. How, then, and the officer's eyebrows rose to his hairline, had I come to stand before him?

I sensed this immigration inspector would find anything less than the truth to be transparent and not amusing. He might be rude to me. Book me into the local pokey, for example. So I told him the truth, in mind-boggling detail, from my solo flight off the verandah in Kyrenia to the docks at Rhodes, the quality of the cabin accommodation, the storm, the excitement in the radio shack. I chattered nonstop, omitting only an exact description of the boat and its cargo, until my breath ran out. This I did on the principle that this stream of consciousness explanation would bore him, and he'd be glad to get rid of me. It did, and he was, wearily handing me back my passport and demanding only that I report to immigration once a week until I left the country.

In Athens, Frank Scherschel of *Life* and I booked into the Hotel Mercury, a newly built concrete human hive down a back street from Constitution Square and the Grande Bretagne Hotel, where the more affluent reporters lounged in luxury: Morley Cassidy, the *Philadelphia Bulletin*, and his wife, Phyllis, from the Jerusalem crowd; Clare Hollingworth, there from Amman; Drew Middleton, the *New York Times*, and others. Frank and I suffered a lesser hostel because both of us were living on my supply of American Express checks and they were running low. The arrival of more cash from the States for either of us was unpredictable, and Frank was a bit tetchy. So we pinched.

"Drink ouzo! It's cheaper!" he demanded when I ordered my first Greek beer. So I drank ouzo, a licorice-flavored hemlock that scarred my stomach lining beyond repair. Still, I found that a lifetime's indigestion was a small thing to bear for Scherchel's company.

A huge balding, 500 percent American from the north central states, one of *Life*'s most valued troubleshooters and later a picture editor in New York, he lived life in all directions at once, flat out. We'd met in Jerusalem. Recognizing I was a fumbling neophyte, he took me under his wing and guided me to, and through, some pretty exciting stories. Now, he was on his way back to New York, with as many pauses en route as he could dream up, and was stuck with me—and my travelers checks—for at least part of the trip.

Before I could join him in his haphazard trek homeward from Athens, there was the matter of a small-bore war to be covered in the Greek highlands. It took me about a week to travel several hundred miles north into the Grammos Mountains—a most appalling journey—crawl around craggy landscape with the Greek army and the Anglo-American Mission, and return in a hospital-cum-refugee plane to the capital city. But more of that in its place.

This tussle with the elements—than which there are none worse outside central Greece—and coping with man at his least attractive, had left me jaded and ready for a break. Frank was leaving for Rome the day after I returned, and I dropped everything and begged him to let me go along. A few days, I reasoned, quietly communing with the shades of Claudius or Seneca amid the mossy relics of antiquity was just what I needed. What I got was something else.

We stayed at the Quirinal, a top-drawer lodging (Frank's office came across with an ample wad) and sallied forth to "do" the town. We jog-trotted through miles of gloomy catacombs, Frank snapping flash pictures at every turning, just as if it weren't against the law. The hand-wringing anguish and tearful protests of our Franciscan guide merely prompted a cheerful torrent of empty apologies from Frank, who kept on taking pictures, even complaining that the "monk keeps gettin' in the way of the bones."

We shot through the Castel San Angelo, whirled around the interior of the Pantheon utterly oblivious of organ music gloriously filling one of the finest acoustical chambers in the world, and sprinted about the grounds at the Baths of Caracalla. I staggered into our hotel room at dusk, my memory of the day consisting of little more than a tattered collection of blurred images. The next day, Frank went on his own. I went alone to the zoo and Borghese Gardens.

At eventide he boomed through the room door, sweeping the entire day before him in a flood of frenzied description. While he peeled himself out of a tangle of cameras and gadget bags, a tripod, and other impedimenta, I broke in and asked him what he, as a Roman Catholic, thought of St. Peter's, treasury of the world's great religious art and a Sacred Place, which, excepting only Jerusalem's Holy Sepulchre, must have no peer in Christendom for "Romans."

"Biggest goddam church I ever saw," he said.

In Athens, before my up-country trip to watch the war and our trip to Rome where we savaged those golden hours, I had spent a few days coasting idly about the capital city. I'd climbed up to the Parthenon with Morley and Phyllis, admired the Evzones in their tu-tu–like garb change the guard at the parliament buildings and had dozed in the sun in the nearby botanical gardens. I had developed a taste for retsina, the resin-flavored Greek table wine and, escaping the Mercury whenever possible, had poached on the sybaritic marvels of the Grande Bretagne.

My memory of the lounge records it as the size of a ballroom, richly furnished with Victoriana concealed in forests of rubber plants, tiny carnations, azaleas, and aspidistra; of gold-filligreed mirrors on towering pillars and glistening candelabra and chandeliers with prisms that tinkled in the evening breezes that wafted through the front portals.

In the summer evenings the stifling heat of the street outside abated slightly, and since no mechanical air-conditioning systems other than electric fans existed there then, the large revolving door at the entrance was folded flat and pushed to one side. The fresh air was thus allowed to "waft."

To conceal the ugliness of the door's hinges, springs, and other inner workings, heavy drapes hung from the high ceiling, and framed the mechanism like silken columns rooted in greenery and potted blooms.

One evening on my way out I confronted a female journalist of beauty and many talents, coming in. Dressed to the nines, she was interestingly disheveled and tilted a bit to starboard. The night was no longer young, and, as we paused between the framing drapes for an idle exchange, fatigue overtook her. Before I could caution her she had leaned heavily against one of the drapes and vanished from sight.

By the time I'd negotiated the shrubbery, she was being borne up off the Aubusson and pulled in several different directions by a host of eager Latins who threatened her with far more damage than that occasioned by sprawling into the greenery. Having brushed aside assorted

Greeks, I guided her to her room and dutifully tucked the incident away among my mental notes. As I recall it now, it reminds me of a similar embarrassment in another hotel at another time.

I was breakfasting at London's Savoy. The dining room was newly decorated, a posh salon indeed, hushed atmosphere, rich decor, pale-blue carpeting, white napery in snowy abundance, glistening silverware and stern propriety.

Into all this came an elderly lady of Queen Mary demeanor, aloof, chin high, handsome head crowned with a towering, feathered hat. The headwaiter glided hurriedly toward her, urgently raising both hands in an obvious warning gesture. But it was too late.

She failed to see a step down, calmly swept out into the space and with the leisurely grandeur of a felled northern pine, plummeted forward, full length. The sound, as she struck, was of a large bolster dropped from a great height, followed by a strangled grunt.

Seldom have I witnessed such self-possession. She struggled upright with astonishing speed for one of her advanced years, silently thrust away the sniveling headwaiter and breathless, beet-red, her feathered headdress askew, gathered herself, and, through the deathly hush, floated forward, head high to her table.

My comely young journalist of the Grande Bretagne couldn't have matched the Queen Mary dignity if she'd tried. Rather, she did it all her way and the next morning accosted me in the lobby, embraced me firmly, and, satisfied I'd been amply repaid, rushed off on a story, which, she archly informed me when I asked, was none of my bloody business. So much for chivalry.

I, in turn, took off for my last report to immigration before leaving with Scherschel for our Roman holiday. On a previous visit to the authorities, I'd been obliged to recount, ad nauseam, details of the voyage from Limmasol, a tale they obviously considered a likely story. This time, however, it was different.

"You will repeat me a description of your boat, monsieur?" the fat, frog-shaped official grinned eagerly, leaning forward over his desk.

I'd been ushered into The Presence directly after I'd arrived, not kept waiting in the dark, moldy corridor as before; he'd asked me to sit and now here he was actually doing his smiling exercises.

"Again?"

"Once more, monsieur, if you be so kind."

I did: about forty-eight feet, wooden hull, beam unknown, twin Perkins-type diesels; painted peeling gray, no decipherable name, Greek ensign. I'd have stumbled on, but he held up a restraining hand.

"Well, monsieur," he rose, hands clasped prayerfully under his chin, lips pursed. "We find this boat, finished, on small island, Kasos, down from Rhodes; boat empty, but," and he produced a mild "aha! There is enough," he said, and added ominously, "with other things, to tell us a story of small but very bad smuggling of arms and people, of nighttime changes in the sea from boats your size to big ones.

"The people paid much money and then, sometimes," he slit his throat with his forefinger and grimaced horribly. "Mostly the guns arrived, but not always the people."

Why had the captain risked having me, a journalist, aboard, I asked.

"Ah, monsieur. The dollars. And because you no problem. You a problem, well, then," he paused, rolled his eyes, and used that deadly forefinger again.

I wondered what I could have done that might have identified me as a "problem," and all at once, standing there in that musty office, I felt quite sick. I suppose I had known all along what was happening. I'd simply brushed the suspicions aside, afraid to go after the story. All I'd been after was safe arrival in Rhodes. I'd chosen to ignore the chilling evidence of the emptied deck that morning, and, describing the voyage to my colleagues, I had conveniently skipped the brutal details.

Later, back at the hotel, I confessed all this to Scherschel. He was comforting.

"Listen, stupid; how would *you* have known about the baddies? You just left off doing social notes for the society ladies a month ago," and he snorted contemptuously.

"Come on." He rose and slapped me on the back. "We've got to turn in our Greek money," and he did say "our." "It's against the law to take it out of the country, as if anybody else would want it."

Turning the drachmas back into dollars was much less confusing than the reverse, an exercise we'd sweated through with Noderer a week before. At that time it had taken the entire morning.

In the National Bank Building on Venezelou, we'd felt our way through the murk to the "Échange Étangère" window. I'd presented my hundred-dollar travelers check to receive in return National Bank certificates of a drachma value matching the hundred dollars. No money. Just this embosssed parchment. Several minutes of ill-tempered instruction in Greek got us nowhere, and Scherschel was about to jerk the clerk through his cage grill when a passerby aimed us across this gloomy arena of high finance to another window.

There an aging medusa of faltering intellect finally delivered to us Greek government bonds in exchange for the first batch of paper. The bonds were denominated in Greek drachmas of a value equivalent to one hundred U.S. dollars.

Our next trip back across this echoing hall was to a counter where we sold the bonds back to the bank and received 502,000 drachmas in currency of various denominations after deducting numerous commissions and service charges.

This perplexing procedure, we learned, was designed to inhibit black market traffic in dollars. The extent to which it succeeded we never learned, but we had seen a lot of paper money change hands all over Athens, in back alleys, men's rooms, and under restaurant tables. Since the Greek buyers gave twice the official rate of 5,020 drachmas to one dollar American, this devalued the country's tottery currency still further at a time when war was costing millions in foreign-arms purchases. This had upset the government, and it decreed the elaborate exchange control measures.

This kind of "devaluation," the rotten fruit of greed, increases in inverse proportion to a country's economic stability. The healthier the country's economy, the fewer the furtive touts with money to sell, although it is still a thriving business in the "underground economy" of most European and all African countries. And these grubby freebooters can take their trade very seriously.

Some years later in a Casablanca back street I nearly got myself punctured by a knife-wielding money merchant infuriated by my refusal to swap my dollars for his Moroccan francs. He'd persisted for several blocks, repeatedly grabbing me by the arm, until, having had enough, I turned on him, threatening to snap off his fingers one by one and stuff them up his nose, among other orifices.

To my surprise he took this picturesque proposal at face value, suddenly producing a silvery blade and loudly appealing to the gathering throng with screaming variations on the "Yankee Go Home!" theme so popular in those times. I was, he shrieked, an arrogant American insulting his country. How he'd conjured up this non sequitur I couldn't think, but, miraculously, this harangue elevated the wretch from a petty crook bent on fraud and murder to a deeply affronted Moroccan patriot.

With uncanny speed, he zeroed in on my favorite stomach. I'd dodged a few of his wild passes, one of which took a few buttons off my fly, when his grotty compatriots, seeing constables round the corner on the run, dragged him away and disappeared into the milling crowd. Even the audience, so keenly interested in seeing my gizzard dissected, sank out of sight, apparently into the cobblestones.

Obviously transactions in hot cash can be tricky. This plainly was known to Scherschel and Noderer, who had prudently taken the official route rather than chance clandestine meetings in the city's public conveniences.

After leaving the Greek bank, our bundle of drachmas carried in a paper sack, we decided to pause briefly and try out our new money, climbing the stairs to a second-floor bistro with a balcony overlooking the busy main street. Drinks ordered, we examined the bills, quite stunning works of art. Indeed, most European currency for sheer beauty of design, and this includes the businesslike British pound, puts American money to shame.

> The average Italian bill [I wrote sometime later] is gorgeous and about the size of a Van Gogh landscape. Belgian and French paper money is magnificent, classic masterpieces every one, although, as the Italian, it's about the size of a popular tabloid. And tissue thin.
> I recall that Art Buchwald, the columnist, writing then for the *Paris Herald,* did a story on these perishable banknotes. They tore too easily, he noted, and forever had to be stuck back together. He concluded by stating that at one time the cost of the scotch tape on a note he passed was twice the value of the note itself.

In the piece I'd written, quoted above, I'd also recounted the ordeal with the Greek bankers over my $100 travelers check and had described the second-floor refresher stopoff that Noderer, Scherschel, and I had made:

> Our flagging morale renewed, we'd descended into the street, only then discovering that we'd left the paper sack full of drachmas on a chair at the table.
> Scherschel raced back up and in a playful mood tossed the bag over the railing to Noderer. Who missed it. It exploded on the sidewalk and some 500,000 drachmas suddenly were floating about as in a tickertape parade.
> One would have thought half the population of Athens would die in the scramble for all this loot.
> In fact, a news vendor, three pedestrians and a shoeshine boy languidly detached themselves from the hustling crowd and joined us in a desultory recovery of this legal confetti, handing what they collected to us in grubby wads.
> Some of it disappeared, glued to passing motorcar tires. Some remained airborne and when last seen was eddying upward over the ancient rooftops.

CHAPTER XIII

Pungent Antiquity!

I had briefly considered suggesting to Frank that we charter a small boat and wander the islands of the Adriatic en route to Italy. Yet the memory of the sea trip to Rhodes remained sour, and I'd dropped the idea. In fact, I didn't try seagoing again for several years.

Not that there weren't to be opportunities aplenty on a variety of vessels: Casablanca to Dakar by freighter (too slow); Dakar to Monrovia in Liberia, also by freighter (sank in Dakar harbor before I could book passage); Takoradi in the then Gold Coast to Lagos by packet (leaky, filthy, and prey to pirate raids). Hence, it had been easy to avoid ocean voyages until, I suppose inevitably, I found myself afloat once again.

I was doing some work in the wild regions of southern Africa when I let myself be persuaded to board an aged boat that plied the Indian Ocean coast of Mozambique. This derelict ketch, sails luffing, auxiliary diesel gasping spasmodically, regularly navigated from the port of Beira southward, stopping at native communities along the mostly uninhabited shore. Our destination, 120 miles distant, was the village of Villancoulos, a wreck of a place matching most villages in that part of the world. Yet this very decrepitude, ancient as it was, was what appealed to Reg Francombe, an architect friend of mine badly in need of a holiday from a barren draughting board. He was unwell, he said; needed a companion for the kind of jaunt he proposed; and asked me to go along.

What he proposed in September, 1953, was a step back about 300 years in time along a section of the continent, variously occupied for thousands of years and about which very little was known. Even the cartography was rudimentary. For me it could mean stories, and I accepted, a mental lapse I was to regret.

Below the port of Beira, over the ancient territory of Sofala, the southeast tradewinds blow, as a book on the area points out, "on and off most of the year and provide dangerous and uncertain conditions for small sailing craft," a flattering description of the forty-foot tub we eventually took. And there was no question it was forbidding territory on other counts as well.

Not only was the weather treacherous, but the seaboard and immediate inland country was desolate. Unless a traveler, forced to beach his craft, happened on one of the few squalid villages, he could be dead a long time before his remains were discovered. During the affluent and balmy days preceding the bloody warfare that ended Portuguese rule of Mozambique in the mid-1970s, gaudy holiday camps bloomed on the sands, a coastal roadway of sorts served these dubious pleasure domes and airstrips were common. But when we visited the area in the fifties, none of this tacky incursion had taken place. There was only the pristine misery so beloved of crabs, scorpions, and hysterical conservationists.

Millions of years before we got there, the region had been located miles inland. It had only begun breasting the seas when a huge chunk of its eastern border broke off, wallowed for six hundred miles, and finally bulged to the surface as the island of Madagascar (Malagasay). So far as could be seen when we did get there, not much had taken place since that alteration.

Sofala had once hosted seaboard terminals serving the gold trade in the upcountry land of Monomotapa, first visited by Portuguese monks in the mid-1400s. It hadn't been a consistently successful venture, what with the more experienced Arabs slicing across the route deep in the bush, but it did flourish for a time. South from Sofala, at the time we planned our trip, the interior was believed to be dotted with the remains of ancient encampments established by King Solomon's minions, sent there for gold and slaves and ostrich feathers. Many of these places were still inhabited, some of them by the descendants of the original Semitic vanguard. Among the most active settlements were those dating from the fifteenth century, the era of Bartolomeu Dias and Vasco da Gama.

So many unknowns to contemplate heightened the mysteries abounding in this ancient quarter and even had me enthusiastic enough to overlook, temporarily, the fact that we'd be in a boat that would only skirt the outer reaches of most of this fascinating history.

Among the certified legends about forgotten civilizations in this part of Africa are those describing a string of trading posts running from the Indian Ocean below the equator diagonally across the continent to the southwest, thousands of miles distant. It is thought that these were garrison communities defending and provisioning merchant caravans trafficking in slaves and gold, ivory, and precious stones. These camps, the reasoning goes, eventually settled peacefully into civilian towns, absorbing the local populations and their pastoral and agricultural pursuits.

Reknowned among these was Zimbabwe (from the Portuguese word

"Zimbao" meaning "great stone house") in what was then southern Rhodesia's Eastern District. Marvelously constructed of mortarless stone walls, some of the defensive structures reaching heights of thirty feet and fifteen feet thick at the base, the complex encompasses shrines, priestly dwellings, and what appear to be family quarters.

Zimbabwe, from which Rhodesia took its African name after black independence from the British in 1979, was discovered by Adam Renders, an American hunter, in the 1860s. Southern Africa was acrawl with prospectors in the great gold rush of those years, and the word of an ancient ruined city, ostensibly crouching over a fortune in gold and precious stones, brought scavengers to the remote badlands in droves. Some gold there was: coins, jewelry and figurines; and jade, Chinese pottery, iron and bronze weapons, beads and stone carvings. Most of it was swept up and disappeared with the departure of the earliest gleaners.

So disturbed was Zimbabwe's soil strata, laid down over the centuries, that archeologists, who read the striations to establish a sequence of events, have been hard put to establish its age or origin. Africans, anxious to identify a native heritage, claim it as Bantu. Cynics, who insist primitive Africans couldn't have invented the walking stick, claim that the Phoenicians or the Arabs or perhaps even the Indonesians built not only Zimbabwe but the other links in the chain across the continent.

Although Francombe and I were interested in these speculations and knew we'd probably be visiting territory on the fringe of this long lost world, we had no plans to go lunging off on an archeological expedition into the Mozambique wilderness. Francombe reminded me that our holiday was to be a sea change and nothing more, emphasizing that a trek into the bush could set back his recovery for months. For Reg, even a picnic was a brutalizing experience.

After several weeks assembling the kind of gear Francombe felt would be appropriate for gentlemen going yachting, with khakis and walking boots tossed in for unavoidable pauses on shore, we and some friends who expressed confidence they would never see us again were gathered on the station platform at the Rhodesian border town of Umtali. It was early evening, and it would take the train until dawn to travel the distance to Beira and our waiting "launch."

Just as the streetlights were flickering on, the asthmatic wheezing of the old engine picked up, its whistle blew sharply, and we climbed aboard to settle in a compartment where comfortable beds already had been made for us.

Beira in the early 1950s was a disreputable town sprawled along an outsized sandbank between the Pungwe flats and the sea. Some two-thirds of the population of about 40,000 were classed as "noncivilized" or unassimilated into European ranks. These worked the docks and in related blue-collar jobs. The balance, the "civilized," about half of whom were white, were employed in the export/import houses, the banks and casual commerce, knick-knack emporiums and in the often arrogant, always feeble, Portuguese government administration.

No color bar existed in law as it did in the Union of South Africa and in the Rhodesias. This hardly meant all Mozambicans loved one another as equals, but intermingling at all social and professional levels was legally allowable.

The town's reason for being was as a major harbor and railhead for the landlocked British colonies of northern and southern Rhodesia and Nyasaland. It was also, increasingly, a holiday resort for upcountry visitors.

"The Estoril" seaside camp on Lighthouse Beach, a magnificent sweep of ivory sand, and the only such haven of any consequence, took in about 600 vacationers during the entire three-month season in the midfifties. Five years later it would grow to easily provide for 38,000. So things in the fifties had begun to move. A bit frantic and disorganized but on the move.

The town would remain grubby and become increasingly jerry-built well into the 1960s. The rich, mostly whites, lived in the beachfront villas along gardened boulevards. The "assimilados," some of whom shared this affluence, lived for the most part back in the commercial areas. The vast mass of "noncivilized" squatted in the "bidonvilles," the tin-shack slums, bordering the swamplands, human dumping grounds from which the sweated labor came.

Out of this awesome inequity, steeped in hypocrisy and born of arrogance and weary indifference, the fifties began to produce a hopefulness, the first, faint hints of better things to come for this ancient backwater.

In the van of this advance and personifying this newness were more and more men of the stamp of one Carlos Abel Henriques de Souza e Brito, a once nearly penniless postal clerk with big ideas and of whom I wrote for the *News* at the time:

> Persuading a Beira builder to risk $30,000 in holiday motel facilities on the beach, this madman took over as proprietor and one year later paid off the entire amount plus 10 percent.
>
> Seven years later he had parlayed that initial risk capital into $1,120,000 in restaurants, a motel complex complete with refrig-

erator and radio in every room (inexpressibly modern then), beachside chalets, dance pavillion, and snack bars. All this in a part of the world where the population largely had shuffled about, half-dead on its feet, for 400 years.

The slummy Beira dock and commercial districts would also be spruced up when all this excitement arrived at the opposite end of town from where the villas grew, but Francombe and I were a few years too early for that.

We fell off the Umtali train at dawn, unslept and violently dyspeptic from an excess of raw malt scotch and red hot peppers. Most of an unseasonably rainy day we passed hiding in a waterfront dump that specialized in spiced boiled prawns and lobster tails, a variety of stimulants, and a piratical clientele that lurked in the gloom. Occasional forays out into the downpour to visit the Alves shipping company offices for information about departure time and pier location kept us just this side of comatose until midnight. At the witching hour, a giant blackamoor slammed through the pub door, swept up our luggage, and motioned us to follow him. Outside it was blacker than he was and ducking against the wind, we followed at his heels down a labyrinth of dimly lit alleys to the wharf.

Sheets of rain lashed the aged wooden dock and below us, in a tumult of shadows, a bargelike hulk wallowed violently in the sea. We kept a wary eye on it, and when, shuddering against the pilings, it rose apparently as high as it was going to, we threw ourselves at it before it fell down into the blackness again.

Strong arms carried us across the heaving deck and into the only cabin, a pooplike affair; our kit was tossed unceremoniously in behind us and the door slammed in the wind. In the darkness we groped for beds and found them, wooden pallets with sides to keep us in, like open coffins.

I lay there wondering if I might remain thus, ready for burial, all the way to Villancoulos and then must have passed out, for, when I could see again, it was becoming light around me. In the gloom my watch gleamed five o'clock. My awakening was reluctant, and only after I gave up trying to keep the new day from arriving at all did I look for Francombe. In the murk across from me I recognized his large, recumbent form shifting gently in the wooden sarcophagus as we rolled in the swell.

As the beginning of a healthful holiday cruise in the warm azure waters of the Indian Ocean, it did rather lack something. But it certainly set the stage.

Judging from what I could sense, the bad weather had passed. The shrieking wind and the slap and clank of the rigging had given way to new alarms. A monotonous thumping and rhythmical quiver rattled the door latch, and a steady squeaking came from everywhere, background to Francombe's weak snoring noises.

I sat up in my box and, feeling less than fighting fit, surveyed our stateroom. It was not an inspiring scene.

It was cramped for space: I would be able to stand erect, if I ducked a bit, and swinging a cat full circle I would have just missed the walls. The whitewashed interior had corrupted to a gray-green mold, and the split teakwood flooring had seen better days. A kerosene lantern vibrated from a hook in the ceiling, and the furniture consisted of our two wooden biers, one gangrenous leather-bound sea chest, and a straightbacked wooden chair screwed fast to the deck. The glass in the portholes, one on each side, appeared to have been sprayed with brown stain. Both were stuck firmly shut.

On the off chance that the air topside might be less dense than it was in the cabin, I left Francombe rocking to and fro and crouched out through the door.

The boat was rigged more or less like a ketch, with our makeshift cabin set just abaft midships, between the main and mizzenmasts. Overall length probably was no more than forty feet, but getting from bow to stern was a slow process. Like stumbling about in the municipal dump.

Everywhere, as if it had poured down a chute to the deck and been left where it landed, was a flotsam of drums of diesel oil, gasoline, kerosene, automotive greases and tubs of lard, coils of hemp and wire rope, kegs of nails, crates of red wine in five-liter amphoras, bundles of lath, gum-tree pit props, boxes of cheeses, and sacks of dried fish. Underneath it all was a gummy residue from previous equally catholic cargoes.

Some of the crew of six had a fire going on an oil-drum lid raised on bricks not much above the obviously inflammable decking. A pot swayed over the flames on miniature sheerlegs, and into it went random pieces of vegetable, chicken corpses, red peppers, and reeking chunks of barracuda. What sea breeze there was preserved its purity by fluttering past well clear of our contaminated craft.

My first encounter with the master of this floating slum occurred just aft the mainmast beneath the boom, along which dirty yellow sails were bunched like bodies hurriedly sewn up for burial. In the sliver of shade it cast, the captain, whose wrinkled jet visage featured a huge broken nose and a week's stubble of stained beard, was working a pump handle. The oil scum it threw into the scuppers came, he gasped, from the bilge, the outgo apparently just surpassing the leak-in. He and his crew took turns pumping the boat afloat, he said, the Portuguese owner having decided that it was cheaper to periodically hire another pumper than to dry-dock and plug the multiplying holes. Little wonder we hugged the shallows, never beyond the sound of the surf, at a speed approaching four knots.

Even this leisurely gait was maintained only by heroic effort from a crusted Hanomag diesel, lifted, I was told, from a defunct bulldozer and converted to sea duty. Handling sails obviously was considered too much work, and it was my guess that they'd stay furled pending a complete mechanical collapse.

Adding to the diesel's handicaps was a bent prop shaft. This gave the boat a violent stern shimmy that threatened to dislodge the head and shake it into the sea.

This excuse for a comfort station, the only one on board, was a one-hole, pitch-dark outhouse standing unsteadily on the afterdeck just beneath the mizzen boom end and somehow suspended above the boiling wake. The hole was so large that one could have settled on the seat only at the risk of falling straight on through. The only recourse was to balance gingerly above it and this was quite a neat trick.

Francombe and I, electing survival as our prime concern, cleared a spot of deck and lolled about in the warm sun. The voyage was scheduled to take eighteen hours, Beira to Villancoulos. Actually, it was eighteen hours before we made it to the first landfall, an aged trading post several miles up the Sabi River.

The captain sashayed the boat in over a shallow bar at the mouth of the river late one evening and headed for the village of Mbabane about a half-hour away upstream. As we slid off the inside of the bar, the wind dropped. In the still air of the sheltered roadstead, we ran into a fog of mosquitos that settled on unprotected skin in a black layer, and I must have inhaled at least a cubic foot of them before I got my mouth shut. I was bitten inside and out.

The farther we went, the thump of the laboring diesel echoing off the thickly wooden riverbanks, the hotter it got. The debris we carried, as cargo and decor, ripened by the minute. There was nothing for it but to keep on the move and counteract the everpresent tendency to throw up. As the old scow sidled toward the end of the wooden landing at Mbabane, we jumped off and worked our way through a jabbering mob toward a sign reading "Hotel-Bar," obviously a rank misnomer. In fact, almost everything at Mbabane was rank.

Mbabane had been there, in one form or another, since a few months before that day hundreds of years earlier when, as a military camp, it had bidden farewell to a company of Portuguese soldiers and native levies, off to raise the king's standard over newly conquered lands in the far interior. In full armor, flags flying, the officers grandly mounted on horses never seen in that tsetse-fly country, the procession paraded through town and disappeared into the forest. Forever.

Although a main base later was established sixty miles higher up the Sabi and the hinterland was combed exhaustively for several years, no trace of the column ever was found. Bits of breastplate and the remains of a crested helmet are said to have surfaced in the frantic excavation for gold at Zimbabwe but no connection with the Mbabane expedition has been confirmed.

After the abandonment of this outpost in the late 1700s, the Mbabane community became the only Sabi emplacement, seldom visited. Its condition when we arrived was remarkably good, considering the neglect.

The "hotel," a trading store, a police camp, and a scattering of public works department houses for the few resident whites, clustered together a few hundred yards from the riverbank. The oiled streets were drained, and the main roadway leading out of town to inland farms and mining camps was well kept. On the outskirts of town there was a small stone church and in the well-tended yard and cemetery there were memorials and headstones dated in the 1700s.

The "hotel," within a few yards of the river, was of green-tinted stucco with a rusty tin roof. It boasted six rooms with beds and was, overall, perhaps the least romantic antiquity I have ever visited. In cloistered gloom that passed for a shaded patio, the sour dankness of centuries collected in a palpable haze, and only the chatter and clink of glasses from the bar saved it from rivalling the churchyard for melancholy.

During the thirty-six hours we loafed about this aged settlement, very little was unloaded from the Alves coaster, and what went aboard, destined for Inhasorro, a beachfront halt en route to Villancoulos, very nearly pursuaded us to jump ship.

Each of the two nights, working in the light of hissing Tilley lamps in the courtyard outside our bedroom window, porters had heaped up bales of dried elephant meat. Laboring through the night might have been cooler than under the blazing sun but the rhythmical chanting that eased their efforts hardly lulled us to sleep and the stench of indifferently salted chunks of dead pachydern beggars description. Even the flies that took refuge in our room were gagging. And it was this packaged offal that went aboard the coaster, adding a new flavor to the vessel's already unique aroma. Twenty bales on the forward deck produced a sickening and almost visible miasma that misted aft for two days and a night.

At Inhasorro we landed by simply grounding the craft on a sandbar outside the fringe of wispy surf and wading ashore. The stinking merchandise was shifted to the general store by porters, who carried the stuff on their heads.

Francombe and I were curiosities. No white ever traveled this way, especially on the coaster, and we spent a cheerful two hours conversing in a mixture of English, Portuguese and "Kitchen Kaffir," a lingua franca constructed of half a dozen languages including Zulu and Swahili. We toasted our hosts in hot Orange Crush and took snapshots of the happy assemblage, tripled in volume by the time we left. Looking back, I think I would have found it hard to accept at that time that any one of these would cheerfully have slit out throats in the "troubles" that hovered just over the horizon.

We arrived at Villancoulos well after dark and only a few hours short of four days after we'd departed Beira. This was a bit behind schedule, admittedly, but I don't recall that I gave it a thought. The captain literally groped his way into the small harbor through blackness that was complete except for a sprinkling of lantern lights along the shoreline or bobbing on the prows of the small boats that clustered around us. The general din and disorder, strangely disembodied in the darkness, gave promise of an all-night thrash in the middle of the little bay with no thought of docking until dawn.

Entranced for a time, we soon tired of the aimlessness and threw ourselves overboard and swam to shore, frivolously consigning our valuables to the ragged crew and their stevedore henchmen. This blunder occurred to us only as we started up the long flight of steps from the harbor. Not that we were afraid they'd be stolen. There was very little theft in Mozambique in those days.

The authorities still employed the "bastinado" as standard punishment for minor felonies. This was a beating on the palms of the hands or soles of the feet with a flat, wooden bat with slits in it. After a few strokes the skin broke and at each following blow the flesh was forced up through the holes. I'd seen hands so torn and swollen they looked like ragged, bloody gloves, puffed out to almost twice their normal size. And excruciatingly painful. Sometimes the blows permanently damaged bone and tendon, and the limb became a mere lump.

I never saw this torture inflicted but I'd been told it was normally done by black warders; few whites could face it. This willingness to inflict severe pain on other blacks was common everywhere in Africa not because of any essential black brutality but because, traditionally, tribal discipline and challenges to manhood involved acute suffering. During this execution of sentence and as long as he retained consciousness, the victim was said to bear the agony without a whimper. Nonetheless, few invited it, and theft was uncommon.

What concerned us about our neglected wallets was that we had no identification, no money for the night's lodging or for food and drink. We needn't have worried. The black hotel proprietor laughed loudly at our concern, said he'd been told to expect us and even granted that we could wait until morning to complete police formalities.

All our effects arrived safely about breakfast time and our three days in the old village and the islands offshore were idyllic. The hotel was newly built and blessed with all "mod cons," hot water, large clean rooms, and comfortable beds. And electric light. The food was violently spicy but varied. We even had fried eggs and bacon when we wanted them, although, as is the continental custom, the eggs were cooked in olive oil and had a special flavor and rubbery consistency.

The little village, which managed a neat white sparkle in the sunshine in spite of the corrugated iron roofing and dusty streets, sat atop a high bluff. Below it, white beaches, broken here and there by protrusions of black basalt boulders, stretched to the horizon in both directions. The bay we'd entered was an almost perfect natural harbor at the base of the bluff, and its narrow entrance helped break up the Indian Ocean rollers that swelled around the offshore islands.

Principle feature of the town, an administrative center for coast guard, customs and police, was a tiny stone church. Believed to be some three hundred years old, its nave was no more than twenty feet from entrance to sanctuary and about the same width. The interior was lavishly if crudely decorated with brightly colored paintings, and the little altar was richly equipped with golden ornaments. Already, for the few visitors, it had become a "tourist attraction," or so the hotel proprietor told us.

The community would, before too long, succumb to "developers" and become a resort catering mostly to wealthy South Africans. But that was still several years in the offing, and we had the place almost to ourselves.

It was advertised as a big-game-fishing haven, but this was mostly pretense. A Cessna-sized airstrip had been grassed on the edge of town; and the hotel had been built with tourists in mind, but there had been no rush to use either.

The island of Santa Carolina, later to be named "Paradise Island," was a few acres of palms and pines and grassy dunes about twenty minutes by dyspeptic launch from the harbor. Once a penal colony with a Devil's-Island reputation, it had been the final home on earth for the hundreds of criminals transported from Portugal. Francombe and I spent hours poking about the ruins from which much of the stone had been carried away for use in the village.

The ghost of the warden, said to have been driven mad by the wretched tedium of the settlement and to have thrown himself from the battlements, was believed to roam the island. The natives gave the place a wide berth after dark, and we had to make our own way out to the sheltered inlets by bumboat borrowed from the hotel. There we conducted mild revels around a campfire over red wine and cold, spiced lobster tails and great chunks of Portuguese cheese and bread.

When the "Paradise Island" resort that destroyed this simple tranquility did take over, it was only for a few years. In 1964, after decades of growing black discontent, the native population exploded into revolt under the leadership of FRELIMO (Front for the Liberation of Mozambique). During the ensuing ten years, all semblance of normal life gave way to a bloody conflict that was to leave 17,000 dead on both sides. The Portuguese administration was torn out by the roots; most of the survivors among the 300,000 whites left the country, and Mozambique declared for Black independence under FRELIMO leader Samora Machel, on June 25, 1975.

The new black regime could not manage the sophisticated infrastructure needed to carry the rudiments of modern economy, much less the holiday camps. During their three-hundred-year rule, the Portuguese had done little to prepare the native population for such a role, and the country quickly collapsed into near chaos.

Places like "Paradise Island" and the sprawling resort that at one time took over from the putrid elephant meat depot at Inhassoro, will no doubt return one day. There is one attraction that can never be duplicated: a passage on a two-masted Alves coaster.

CHAPTER XIV

Through the Back of Beyond

Some years before the Mozambique adventure, I had, perforce, to make a trip from the Gold Coast Colony to Lagos, port capital of Nigeria. My choice of transport was among air charter, which turned out to be too expensive; a leaking, filthy packet which was vulnerable, as noted before, to attack by pirates; or overland African "bus," dependable but notably short on comfort. The distance wasn't great, a few hundred miles, and eventually, given pirates or discomfort, I picked the last.

The Gold Coast as a place for a casual stopover in the winter of 1949 was what is best described as a modest choice. On the surface it did have a primal charm. Essentially, however, it was a colonial enterprise at its most businesslike and grubbiest. And for me no haphazard holiday.

I was there because the British colony had suffered the early onset of an independence movement which had upset several centuries of relative calm, broken only by the Ashanti tribal war and other minor differences with the natives. It was to become the first colonial possession in Africa to be granted independence, and, although that was still eight years away when I arrived, the threat to violently sever the ties with the mother country was building. In those days this constituted a phenomenon and was worth a look.

It was not a situation readily understood by a newcomer, and I would have to settle for a while and study the details. Settling meant, first of all, finding lodging, no serious problem.

There were only two hotels, a backstreet hovel better left nameless and the Seaview. This ramshackle relic was a two-story, U-shaped structure with rooms on both floors except on the seaside leg of the "U." Here the second story was an open veranda, roofed, and used as a residents' lounge and bar and boasting the meager view of the ocean that gave the place its name—meager since the view was largely blocked by the tin roofs of mercantile establishments, government buildings, and warehouses. Everything about the hotel was rusty and jerry-built, and the warm odors of the salt sea, decomposing fish, petroleum products, sweat, and floor polish were everywhere.

The proprietor was a giant Greek named "Connie" Constantos who'd hosted scores of American servicemen during World War Two when Accra was a stopoff airfield on the ferry run from Brazil to the Middle East. Connie's experience with "Yanks" obviously hadn't been too off-putting. He was friendly, and a mine of gratuitous tips and general information, much of it conveyed over a river of gin-and-bitters in the hot evening gloom of the veranda lounge. The nasal honk of car horns in the avenues below, the distant boom of the surf, and the sound of the whining, repetitive African music from the ground-floor cafe in the center of the "U" forced us to shout at one another. The atmosphere didn't make for learned exchanges, but then neither did the gin, and we accepted the limitations. It was just one compromise among many.

Illumination in the first-floor cafe was provided by strings of multicolored "fairy lights." In our upstairs lounge it came from meek electric globes vaguely present in the ceiling. Yet even this wan yellowish glow attracted bugs from miles around. There were, of course, mosquitos against whose bite I took daily doses of Aralen, an antimalarial that partially deafened me and occasioned the "hey?", "what?" and "how's that?" with which our conversations were punctuated. But among the scores of insects circling in clouds above the table, most interesting were the hardback beetles and praying mantis.

The hardbacks were the size of .110-gauge shotgun shells (a bit shorter), had a covering the consistency of amber, and flew blindly at the speed of sound. Hardbacks striking the green metal lampshades rang the tocsins from dusk until the lights went out. They struck walls with a crack like a smallbore rifle and mushed right through the lacelike metal screening. To be struck on the head by one of these insectoid projectiles was like suffering a blow from a rubber hammer.

The praying mantis was a different kind of menace entirely. In the Gold Coast an everyday common or garden mantis would easily stretch its spindly figure to eight inches. Its mandibles, claws and serrated inner elbows, used to hold its prey as it tore it apart with spiky fangs, were magnified, as if under a microscope. The things have little appeal, really. They eat their mates and hence operate largely as loners, attacking recklessly out of the shadows, rustling and crackling, to occasionally slap against one's head. When this happened, the gangly, saw-toothed arms and legs became tangled in one's hair and, so trapped, they flailed about, emitting a strange, mewing sound.

My first experience with these flying horrors froze me in fright. Connie reached over, extricated it, and casually tossed it into the night. After a while I, too, grew blasé. If one blundered into my then generous pompadour, I plucked it out without so much as a pause in the conversation.

Inevitably, we made friends with one of them, identified by a darkish patch on a green mandible, a mark that set him apart from the others. We called him Sidney, and he joined us frequently for his share of the pink gins, a drop of this titillating libation on the end of a wooden match stick.

What I know about the metabolism of a praying mantis is limited. The conversion of this alcohol into food and stimulant in its insect insides is a mysterious process, but the outward and visible signs were entirely recognizable.

He drank the drop and a few more, lay supine on the oilcloth table cover, his arms and legs in slow-motion gesticulation, then staggered to feet that resembled Turkish slippers, and, wisely refusing to try flight, floated about the surface of the table in a reasonable imitation of what I presumed was insect ecstasy. Occasionally he'd fall and struggle upright again with odd little scratching and tapping noises.

He came back for more night after night. What he did when we weren't there, only God knows. Engagements that took us elsewhere and left our special lounge table bare of pink gins certainly saved him from becoming the first known arthropod alcoholic.

Other distinctive characteristics of the mantis were attested to one evening during an up-country visit. One of them, about Sidney's size, rattled into a dining room Tilly lamp, fell, dazed but undamaged, to the table and was gingerly removed by my dinner companion, the black editor of the local paper. He set it free, explaining, tongue-in-cheek, that if the insect died it must be buried in a grave in the ground.

"Like you," he said, pointedly.

If this formality was overlooked, he went on, the soul of the insect would return in the form of clouds of angry praying mantis to haunt those present when it died. Madness, he assured me, would follow.

Not that this was necessarily bad, he added. An unsound mind was a release from life's miseries, he noted philosophically, and anyway there were so many "nuts," mostly white, in the Gold Coast that a few more, of any color, wouldn't make much difference.

He was right about the "nuts" in the Gold Coast. For years the country was known as the "White Man's Grave." Malaria and cirrhosis of the liver were endemic. Those not written off by these afflictions went "round the bend," his phrase, trying to cope with the conviction that one "must never face up to a problem that someone else might get around to solving tomorrow."

I had some experience with this when I hired a car.

With the "good old Dodge of the 1940s" repeatedly proclaimed as the only car for bush travel, the one vehicle I could get was a small English car, better unidentified. It was to take me on a trip into the interior. It did. For three hours. At that point the left front suspension snapped, and we careened off into a ditch.

"Nothing bad," the driver cheerfully promised me, mopping blood from a wound in his head. He would be in touch with the Accra agency to sort things out. The following day, help arrived in a small box from the coast with an explanation that "this kind of thing happens all the time" and that the enclosed special clamp, provided by the factory for "just this sort of accident" would get me back to Accra. It did, as it had scores of others in like trouble, and as it would until the death toll began to attract the manufacturer's attention and the design was changed.

My month's research finished and having refused boat travel to Lagos, I had chosen to leave Accra by what was called a "mammy wagon." Beginning a few months after this ride, I was to start a trip that would bounce me over thousands of miles of Africa's bone-cracking bush trails. For that, the "mammy wagon" excursion was splendid preparation.

Among the Ga, the tribe inhabiting the Gold Coast colony's seaboard, petty commerce was strictly the purview of the women. The males inclined toward the professions, teaching, the law, taxi-driving, gin-and-cards, and meditation. The women ran the fruit and vegetable marts and the ubiquitous gimcrack general stores. Nor were they mere employees. They personally qualified at the bank for business loans; they kept the books, did the buying, and managed the shops. The works. They were large, loud, tough as old boots, and unaccountably cheery. With "woman's liberation" decades away, they had long since established a preeminence in the moneymaking trades, including transportation.

The "Happy Days Are Coming Omnibus Company," the "God Is Good Transit, Ltd.," and the "Keep Smiling Coach Service," among others, vied vigorously with one another for cargo and passengers, and with larger company lines such as "The Inter-Colonial Transport Services—Accra, Lagos, Sudan, and Mecca." All were owned and operated (but not driven) by Accra's "mammies."

The "Inter-Colonial," my choice, as well as the trip to Lagos made the run to Mecca, 5,000 miles across desert and bush carrying Moslems to the Holy Shrine and back. This round-trip through hostile country and often murderously unfriendly tribal territories was a chancy business at best. Organizing fuel supplies, maintenance, and repairs was daunting, and roads through mountain country were a cruel joke. The loss of an entire busload of pilgrims if an aged vehicle lost a braking system and shot out into space was not infrequent. Nonetheless, it was considered worth the risk by thousands each year. Once safely returned from this harrowing junket to kiss the Q'Aaba stone and worship in the Grand Mosque, the zealot was perforce a "Hajji," or pilgrim, the title of honor that raised him cubits in neighborhood status.

Equipment run by the "Inter-Colonial," as by all other such undertakings, was improvised out of need and inspiration. My "bus," carrying twelve others and heaps of their personal effects, was a Ford pickup hauling a half-ton trailer. Planks provided the seating across the width of the truck bed under a wooden top with open sides. Most of the luggage was crushed into the trailer, but bundles of food and clothing for the trip, a score of chickens in crude wicker baskets or flapping free, and two small goats somehow made it into the back of the truck along with the human cargo. Assembling this variety of freight and human beings and readying for takeoff was roughly similar to the evacuation of Dunkirk, only noisier.

The bus collecting point was located on the edge of the dusty main marketplace, explosively alive even in the dimness of early dawn. Wind-up Victrolas and radios, shouted conversations, shrieks of laughter, and barnyard bleats, cackling and barking noises shattered the peace.

I paid an extra ten shillings for a seat next to the driver in the cab, knowing my boney backside would never survive the trip on the wooden planking, climbed aboard, and waited. An hour. At 6:30 A.M. an hour and a half behind schedule, we pulled away into the already suffocating heat.

Two days later I dumped my belongings at the Royal Hotel, a crusty waterfront dump on the edge of Lagos, and promptly went out to see if I could find something better. As I trudged wearily through the littered streets, I mused about the trip just completed and shuddered. Behind me was three hundred miles and thirty-six hours of corrugated, potholed roadway, a dreadful hostel wryly named the "Bon Plaisir," and two river crossings, the Volta and the Grande Popo.

The Grand Popo one was made on a barge pulled across by chanting navvies hauling on a rope. The driver, and other executive officers, had miscalculated the tides for the day, and as a consequence we stuck fast on a sandbar in midstream. This oversight suspended us for three hours in a dense cloud of ravenous, man-eating mosquitoes that covered me in a furry blanket. In no time the things were biting bites.

The pains of the trip did not, however, go unrelieved. There were times, through Dahomey, that we spent skimming gloriously over the hard sands of the beach, along avenues of palms and sweet-smelling blooms, and through showers of tree orchids in full blossom.

There were some pretty bad customs delays at Lomé in Dahomey and Contonou in Togo, both lushly tropical, with inhabitants drifting about, half-asleep. At each steamy post, the pickup and trailer were laboriously stripped of all personal effects, prodded by black officials newly-appointed and reveling in their authority.

Through all this arrogant mistreatment, the passengers had shown a cheerful patience and general good humor that shamed me and succeeded in checking my predilection for flying off, screaming, in all directions.

I never rode the "mammy wagons" again. Indeed, it was almost the last time I used public transport on the continent until the Umtali to Beira train five years later. I did ride the steamer *Kivu* on Lake Victoria and *Illala* on Lake Malawi, but for the most part I managed to get about pretty much on my own.

In Lagos I bought a Land Rover, the first British product in the "Jeep" category. It was a twelve-point-something brake horsepower, and, in high gear, could hardly pull your hat off if you raised your eyebrows. Yet, with all four wheels at work in low range, it could climb the side of a cliff. In it I rattled southward from West Africa to the Indian Ocean port of Durban in the then Union of South Africa, a distance of some 7,000 miles, side trips included, without serious mechanical trouble.

Travel about Africa in that era was demanding but safe from the violence that would tear things apart before another decade passed. The continent in 1949 and 1950 may have been at a slow boil, politically, with black and white coexisting uneasily in most colonies, but the revolutionary upheavals that would leave hundreds of thousands dead and the administration of entire territories in chaos were six or seven years away.

The native peoples accepted *power* as sufficient reason why the European ran things. If they found this stultifying or degrading, they accepted it. There were no effective alternatives available. Not then.

Thoughtful whites foresaw the end of the colonial systems as in the order of natural and inevitable change but fervently hoped, and often believed, the passage would be peaceful. That they would be proved terribly wrong few even imagined.

Law, enforcing order, kept the lid on through most of the fifties, and there was little threat to life and limb for white travelers then. I even met an Irishman deep in the Congo happily pushing his bike along the middle leg of a cycling tour from Cape Town to Dublin. He was perfectly at ease and, preferring his own company to mine, turned down my offer to share a meal and a night in camp.

Hungry animals were quite capable of chewing up the odd visitor or might attack to defend a family, but most of the wild beasts avoided man. A chance encounter could, of course, get sticky, as will be seen, but such events were rare.

My planning for the journey was scarcely faultless, but the trip from Lagos to the then Rhodesias, several thousand miles away, made only minimal demands on foresight, and what advance preparation I'd made seemed sufficient.

There were times, of course, when lack of attention to detail did prove embarrassing.

Most roads in Nigeria are unpaved, and the surface is laterite, granite in its latter stages of decomposition. The dust it produces is dense and reddish-brown and in the Land Rover (locally called the "Land Hoover") it was sucked into the back through to the driver's seat by the vacuum created behind the vehicle. Nothing escaped the gritty powder, and after a really sweaty trip a brown mudpack was glued to all uncovered hide, and hair was ruddy and stiff with it.

Arriving late at the inland town of Abeokuta, about sixty miles from Lagos, I was urged by an agitated district officer to hurry and make ready for a special dinner. The resident (senior official in the area) had heard from government public relations in Lagos that an American newsman was on the loose in his community. His invitation to me apparently had been suggested by Lagos, and he, in turn, had instructed his junior officer, the harrassed D.O., to produce me.

I'd had no time for a proper bath; only for a quick wash, rinsing off the visible areas. I'd run a wet comb through my hair, donned my "ice cream suit" seersucker creation that was less than suitable for formal wear, and was off.

Ivor and Anna Schofield, the resident and his madam, were charm itself. Crisply uniformed servants produced an excellent meal on starched white napery complete with shimmering silver candlesticks, and brandy and demitasse in the lounge.

Responding, I rose to unbelievable heights of wit and amiability, pulling out all stops to disarm them with scintillating chatter or leaning forward to listen with rapt attention to every word Mrs. Schofield uttered. I all but bowed and kissed her knuckles when I departed.

Back in my room at the D.O.'s, smugly satisfied with my evening's performance, I discovered when I removed my jacket that its collar was stained reddish, as was my shirt. Worse still, the mirrors in the bathroom, to which I rushed in mounting horror, threw back an image that showed little runnels of dirt etched down the back of my neck.

My hurried whip-through with a wet comb had obviously initiated a slow laterite flow, like cooling lava, and during the course of the evening as I gestured expansively and waxed eloquent it had progressively smudged its way downward. Suddenly chilled through, I recalled a moment at the meal.

The resident had asked me what I did in the open Land Rover, top off, when it rained.

"I get wet," I'd replied shortly, at which dubious bon mot he'd fairly split his sides laughing and then, he'd said, still wheezing: "You must be henna'd everywhere from head to toe!"

I'd been hard put to see this as exceptionally funny but had easily joined the raucous laughter. Only when I'd looked in the D.O.'s mirror had I seen his point.

Dust and embarrassment were not, of course, the sole indignities suffered in thousands of miles through pretty wild country. As I've indicated, few of the travelers meandering about in the early nineteen-fifties were chopped up by the locals or dropped dead of basic privation. Yet such a trip was no Sunday promenade, as stories I wrote for the *News* patently show:

> *Bangassou, French Equatorial Africa, May 1950 (by airmail).*
> Motoring down the backbone of the African continent requires a strong back, a flair for the unexpected, and a hard head.
>
> Let the ghosts of Stanley and Livingstone snort contemptuously at "modern" Africa with its roads and resthouses and cowed natives if they will. The contemporary human constitution that goes with it is jerked rigid by the experience.
>
> An overland trek is taking me from Lagos, seacoast capital of Nigeria, up into the northern provinces of that country, east along the southern fringe of the Sahara Desert to the Congo and south through the Rhodesias to the Union of South Africa, a total distance of 7,000 miles.
>
> The vehicle is a Jeep-type British car, a Land Rover, first of its kind to be made in England, with a low-range gear that is working overtime.
>
> On roads that would shake the tracks off a tank, the little car has jittered itself into what seems like a permanent palsy. In the back a 900-pound load of supplies and equipment thunders about like panicked cattle in a boxcar, and I am repeatedly showered with miscellany.

What one carries on a trip of this kind varies with personal tastes and the purpose of the journey. Standard basics include water, water-filtering equipment, gasoline and oils and greases, mosquito nets, and the usual camping-out paraphernalia. To these I have added a snakebite kit with syringes, needles, razor blade, potassium permanganate, bandages, and serum for cobra and adder poisons. I could die a thousand writhing deaths before unearthing it from the back, and, as for my matching the serum with the snake . . . ?

I also carry enough spare parts for the car to start my own business and a .12-gauge shotgun with ammunition numbers 4, 6 and SG shells, also buried somewhere near the bottom.

Through most of Nigeria and French and Belgian territories, night accommodation can be a resthouse or "casse de passage," or, in the Congo, "hotel de brouse." These are opensided huts of mud or breeze-block construction, sometimes thatch, usually under the indifferent care of an aged pensioner and bare of amenities other than a 45-gallon oildrum of bathwater, churning with swamp life.

It's best to carry one's own provender, although bananas, pineapples, pawpaws, tiny potatoes, and some pretty exotic greens can be bought along the way. Mistakes can, of course, be made.

I bought a plantain, thinking it was a banana, took a large bite of it raw, and coated my teeth and gums with a layer of what felt like thistles in wall plaster. An egg must be tested for freshness by dropping it in water. If it pops back out again it's mostly gas. I learned this the hard way.

This location, Bangassou, is about 2,500 miles from the starting point in Lagos. Most of the distance has been through deep sand and scrub, at the desert's edge with the thermometer in the 100s. Getting near to the equator, about 700 miles by road south of here, the temperature is crawling steadily upward. The air is heavy with moisture. Bamboo and palm groves arch darkly thirty and forty feet above the trails.

The people and their customs are changing as well.

The story had been cut off abruptly and been paired with another I'd written later.

Bondo, Belgian Congo, May 1950 (by airmail). After 3,000 miles and more than a month in West and Central Africa I've come to the conclusion the native just isn't living up to expectations.

He's a changed man, from his Birmingham (England) print wraparound to his American haberdashery.

Following tradition he should be scantily clad in monkey skins as he slips noiselessly through the jungle heaving spears at bellowing gorillas when he isn't carving up the tribe next door. At best he is supposed to leap about great bonfires chewing missionary leg-bones.

It is true he still hunts his food with spear, bow and arrow, and antique flintlock. There is also evidence that now and then his neighbors do contribute to his sacrificial worship of some gory fetish with a thighbone here, a leg there. And, if he's a pagan, more than likely he'll wear a short skirt of leather thongs or simply ochre and bangles. And he dances when the spirit moves him—literally.

In the northern territories of Nigeria where the Moslem emirs rule an ancient feudal society, what tribal mores remain are being undermined by British insistence on a representative council system.

Where once he collected villages, wives, and sometimes heads, now the emir takes pride in his American automobile. At a recent council meeting in Kaduna, of nineteen shiny cars, seventeen were chrome-plated Detroit products, the gold-and-ivory scepter of the emirate bolted to the left front fender.

Under his flowing Arab robes, the emir jerks up his Bond Street trousers when he sits down at ceremonies to watch his mounted tribesmen charge by in coats of mail captured from Crusaders in the Near East centuries ago.

The African is no effete salon product of tender nurture, but he's changed.

To the east, in French Equatorial Africa, the pagan hunter may still wear little but the warm tropical air (plus a basketweave cover over his vital zone and shaped a startling likeness of the items it protects). But passing him in the bush is his cousin in white duck trousers, cotton shirt, and pith helmet.

A secret women's society may cavort to the rattle of drums and clappers and showers of goats' blood, while in the audience there is, in one instance I know of at least, a man in white shorts, yellow sport shirt, and "tackies" (tennis shoes).

In Bangassou, a small town along the Oubangui River, I had my French corrected by a young African who was at home in that language, English, and, of course, his own.

Being articulate in a foreign tongue and wearing khaki shorts and sneakers doesn't, ipso facto, reflect expertise in the infrastructures of modern societies. The African has a way to go. But in small things he's changing.

An incident on the ferry crossing the Oubangui River into the Congo is an example.

The Jeep trundled up two parallel planks and dropped onto a

platform laid across six, thirty-five-foot-long dugout canoes. We eased out into the softly gurgling stream, the craft precariously balanced, even in the sluggish current. In one of the canoes, a native drummer sat pounding out a monotonous rhythm on a funnel-shaped log, booming an even beat for the men wielding the poles and long, spearlike paddles. As he drummed, he wailed a weird, tuneless singsong.

I lowered myself into the drummer's canoe to get a closer look at the instrument and the label on his cotton shirt caught my eye.

On it, it said: "Packard Shirt Company, Fort Wayne, Indiana."

Actually, the unexpected became the common denominator of experience over those 7,000 miles. Very little lived up to popular conceptions. The strange, dark land was characterized by contradiction as this story for the *News,* reveals:

Elizabethville, the Congo, April 1950 (by airmail). The usual picture of the Congo as a giant forest of spiny undergrowth dripping in a perpetual hot fog of swamp and bog inhabited by maneaters, human and animal, belongs with sketches of Columbus's ships falling off the edge of the earth.

"Impenetrable jungle" there is, and rotten roads and poverty-stricken, witchcraft-ridden natives struggling to stay alive much as they have for centuries. In large areas the wet heat is killing.

Yet there are also high plateaus where thousands of acres of corn and wheat and cotton sweep away to the distant horizon. Rubber, palm, and banana plantations dot rolling open country. There are brightly painted, tidy European and African villages of brick and stucco, and the chrome and copper mines of Géomines have built modern towns and suburban communities near the smoking smelters.

Great mountain ranges dominate the northeastern provinces. Almost sliding off the steep slopes are horticultural nurseries and hundreds of square miles of truck farms growing tons of vegetables annually.

All of this was ripped out in the bloody violence that overtook the Congo in the sixties. To my eternal discredit, none of the stories I wrote long before that time even hinted at the tragedy to come. While I often was made uneasy by the arrogance of some colonials and the sulking response of the natives, I never plumbed deep enough into those responses to detect the hatred. A rueful comment appears on the margin of my 1949

Congo notes, a cryptic notation dated January 1966: "I missed the genesis of all this! How?"

After the rigors of the Congo bush, relieved only by the wonders of the Grand Hotel Leopold II in Elizabethville near the Northern Rhodesian border, the trip on through the Rhodesias and into South Africa was a breeze. Once I was back in British territories language ceased to be a serious problem—and the pidgin French spoken by Congolese natives had certainly raised a few serious problems. Difficult British bureaucrats could be unhelpful but at least they used the mother tongue. Something resembling hotel lodging was available at regular intervals, as were post offices and cable facilities. In short, the wherewithal a reporter needs to get things done were once more predictably accessible. Even getting from "A" to "B" was consistently easier.

Most of the main road became nine-foot tarmac mat or, in Southern Rhodesia, consisted of twin macadam strips each eighteen inches wide and laid out roughly parallel to provide hard-surface tracks. They were the results of make-work during the Great Depression of twenty-nine when impoverished whites joined African laborers at pick and shovel work. They provided all-weather communication, opening up large areas of the country that would otherwise have been isolated by rainy-season bog. So important were they to southern Rhodesia's survival in the early days that, when highways were fully surfaced, some stretches of the old strip roads were preserved and enclosed as national monuments.

Beyond the "great, green, greasy Limpopo River," the border between Southern Rhodesia and the Union of South Africa, all facilities improved steadily until, in Johannesburg and onward to Durban, they became positively civilized. This unfamiliar condition produced in me, at one and the same time, a sensation of great relief and a wistful hankering for the self-dependence I'd known in the vast aloneness of middle Africa.

CHAPTER XV

From "How-to" to "What"

The techniques of foreign-news reporting during the decades immediately following World War Two employed tools of a time my children would scornfully refer to as the "olden days."

We didn't exactly depend on travel by windjammer nor tap out our stories in Morse code after accompanying grenadiers into battle behind flying guidons and pipe and drum. But, 'tis true, we didn't cross the North Atlantic in three and a half hours nor did we know instant transmission by satellite. And we were still "the press," not "the media." Yet the "reporting job" remained essentially the same.

Frank Scherschel told me of a crusty old news photographer, a genius with a Speed Graphic, who, when asked his secret for getting good exclusive pictures, had a curt reply: "Your camera set at a hundred at eleven and be there." For the reporter, the last half of that dictum has always been the same.

Up to now, this, my personal case history, has largely concerned itself with how to "be there," the mechanics of getting to the scene of a story, establishing bona fides and keeping body and soul together while going after it. But that's just a part of the play. Before I turn to the rest, the real substance of this narative, however, permit me a digression. My reason for it will be clear.

One of the radio series I have done was a thirteen-week program titled "Genesis in General, the Beginnings of Almost Anything." It was aired by the Rhodesia Broadcasting Corporation and included an angry comment under the heading of "Journalism," and it went like this:

> Journalists, of my vintage anyway, have grown a bit weary of unthinking, public condemnation of "the press," of the charges aimed at the institution itself, identified as consisting of the "monopolies," the "yellow rags," or the "right-" or "left-" wing

"propaganda sheets" and all published by greedy men, numb to the tragic state of the human condition.

Sadly, such papers, and publishers, do exist, but they are in the minority. For well over a century, great papers the world over have protected and educated a public that needed both.

Mindless attacks on "the press" pillory the newsmen who work for it. That includes me. More important, it includes my colleagues. I've had some who weren't worth the effort to pillory them. But I've known far more whose only reward for intellectual brilliance, courage and dedication has been death from machine-gun fire or simple exhaustion. Goodness knows, not money. Newsmen are the worst-paid professionals in the world. Nor is it "power" or "prestige." Journalism counts more unsung heroes than any other calling.

One of these I knew well. His name was Morley Cassidy, and he was a newspaperman for five decades. Half of that time he worked a local "beat" in America. When his only son was killed in World War Two, he arranged to be sent overseas as a correspondent. Not just as a kind of "replacement" for the boy, but because he felt, deeply, that the story needed better telling. He turned out front-line coverage from every major American battlefront on the European continent.

When I met him, he was being shot at again, in Palestine and then in Greece. Later I worked a more peaceful assignment with him when he was editorial-page editor for the *Philadelphia Bulletin.* For most older newsmen this job is a pain or it's cushy, an earned rest period. For Morley Cassidy, it was an assignment to produce responsible and enlightening commentary.

He was a wispy little man, faintly cadaverous, soft-spoken but tough and hard on himself . . . a keen observer of the human condition.

Morley Cassidy's dead now. He died a few months ago. Sixty-seven. Not a bad age. He'd been missed by the machine-gun fire and the other things the world threw at him, and died, I think, of simple exhaustion.

Morley was my colleague as he was the professional associate of all newsmen who try.

He didn't have to die to make me more aware of witless criticism of "the press" and be angry. But thinking about Morley's example would make any journalist, of my vintage anyway, a bit weary of what has become a surfeit of half-witted carping.

We shall meet Morley Cassidy, briefly, in the pages that follow, but I haven't digressed just to introduce him. I digressed because of what my rather rough eulogy had to say about newsmen in general. And I like to think it's in the Morley Cassidy tradition that the stories that are to come were sought out and recorded.

•

CHAPTER XVI

Deadly Mountain Warfare

Out of my first foray into foreign reporting several experiences loom in my recollection. After a few decades more they will, I suspect, still be looming. One is the sadness in war-ravaged Greece.

The mood of the Greeks in the summer of forty-eight was taut and bitter. And they were weary.

> While enthusiasm about the ten-day-old offensive [I wrote for the *Indianapolis News* below an Athens dateline] seems to have brightened spirits here, it doesn't show much. The Greeks are very tired.
>
> Even in the bustle of Athens, where American and British missions hold forth almost as an interim government, the affluence of the capital is somehow tainted and the exhilaration is phony.
>
> The city is bulging with too many people. If one more refugee takes up residence here, I suspect the end of the peninsula will break away and drift across the Mediterranean.
>
> From a pre–World War Two population of approximately 500,000, the city has grown to a mob of close to two million. Down from the troubled areas in the north at the beginning of the war, small streams of evacuees trickled toward the southern coast. This freshet became a swollen torrent. Today this is a city of displaced persons.
>
> Inflation is numbing. A hotel bill of 223,000 drachmas for three days is common enough. It's only fourteen dollars eighty-three cents American, but for the Greeks it is 223,000 drachmas. Clothing and food are costly and scarce at any price. The efforts of the Greek government to raise up a country battered to its knees by the German wartime occupation are admirable. But inadequate and pained.
>
> Testifying to this underlying hurt was the recent shipment of

orphaned children from the northern towns to the Dodecanese islands in the Aegean, a move made ostensibly for "security" and humanitarian reasons. Families had been split up in guerrilla raids; children died in the fighting.

I had been in Rhodes when one contingent arrived. Out of the gaping mouth of an American L.S.T., the miserable little band had stumbled, dutifully singing a whining rendition of a song about the wonders of Greece.

In the lead a sad-eyed little girl dressed in ragged brown, an orange kerchief almost hiding her tear-stained face, carried a placard. Translated, it read: "We are happy to be in our new home. We will learn to know our new neighbors and to live happily with them." Not exactly spontaneous.

The Greeks who greeted them sensed the tragedy. One of the conducting officers, tight-lipped, shook his head angrily:

"This is necessary but it is terrible. Look at that little thing, perhaps four years old. She is frightened half to death. Always she keeps crying to go home."

Stuffing a piece of dry roll into her mouth with grubby fingers, she looked up at me as she shuffled by. The glance was a fleeting one. Her face was pale, her eyes swollen and red from crying, desperate, searching, the face of the twentieth century.

Later on, settled comfortably in the posh lounge of the Grande Bretagne, Morley Cassidy, his wife, Phyllis, and I playfully flicked peanuts into the air and snapped at them as they fell, drank a lot of excellent scotch, and made a wager.

We were both headed for the battle zone 200 miles to the north, I the following day, Morley two days later. In an uncharacteristic fit of bravado, he bet me fifty dollars that, giving me a two-day start, he'd still beat me to the forward positions, somewhere around a place called Koziani.

I rashly agreed on the spot and, on the spot, was appalled at my folly.

If I'd been a crow, the distance I'd have calculated to Koziani would approach 200 miles. Over Greece's tangle of mountain roads, the mileage would double. Air travel, where available, would consume perhaps one hundred miles to one of the few safe landing strips from which Anglo-American Aid Mission supplies were dispensed overland.

I suspected that Morley, shrewd and vastly experienced knocking about in impossible situations and known and respected by upper ranks in the government and military, had already laid out his line of march. All I had going for me were documents, Greek and Anglo-American,

140

stating simply that I was an American newsman.

In Europe, journalists, I learned, have aspired to qualify for Richelieu's fourth estate, and many have made it. This implies no mean status. From medieval times, the other three have been the clergy, the aristocracy and the parliament or Commons, the bourgeoisie. Indeed, peopling the ranks of the fourth estate at one time were scholars and others of esteemed rank and exalted position. Today these lofty qualifications are not always possessed by the claimants. Certainly, I have met a plethora of journalists archly identified in high places as "Doctor" and even "Doctor Professor" who actually had toyed with the wonders of Academe with even less success than I'd enjoyed.

In America, generally speaking, reporting is historically a rough-and-tumble craft, its ranks replete with brilliant social historians and critics, good recorders and, no less, by unscrupulous hacks. All categories are acknowledged as wielding influence and are not to be ignored. Overseas, as I've noted earlier, newsmen without a "name," either their own or their newspaper's, may have to push a bit harder. Still, if one did "push" a bit, it was acceptable. Then, in the forties, before "investigative" muckracking made them congenital antagonists, relations between newsmen and the political and military establishments were fairly congenial.

In any event, without benefit of but the faintest status, much less a "Doctor Professorship," and counting entirely on dumb luck, I blundered into the American air force base on the edge of Athens about noon the day following the bet. My only "credentials" were some dubious documents (some in Greek) in my pocket, my portable Hermes in one hand, and a ragged musette bag in the other. Apparently my pathetic demeanor did for me what prestige did for my competition, and with entirely friendly dispatch I was whipped through formalities and waved to a waiting plane.

A fleet of old C-47s (Dakotas) made milk runs daily to the north, and, after I'd signed a paper relieving the air force of responsibility for my death or maiming while in their care, I squeezed aboard one crammed with supplies.

The C-47 has been the mule of the air the world over, dependable and tough, apparently unafflicted by such original ailments as "metal fatigue." Some were still pounding off bush runways into the air in the nineteen-eighties, millions of air miles and a few new engines behind them. It was comforting to fly in them, if rarely comfortable. On flights over rugged country, they bobbed and swooped about alarmingly, buffeted by the winds, and they were noisy and cold and cramped for space. But they arrived.

I sat on my musette bag surrounded by wooden boxes and cardboard containers bearing bewildering military labels. Roughly translated they indicated the cargo consisted of hand grenades, assorted mortar bombs, .303 and .50 caliber ammunition, packets of gelignite, blankets, long underwear, and condensed milk. I had been prepared for the soft goods, but the presence of explosives was disconcerting. These planes are easy to hit with rifle and machine-gun fire from the ground. The slugs normally rattled on through and out the aluminum skin on the off side, but they'd been known to come up against solids en route, like TNT. This could get me to my destination well before Morley but not in working condition.

My anxieties were short-lived. Nothing hit even the canned milk in the forty-minute flight, and we landed on the top of the world at a place with no name.

"We're not supposed to say where we are. And I couldn't pronounce it anyway," the sergeant pilot from Brooklyn laughed as he handed me out through the hatch and tossed my musette bag after me.

"You're on your own from here, Mac. Koziani is about thirty miles. Fokin' awful road. Somethin's always goin' that way, though."

I thanked him and, dodging army weapons carriers that roared in to unload the craft, I found the message center operated by combined RAF/USAAF units.

Out of the July sauna of Athens it was crisply cool even at midday, and a light breeze swept the place clear of the dust thrown up by the military traffic. The airfield was centered in a dry, stubbled tract mostly treeless and edged with rough stone walls. In all directions, jagged granite peaks marched in disorder to the horizon.

A cockney mess sergeant wearing a filthy apron, his sleeves rolled up, was sole officer in charge. How could I get to Koziani?

"Easy, mate," and he waved my credentials away, shouted out the window of the hut, and, somehow, produced a Jeep with an American second lieutenant at the wheel.

" 'E'll take yuh to Koziani, Guvnuh," said the sergeant, opening the door of the shack. "Goes there every dye 'bout now, 'e does. Greek H.Q." And he walked me out, carrying my typewriter and bag, handed them into the back, and waved us off. The young officer merely nodded my way, slammed into first, and shot off down a dirt track.

Even with this mute wildman at the wheel, it took us two hours to do the thirty-five miles. Although washouts, herds of assorted domestic animals, and crawling convoys were all treated by the lieutenant as a personal affront and a challenge to his driving skill and fearlessness, they nonetheless forced us into the lower gears from time to time, and we only arrived as it was getting dark.

Koziani I recall as a huddle of stone buildings, more or less white, around a village square and marketplace converted by rain and military traffic to a swamp. The main roads into and exiting the town and the winding side lanes were ankle deep in mud, constantly churned up by heavy equipment, herds of goats, and what appeared at times to be the entire population of Greece, milling aimlessly about, aged and bent and clothed in tatters.

The lieutenant broke his vow of silence long enough to introduce me to the Greek billeting officer headquartered in a sequestered inn of great age. I got a bed in a dark corner of a candlelit barn, redolent of the ammonia reek of farmyard and, judging from the luggage heaped about, already booked to the rafters by other losers. Later I ate an army meal from a borrowed mess kit, lining up with others in a chow line stretching the length of the town hall veranda.

A bottle of retsina shared with a captain from Griffin, Georgia, in an almost empty cafe lit by a single kerosene lamp rounded off the riotous evening in Koziani. The windows and cracks around the doors of the cafe had been blacked-out with strips of canvas; otherwise, the captain told us, snipers practiced their night marksmanship on the place.

With this in mind we slipped out quietly and stepped out briskly for the barn. As we squelched through the muck, the roar of the trucks and racket of shouting herdsmen and bleating goats had stilled. It was a dense black night under a heavy overcast, and that's the way I remember Koziani: mud and blackness and dirty white and the stink of the slop in the dead village square and in the lane outside my bedroom door.

I spent the next day out in the district with the military and wandered about the town in the late afternoon and then wrote this story for the *News*:

> *Koziani, Greece, July (by airmail).* From the "Hill of Fools" to the "Mountain of Sand," the Greek soldier is fighting a gruelling battle against a too numerous communist enemy in "free Greece."
>
> The battle he fights is not a thing of hit-and-run raids, or guerrilla ambush and counterattack. It's inch-by-inch conventional warfare.
>
> Approximately 75,000 men in six divisions, mountain and regular, are deployed against a "bandit" force of only 8,000. What evens the odds is a nightmare terrain, every foot of it known to the terrorists.
>
> American army observers state the Greek fighting man is superb. It is said his endurance, courage, and initiative, without peer, make up for lack of adequate training. Supporting him he has

American, British, and Canadian personnel and materiel. It's a formidable mixture, and it will win the day.

Yet behind this front the nation barely survives in the debris left by the German occupation and, now, the ruin spread by this new conflict. Athens, city of the displaced, rotten with avarice and incompetence and the dead hand of a past still clung to, is nonetheless flourishing compared to the rural uplands. In the hill villages the country is in a coma.

This town is headquarters for a Greek division committed in the latest offensive of many. Normal population is 15,000. Today it exceeds 35,000, not including the army and a host of camp followers. Most are refugees from Communist-held territory. Here they work for subsistence in the nearby fields, the leather and tinware shops, the basketry and ceramic works.

The fighting front is thirty miles away. Between that ragged line and this village, there is a bloody, running contest with terrorist harassing units. The day I arrived, a convoy moving forward from here lost half a ten truck section from teller mines missed when the road was "swept" the night before. The "shoe mines" are everywhere. This is three pounds of TNT and loose gravel or bits of metal scrap set in a wooden box not picked up by a mine detector. They are buried in roads and paths each night. A few pounds' pressure sets one off, and it jumps to waist height and blows a man, or a woman, in half. Everyone walks with dread until the mines are found. One way or another.

I followed a convoy of American two-and-a-half-tonners moving Greek troops to a place in the mountain passes where they debussed and trudged ahead on foot. They swung through a tiny village singing what sounded like "The Battle Hymn of the Republic." To the villagers, the men were invisible. No one shouted encouragement. There was not even interest from the children, who, not looking up, went on with their games. When the soldiers had gone, it was silent again, the quiet broken only by the laughter of the youngsters and the screech of a two-wheeled cart loaded with a few belongings salvaged from a burnt-out hut not far from the village.

I still had thirty miles to go from Koziani to the front, and Morley's fifty dollars. Troop convoys I might have joined were easy marks for bazooka fire from ambush and, of course, the mines. Any one of these could slow me up. Permanently. As a prudent alternative I chose a try at a small-plane hop from a local airstrip, asking the first men I saw if anything was going forward.

"Right away, laddie," an R.A.F. pilot answered, pointing to a small low-winged Proctor standing on the runway. "Just gie 'im a shou' and see."

The flyer was already climbing aboard, and I broke into a dead run, breathlessly reaching him just as he dropped back off the wing.

"Why, of course. You're very welcome, lad," and he threw open the engine cowling. "Toss your stuff in," and he ducked into the plane's mechanical innards. And reappeared almost instantly.

"You don't by any chance have a screwdriver, do you?" and he cocked his head a bit as he raised his eyebrows, a perfect admission that, yes, he agreed, it was a pretty stupid question. He was curly-blonde, weatherbeaten, about thirty.

I did, a Swiss army knife I'd carried for years. Bottle opener, corkscrew, and the like, including two sizes of screwdriver.

"Jolly good!" he snatched it and ducked back into the works. All I heard of his muffled commentary were snatches that, summed up, seemed to imply that "this ruddy thing is forever stalling in midair."

"Well, that ought to do it." He slammed the cowling into place. "Keep your fingers crossed"; and he tossed me the knife, waved to the bystanders, pushed me into the only other seat, aft of his, and climbed aboard himself. It was like being squeezed into a slender perspex-canopied torpedo.

Once airborne, the engine making a numbing if gratifying amount of noise, I relaxed. How, I'll never know. It was the most terrifying fifteen minutes I have on record. I suppose I must have accepted I was totally helpless and simply turned myself over to God and the driver up front.

Almost as soon as we were aloft, the plane seemed wildly out of control, rising and falling thousands of feet in seconds, sashaying and ducking invisible forces. I toyed with the notion that it wasn't us after all; it was the ground that was misbehaving. Ragged, sunburst peaks thrust suddenly up at the plane's tender underbelly, passing a few feet beneath my seat and as quickly fell away to reveal a tiny sliver of river far below in the shadows of a deep valley. Entire tilled fields appeared from nowhere to whisk by just missing the undercarriage. Then nothing but rolling clouds. As we proceeded on an apparently even keel the entire world writhed in spasms below us.

That there were flat spots atop these heights, even if they did slide by with breathtaking speed, was of some comfort. The engine sputtered a lot and "stalled" once, an annoying development the pilot countered by diving headlong into the nearest gorge. Just about the time my stomach had arrived at larynx level, the propeller, driven by the wind, cranked us up again, and we zoomed over the lip of a cliff, collecting a few of the native eidelweiss on the axle.

Our arrival near the village of Nestorion was bumpy but uneventful. I think. I was so benumbed I hardly noticed. The pilot was charm itself as he helped me out and bade me a cheery farewell. I did have enough presence of mind to thank him for bringing me, in those few minutes, over what could have taken me three days through the passes of the massif below us.

I joined a Brigadier General Thomas Pentzopoulos and his Greek staff in a forward post; greeted Morley when he arrived, modestly absorbing his effusive praise for my ingenuity; collected my fifty; watched the war for a few days; and then started back for Athens, taking a Jeep all the way back to the combined operations airbase south of Koziani.

The C-47 from there to Athens flew a combined hospital and refugee evacuation flight. The blood-soaked lumps of men, prostrate beneath clusters of intravenous feed bottles swaying from the ceiling, were packed into the forward part of the compartment over the wing. All the furniture had been removed but the metal jump seats fixed along the bulkheads. With the injured concentrated where the ride was smoothest, the rest of us, huddled together on the afterdeck, were soon a sorry sight.

Among the refugees, children and the very old, mostly women, not one had seen a plane on the ground, much less actually flown. All were ill-fed and sick for one reason or another. Fright and debility marked them, the old faces pale and vacant, their bodies so obviously fragile beneath the dark, threadbare clothing. The children seemed numbed into silence, wide-eyed and wary.

Stricken with sympathy, I'd settled on the floor in the center of this throng and, hoping my behavior could be seen in the dim light, put on a show of being perfectly at ease, smiling broadly and chattering cheerful sounds at the little ones and otherwise behaving like a total nitwit. If anyone understood what I was trying to do, he had little time to acknowledge it.

We'd hardly rocked off the ground, the compartment flooring vibrating and rattling ominously, when we plunged into rough weather. Within seconds airsickness hit like hysteria. Excepting me, not a passenger escaped. I busied myself distributing sick bags and reassuring any who could care and managed to keep down my own breakfast. I recall putting my arms around an old woman, a black baboushka on her head and an ankle-length black woolen gown hanging like a shroud from her shoulders. She was convulsed by the sickness. I sensed she had been a large woman and strong. At the time I took her in my arms she was so wasted I embraced a thing almost without substance, a wickerlike frame beneath the robe.

It was a short flight but long enough to accumulate a palpable aroma, even in the freezing confines of the plane. The young airman who opened the hatch in Athens turned visibly green, and the cabin had to be hosed down and disinfected. Back at the Mercury Hotel, I paid a ransom to have my clothes laundered and dry-cleaned and fell into a long soak in a hot bath. It dispelled the acrid stench but not the memories of it. Yet, for me there was always escape. I observed, reported, and then went away, leaving behind Kozianis and Nestorions and Ramat Rahels and the sick and the fearful everywhere.

CHAPTER XVII

Boneyards, Battlefields and Crypts

The Gramos Mountain story was the last organized warfare I would cover. Perhaps that's why it has retained a special chilling stridency of its own in the echoes of my mind. And always will.

Nearly as intrusive a recollection but for quite different reasons has been a trip taken back into the past during a stay in a ghost town on the North African coast thirty-five miles west of Algiers.

I'd first heard of an archeological dig at the newly discovered ruin of Tipasa from an acquaintance in the Department of Fine Arts and Monuments in Algiers and with his help had located the place in the Cherchel area, in ancient times a garrison community for the Roman legion "security forces." After some weeks of pleading for official permission to visit the place, I was assigned a guide by the Fine Arts Department and given carte blanche to wander the place at leisure, including those areas "off limits" to the general public.

En route to the site and my rendezvous with the man from Fine Arts, I'd decided to digress and visit some of the Hotel Plan people at a beachside villa in Staoueli, not far from Cherchel. The stopover had little to do with the ghostly past I was preparing to plumb, but as a diversion it produced its own special excitement.

Late that night a burglar slipped into the villa from the beach and might have made off with an impressive haul if fate hadn't dealt him a run of bad luck. My bellow of alarm as I spied him creeping into my room behind a pale-yellow flashlight beam had completely shattered his professional aplomb.

He'd shrieked with fright and became entangled in a window curtain as he scrambled for the doorway, scattering African curios and a clutter of my personal effects along his line of retreat.

I could argue that this rubbish slowed my pursuit but this would suggest that there was one. In fact, I was proceeding with extreme caution.

Visions of a dirk in my diaphragm or a scimitar peeling my adam's apple left me vaguely irresolute. Only when I heard the slap of his bare feet down the corridor did I even risk peering around the doorjamb.

I was just in time to see his shape disappear into what he obviously thought was an exit but which was, in fact, a larder. (No inside job, this.) There followed a racket compounded of screams of pain, astonishment, and rattling buckets and a deafening sound similar to that produced by a large crystal chandelier falling from a great height.

He emerged on the run and took off down the hall still wearing my curtain and decorated with the contents of a bag of flour.

The household, by now fully aroused and armed to the teeth, swept the area like a SWAT team to find only traces of the intruder's retreat. Some bedsheets and a bag of semolina, found outside, were all that was taken.

The next morning the village gendarme automatically arrested the entirely innocent houseboy, Sherif, a meek little man from Ouargli some 300 miles south in the desert and only recently come to the bright lights to make his fortune. That he was patently without guilt was considered irrelevant, however, since "they're all alike: thieves and cutthroats," the policeman said, and the poor man was dragged off to jail to be beaten and imprisoned as proxy for his fellow-countryman. This struck me as a bit unreasonable, and I said so. The gendarme dismissed my protest with a shrug, observing that Sherif'd probably stolen something at one time or another anyway and not to worry. I recall wondering during the ensuing few days in the ruined city of Tipasa if its long dead Roman inhabitants had treated the natives then with the same cavalier injustice. If so, they'd got what they deserved.

At Cherchel I'd met the department guide, a mincing, professorial little man, bald with gold-rimmed spectacles and a soft mellifluous voice, obviously no ordinary dragoman. Sadly, my notes show no name. I'll call him Sagesse.

Over coffee, brandy, and croissants before we left for Tipasa, Sagesse detailed the history of the place as far as reconstruction had revealed it. His English was fluent.

The presence of the ruins had first been suspected in 1934, he said, when a local antique dealer had taken a small stone carving of a human form to the gendarmerie. The man had bought it from a laborer who'd said he knew where he could find more such relics and asked the dealer to make it worth his while. When the laborer returned, he was collared by the cops and hastily agreed to lead them to acreage on the seaward side of the present-day town of Tipasa. There, ten feet below the surface, diggers had uncovered a magnificent marble sarcophagus.

Working landward from this spot and around the periphery of the existing town, the Beaux Arts people had ultimately delineated an area about a mile square. Barely two years of preliminary excavations had revealed evidences of a large cultural and political center when World War Two suspended operations. The results of subsequent digs, he concluded, his eyes lighting up, had been more rewarding then he could describe.

On our drive there he elaborated. Apparently the first settlement had been headquarters for a Roman hydrographic field section commissioned to study the inland desert country with a view to reclaiming wasteland for wheat culture. From a population of several thousand Romans, their servants and slave labor, this town had grown quickly to a city of 40,000 and in time to 80,000, a metropolis and a "Rome" away from Rome.

When Sagesse and I'd arrived at Tipasa, in 1949 a town of about 7,000, two thousand of them Europeans, we parked near the municipal gardens edging the community on the northwest and began our visit into the past.

The first buildings we encountered were villas built by the rich. Constructed around spacious inner courtyards, they had been single-story structures of stone with marble facing. Only the lower walls remained standing but still were clearly ornamented in paint and bas-relief with vigorous hunting scenes. They had all been resurrected, Sagesse said, from beneath ten feet and more of overload. In some of the larger dwellings, gold bracelets, pendants and rings, and gilded ceramic plates had been scattered about amid a moraine of trinkets in marble, bronze, glass, semiprecious stones, and even ivory.

Keeping the homes and some of the public buildings warm in the winter had been accomplished with hot-water piping. Each home had its own "boiler," the hot water fed into a lacework of tubing under the floor. Similar Roman heating systems, he said, have been found in the United Kingdom and on the Continent.

The Old City center, now slowly emerging from beneath tons of rocky soil, had been the focal point for the community's cultural, business and political life. Hub of this had been the main marketplace surfaced with some 8,000 square feet of paving stones, worn and grooved but so level and precisely joined that they seemed almost newly laid. Edging the square were the remains of great buildings; on one side, Sagesse told me, the Palais de Justice; on the other the theater, identified by its now roofless cellars, orchestra pit, and backstage areas.

This building, in its heyday covering two acres, was, Sagesse pointed out, a most remarkable "mécanisme." Not only had it seated the audience in banks of raked rows, but about 3,000 flues had been used to float

151

perfume out over the spectators. Theater records were nonexistent, but research and evidence elsewhere suggested that the scent had matched the mood of the production, light and fleeting for comedy, dense and clinging for the gloomy bits. The backstage pit, some fifteen feet deep, had been covered, and the pillars now visible to us as free-standing piers had at one time protruded through the stage flooring and were topped by busts of the gods. The "curtain" was a "fly" that did not rise or part in its middle but dropped into a recess.

From the town center we'd walked up to a promontory overlooking the sea, where the cemetery had been positioned, as if to give the dead a view forever toward the Italy they'd left behind.

It had been a massive undertaking, this necropolis. Almost a companion community. Several acres in extent, it comprised three levels of catacombs as well as the mausoleums and other monuments on the ground level. In one corner was a huge, unroofed, and unmarked grave Sagesse said had held the bones of perhaps 15,000 of all ages, tossed into the sepulchral barrow, victims of a plague that had ravaged the city. Somehow Tipasa survived that scourge, and the catacombs had grown deeper and more extensive, cut into the rock in tiers of crypts holding 4,000 stone and marble coffins.

In a shallow excavation, we had come upon a stone coffin that caught my interest, and, as a final request, I had asked Sagesse if we might see inside. While the laborers sweated to remove the heavy lid, I'd climbed out of the hole and surveyed the scene around us.

It was early evening and on the distant southwest horizon the bulk of Mount Chenois was haloed by the setting sun.

Away from us to the north lay the incredibly deep blue of the Mediterranean. The air was still and soft and mildly cooling. It was one of the rare moments when a journalist consciously suspends the search for fact and enjoys a neutral interlude, a time for assembling the parts and judging the whole. These periods are hard to come by.

In the coffin we found the remains of five young children thought to be victims of the plague. The bones were chalky and frangible, the tiny finger bones like bits of chaff, the skeletons resting side by side. There were a few stone and metal trinkets and no doubt there'd been wooden playthings and dolls of cloth long since fallen away to dust. I lay the palm of my hand on a small skull and was startled to find it felt strangely warm.

After this we picked our way back through the litter of the dig to where we'd left the car. Across the gray ruins in the near distance the modern village was a huddle of white stucco and red tile and splashes of floral color, fragile and impermanent and doomed, too, to one day fall in upon itself.

That's a corny observation, perhaps, but no less arresting for being unoriginal. Indeed, much of the same sort of experience had been mine once before when the past had reached out to me with a similar message, during World War Two in eastern France.

It was just such a mild evening four years before the visit to Tipasa. My detachment had halted for the night as the U.S. Third Army slowed in its dash for the railhead town of Nancy and for Strasbourg and the border of the Third Reich. We were just north of Verdun where the French army in the 1914–18 war had made their gallant and suicidal stand against another German army. The sound and glow of battle was far to the east of us, but in our forward rush we'd bypassed pockets of enemy troops. Suspecting they'd try fighting their way out through our position, we dug in.

In spite of the somewhat tense atmosphere, we idled in the warmth, and it was during a moment of this contemplative scratching that I unearthed the thing, a bayonet, a mere fragment of a blade and the rotted wooden grip. As I dug, more appeared: a rifle barrel and breech, the old 1914 Lebel issued French units; a ridged helmet, a bullethole above the right ear and bits of moldy leather still wadded against the inside rim. More scraps, a rusted belt buckle, the screw top of a water bottle.

Some of the other men had found similar relics, and we'd lain in the darkness and speculated about what might be found still farther down. The War of 1870 had passed this way; before that Napoleon might have camped units of the Grande Armée on the lower side of this ridge. Indeed, all the continent is a vast burial ground of wartime artifacts, especially near Verdun and eastward to Baden and Hesse, continuing evidence of civilization's penchant for falling in upon itself.

CHAPTER XVIII

Colonialism's "Terminal" Spasm

Scores of American and other newsmen, in clumps or alone, "fanned out" all over the globe in the nineteen-fifties, sent to cover specific trouble spots or just "fanning out."

As the world staggered back toward what it expected might be a semblance of tranquility, these peripatetic men and women encountered tottery governments and inexperienced and brutally venal politicians humbugging their way along by guess and by god. They also met and were absorbed by deeply anxious peoples, bewildered and angry amid the ruin of familiar values and comforting traditions. And it was these people that our stories were all about.

Mostly alone, I found the same sort of thing—ferment and instability—but I found it rather far off the beaten path, in the reaches of empires being consciously pulled down or simply collapsing of their own enfeebled bulk. Most of my experience was in Africa, a continent little fanned-out-over by the world press and hence relatively virgin.

I had seen the Near East begin its slide into becoming the Middle East in a state of endemic convulsion, and I was a spectator as Europe struggled back to its feet, revitalized by the Marshall Plan. But Africa is where I lived and worked for the best part of twenty years. As a professional observer and as a "settler," I passed journalistic judgment on and took part in, often simultaneously, the happenings that found native blacks and colonial whites perplexed and bedevilled by unfamiliar freedoms and, paradoxically, constricting opportunities.

Britain, bloodied in Kenya, disgraced in the Gold Coast, and despised in Southern Rhodesia, was backing out of the continent. This precipitate abandonment, while not entirely her own fault, produced disappointment and scorn.

France and Belgium sensibly pegged out hidden preserves they could secretly hang onto, and then made a great show of retiring. Sometimes they left behind a rear guard to vent white bitterness by looting and wreaking as much physical and administrative havoc as opportunity permitted, even to ripping the telephones off the walls of public buildings in Senegal.

The Portuguese colonial bureaucrats, farmers, and businessmen, deserted in 1974 by a government in Europe thrashing itself out of recognizable shape, were bloodied and humiliated even more than Britain had been when she was plagued by the Mau-Mau in Kenya.

In the vacuum left behind in each case, it was open season for the bully boys and the misfits found in any society. Normally such elements are inhibited by law which is enforced by stable governments with some practice at being the boss. There were, however, few such restraints in the aftermath of colonialism, and without them the bad boys, aided by the opportunists and the misguided "good chaps," literally slaughtered their way to prominence at the top. And since tenure at the top was tenuous at best, anarchy was the order of the day.

Of a total of forty-seven nations (omitting the Indian Ocean island states of Malagasy, the Comoros, and the Seychelles) there were one hundred thirty-nine attempted coups during the fifteen-year period beginning in 1961, forty-six of them "successful." From the starting gun fired in the Gold Coast (now Ghana), the first Black African country to gain its independence in 1957, until the early eighties, seventeen one-party regimes were set up, and nineteen military dictatorships seized power. One third of the continent's population of some 300 million lived under military administrations of one kind or another.

One country, Dahomey, through which I had bounced in a "mammy wagon" in balmier times, had five violent revolutions, Nigeria suffered three, and four other countries two each. These were rousing times. And incredibly bloody. Half a million were butchered according to conservative calculations and an unknown number were dead of starvation and disease.

In 1974, by which time this lethal free-for-all had thrashed about all over Africa for seventeen years, the cynical leaders of the "new" land of Sierra Leone, in an obvious tongue-in-cheek gesture, thumbed its nose at colonialism with what had to be calculated silliness.

On May 7, the president of this one-time British colony of about three million announced the creation of "The Order of the Mosquito." This bothersome bug, turned killer as carrier of various protozoans, was being officially honored for having made the country the "white man's grave," thereby preventing Europeans from settling and "establishing another Rhodesia." The award was created, along with seventeen other tributes, for ceremonies in the capital at Freetown. It would go to persons for outstanding acts of civil or military gallantry.

Whether or not, since then, Sierra Leonians in large numbers have trampled each other into the swamps in competitive feats of derring-do, I haven't noticed. What I do know is that this birdbrained idea was one of the few civilized acts to grace more than a decade of savage mayhem.

As for birdbrains: the United States, tossing out the baby with the bathwater, loftily inveighed against the "evils of colonialism." She hastened the departure of the European powers by censorious prating in the halls of the United Nations and by outspoken support of what often developed as grossly inept—when not downright malevolent—regimes too numerous to list. One of my Australian friends, living in Rhodesia, a retired military man with a decade and more of service behind him, some of it in Africa, was blunt and accurate: "The Yanks made a proper balls-up from Suez in fifty-six to the Cuban walkabout in Angola in 1975." He was too generous.

Indeed, it was to be an era of almost unrelieved hypocrisy, of duplicity best described by William Murchison, editorial staffer of the *Dallas Morning News* in a column appearing December 18, 1979. The black takeover in Rhodesia was beginning in earnest:

> To the the last Living American—namely me—who thinks the British Empire was God's way of underwriting peace, sanity, and civilization in the world, the sight of the Union Jack flapping once more over Rhodesia should be a wholesome one.
>
> It is, in fact, something less than that. The British are back in Rhodesia, this time not to rule but to preside over the latest attempt at sanitizing that country's form of government. It is an attempt that may work. Indeed, all men of good will should hope that it does.
>
> The fourteen-week-long peace conference masterminded by Britain at last pursuaded Rhodesia's whites, who used to run the country, to give up what powers they retained after bowing out in favor of Rhodesia's moderate blacks who run the country now. The Soviet-backed guerrillas operating from Zambia and Mocambique were all but pursuaded to stop fighting and take part in the elections and formation of a new government. They have balked over details of the ceasefire but may come around yet, as their war isn't going too well.
>
> The consequence—some day—may be a peaceful Rhodesia (renamed Zimbabwe). But has all the agony been justified? It is hard to see how.
>
> Rhodesia has always brought out the two-faced worst in world

leaders. Ah, the crocodile tears that were shed while it languished under the rule of Ian Smith!

It scarcely mattered that Smith's rule, whatever franchise restrictions underlay it, was milder, more respecting of genuine human freedoms than the governments of nine-tenths of the world.

With the constitutional arrangements of Uganda, where Idi Amin held bloody sway, or of the "Emperor" Bokassa's Central African Empire, the world thought it unseemly to interfere. But Ian Smith was worse than a murderer, worse than a demon. He was a white man governing a mostly black nation.

Smith's succesor, Bishop Muzorewa, fared little better with world opinion. He himself might be black, but he allowed the whites the power to block constitutional changes. Nor had his government any guerrillas in it. No, the bishop wouldn't do at all.

To be sure, Jimmy Carter could declare Communist China worthy of recognition, its totalitarian nature notwithstanding. After all, Deng Tsaio-Peng doesn't discriminate. He represses everybody without regard to race, creed, or color.

Indeed, in all the world, Rhodesia was the only nation whose form of government all the world sought persistently to change. Its sin—and it is a heinous sin in the twentieth century—was to allow whites a disproportionate voice in government, never mind what principles of civility and justice that voice might declare.

So long, Rhodesia. It was a nice try. Had you not tried in the most hypocritical era that comes to mind, you might have made it.

His ringing Huzzahs for "Empire" may prompt unsympathetic reactions. Such as the attitudes on the subject expressed by the Irish Republican Army, Jewish graduates of the Stern Gang, erstwhile Mau-Mau zealots and the shades of Gandhi, to name a few.

But then, nobody's perfect.

The transition of Britain's African possessions from foreign rule to self-government was not entirely peaceful. Some of her former colonies let things get out of hand. Nigeria fell into near genocidal war, Uganda was to become an abattoir and Rhodesia in the seventies lost 27,000 killed in a decade of savage violence. Yet, allowing for these bouts of unreason, The Empire territories managed, at worst, to do better than most. The continent's longest death rolls were not compiled at Westminster. In the nineteen-sixties Belgium's Congo and Uranda-Urundi alone saw the toll rise into the hundreds of thousands.

The first intimations of impending continental upheaval rustled into

West Africa in the late forties. Those found guilty of intemperate rhetoric were tossed into jail for brief if salutary periods. "Revolt" was not permitted to exceed a hum of discontent in the native quarters or in university halls.

Yet, the sense of disquiet was eloquent enough, especially to a visiting American newsman for whom the antagonists, ruler, and ruled, learned quickly to assume truculent postures. For these adversaries the gut issues translated racially: the "native" is unprepared for freedom; the white man is a tyrant.

I'd observed this simplistic racial polarization beginning in Algeria; had seen it demonstrated in Senegal, and become the butt of it in the Gold Coast.

This last took place in Accra. One morning black stevedores near the docks, seeing me approach along a sidewalk, had bunched together and forced me off into the street.

"Off the pavement, white boy."

And one Saturday night at a black hotel I joined resident whites in what, admittedly, could only be described as "slumming." There was a dance, the "music" an endless repetitive tenor-sax shriek that later became known as "skokiaan." And there was a lot of beer. Early in the evening the African men, dressed up in suits and neckties, were orderly and if not overly friendly tended to keep quietly to themselves. The African women were "ladies of the night." No self-respecting "mammy" attended these thrashes.

As the beer reached red-eye level, there was a subtle shift away from this cordial calm toward a nervy readiness to take offense at imagined slights, to block a white man trying to work his way to the bar, a "who you lookin' at?" hostility.

I was quite ready to pack it in at any time, said so, and as a gesture made a purposefully final trip to the Augean sty that passed for a men's room. Exiting back out on the crowded veranda and shuffling through the crowd, I was confronted by three very large blacks. They were tastefully turned out and were quite out of character as "heavies" in the accepted sense. Yet, the message was clear enough.

The "point man" of this trio slowly and deliberately snapped open a businesslike flick knife, shut it, dropped it into his pocket, and stared me down.

I recall saying something about joining my companions, put up a show of bravado that got me back to our table, and we left with as much haste as some show of dignity permitted.

It was patently obvious that the cowed colonial native who "knew his place" already was a thing of the past. This move up from what was often a state of shame was an improvement in man's treatment of man that I would promote as a newsman on a Rhodesian country paper years later. In these early days in West Africa, however, I was a neophyte and saw only ominous defiance.

White reaction to this change and, later, to the bloodletting of the deadly independence celebrations, was predictable. Some feigned indifference, and others pretended that, if ignored, all this unpleasantness would go away. Others went "home." Some resisted and fought back with mounting anger. And some climbed aboard the bandwagon and rode it for all it was worth, most of them rather scabby opportunists. Some, the wisest, simply adapted.

Among the blacks, the vast majority kept a low profile and devoted themselves to the rudiments of survival. A minority took part in the gory maneuvering of the new leaders, many of them joining the tribal goon squads recruited as bodyguards and all-purpose bully boys. Most Africans, while accustomed to the ritual brutalities of secret societies, were stunned by the general lawlessness and suffered at the hands of these thugs.

Over the years I would encounter the gamut of responses to change by both whites and blacks. Closely. In the beginning, of course, it was the whites I was able to observe and understand most readily.

The poseurs who affected to scoff at the growing tumult were the most numerous. "If one carries on as before, all this will starve and die from lack of attention." With many this pose did nothing to conceal the fear it was supposed to hide, but there were past masters who transformed it into an art. One who surpassed them all, who accepted that what he did in this life was mostly fraudulent anyway, was Lothian Alfred Littlewood.

Alfie, I met and savored for too short a time on Ikoye Island, Lagos, Nigeria, in the winter of 1950. He's long since gone to his reward, rest him, but in those days life was forever. He was cockney and spindly thin with a wispy shock of blondish white hair. A large, very red nose graced a wasted visage permanently puce from the ravages of the African sun and gin. His eyes, watery blue and kindly and laughing, entirely made amends for the rest of him.

Alfie could be found most often sagging deep into one of the overstuffed armchairs that disgraced the lounge of the Bristol Hotel, the only faintly acceptable hostel in town.

A fully qualified "coaster," Alfie'd spent eighteen years as a roustabout and as a free-lance newsman and stringer for, he said, the Associated Press. And well he might have, for he was no untutored buffoon. At the time I met him, he was proprietor of, he said, "a high-class dump, The Palm Tree Hotel, across the bridge toward Yaba and, me lad, an asylum it is for humanity's dregs."

He had a loud leaning toward verse recited basso profundo, anywhere and at all times. Byron, snatches of Shakespeare, bits of Kipling, Oscar Wilde. Catholic tastes. Much of the liquid fuel for these oftentimes marathon performances was provided by Tony Basmadjian, Bristol manager, whose pièce de résistance was a morning-after concoction that both fed and stimulated. It consisted of coconut milk, two ounces of gin, and an ounce of Cinzano or Dubonnet, and was lavishly garnished with cucumbers, radishes, and mint. So stoked, Alfie could soar with the muses to great heights, often from a barstool upon which he perched during at least some of the spare time that so easily overtook his working hours.

When he wasn't holding forth a cappella, he was roundly and colorfully cursing the huge West African gray parrot that unceasingly screeched bits of the scores from "Colonel Bogey" or "Dixie," never completing either of them. Relegated to a barren, cement courtyard that acted as an outsized flue for the hotel's inner bedrooms, this unwinsome bird hyphenated these tantalizing fragments with shrieking runs up and down the scale. All day and a good part of the darkness. The thing had no name that I recall, other than the scurrilous ones Littlewood invented for it.

Exhausted ultimately by all this exertion, Alfie would leave the stool to sink, as heretofore noted, into the calico folds of the most convenient armchair. A slender, freckled arm with a glass at the end of it would often be seen waving above this huddle like an insect antenna. If the goblet, once emptied, wasn't instantly snatched away for a refill, Alfie rose slowly from this upholstery wallow like an emaciated brontosaurus from its swamp and roared something like: "Bhhoy! ! you sightless, time-serving, gormless black son of Satan!"

Not surprisingly, there were those African patrons who flinched at this incivility. But not for long. Those who didn't know Alfie, or about him, were soon apprised.

The little cockney had fed, clothed, housed, and staked more black and white deadbeats than ever paid him a shilling at the Palm Tree Hotel. It was generally accepted that to disregard his bellicose rudeness was by way of payment to him in return for his unnumbered acts of kindness over the years.

Alfie's mentor and guardian while I was there was a giant named Cooper, 250 pounds of well-born Englishman who headed up the Lagos branch of the British Consul, a government office commissioned to spread the wonders of British "Kultur." For him the cockney's poetic excesses were comic relief and an opportunity to test his own memory. Often Cooper matched him verse for verse or vied with him in dialogue. Sample:

As Wilde's Lady Bracknell in *The Importance of Being Earnest:*

COOPER (entering the Bristol Lounge): "Good afternoon, dear Algernon. I hope you are behaving well."
ALFIE (buried in his armchair): "I'm feeling very well, Aunt Augusta."
COOPER: "Ah! that's not quite the same thing. In fact the two things rarely go together. . . ." Followed by all sorts of ponderously well-mannered ribaldry in fruity tones to the fascination and awe of assembled guests.

As an ode to his wizened little colleague and a tender commentary on Alfie's refusal to admit that the old "coaster" days would soon catch up to him and embed him forever in an unforgiving Africa, Cooper wrote this takeoff:

> To Alfred Littlewood,
> with Apologies to Lewis Carroll

I'll tell you then everything I can
Now that the weather is cool
I saw an aged aged man
A-sitting on a stool.
Who are you, aged man, I said
And how do you survive?—and
His answer buzzed around my head
Like bees around a hive.

He said: I look for potted prawns
That swim in the lagoon,
I curry them with peppercorns
And roast them in the moon,
I sell them unto men who drain
My beer and spirits dry,
And that is how I continue sane
And help the time go by.

I burn the candle at both ends
To see if they will meet.
I whisper poems to my friends
Then kick them in the street.
It caused me wonder to suppose
How could he stay alive.
I struck him on his glowing nose;
Pray, how do you survive?

His beery voice succeeded mine:
There is little to relate
I answer to the Duke of Windsor
Upon the telephone
I feed the Africans on whales
And play the dulcitone.
I beat him hard upon his head
Until his brain was blue.
Pray, how do you survive, I said
And what is it you do?

I sometimes sing a little song
An opera, two or three,
I smoke tobacco all day long
And go to bed at three
And that's the way—he gave a sigh
And shed a bitter tear—
I try to manage and get by
And have a glass of beer.

––*

And now if e'er I sit
Beneath a torrid sun
Or fall down in a frenzied fit
And chew a currant bun
Or if I ever try and bite
A bowl of gooseberry fool
I reminisce with much delight
On that old man with hair so white

*Whose speech so blurred, eye so bright
Whose nose was practically alight
Who wore a glass to aid his sight
Who always seemed a little tight
And cried Ponti-ous with all his might
Whose manners were most impolite
Who took offense at any slight
And sometimes tried to pick a fight
Who drove the African to flight
Way back upon a summer night
A-sitting on a stool.*

CHAPTER XIX

"Characters" and Cobras

There were white expatriate settlers faced with mounting turmoil who contrived an indifference to Africa's spasms, who displayed a counterfeit composure in the face of catastrophe by cultivating eccentricity and hovering ostensibly aloof from the banalities. This was most easily done, of course, by those who qualified as uncertified loonies, of which there were aplenty.

In the early nineteen-fifties Southern Rhodesia enjoyed an unprecedented economic boom. Investment millions poured into the country to build fabricating plants, to open mines, develop agribusiness, and even support an exciting national stock exchange. Race relations were a bit uneasy but in a way that was a plus, because it stemmed from government efforts to experiment with "partnership" between the races, opening opportunities for blacks to compete in commerce and the professions. Generally, the climate was one of optimism about the future and a growing pride in the new nation.

It wasn't long before the "pioneer era of conquest" was being thought of as the early part of the country's modern history instead of the only history it had. Not that it wasn't worth chronicling. It represented the beginnings of what seemed a limitlessly promising tomorrow. An imposing archives structure went up in the suburbs of the capital city of Salisbury to house the accumulating records and act as adjunct to the town's existing Queen Victoria Museum and the older, 1901, National Museum in Bulawayo.

It was a period of glory or humiliation depending on whether you were white or black, but either way it was definitely yesteryear and worthy of all this feverish attention. Except, that is, for a few who considered this fuss about a glittering past to be pretentious nonsense. I met one who had strong views on this topic.

Following up a story on the Meikle family, the Rockefellers of the

Rhodesias, I'd stopped a few nights in Bulawayo, which in addition to hosting the National Museum was also the country's burgeoning commercial capital. I'd managed to book into the Bulawayo club, a comfortingly stuffy and private preserve open to me under terms of reciprocity with my Umtali Club in the eastern districts. This gentlemen's exchange of courtesies extended, too, to such illustrious precincts as the Rand Club in Johannesburg; the East India Club, St. James Square, London; club Baur au Lac in Zurich; and others, all very exclusive and civilized and, in Bulawayo, successfully concealing Rhodesia's brash and nouveau origins behind a cultivated pomposity. I wallowed in it.

Lounging alone in the bar one evening, cosseting a brandy ginger and contemplating nothing in particular, I was startled to see an aging giant fill a large part of the other end of the room. He was well over six feet, broad under a tattered, tentlike safari jacket with valise-sized pockets and voluminous khaki trousers belted tightly around his bulging middle. Atop a florid and wrinkled visage, featuring a stained white handlebar moustache, was a wide-brimmed bush hat that had seen better days, and on his feet were what used to be called "mosquito boots," lightweight leather footgear into which bottoms of the trousers were stuffed.

And dead center, protruding from his waistband, was the butt end of a big revolver I recognized as a Colt army model, long barrel .44 six shot, manufactured in 1860, a formidable weapon.

He knocked back a tumbler of neat whisky, after raising it to me in silent toast, and then lumbering the length of the bar slid onto the stool next to me. Waving to the barman, he repeated his order and, looking me hard in the face, told me—just because I'd probably ask him anyway, he said—that he was six feet five, two hundred fifteen pounds, born in Australia but came here in 1890 when he was a lad, was now "as old as God." . . . and would I join him in another drink? We never exchanged names.

I said I would and asked him the obvious question: Why the gun in these enlightened times?

"Enlightened times, my ass!" he snorted. "Hasn't changed a bit."

"There was a native uprising around here," he went on, "in the nineties. Our family farm out near the Matopos, not far from here, was a laager. Everyone moved in on us when there was trouble, and," he added, "there was a hell of a lot of that."

"The bloody Kaffirs at us two days before they got the place afire"—he was staring far away into the mirror behind the bar—"and then butchered the lot."

"Me," he shrugged, "I got away into the kopjes with two other kids." He finished off his drink. "You couldn't trust them Kaffirs then. . . . Some of them worked for us for years. My mother cared for the sick, delivered the bloody picanins; they hacked her to bits.

"Like I say," he called for more drinks, "you couldn't trust the buggers then, and you can't trust them now. Could be a Kaffir you see dressed like a banker, shoes and all, has a cane knife up his trousers," and he grinned at me without smiling.

And then there was Arthur ("Ginger") Davison.

Research on the story I'd been assigned by *Pathfinder News Magazine* on the Meikle family began in April, 1950, in Ndola, a copper-mining community just south of the then Congo border in what was still Northern Rhodesia. The magazine's South African stringer, name of Wentzel, had been rebuffed by the publicity-shy Scottish merchants and the job had fallen to me.

Although, years later when I'd settled in Southern Rhodesia I was to meet Meikle women and find them clever and vastly attractive—Joan, in particular—in the early days, I ran head on into a defensive phalanx lead by an in-law autocrat who threatened me with legal action if I "printed one word" of my findings. Thanks to forewarning and the helpful contacts beginning in Ndola, those findings were by then considerable. Irked by this pompous posturing, I fed *Pathfinder* the full text, which they "printed," and I sent numerous variations of what was a good story to other publications. I never heard from the Meikle attorneys.

In Ndola, a facsimile cowtown tucked under the lee of scrubby hills rolling northward above some of the world's richest mineral deposits, my first professional call had been at the editorial offices of the *Northern Rhodesia Advertiser*. The staff was courteous and helpful. There were two people to see, they told me, old-timers, "a bit touched" but approachable: Arthur "Ginger" Davison and Chirupula Stephenson. Stephenson was about a hundred miles south out in the bush on the Great North Road near a place called Kapiri Mposhi. Davison, they said, was in Ndola, "probably working on his castle," a monstrous gray pile he was building with his own hands on the outskirts. Unable to reach him by phone, I sent a message inviting him to dinner and received a reply, by return messenger, agreeing to join me at Rutland's Hotel.

There is little I can recall in a long and full life that has been more loathsome than a meal at the old Rutland's. It had clean, bright rooms, the most comfortable beds in Africa, a cheerful and helpful staff and the world's worst table.

The standard opener was Brown Soup, lukewarm, lightly burned, and the consistency of oatmeal. The fish course consisted of a rock-hard cake, the flavor of a hockey puck under ketchup. Entrées invariably arrived cold and tough as old boots smothered in a clotted scum that passed for gravy; the vegetables were tinned, as were the pears or peaches dished up as dessert if the sagging crème caramel or gluey tapioca had run out. And this in a tropical fruit-growing Mecca. "Coffee in the lounge" featured a brackish fluid served in individual metal pots that resembled battered bailing buckets.

For "Ginger" Davison, however, this poisonous repast was central to a "night out," and what I gagged over he consumed with relish.

Squat and square-built, "Ginger" had piercing blue eyes under ginger-tufted brows, the only hair on his head and responsible for the sobriquet. His handshake was bone-crushing, but his voice was soft and English north-country and his manner gentle. As Alfie's had been, his complexion was mottled cerise, but unlike Alfie the cause was an external burn. More than twenty years of tropical sun had seared his pale skin until he looked like a permanent casualty. He was a bachelor and freely admitted to being sixty-eight and "not the man I once was."

That man had been a young engineer come first to Central Africa from South Durham, England, as an apprentice employee of the Cleveland Bridge Company building the railway span across the Zambesi River below the Victoria Falls. After that, he'd been a ganger supervising crews building the railway north as far as Elizabethville in the Congo, where he quit and settled in Ndola. He'd coasted along the last twenty years, supporting his slim needs by land speculation and engineering consultancy. And by toying with his "castle."

Built overlooking Ndola in an area then called the North Rise, this unlovely monument to eleven years of sporadic labor was gross and obviously permanent. (The municipality later condemned it and spent a fortune in gelignite trying to demolish it.) Great, rough-skinned slabs of reinforced concrete and heaps of granite masonry, loosely associated in an upward-reaching frenzy, had created a surrealist structure destined to be forever growing, changing, and never finished.

Inside it was dank and drafty ("airy" he called it) rather like a crypt above ground. It had grown as the spirit moved him along narrow dark passageways connecting a miscellany of obviously unplanned cubicles that were more cells than rooms. His "airy" blasts were admitted through square, unframed openings in the concrete, to be trimmed up "sometime" as windows. Precipitous winding stairways, some steps eighteen inches high, others eight or twelve, generally wandered from one story to another. The place was entered from a concrete platform partially cantilevered out into space over the hillside and designed as a veranda but with no railings or balustrades to prevent the unwary from plunging out into the abyss. On the top floor, there was a large, alarmingly open "great hall" from which yawning gaps, planned to accommodate french doors, opened onto a balcony and provided a breathtaking view of Africa to the south. A large, walk-in fireplace with the bricked hearth extending into the room filled the opposite side.

Throughout the building all surfaces were rough cast, no plaster. There was almost no furniture, no carpets or hangings in any of the halls, nooks or chambers. Only the "great hall," part of which he said was his "office," had any furnishing. There was a battered couch that looked as if a horse had slept on it for years, and, except for a large shapeless heap that had been an armchair, seating was provided on straight-backed wooden antiques, of value to collectors but not visitors.

Yet in spite of the sensation one was in a wartime pillbox, this truly charming old man, surrounded by piles of documents and newspapers and books on sagging shelves all around him, warmed the room and furnished it luxuriously with his presence.

The future of his gruesome hovel seemed to prey on Ginger's mind. His most improbable dream had the place becoming an "exclusive gentleman's club with billiard room and card parlors, and a fine long bar and excellent food." There would be finely appointed rooms, he said, "for women who got drunk to sleep it off." Certainly they "couldn't be carried abroad at night to their homes; the place would get a dreadfully bad name." Ginger had the same view of women en masse as, he told me, old Tom Meikle had about gold mines: "holes where ordinarily sensible men threw their money," which sounds rude and was.

We reminisced about the Meikles family, about "Old Tom," patriarch of the clan, and about Ginger's life. And his future. There obviously was no room in it for the kind of change that was coming. For Ginger Davison, only his death could be permitted to intrude on the serene routines he'd established for himself years earlier. Toward the African, his attitude, about which he'd given very little thought in any event, was entirely, and rigidly, paternal.

"They're like children," he'd said, echoing sentiment I'd encountered since Algiers, "and must be taught and cared for and punished when they do wrong." Sometime in the distant future they might "catch up," and "in the meanwhile they may—indeed they should—aspire, but they will not achieve."

Africa was to convulse all around Ginger's castle before he died, sometime in the sixties. I never saw him again, but I suspect that during that decade he often sat alone, high in the "Great Hall" amid the familiar clutter and, drawing his warming convictions around him, dozed oblivious, above the bedlam of this century's barricades.

The morning following our meeting I found a note from him at the hotel desk introducing me formally to Chirupula Stephenson and telling me how to reach his home. The message went on, almost compulsively, to describe the Great North Road, the wondrous passage I would take, and the route from the Congo border and the middle of Africa to the Antarctic waters of the Cape of Good Hope.

"The highway is graveled here in the north," he wrote, "but often changes surfaces. From Ndola it pushes through thinning jungle into scrub country and then onward to fly three times over great rivers and struggle through rugged lands gashed by granite canyons half a mile deep.

"Its progress eases," he went on, "as it slides dead straight across barren plain and through head-high stands of grains, then out across neatly cultivated farmland, orchards, cattle ranches, the strange wastelands of the Karoo, and into rolling vineyard country.

"At its most beautiful, it will sweep down the mountainsides of the Cape to the town and the sea, more than two thousand five hundred miles away."

I covered a microscopic fifty miles of all this before, following Ginger's directions, I wheeled left toward the northeast and began another sixty miles up the main mail and transport route to the entrance to Stephenson's home. This road was, for the most part, smooth-going and fast and an indescribable relief after the stream-bed tracks of the Congo. Yet, there was one place on it that came close to being the last stretch of highway I'd ever travel.

Filled to the back teeth with frothy Lion Lager after a "tea" stop at Kapiri Mposhi (where I'd made the left turn) and in need of a "rest" halt, I pulled to the edge of the roadway and switched off. As the sound died, a heavy, cloying calm, silent as only a sun-dappled tropical forest can get, took over, the hush broken only by the cracking of the overheated engine block.

I walked a short distance through the thick growth of fern and low brush, and, one urge prompting another, found concealment behind a high fan of elephant grass and dropped my lederhosen, the Bavarian leather shorts I'd worn to a burnished shiny black as my everyday dress. They had scarcely hit my boot tops when I sensed movement behind me and off to my left. There was no sound to speak of, just a presence.

Frozen in mid-crouch, taut and barely breathing, I slowly turned my head and saw, not four feet away, wavering at least a foot above the fringe of undergrowth, the scaly upper body and hooded head of an Egyptian cobra.

This was not my first experience with snakes, but it was the first time I'd confronted one—if that's the word—with my bare backside. And with my ankles firmly hobbled. The odds against my surviving this humiliating encounter were stacked against me.

A few weeks earlier I'd done a story in the pygmy country along the Congo's Ipule River. Assorted reptiles had played a part in the piece, and I'd made it a point to learn about them in detail from an expert, an American named Putnam, who doubled as resident zoologist and clinician in charge of a jungle infirmary serving his stunted neighbors. The little bush hunters were bitten often, and over the years he'd built up a wealth of lore about snakes, pin-pointing the lethal ones.

If the snake now hovering behind me was the banded cobra I thought it was, I was in big trouble. From the flat top of his hood to the ground I guessed to be about four feet. Since a cobra of this kind rearing up for a better look could raise half of its total length into the air, this angry specimen had to be between eight and nine feet long. Its body girth, or what I could see of it, was roughly that of a municipal fire hose.

Members of the cobra family are equipped with two hollow fangs permanently fixed up front. Through these tubes the poison, a nerve-paralyzing drug, is injected with a syringelike action, a contraction of the muscles of the throat acting as a plunger. Not satisfied with merely puncturing the flesh, the cobra, unlike most species that strike and pull away, will hang on and worry the wound as if it were shaking a rat. It eats rats, and toads too, and even fish. An enthusiastic carnivore.

I don't, of course, remember giving much thought to specifics such as diet, neurotoxicity, and the like. I do recall being aware the thing would probably chew on me if it once got a grip, even though I'd be dead within minutes if it just perforated me and pushed off.

Putnam had told me dying this way was a poor way to go. Paralysis of the nerves that activate heart and diaphragm muscles pretty quickly gums up the machinery. This is very painful. And then coma. In short, I could be converted to a world statistic in a flash, one of more than 5,000 dead each year from attack by cobras. Not just "snakes." Cobras.

I got some brief encouragement from the recollection that most snakes are at heart shy and unassuming. All this raising up and puffing out is defensive, not aggressive. Since snakes, like most animals, are forever foraging for food, this stand-up balancing act is really the better to see a meal. If whatever it is that's attracted the snake's attention—in my case, a glistening backside—is neither dangerous to it nor obviously edible, the snake quickly loses interest and collapses back on the horizontal. Furthermore, in addition to preferring a life minding its own business, the common Indian cobra can be quite reasonable. Or so an Englishwoman who'd lived all over the subcontinent for years had once told me.

Normally, she'd said, in Madras, the springtime finds the atmosphere cooling but still heavy and she used to let her eighteen-month-old son have his meals in the veranda breezes. One evening, the woman said, she overheard her child squealing with laughter and, curious, she opened the door to the veranda near where he sat in his high chair. And froze in her tracks. What she saw is scored into her memory for life, every detail.

The child sat in the chair, a bowl of milk and porridge on the tray in front of him. Coiled up the leg of the chair and arching over the edge of the tray across from the lad, its head dropped as if it were resting its chin on the lip of the bowl, was a large cobra, its "cape" only loosely distended. Even as she watched it ducked its head into the bowl and began lapping, "or whatever it is a snake does," oblivious to the happy racket the child was making, and the blows it rained on its head with a spoon. At one point the child reached out with its free hand and pushed roughly at the thing trying to attract its attention. The snake merely flexed slightly and went right on feeding.

At a loss to know what to do, the mother, faint and shaking, remained rooted in the doorway and watched the baby repeatedly hit the snake "a right good wallop" with the spoon, giggling hysterically the while. Finally, the child, tiring of the play, simply sat and watched. The reptile, sated at last, withdrew, pulling back with a silken slither to the granolithic floor, over the edge of the veranda and away into the bordering flower garden.

The woman told me that, close to hysteria, she'd snatched up her child and rushed into the house. Her fright and wild retreat scared the babe and his happy laughter gave way to howls of alarm. Soothing him, she calmed herself, she said, and realized that the snake must instinctively have sensed that the child had meant no harm, that there had been a form of extrasensory contact. What's more, she insisted that the snake had, in her words, made a judgment and opted for restraint.

Whether this slavering predator behind me would choose to be reasonable or would fly at me and start chewing was a judgment I couldn't wait for him to make. Yet I was forced to remain in that ridiculous posture while I pondered the limited alternatives.

Putnam had told me that this species could strike a distance equal to about half its length. At this range he could hit me and be munching away in a split second. Since it was therefore obvious that I could definitely be hit, my only recourse would ultimately be the supply of antivenom I carried in the Jeep.

This hope faded as rapidly as it surfaced.

As I have noted earlier, thousands of miles away in Lagos I had bought a snakebite kit. It was equipped with cobra antidote, a razor blade to slash open the punctures to promote bleeding, potassium permanganate crystals to stuff into the wound as disinfectant, a tourniquet and a small pamphlet detailing the horrible death invited by failure to follow instructions carefully. This emergency gear, along with the .12 gauge shotgun, was stored in the back of the Land Rover beneath hundreds of pounds of gear.

Obviously all this wide-ranging review of snakehood and speculation about my immediate future had consumed less than a few fleeting seconds. The brute still hovered uncertainly, its flat head swaying gently, the forked tongue ceaselessly flickering past those tubular fangs, ready to plunge into my meaty buttocks, waiting way down there in the back, all unsuspecting. And I remained unmoving, not a tissue a-twitch.

Yet, obviously, this couldn't go on. Not in this bent-over posture. Any moment my strained muscles would start to jerk and give way. And that would be it. An instant decision was called for.

Frantically and without much thought, with a grab at my lederhosen, I made a wild lunge toward the roadway, throwing myself out into the dust behind the Jeep. My vital parts were savaged by thorns en route and lacerated by laterite chips as I hit. But if the snake had struck out, it had apparently missed me.

From there over the top of the door into the open Land Rover called forth my athletic prowess at its best. The engine cranked over, the car roared backward, all wheels spinning, and stalled in the center of the road. I couldn't see any snake, but there was no certainty it hadn't followed me and might not, right now, be scaling the canvas sides.

With my leather shorts still unflapped at half-mast, I somehow managed to restart, switch gears, and leap the Jeep forward. At that moment the snake stood up swaying erect a good four feet above the dusty surface of the berm. As I swung past, it lashed out, striking the left front fender a hammer blow.

After some twenty yards, I slid to a halt and looked back. The snake had dropped to the ground and, its full length twisting in a frenzy, was skating down the road in my direction, its upper body bobbing and swinging a few inches above the ground. How I'd ever managed to escape this beast I'd never know. Confident now I could stay away from it, I eased the car slowly forward and studied the reptile over my shoulder.

Using the height of the fender, I laid off that footage down the length of the body to reach an estimate of no less than nine feet long. The girth I guessed at ten inches. A big snake.

It took about six miles of travel for my body activity to return to something like normal. I could breathe freely again; my heart stopped pounding in my throat, and the clammy pallor that had winked back at me as I'd looked into the rear-view mirror gave way to my customary puce.

CHAPTER XX

"He Who Beats"

Sixty miles from Kapiri Mposhi, I came upon Chirupula's name etched on a strip of rawhide stretched between two msasa saplings. Set back in the bush at the end of a half-mile of sandy track, the house was a cluster of two-story towerlike structures, mustard-colored stucco under ragged thatch. It sat in a clearing swept clean and bordered by banks of purple bougainvillea and honeysuckle, a sweet-smelling fairyland of a place. And Chirupula, who'd apparently heard the car approach, stood in the doorway, an archetypal gnome matching the surroundings.

Resembling a miniature Jan Christian Smuts in a baggy white linen suit and solar topi, Stephenson shook my hand warmly in his wrinkled brown paw, took Davison's letter, read it and invited me in "forever."

Inside, the house was a warm, bric-a-brac–strewn counterpart to Ginger's drafty cave, rooms partitioned by hanging drapes, and, in one instance, a hallway closed off by a slab of corrugated iron. Carpets, throw rugs and reed mats were everywhere across the floors and up the walls. We finally settled down in his study on the second floor, a narrow apartment, one side glassed the full length and letting in a golden glow.

Much like Davison's hideaway, Chirupula's was cluttered with heaps of yellowing newspapers, magazines, brochures, and, he explained to me, past issues of a newsletter he composed periodically, running it off on an antique duplicating machine and mailing to his friends worldwide. He wrote about a lot of things, from the atom bomb to Egyptian pyramidism. Books from floor to ceiling were a catholic selection: Meaterlinck's *Life of the Bee; Commercial Fruit and Vegetable Products,* by Creuss; *All about Gold,* by Bert Seymour; *Moore's Family Medicine in India;* Herodotus' *History; Trade Unionism in England;* Grimm's *Fairy Tales.*

In my notes he's introduced as a "little old man, a chuckler-to-himself with a pearl-gray goatee and carefully trimmed moustache. In repose, with his soft, tanned, wrinkled face he looks a wise old elf.''

The description was close enough, as far as it went, for Chirupula Stephenson was a rare and awesome original, a quintessential Englishman doggedly reordering the world in something like his own image by power of will, humor, and absolute confidence in the right as he saw it.

He had penned an autobiography, *Chirupula's Tale*, published by Geoffery Bles, London, in 1937, with a planned foreword by, appropriately, Jan Smuts. Written as a letter to "My dear Stephenson" in 1936, when Smuts was Minister of Justice for the Union of South Africa, the letter states:

> The extracts of your forthcoming book appearing in the local press are so extraordinary that some may doubt your account of strange happenings in the interior of Africa and may even doubt your very existence.
>
> To me and to others, however [the letter continues] who are conversant with the affairs of Southern Africa during the last half century, your part . . . is well known, as is also the fact that you acted on the instructions and on behalf of Cecil Rhodes in connection with his northward scheme.

Smuts concludes by commending Chirupula "as one of the chief actors" in the drama opening up Africa. And he signed it, "Yours Sincerely, J. C. Smuts." Sadly, this flattering testimonial was "mislaid during the editor's illness," according to Stephenson, and missed the publication date.

Chirupula was immensely proud of this letter. After he'd shown it to me he tenderly tucked it away in a mare's-nest filing system consisting in part of stacked tea chests. After that, the subject of the book fell behind us, swirling away, as did so many other topics, like jetsam in the wake of his reminiscences. Discussion of the Meikles, the real reason for my stopover, became a minor part in a rambling review of his personal history.

During the several days I was his guest, he harked back over his fifty years in the Kapiri District, much of the time as Rhodes's administrator and local agent for the British South Africa Company (BSA Company); back further yet to his first arrival in Cape Town in 1896 to take on a job as post office telegrapher; and ultimately back to his first arrival anywhere: his birth, John Edward Stephenson, in the village of North Shields (eight miles from Sunderland), Northumberland, in 1876.

Absorbing as I was to find his autobiography and a later biography by Kathleen Stevens Rukavina (Exposition Press, Inc., New York, 1950), far more engaging for me were the hours spent listening to him chatter and chuckle his way down the byways of his memory.

He had been, literally, a pathfinder for the BSA Company when Rhodes was the colossus astride Southern Africa at the turn of the century.

"I didn't know him personally, mind you," Chirupula flapped his hand in dismissal, "I worked for him here; was a kind of district commissioner; kept the natives reasonably honest; policed the area, spanked the naughty ones; collected the taxes."

He'd first arrived in Northern Rhodesia in 1900 with "Francis Emilius Fletcher Jones, from northern Wales," carrying instructions and authority from Rhodes to "open up the territory."

That part of Rhodesia for which the two men were responsible was 150 miles long, 70 miles wide, encompassed a goodly portion of what became the famed copperbelt mining operation and was inhabited by, Chirupula said, the Lalas, some Lambas, by offshoots of the Angonis, themselves fugitive relatives of the Zulus in the far-off Indian Ocean province of Natal, and by other, lesser "families," "all of them bare-ass primitives, if you'll excuse my French."

At first he was known only as John Edward or Bwana Stephenson. He lived among the Lalas, shot game for the tribal pot, enhancing a great-white-hunter reputation by shooting five elephants in one day ("the natives climbed right inside the huge rib cage and tore out the insides. Ghastly!"). With an ear for languages (most un-English), he soon spoke like one of them and within two years was initiated into the tribe as a "great one," he said, "all five feet six inches of me." He declined to discuss the "initiation."

As the tax collector, a job he hated, and as "sheriff, police chief, the FBI and M15 rolled into one," Chirupula was "Authority." He was prosecutor, judge, and jury. He also doled out the punishment, most of it for failure to pay the tax, in those early days a quota of hides or ivory. Later, when the copper mines opened and paid money wages, taxes were met in cash.

Tribute, for such it was, was no new thing imposed by the white man, Stephenson pointed out. In parts of Southern Rhodesia, for example, it had long been paid by vassal tribes to the courts of the Matabele, Mashona, and Manyika nations, often as porcupine quills filled with gold dust or as slaves and concubines—"goods" that were in turn marketed to the itinerant Arab traders.

If a tribe failed to pay him, as often happened before Stephenson established his authority, he selected one of the elders and whipped him, publicly.

"With a 'cat,' or something like it," he explained—a bamboo handle with thongs attached.

"My 'cat' hurt," he admitted. "That was the idea. But it was nothing like the Portuguese East practice of bastinado, which could cripple for life. We meant to punish, not terrorize.''

Although, he said, he was forced to inflict pain and, worse, to humiliate the tribal elders, they accepted the principle that one must "pay up for wrong things done, for orders ignored.''

"For example,'' Stephenson pointed out, "they well knew that one ignored the rules of bush survival at one's peril. Death from thirst, starvation, mauling by a lion or hyena—these things follow as the night the day a breach of established practice. In such things the native is quick to associate cause and effect.

"For these beatings,'' he went on, "I was annointed with the cognomen 'Chirupula.' It's not a particularly affectionate title, not even respectable. But it's plausible. It means 'he who beats.' Most of these native 'pet names' are a bit brutal, but they hit the mark dead center.''

In 1906 Stephenson took the six months' leave "home'' allowed by the BSA Company and returned to Northumberland. The cold, gray English days depressed him. Add to that, he said, mounting homesickness for his Lalas, and he couldn't stay the course. He came back to Rhodesia a month early, never to leave Africa again.

His tours of duty took him through Lala territory and into Katanga, that Congo pedicle province protruding down into Rhodesia, "a bit of land we lost to Belgium through incompetence and bad luck.''

Unfortunately my notes don't deal much with this bitter topic. Katanga, first a part of the Belgian Congo and now Zaire, holds one of the world's richest concentrations of copper, cobalt, uranium, lead, and zinc. Hence, Chirupula's charge of British bungling was both original and fundamental, especially as applied to the European scramble for power and riches in Africa during the late 1880s.

What I did make note of was that, in 1890, an Englishman named Sharpe was sent, according to Chirupula, by Rhodes, to make a treaty with a Katanga chief and was rebuffed. Later the chief relented and sent word to Sharpe, asking him to return. This communication was intercepted by a Capt. W. G. Stairs, who tipped off the Belgians, determined to block Rhodes's push into the area. As a result, the Belgians got to the chief before the British. According to Chirupula, Stairs, commissioned in Britian's Royal Engineers, had been "bought'' by the Belgian king and was a "traitor who cost his country wealth and strategic advantage in the battle for Africa.''

At the same time, Chirupula said, making no effort to mask his disgust, another British envoy, Thompson, working with Sharpe and on Rhodes's instructions in a two-pronged maneuver to get to the Katanga ruler, "made a treaty with the wrong man, Musiri of the Lambas instead of Mushidi of the Katangas *and* in the wrong place, 300 miles short of the Katangas' kraal!"

Loss of so large a chunk of what could have been part of Britain's copperbelt was particularly galling to Stephenson. Not only had the English been tricked out of Central African pre-eminence; they'd also lost what he was convinced were some of the prehistoric mines of the ancient Land of Ophir, source of the wealth of King Solomon and of the early Egyptians. Aged workings existed in the vicinity of what was now the Bwana Makubwa Mine in Britain's copperbelt region. Many more such early pits had been located north of there in the Katanga area, probably the first copper mines in Africa.

"The malachite, the copper ore, was mined for itself, for its intrinsic emerald beauty," he said, "not just as the beginnings of refined copper.

"It was carried overland from the middle of Africa thousands of years ago to the Nile Valley," he said, "where the Egyptians floored some of their temples with it to represent the green produced by the river's life-giving floods.

"Part of the booty found aboard the remains of an Egyptian warship sunk in the Red Sea about 1500 B.C. was identified as the 'green gold of Emu,' " and his eyes lit up, "and Emu was the island of Lamu in Lake Victoria, not far from here, a depot for the caravans transporting the malachite, ivory, and other loot."

On the subject of his personal life, Stephenson told me he'd been three times "married" to "high-born" African women, the last two sent to him by the tribal chief. The first, with the melodious name of "Chisimongana," an Angoni woman captured by the Yao in a Nyasaland tribal war, he bought for "about ten shillings" to rescue her from a slaver. His last wife, with him when I was there, a handsome, light-skinned lass, I saw only when she limped in and out with teas, evening drinks, and food at mealtime.

She'd been born with a club foot, Chirupula explained. By custom she'd have been left in the bush for the hyenas but, because of her relationship to the chief, had been spared. Chirupula'd felt sorry for her, asked that she be given to him, and the chief had agreed.

By every point system known she was a high scorer: gardener, cook, concubine, guardian, and general handmaiden. And good at all of them. She was not, however, permitted to join us in conversation or to eat at our table, because, as Stephenson noted somewhat testily when I asked, "this is the custom."

He said nothing of children.

As I prepared to leave, we stood outside his home as workers from the orange groves ("California navel!") loaded the Land Rover.

"I am considered a crazy old fool," he chuckled. "Once I was the 'Great One' and 'The Law.' Today I am a silly, disreputable old man who's 'penga,' crazy, and has gone native. Well, perhaps."

During his fifty years the Africa around him certainly had begun to change. Yet it hadn't changed as much in that half-century as it would in the two decades to come. So far Stephenson had absorbed what changes there'd been—indeed, had even been the cause of a few of them. But imminent was a violent conflict that would claw at the continent's ancient visage, mutilating it beyond recognition for the likes of Chirupula. He knew this, I'm certain, but knew as well that if he could no longer participate he still had ten thousand square miles of primal jungle in *his* "backyard," well off the beaten track.

Most of his lifetime had been spent defending the black against white exploitation and cultural encroachment. The twain would never meet, he argued. The races, he insisted were "different."

"Thousands of generations have produced divergent idiosyncrasies," he'd written, "culminating in different religions, different lives, different manners and responses."

"It is not a question of better or worse," he'd said. "The whites' arrogating to themselves a racial superiority, loftily preaching downward a newfangled doctrine of 'uplift,' is as wicked as turning the country back to the natives," a development he saw coming soon.

"Paternalism," the father-knows-best guidance of his African "charges" by the white that so aptly described Chirupula's relationship to "my people," would become a dirty word characterizing an attitude all the more evil, it would be charged, because it was hypocritical and only pretended beneficence. Chirupula might not have accepted that the term described his cast of mind, but he would have vigorously defended the early definition of it as honestly kind and bounteous and genuinely intended to enlighten. Perhaps this might be viewed as restricting new "freedoms," but it could hardly be termed "evil."

In an epilogue to *Chirupula's Tale* titled "Retrospect," he wrote:

> I have set down much that will mean little to my readers. My excuse must be that to me at least it meant very much, those early years in Africa and among those Africans that I love.

Most of the "Retrospect" is in memoriam for Mwape-Chiwali, given to him by a Lala king to be a "masanu," a junior wife to Chisimongana.

"More than thirty years after" she came to him "on May 15, 1934, she left me to live forever in her spirit world, to intercede with God for those she loves.

"She was ever true, ever affectionate, ever patient. She was not strikingly beautiful, but she understood a thought before it was uttered. She knew when to laugh, when to be silent, when to give counsel.

"She would never leave me whether in the Congo where the poisoned arrows pattered through the leaves, or nearer home where a 'good' white woman sought to drive her forth at the point of a revolver. And when death stalked me and nearly took me for his prey, it was she and Chisimongana who held me to earth and would not let my spirit leave them.

"The sun shines here still, and at night the breeze ripples through the trees across the little stream; the stars burn brightly and from the forest come the voices that I know. But they will never be the same again."

CHAPTER XXI

Losers, Good and Bad

Excepting in communities along the Mediterranean littoral and at the southernmost end of the continent where he's lived for thirteen generations, the white man has remained an outsider in Africa. He or his immediate past relatives have come from somewhere else and could return there.

Yet for all this "settler" or "expatriate" status, he often considered himself a permanent resident, his livelihood fixed in his new home, his allegiance to it total.

For him the assessment of the changes mauling Africa from the nineteen-fifties presented bewildering problems, created harsh alternatives.

He could, as noted earlier, pretend nothing was changed; fight back and try and retain his "vested interests"; compromise, which almost invariably meant sacrifice; or he could pack up and leave. If he had the money and still had a country to go to.

The Africans, on the other hand, the "establishment" kings and chieftains and headmen and advisory "indunas," could only resist or compromise. Even these alternatives differed from those facing the whites. Often the leaders were targets of nationalist fanatics no less than the whites. To fight back against these odds, and many did, earned them only a gallant death. As for compromise: equivocation in such primitive societies was scarcely less suicidal.

In a strong and numerous tribe, there was, of course, a chance one might survive long enough to adapt. As a member of the "establishment", one might be strong enough to pretend nothing out of the ordinary was going on. Such a black man, one who chose to ignore the portents, I had met earlier in the Gold Coast.

Upcountry in the city of Kumasi, I was on an unlikely mission searching for the "Golden Stool of the Ashantis." This is a three-legged wooden seat believed to embody the souls of the tribe and I had, perforce, to see the chief in whose care this relic rested.

The significance of the story for me lay not in the fetish as such but in its continuing importance to a large, warlike and influential tribe in a country moving with speed toward "self-government," a proposed democratic-style regime that would demand of its electorate rather more than superstitious dependence on a wooden talisman, however extraordinary.

Nonetheless, I did have to admit that from what I had learned the stool was no run-of-the-mill graven image.

Early in the eighteenth century, tradition has it, Osai Tutu, fourth King of the Ashantis, was chatting to Anotchi, his head magician, who told him that Onyame, god of the sky, was planning to convert his subjects from a scattering of subsistence farmers to a great nation. And, lo, even as Anotchi spoke, a large black cloud hovering overhead exploded in thunder and lightning and a wooden stool, ornately gilded, emerged from this chaos to float slowly earthward, settling on Osai Tutu's knees. Anotchi immediately proclaimed it to be the "sumsum" or soul of the tribe and declared that if it was destroyed, the Ashantis would perish en masse; if it prospered, so the tribe would become great.

It prospered.

Laden with gilded gaudery, including a pair of delicate bells that sang in tinkling tones, the stool was never allowed to touch the ground but rested on an elephant skin. And to the gold bells and original gilding other riches were added.

A facsimile of the stool had been manufactured by a blasphemous competitor chief, and this unfortunate's head was promptly lifted and attached to the stool. There it joined the grisly sconces of the once paramount king of Denkirya and his wife, taken because, without first receiving King Tutu's permission, they had demanded too much in annual tribute, to wit: the comeliest lass in Ashantiland and a plateful of gold dust. The Denkirya king's golden fetters also were added to the abundance of riches which by now nearly concealed this simple wooden object.

Interest in the stool naturally increased in direct proportion to its mounting value, and the Ashantis were forced to find places to hide it when it was not in ceremonial use at "court."

The ambitions of the Ashantis also rose, and soon, in the 1890s, with Prempeh I as king, they were conducting repeated forays against British trading posts. These depots had been operating along the coastline, trading in slaves and as clearing houses for gold transactions, as far back as 1553. Since most of the time things had been peaceful, this Ashanti misbehavior was greeted with some pique by the whites.

In 1896 Sir Francis Scott marched on Kumasi, seized and exiled King Prempeh I and conducted an extensive search for the sacred relic. He never found it. Three years later, Sir Frederick Hodgson, Gold Coast governor, took a detachment of soldiers and followed a dissident Ashanti deep into the bush north of Kumasi. This mercenary guide had promised to show them where the stool was hidden but lost his nerve short of the mark and slipped away into the night.

Hodgson was convinced that if he could locate the stool, Her Majesty's government, and Sir Francis Hodgson, would be somewhat richer, and he would possess the embodiment of the "sumsum" of the Ashantis. Once he had it, he had only to park his ample backside on it to effectively control its owners.

The suggestion Sir Francis might actually sit on the stool threw the tribesmen into a fury. Traditionally the stool never was sat upon but held a preferred place at tribal "indabas" next to the chief, who might, if he wished, rest his arm upon it. But no more.

In the joust that inevitably followed, Britain lost 1,007 men, mostly Hausa tribal levies, with nine officers dead and forty-five wounded. Ashanti losses are not known, but they must have been considerable. If nothing else, the war was a measure of Ashanti indignation and British determination to retain control of the interior.

In 1920 a tribal quarrel about land ownership grew so bloody that the British governor of the time intervened. Fearing another attempt to steal the stool, its keepers moved it from the court at Kumasi and concealed it so well they couldn't find it again.

Road builders subsequently ran across the wooden box in which it was stored, but, before they could break it open, they were talked out of it by one Yankirya. He convinced them it might be a smallpox fetish that could be dangerous to their health and took it home with him. In time he inveigled a onetime "stool carrier" and friend of his into opening the crate, promising the man a share of the loot. One of the golden balls, with which the stool was literally festooned by now, was melted down and sold. Denkirya's gold fetters were pawned for the equivalent of five dollars, and other items went for similar prices.

When word leaked out about desecration of the stool, a new Ashanti war threatened and was only averted when Yankirya, in company with a trio identified as Danso, Seniagya, and Yogo, was hastily put on trial. No kangaroo court, the proceedings took some weeks, and the judges deliberating were drawn from numerous religious denominations—animist, Christian and Moslem.

They found three of the eight persons finally placed on trial to be guilty of "debasing the name and fame of Ashanti, much to the annoyance and provocation of all people, young and old, thereby giving occasion to disturbances and bloodshed, . . ." Sentence was to be death, commuted to banishment, which was essentially the same thing in those days, since once beyond their own tribal boundaries the thieves were fair game.

Of the eight accused of buying the relics, five were acquitted and three were ordered to "swear fetish," and each paid a fine of seventy pounds sterling, one live sheep, and two bottles of gin.

To "swear fetish" was a ceremony using two brass bells held against the mouth of the accused, who asked the "fetish" to strike him dead if he lied. He was then required to reply to an accusation, in this instance: did he possess any more of the treasure beyond those pieces he'd admitted to? They all passed the test.

Following this celebrated case, the stool, or what was left of it, was returned to the royal family in Kumasi. The British, accepting that its significance was intrinsic rather than having some relationship to a symbolic throne, agreed to let it remain there as totem of the Ashanti.

When I arrived in Kumasi, neither British civil servants on the king's staff nor his African bureaucrats would say where the stool was or even admit it existed. It was obvious I would be forced to gain an audience with the king himself, an achievement tantamount to walking on water. Yet, luck was with me.

At the Grand Hotel, which is overstating it, I had met Dr. R. E. G. Armattoe, Gold Coast–born and a medical man and anthropologist of accomplishments, including lecturing at universities in, he said, Hamburg, Lille, Paris, London, Chicago, and at Temple, Cornell and Johns Hopkins, all of which was name-dropping in earnest. No matter. His success had mellowed him, and he was sympathetic to my problems, promising to help.

Within twenty-four hours, dressed in my "ice-cream suit," I was sitting on the veranda of the king's "palace" with Armattoe and an edgy, disapproving British official, awaiting His Majesty's arrival.

The "palace," I read from notes I took at the time, was "a large English-style stone-and-stucco bungalow, whitewashed and surrounded by magnificent gardens; there is a tennis court on which the forty-nine–year–old king plays 'very badly,' according to Armattoe; where we sat, the furnishings were reed mats and wicker chairs and sidetables and a calico-covered bench swing suspended from hooks in the ceiling, all very summertime suburban and 'middle class.' "

When he made his entrance, bounding up the steps from the garden,

King Osai Agyemon Prempeh II, Ruler of all the Ashantis, sported a cream-colored cotton spencer or singlet, buttoned up to the chin, under a flowing, pin-striped black robe. He was short, five feet six inches, I'd guess, slender but with big bones, large hands but soft. On his feet were simple leather sandals; his head was bare, his hair tight-cropped. (The "Afro," symbol of roots in the African continent was invented a decade later in the United States.) He had a long, bloodhound-like dark-chocolate face.

He shook hands formally all around before settling with regal deliberation into a large, high-backed basketwork chair. He was thoroughly charming in a quiet, worldly way; smoked Senior Service cigarettes; drank a small whiskey water served him by an African servant in whites; and chatted easily in a deep, booming voice.

He slyly dodged my query about the Golden Stool by announcing he had spent three years writing a history of the Ashantis, to be finished ere long, and coyly suggested I buy one. Without pausing he countered with: "Why does your country buy all my gold and immediately put it back in the ground in Kentucky?"

"One day," he went on, "the atom bomb will destroy this civilization, and the new people who come will have a ready-made gold mine."

He well knew the answer to his own question, for the king was not naive in things financial. He was rich beyond the dreams of avarice, to coin a phrase; income from timberland, diamond mines, gold caches, added to cash perquisites from the British Crown and tribute traditionally levied on his subjects fattened an already healthy royal exchequer at a rate of some $600,000 annually and on which, I was told, he focused a miser's beady eye.

Apparently a hapless Scot once had tried to win a generous gold-mining concession by deprecating the value of the holding. The Asantehene, suspicious, slipped out to the spot on a weekend when Jock was away and collected samples. Finding the ore plentiful, he multiplied demands for a security deposit and royalties by ten times. The applicant couldn't meet the terms, and the king moved in.

Out on the grounds surrounding the veranda where we sat, the "palace" guard in red-and-green uniform and armed with polished if ancient Enfield rifles, stood completely at ease. Gardeners who passed the veranda faced the monarch and dropped to the ground face down, crabbing sideways until reaching some presumably specified distance away before rising again.

On a walk through the "palace," richly ornamented in the Victorian manner with brocaded purple and scarlet velvets, gold and ivory ornaments, the king, in clipped English, talked of the past glories of the

Ashantis, the riches in gold and jewelry won in battle, the heads of rival chieftains taken and displayed on poles at his "field HQ." Padding quietly through one heavily carpeted room, he pointed to a photograph of the Golden Stool, nearly invisible under a plethora of geegaws including two gilded skulls suspended on either side by golden chains.

The Asantehene had been presented, in frock coat and topper, to King Edward VII at Buckingham Palace (and had a photograph that stood near the Golden Stool picture to prove it); had been courted on the Continent at the spas and tinseled hangouts of the mighty; at home his people prostrated themselves in the dust as he passed. Yet, Armattoe told me later, he seemed to accept this adulation and his exalted role for the transient thing it was. In the agitation in his country for "self-government" and in the "democracy" that might follow, there was no room for a king whose showerbath floor was inlaid with the skulls of his enemies. He seemed to understand this, but, as Chirupula did, he found it easier to pretend that, however precarious his venerable status, it might outlast him as an institution.

In 1954, his country in political turmoil, he would drop his pretense long enough to support a National Liberation Movement, a conservative Ashanti faction opposed to the policies of Nkrumah's left-leaning Gold Coast Convention People's Party. The movement was short-lived. The extremists ultimately were victors, and Prempeh retired. He is a long time dead now, gone to what can only have been a second-rate reward after all those earthly honorariums. This is proof, if it were needed, that for some the past is the best there ever will be and, once gone, is really buried.

There were, of course, many more thousands, black and white, who preferred to pretend, as the Asantehene did, that the upheavals of the nineteen-fifties and -sixties were aberrations and that the old normalcy would return when sanity did.

Less numerous but virulent because moved by a special desperation were those, almost exclusively whites, who openly fought back, who reacted to the threat of black ascendancy with bitterness. I'd met a great many, but my first, and the most resentful, I'd encountered in Senegal.

The city of Dakar, at the point where the continent bulges outward into the South Atlantic and the region's capital, was, in the winter of 1949, in a state of near-total administrative disarray. The angrily departing French hadn't yet ripped the phones off the walls. That was a decade away. But the place was a shambles.

With the mostly white pre–World War Two population of 5,000 swelled to 20,000 and added to an influx of 16,000 natives, Arab and black, crammed into stinking "bidonvilles"—literally "tin-can villages"—the town's community services were noticeably overtaxed.

At the Air Hotel, owned by Pan Am, a two-night stay had been set as a limit to provide a turnover, making space for new arrivals. As a mysterious favor I hadn't earned and never returned, I was accommodated for a week. This kept me off the streets, which was just as well. Considering the streets.

Many African cities have long treated sanitation as a Western whim. In Dakar at least it was accepted as a problem requiring attention, albeit in a picturesque manner: the indigenous vultures were the town's garbage detail.

Like tatty gargoyles these huge fowl hunched in ranks along roof ridges and periodically swooped into action to snatch up the newest revolting tidbit. Walking the pavements was risky. The great birds dive-bombed into the narrow avenues, huge wings beating up clouds of choking dust from the grimy cobbles. More than once I was stopped dead in my tracks as one of these airborne trolls slammed into the sidewalk at my feet and then pirouetted away in a whirling, feathery stench.

Perhaps it was the debilitating effect of this decay that ignited the smoldering ill will of one Jacques Ceuesnon on an evening at the Marie Louise bar across from the Air Hotel.

Ceuesnon was a French surveyor forced by circumstances to work in the barbaric climes outside the confines of Paris, the abode of the blest and, of course, beyond which all is limbo. And for Ceuesnon the worst of this was Africa. Having spent his last two months on a job inland at Bamako ("city of the crocodiles") after a year on the continent, his meager store of charity had run out.

I was a godsend for Jacques, a convenient whipping boy taking the lashes he'd have preferred to rain on the personnel of the U.S. Department of State. By Jacques's lights, even allowing for the usefulness of Marshall aid to postwar France, America's foreign policy was based entirely on ignorance, arrogance and a mindless stewardship by a witless staff at all levels, in Washington and overseas. I didn't know it then, but at least in foreign fields I was to find his assessment pretty accurate.

From Algiers to Durban in South Africa, there were a score of American embassies and consulates and the offices of honorary consuls. In my trip during the winter of 1949 and 1950, covering some 7,000 miles, I visited a dozen of them. I found three in which the staff understood their appointed task, liked doing it, and were courteous and helpful to fellow countrymen in need. These were the consulates in Rabat, Dakar, and Durban. In between, as far as American representation went, it was a vast wasteland. After several fruitless sessions at these offices, I took to going to the British or the French when I needed an intelligent briefing. One example may serve to indicate why.

In the Congo, beginning to throb with racial, tribal, and international political problems, the United States had filled a sensitive post in the center of the country with a Georgian who made no bones about his contempt for "the nigras." His intelligence-gathering duties were understandably unrewarding, his value to the State Department nil.

None of this knowledge, to be so painfully acquired, was mine, as, in Dakar, I submitted to repeated bludgeoning by Jacques. I would have cut short this dubious association forthwith if I hadn't already grown accustomed to being mauled. Clawing Americans as idiots or gangsters was, and probably still is, a fairly widespread overseas parlor game.

What's more, Jacques was generally informative and good company when he wasn't riding one of his meaner hobby horses. One of these I did, however, find it hard to manage: his hatred for the black man "en-principe" as a "bête farouche" a "parasite and scavenger." On this subject his rages were unnerving. When encountering anyone espousing a "native" cause or when confronted by a black Jacques considered had failed to "keep his place," he lost all control.

That night at the Marie Louise two unfortunate Senegalese were whipped off their bar stools and frog-walked out the entrance by Ceuesnon, muttering grimly, and two others left quickly when he burst back through the entrance. The barman, a native Parisian who hated Dakar, disappeared into the rear ostensibly to replenish beer kegs and left Jacques to run amok unhampered. For a medium-sized, middle-aged Frenchman he produced a prodigious furor.

At a nearby village the next day, as we made a vain attempt to dampen intestinal fires lit the night before, a native vendor made the mistake of laying out his leather wares on the pavement near our sidewalk cafe table.

Shouting epithets and close to frothing at the mouth, Jacques shot to his feet and sent the merchant flying, his armful of quite handsome goods scattered into the street. Before this outburst, he'd sat staring vacantly at the old man, tensely waiting until he'd completed his display. This premeditation made the attack, when it came, that much more vicious. And not content with knocking the trader down, Jacques set about kicking at the pavement exhibit until there wasn't an article within thirty feet of where we sat.

The old man silently collected his merchandise and went away without a word, his loathing for us almost an aura around his bent form as he moved off. A group of desert men in robes and kafiahs gathered in the shade of the cafe building suddenly were deathly still and eyed us balefully, as, at my urging, we got up and left.

Jacques drove us back to the Air Hotel, and, as I got out, he leaned out the window and looked at me.

"You, my friend, find me hateful to my fellow-creatures, do you not." It wasn't a question. "If you think I'm hard on them," he went on, "study how they will treat each other. One way to study that is to ask about 'L'Isle Sinistre,' " he grimaced. "Out in Dakar harbor, d'accord. My ancestors were there, but so were theirs," and he slammed the old Citroen into gear and screeched off sending up a cloud of vultures.

I never saw Jacques again. Which was extraordinary.

In Africa in those days, a farewell was invariably prelude to another meeting, somewhere. Salesmen met in Casablanca were seen again in Kano, Nigeria; a hotelier known in Lagos would be throwing his arms around you at midnight outside a pub in Cyprus, and a policeman befriended in Accra might reach across in front of you, all unexpected, to pay for your drink in "The Rose Revived" near London. But Jacques I never saw again. He simply vanished, taking his sour spleen and explosive bias with him.

I did take his parting advice, and wherever he is now he is to know that I'm grateful for it. The lesson the Sinister Isle had for me was rather different from the one it had for him. But it was worth the trip.

CHAPTER XXII

Slave Pits and Palaces

Notes I took about L'Isle Sinistre at the time state: "The Isle de Gorée, an island just off Dakar Harbor, was once a Portuguese slave-running depot and heavily armed fort. Scattered everywhere are ancient cannon, some half-buried under the dusty paths, their muzzles angling upward; others are in heaps next to the crumbling village buildings, and more heavy guns this time are in an untidy pile near the rusting machinery once used to lift them into position and train them on a seaborne enemy.

"The island is in a sad state of neglect," the notes continue, "and although U.S. Consular people here tell me the fort at the high end of the island, in the caves well below the surface, is loaded and 'ready for bear' most of the place belies it; rather it's a kind of cemetery, a burial ground for unhappy memories of long ago, foreboding and dismal."

I studied the history of Gorée, leafing through the dusty, meager materials in the local library, visited the island several times, and wrote a story for the *Indianapolis News*. A few years later I adapted it as a radio script for my "Information Plus" program and Station WILZ's St. Petersburg, Florida, listeners. The following script was prompted by newsworthy developments in Senegal at the time, but the substance of the earlier story about Gorée remained unchanged:

> Four miles into the South Atlantic off the Senegalese port of Dakar there's an island called Gorée. It's an inhospitable, volcanic chunk, baking in the hot sun, reddish dust, scraggly undergrowth, exhausted palm trees that have given up and lean with the wind, their parched fronds rattling. At one end there's a leftover French naval base and at the other a crumbling heap that was once a castle. And a depot where slaves by the thousands were collected to be shipped to America.
>
> The first human habitation was by Phoenician traders from the

distant Levant who used it as a waystop on their West African journeys. Thus began the island's more than two thousand years of history, six hundred of it recorded. And most of it frightful.

When I rolled out there in a bum boat a few years back, only a score of natives remained. They fish or rot peacefully in the warmth, and at night they lock themselves in against the spirits that haunt this desolation.

Because it is a strategic location on the northwest corner of the continent flanking the seaways, it's been bandied back and forth among the European powers since the fourteenth century.

Preparing to exploit this historic past, the new African government of Mali has taken steps to turn it into a tourist attraction. Preliminary publicity already has drawn a few black Americans, masochists testing the horrors of their dark beginnings, but the locals don't seem very enthusiastic. A main attraction for the visitors is the island's bloody past, and the natives don't find this especially attractive.

It's also true that the French colonial masters have only left a short time ago and the sense of subjugation and second-class citizenship is palpable. What's more, back inland from Timbuctu and other centers, the trade in slaves, now a black African monopoly, continues alive and well. Major markets today are in the Near East. Commerce is brisk, as it has been for thousands of years.

On my second trip to the island, an exorbitant bribe persuaded an aged Senegalese to enter the grounds of the old castle and guide me through its decaying innards.

The baksheesh hadn't done much to suppress his fear. He shuffled ahead of me at a faltering trot down the passageways and more than once I had to call to him to slow down. Repeatedly his lantern blinked out around a turn, and I was left in the moldy blackness made more eerie by the distant booming and the shuddering of the ancient structure as it was pounded by the waves.

It was a warren of slippery, cobbled passageways, many dead-ending in the wreckage of armories and storerooms. Narrow channels connected airless dungeons, the rusted iron gratings still hanging across their openings.

One corridor, centered in this maze and larger than the others, sloped downward. As we entered this the guide stopped and motioned me past. As I groped my way down the shallow slope the darkness gave way to a greenish, underwater glow that intensified as did the thundering of the sea. Around a final turn the tunnel plunged down and into a heaving, frothy iridescence that swelled up the passage as if to engulf me to then retire on itself with obscene hissing and sucking sounds.

Through this opening, my guide told me later, when the tide was low, the living were brought from the mainland. And from this portal, on the sea side of the castle, they were herded back out to begin the long, horrifying ocean voyage to distant lands. And from this exit as well, whatever the tide, the dead were thrown to the sharks.

Back out in the sun again, out of the slimy crypts below us, the old man breathed more easily. This island, he told me, had been an entrepôt for slaves, more than eight thousand of them quartered here during the seventeen eighties.

Some lived to be sold on the stone block near where we stood. Others, he shrugged, died. Some, because they refused food; some, of disease. Others, the troublesome ones, were crushed into damp, coffin-sized stone recesses deep in the bowels of the citadel, where their screams as giant rats tore at them could still be heard as a warning to others with mutiny in mind. They were chained and left to rot, the remains dragged down that sloping corridor.

Twice the slaves on Gorée broke out and raged across the island. Overpowering black guards at feeding time, one group ran from cell to cell, releasing the others, and in a rout they poured from the dungeons. Swinging chains torn from the walls, they battered white traders and their families to death. A few of the prisoners made it back to the mainland on improvised rafts; more tried, but sharks attacked and overturned the wooden floats. Those who stayed behind were finally overpowered and shot.

"I have heard there are ghosts, spirits of the dead," I said.

"Ahhh," with a drawn-out sigh, he interrupted me, "they are here," he said. "Many of them; they come sometimes," he went on. "One, the Koba, comes always.

"On clear nights," he said, "one sees it, a black man's face, screaming without sound; it has a reddish cloud round its head."

This disembodied head floats upward from the depths of the ruined castle, he said, and hovers along the battlements, swinging and sliding through the night. Just as the dawn silvers the isle, it vanishes near the sea-level portal at the end of that blood-tainted sloping gallery.

Jacques Ceuesnon's aggressive hatreds certainly typified an antagonism widely shared, a two-way sentiment, it might be noted, its birth in the likes of the Isle Sinistre and in the conflict between alien white cultures and the centuries-old traditions of Africa. But as a gesture of real resistance, Jacques's fits of rage represented a mere petulant twitch.

Nor indeed, were the sporadic horrors of Mau Mau, of the 1973 slaughter in Burundi or the shrieking ecstasies of Nkrumah and Lumumba much more, in the long run, than agencies or consequences in the gut processes of change.

It was in the middle ground, where the revolt was shaped and the planning simmered, that true change took place. And it was here that stoic individual sacrifice matched inspiration in the struggle to shift the scene radically. Here were the genuinely talented and honestly dedicated.

One of them whose personal losses had been high and for whom the penalties had been severe, I met in Rabat, Morocco, in the autumn of 1949. My meeting with him, an Arab, was the first between an American newsman and a leader of the Moroccan independence movement, a resolute underground junta that persisted until it won freedom from French domination in 1956. This was a long seven years after our contact, yet even in October of forty-nine the movement had been a force of consequence and, for me, an important story.

Perversely, much of what I recall of this critical parley involves the near-comic melodrama that was background to it.

Neighboring Algeria, which I'd visited earlier that summer, looked and behaved like the mother country. Metropolitan France. No matter the subsurface tensions, its status as a "colonial" fief was muted, and it was a "départment" of continental France, so obviously French as to be unremarkable.

Morocco was different. It was patently an occupied land. General Alphonse Juin, tough, much-decorated veteran and protegé of the famed Marshal L. H. G. Lyautey of North African legend, had been appointed in May 1947 to replace the more tractable Erik Labonne as the protectorate's resident general and foreign minister to the sultan, Mohammed V. In effect the general was governor in all things, a hard-bitten, nononsense procurator. And it showed: domestic press censorship and rigid control of all political activity were the most apparent.

When I think back on it, the French regimes in Africa, and perhaps elsewhere no less, were paradoxes. At the same time democratic and dictatorial, they uplifted the primitive "indigènes" with massive and enduring doses of French culture and of the principles of "Liberté" and "Egalité" and could simultaneously lash out with merciless supression if their authority was tested. In French territory I always felt the presence of a brutish retribution straining to be unleashed from a taut lead.

In Morocco, France's energies since her declaration of the protectorate in 1912 had been exhausted putting down native uprisings and, when the battlefields fell silent, struggling to keep a lid on incipient revolt. This hardly contributed to a chatty French fraternization with the locals, and, with no love lost on either side, Juin had found it easy to turn the screws whenever he felt it necessary.

The nationalist response, of course, was to go underground. The French knew that's where it went and probably because keeping track of the rebels presented no problems Juin's regime periodically eased off on the pressure. No doubt it was during one of these relaxed periods that I was permitted to make an ass of myself playing cloak and dagger with the Istiqlal. Founded in 1937 by Allal El Fassi, a freelance "troublemaker" subsequently exiled to the southern deserts for nine years and made to disappear again immediately after he returned in 1946, the Istiqlal or Independence Party had nonetheless grown steadily as a revolutionary body.

With the help of one of the only three alert American consuls general I was to encounter on the continent, I was introduced to Ali Bargasch, a twenty-seven–year–old Moroccan described in my notes as "an ardent, intelligent, and thoughtful youth, multilingual, a reporter, and participating policymaker on the daily *Al Alam* (The Flag) and its sister weekly *Rissalat Maghreb* (Mission of Morocco)."

At the invitation of the consul, Bargasch agreed to brave the atrocious dinner fare at my Rabat lodging, appropriately named the Hotel Terminus, and in spite of this painful beginning our association was to develop, for me anyway, into a thoroughly fruitful one.

Among many favors he promised me that evening over our leather mutton was to arrange what he said would be an unusual interview with Ahmed Balafredj, one of the Istiqlal's "executive" committee. This operation would be pretty sneaky, he implied, since the Istiqlal was out of favor with the authorities and any contact with foreigners, especially newsmen, would be frowned on by the French.

As a result we were to employ some highly theatrical shenanigans, tactics I assumed at the time were nonetheless necessary and normal under the circumstances.

By prearrangement Bargasch in his battered old Peugot met me several blocks from the Terminus. We drove sanely enough through a surrounding crush of milling humanity but once in the clear screeched about Rabat in all directions at a road race pace that I suspected was designed to shake any following police. After ten minutes wordlessly wrestling with the wheel, Bargasch, glancing nervously over his shoulder, lurched to a halt in front of an impressively carved teakwood doorway in what was obviously a posh Arab quarter. He leaned across in front of me, opened the door, and whispered me out.

"Wait until they come for you," he hissed, slammed the door, and roared off in a cloud of burning oil and rubber.

The old Peugot gone, the narrow, cobbled street was suddenly quiet and very empty. During the half-hour I waited, trying to act as if lounging about in a deserted back street was perfectly normal for me, not a soul appeared.

When they did, it was in a black Citroen sedan that jammed to a halt, scooped me up, and rocketed off in a close imitation of my earlier mad ride.

Just as I was beginning to weary of being thrown about in the back, we stopped, and my two escorts ushered me through a magnificent doorway from the dingy street into a twentieth-century Eden.

A fountain misted a silvery spray above a pond of lilies and banks of multicolored flowers, and the air was cool and sweet. Pebbled paths led through the greenery that carpeted the garden, and the rest of the world was shut out by high, whitewashed walls.

I was taken through this paradise and into a rotunda, high-domed and airy, the ribbed ceiling an explosion of color above a cornice of deep-blue mosaic. The floor was polished marble across which oriental rugs were scattered and the sole items of furniture were the numerous embossed bronze trays resting on olive-wood stands.

All this was awesome enough. Add to it the assembly of bearded, white-robed elders, crosslegged on cushions around the room and sternly eyeing me in silence, and it was like appearing for final judgment before a conclave of saints.

In the center of this council and facing me, however, sat the man I'd come to talk to. He was short and square of build and wore his hair in a scraggly crew cut, and his bland, faintly welcoming expression and disreputably rumpled gray suit should have put me at ease. And this relaxed demeanor certainly helped. But not much.

I was aware I had been granted this opportunity as a special concession. I had to make the most of it. This wouldn't be easy in my "plume-de-ma-tante" French. I was fluent enough to handle most situations if I could fill in the technical jargon or handle fine distinctions of meaning with the help of a standby interpreter. Now, however, Bargasch having deserted me on that back street, I stood alone.

The import of the story to me, and to the Istiqlal for whom this was a chance to promote American interest in its cause, is revealed in a story I wrote at the time:

> The two American Jeeps careening through the crowded streets of Rabat, French Morocco's administrative capital, raced against

time and an ill omen for the country's eight and a half million Moslems.

On the rear seats, writhing weakly in the grip of blood-soaked attendants, two sheep, throats slashed in the New Year ceremonial "Sacrifice of the Ram," were being rushed to the palace of the Grand Quadi for final rites.

According to custom, if the sheep were pronounced still living by the Quadi, secular head of the faith, the coming year had Allah's blessing; if dead, misfortune lay ahead.

Fortunately, the Jeeps, which in 1947 had replaced a foam-flecked horse and rider, got them to the Quadi in time; the faithful were assured of good things to come for the year 1369 on the Moslem calendar.

Unimpressed by the good tidings, however, were leaders of Morocco's Independence Party, "Istiqlal," in its thirtieth year of opposition to France's occupation of the country.

For although North African nationalist enthusiasm had picked up since the end of World War Two, in Morocco, the French had responded by tightening their hold on this rich protectorate.

To Morocco's nationalists, this means mounting unrest. Only cool heads can forestall violence.

Quietly providing this guidance as secretary-general of Istiqlal is a dumpy little man of forty whose schoolmasterish demeanor conceals shrewdness and experience.

Scion of wealthy Spanish Moors who fled Spain in the late sixteenth century, Ahmed Balafredj, no paupered rabble rouser, lives in luxury in Rabat's Arab Quarter. For him it hasn't always been comfortable.

Active in the Independence movement since 1932, he was deported by the French in 1936. From that time until the war, he wandered in exile in France, Switzerland, and Spain. After the 1942 Allied landing in Oran, he was granted leave to return.

Reactivating Istiqlal in opposition to French policies, he was packed off again in 1944, this time to Corsica. Two years later, under Erik Labonne's lenient "cooperation" policy, he was allowed to return and he plunged straight back into Istiqlal affairs.

Labonne left him alone and General Juin hasn't yet thrown him out again.

This then was the leader, flanked by lordly advisers, I had been spirited down back streets to quiz on the story of his country's fight for independence. And I'd have to ask him some embarrassing questions, such as: "Is the Istiqlal backed in any way by the Communists?" (it wasn't) and phrase them in such a way that they wouldn't put his back up or insult the sheiks assembled.

Without rising but with a reassuring smile, Balafredj motioned me to a free cushion downstage center, and I sank into it with as much grace as such a squat permits, which isn't much. I was also painfully aware that my wrinkled khaki safari suit and worn hobnailed boots were not much of a match for embroidered robes, jewelled kafiahs and intricately hand-tooled calfskin slippers. Altogether it was a poor start. Nonetheless I accepted that I was stuck with my shortcomings and got on with it. My dress may have been vulgar and my French clumsy, but, thanks to the patience of members of the committee and their wish to have the story told, it worked.

Sadly for Balafredj, a warm and genteel personality determined and courageous, the party he'd guided so long was to falter and lose its grip even as it reached its goals.

Independence was achieved in March 1956, and within three years Istiqlal broke apart, divided into conservative and radical wings. The new king, Hassan II, easily manipulated the fractured opposition.

Yet, it was Balafredj who had wrested a plausible independence from the French. It was Istiqlal that returned to the Moroccans and to their monarchy the freedom it would use with considerable skill in a North Africa that was a dangerous place in the years to follow.

CHAPTER XXIII

Politicians as "Messiahs"

Over the great sweep of Africa south of Morocco and other lands along the rim of the Mediterranean, revolutionary black politicians sprang up during the fifties and sixties like toadstools after a spring rain. And just as spontaneously collapsed.

The bulk of them were corrupt or remained captive of tribal practices which by Western judgments closely resembled bribery and extortion. Many who escaped these eccentricities were too untutored to recognize the handles of power or know how to manipulate them if they did.

Not a few of them were mad.

And some of them made it to the peaks of power.

Usually those who did managed it in their own peculiar African way. Often this was unfathomable or distasteful to the departing Western ex-colonials. Nonetheless, some of the new leaders made it work, sometimes for as much as a decade or more, no mean accomplishment.

I met several of these leaders, two of whom were standouts: one, because he rocketed spectacularly to the pinnacle and then failed for all the usual African reasons; the other, who snarled and clawed his way to prominence with no less determination and stayed there.

The first of these was Kwame Nkrumah of the Gold Coast/Ghana; the second, Dr. Hastings Kumuzu Banda of Nyasaland/Malawi.

Writing about the Gold Coast turmoil of the late forties and the country's expectable disorder, I'd noted: "Among the illiterate masses where the press couldn't reach, the cry for self-government-now was raised in person by a short, slight, American-educated rabble-rouser, forty-year-old Kwame Nkrumah."

This curt vignette followed a half-hour meeting with him during which he came across as unfriendly, suspicious, and well-nigh monosyllabic. The session took place in a cell of a room above the *Accra Evening News*. The furnishings consisted of an iron bed beneath a tatty cocoon of mosquito netting hanging from a ceiling hook, two straight-backed wooden chairs, a deal table, and a dirty washbasin. This was a depressing beginning for the man who would, in the not too distant future, christen himself his country's "Osagyefo" meaning "Liberator" or "Messiah," and who would envision and promote by any means a United States of Africa with himself as president.

Admittedly, that January morning in 1950 when I saw him he was newly released from political detention, was awaiting a return to prison for continued agitation, and was wary and self-deprecating. This assumed humility was not characteristic. I saw him another time, and my story for the *Indianapolis News* read:

> Having been banished from Accra by the British administration, after being relieved of a Communist party card, he stayed away a year, returning with fanfare to establish the radical Convention People's Party with the number one demand "Self-Government Now."
>
> The letters "S.G." began to appear on the walls even of up-country bush villages. Nkrumah told me he has the backing of 90 percent of the country's 4 million, perhaps 15 percent of whom speak English or something like it. He claims the support of forty-two native organizations from the Trades Union Congress to the Tri-City School of Dancing.

It wasn't the support of dancing-school pupils that got him a seat in the Gold Coast Legislative Assembly in February 1951 (while he was still in jail) and propelled him to national leadership as prime minister in 1952. It was rather a keen intelligence, mountainous personal ambition, and a population ready to use him to express its "African Personality" (Nkrumah's phrase).

He became president for life of the Republic of Ghana in July, 1961 (the Gold Coast having been granted independence from Britain in 1957, the first black African country to break colonial bonds), and became an African leader of world reknown. Ghana became a one-party state, had eleven Russian K.G.B. (intelligence) agents as high-level advisers, and the "Osagyefo" himself rose to the status of "Messiah" and toyed with the idea of deification.

By 1966 he had spent his country into bankruptcy, and in that year his rule was ended by an army coup. He was on a state visit to Peking at the time, but returned to asylum in the Ivory Coast and died there of cancer in 1972.

When I had seen him in that pathetic Accra walk-up he'd been home from abroad since 1947. Within just under two decades he would aspire to be successor to monarchs of the ancient West African kingdom of Ghana (whence the name of the new state), have gin poured over his sandalled feet by adoring crowds and die in pain and disgrace in a foreign land. I suppose a nineteen-year career encompassing that range of hopes and accomplishments can properly be called "meteoric." Certainly from where I stood it was notable.

Far more enduring because pragmatic was the career of another angry man, this time from the "Switzerland of Africa," Dr. Hastings Kumuzu ("little root") Banda, of Nyasaland and Malawi. If my meetings with the mercurial Nkrumah had been random, my time with Banda was deliberate, and I was able to watch, first hand, a calculated climb to leadership.

Banda's most outstanding contribution to political Africa was to pull down the Federation of Rhodesia and Nyasaland (1953–1963). This political mechanism had been produced by whites over black objections that it would prolong white ascendancy in the region. This it certainly did, but given time it might have achieved the aims of many of its white, and black, sponsors: a multiracial partnership that worked.

To Banda and other black politicians, the Federation was anathema. For them it had to be black majority rule "Now!" In spite of acts that were outrageous and self-serving, the "little doctor" did demand admiration as a clever and distinctly gutsy man. A story I wrote in August 1962 for the *Philadelphia Bulletin* went, in part like this:

Blantyre, Nyasaland (by airmail). To white men living here the duly elected government is led by a black megalomaniac.

To the vast majority of Africans the new leadership is messianic.

Whatever the opinions, the fact of black government headed by a nationalist fanatic is real enough. For most Europeans this is chaos by another name and the man to blame is a fifty-nine–year–old long-time expatriate who, it is charged, "can't even speak the language."

To meet the man, slight and soft-spoken, is to discount the rage of criticism. To argue with him, however, is to encounter the dedication that frightens his detractors. He has been pictured as a "person of great charm" and as a "screaming, incoherent troll." He can be both.

Born a Chewa in Nyasaland's central highlands, Kumuzu Banda shared the endemic poverty plaguing what has been described as Britain's "imperial slum."

At thirteen he left the unfruitful scrub for education in South Africa, went to America with Methodist Mission help, and graduated from Wilberforce Academy, Xenia, Ohio, in 1928. He was twenty-six.

Two American friends sent him from there to Indiana University, whence he transferred to Chicago, earning a Ph.D. in political science. He went on to become a doctor, graduating from Meharry Medical College, Nashville, Tennessee, and British qualifications came to him with licentiates in medicine and surgery at Edinburgh and Glasgow. He practiced in London and Ghana four years, and, in July, 1958, after forty-seven years away from his native land, the last publicly and bitterly attacking the Federation, he returned, by local politicos' invitation, to lead Nyasaland's rebellion against it.

Violence broke out; he was jailed in Bulawayo, Southern Rhodesia, and a year later was back in Nyasaland, leading what was called the Malawi Congress Party, named, as Ghana had been ,for an obscure African empire defunct, in this instance, since the fifteen hundreds. The party organization was rich and disciplined and on August 15, 1961, was victor at the polls with twenty-three of the twenty-eight seats in the legislature.

Three years later Nyasaland was granted independence as the state of Malawi with Dr. Hastings (a name he took from a favorite American teacher) K. Banda as Premier. In 1966 it became a republic and one-party state with "Kumuzu" as lifetime president.

This was no "jumped-up abortionist," as white detractors charged, nor a greedy megalomaniac, but a leader whose goals were clear, a practical man who could publicly pillory the "hypocrite white regimes" of Southern Rhodesia and South Africa but, because his poverty-stricken country needed their trade and expertise, could quietly deal with them freely at all levels, political and economic.

I made several trips to Nyasaland (and Malawi) in the sixties and early seventies. Travel across the Mocambique pedicle jutting up into federal territory between Southern Rhodesia and Nyasaland was most safely done by Land Rover or in my Jeep "Wagoneer," a four-wheel–drive station wagon my family* christened "the Jolly Green Giant." The roads in Portuguese Africa† were unrelievedly dreadful

---

*More about them in the right place.
†Mocambique; black independence in April 1975.

during my nearly twenty years of wandering the continent and the ferries or "ponts" that shuttled traffic across the rivers, in this instance the boisterous Zambesi, were frighteningly ad hoc contraptions. Most of them were pulled across by gangs hauling on huge hausers. This one crossing the Zambesi at Tete, a decayed trading post dating back 400 years, was motor-driven but guided by a cable stretched the width of the flood. Not infrequently it broke, and the fully loaded ferry whirled downstream, usually to come a cropper on one of innumerable sandbanks. Invariably this routine excitement was greeted with delight by the locals and screaming rage among ferry passengers for whom the delay could be crucial.

It rarely dumped anyone in the drink. What it could do was delay arrival at the Nyasaland border post until after it had closed for the night. Until a delightful, small inn was built on the escarpment en route to Chikwawa and the boundary, this was viewed as a disaster. Indeed, a night in the bush was so daunting that ferry travelers running late simply threw away the day and stayed in Tete for the night. This may have been much like sleeping in a combination bus station men's room and evacuation hospital, but it was still some improvement over a freezing night, with insects, on the border.

Once into British Nyasaland, however, there was an improvement in the road surface and Ryall's Hotel in Blantyre was a comfortable landfall for those days.

In August, 1961, at a time when I was working and living in Southern Rhodesia, I safely made it across the pont at Tete to a room at Ryall's and arranged for my first interview with Dr. Banda. He was then out of jail and effectively "chief minister" under the protectorate's governor, Sir Glyn Jones, and was living and working in a Blantyre suburban bungalow dubbed the "presidential palace," in anticipation of better things to come. For me the place was reminiscent of King Prempeh's house way off on the other side of Africa.

I was ushered through iron gates by a red-shirted guard and passed over to a houseman in white duck, who courteously settled me at one end of a glass-enclosed veranda. Furnishings were standard middle class, stolid discomfort, dark wood and petit point samplers bearing homilies like "Home is where the heart is."

In one corner of the room and grimacing evilly was what appeared to be a long, thin, speckled pig. Only the tail and a mouthful of large sharp teeth suggested otherwise. Whatever it was it was certainly an example of whimsical taxidermy, and I could hardly take my eyes off it. When the doctor entered the room, he caught a glimpse of my puzzled expression and laughed.

"Confusing, isn't it?" he gave me a soft velvety hand. "It's supposed to be a leopard. I get a lot of these things," he said, adding, "this one may be awkward looking, but at least it doesn't smell bad during the hot weather, as some things do," and he made a face.

Not much over five feet tall, in dark suit and tie, his broad, flat-nosed visage softened by smiling wrinkles, he opened the interview by talking easily about America.

"Negroes are very much second-class citizens in the States; at least they were forty years ago," he said.

"But it was odd," he paused, "I was just as black as they were, perhaps blacker, but I was from Africa, and that made me different, more acceptable, somehow. I went to white homes, many that were closed to my black American colleagues. I was a curiosity, I suppose," and he laughed lightly.

On the subject of the breakup of the "stupid federation" he found little to laugh at, except perhaps the fact that when it was formed in 1953 Nyasaland had been included as a member state only because Great Britain insisted on it.

"Our whites wanted in, of course," he said, "but our majority blacks didn't. But what's really ridiculous," he went on, "is that the white leaders in the Rhodesias didn't want us in either. We were forced down their throats. And now it's we who are going to pull the whole thing apart."

Although he made his points earnestly enough, a conversational quality began to creep into the interview. Soon I'd relaxed enough to ignore the distracting "leopard" and play devil's advocate.

Surely, I insisted, he must know that there were many white Rhodesians, targets of his sharpest invective, who sincerely supported a genuine partnership between the races and advancement of the African. Wasn't he undermining this hopefulness, so important to race relations everywhere, not just in Africa?

He listened, smiling ruefully, for a while and then broke in.

"You are an idealist," he said. "Of course there are good whites who mean well, but the present system maintains them, gives them security and ensures their superior standing. Take that away," and his smile was gone, "and they will not be so charitable."

He rose abruptly, threw an arm around my shoulders as we walked toward the door. He thanked me warmly, invited me back and suggested that I should attend an open-air meeting on a hill outside Blantyre, where he would address "my people" that afternoon.

The friendliness stopped at the entrance to the "palace." At the gate another red-shirted guard was surly, and the cabdriver, who'd waited for me, truculently demanded, "Who say you can see Kumuzu?" And the atmosphere worsened as the day progressed.

On the outskirts of the town, at the top of a rolling meadow, Banda's minions had erected a speakers' stand. Resting on bamboo stilts, the platform was roofed with leaves against the blazing sun and precarious though it seemed, it managed to hold the doctor and perhaps half a dozen others, including me. My getting a spot center stage hadn't been easy.

Red-shirted squads patrolled the grounds, where several thousand awaited "Kumuzu's" speech and a solid phalanx of Banda's personal bodyguard, the Malawi Youth League, encircled the makeshift dais in a brutish protective ring.

Strung round with tape recorder and camera equipment and pretending authority my khaki costume and dirty boots hardly supported, I barged through the red ranks and hastily climbed the improvised stair to the rostrum. After a moment's hesitation, several of the Red Shirts scrambled after me, and one, muttering menacingly, had seized my arm when Banda arrived and waved him off. The bluff had worked.

For the next half-hour of Banda's two-hour performance, most of it damning "the white man," I hovered near him in the shadows, recording his words and taking pictures. Some of them later appeared in the *Indianapolis News* and the *Philadelphia Bulletin*, so my risks weren't wasted. When I left the security of the platform, however, the Youth League decided to get its own back.

I was surrounded and jostled as I made my way down the hill to the gravel road where I'd left my car. Repeatedly they shouted "Go home, *stupid* white man" (the doctor's favorite buzz word) and emphasized it with a shove or two. As I opened the car door to place my equipment inside, one of them snatched at my camera.

Until then I'd been feigning friendliness and answering the hostility with cheerful agreement on all points, including how wicked the white man was. I was aware a mob like this one could turn murderous instantaneously. My concern was to get into the car as quickly as possible and take off. Now, the tug of war with the camera and the gang forming ominously around the vehicle seemed to have made that fear valid. And then events took the kind of turn that more than once over the years salvaged my dignity, to say nothing of my neck.

"Hello! Master! Master Akson!"

Walking toward the car and surrounded by what turned out to be his "family" was a barrel of a man, his great pockmarked black face beaming in joyful greeting. N'dege, a Nyasalander who worked for me on my small Rhodesian farm, had taken his annual leave a month earlier to visit his ancestral kraal near Blantyre. That he now loomed out of the pall of dust at just the right moment, and hundreds of miles from where I had last seen him, may have been a sort of poetic return of favor.

A year earlier, I had saved his life by getting him to a hospital when, massively stung by a swarm of bees, he was strangling. Since then we'd exchanged an affection and respect which, for black and white in Africa was as close as may be. Certainly it was close enough that afternoon.

Ignoring the Youth League thugs, N'dege pushed through their ranks, bowing formally to me and tapping his palms together in traditional salutation, still smiling broadly. I knew no Chinyanja, so what he and his "family" said to Dr. Banda's "police" I'd never know. Whatever it was, it broke things up smartly. They moved away en masse, and I loaded N'dege and his "family" (which can mean simply members of the same tribal kraal) into the station wagon for a trip back to their village.

On the way he apologized for the Youth League and told me all Nyasaland was a bad place right now for whites, especially from Southern Rhodesia. When I dropped him off at his village he cautioned me to be careful and wished me a warm farewell, adding he'd be "home" and back to work in another four weeks.

I pushed on that night to the town of Lilongwe, later to rise out of the wilderness like a miniature Brazilia, built with South African money as an administrative headquarters when the new black bureaucracy moved from the Blantyre area. Lilongwe was Banda's Chewa tribal home, and the new capital was a monument to "Kumuzu." Located as it was, off in the barren western reaches of the country, it had little other reason for being.

I drove through the night over bush tracks, faintly alarmed by N'dege's warning and determined to make Lilongwe without stopping. Unfortunately, my fuel ran too low for safety, and I was forced to pull up to a black village store after dark. An attendant silently hand-cranked the old Shell "petrol" pump, and I went inside to pay and have a beer. Half a dozen ragged Africans lounged along the counter, playing cards and drinking the thick native brew from cardboard cartons. The room was blue with smoke.

I was sucking in the warm, frothy drink when one of them in more than passable English asked me where I was from. Without thinking I told him and then went chill all over awaiting his reaction. If N'dege'd been right, I could be in trouble.

"Ahhhhh," a long, drawn-out very African sound that can mean anything. The others had slipped off their stools and were standing around me, obviously more curious than menacing.

"You know Boss Pratt?" the one who'd spoken to me asked. When I said yes, he was my neighbor, the man's face lit up, and he turned and chattered to his friends. There was much high-pitched squealing laughter and slapping of thighs, and then he turned back to me.

"Master, I work for Boss Pratt, oh plennnty," he dragged out the word, "maybe three years."

Nyasaland's principal source of foreign exchange came from the country's export of labor to the mines of South Africa and the farms and homes in Rhodesia. N'dege was one of more than 100,000 that year, and my newfound acquaintance, who had pulled his stool up close to mine, was another.

An hour and several rounds of beer later I'd managed to bring him up to date on his erstwhile southern Rhodesia "home" and his friends there, black and white. When I pulled away for Lilongwe, they came outside, all of them, to wish me luck and wave goodbye.

So much for Nyasa hatred of whites.

Yet, what N'dege had said was basically true. The hatreds Banda had stirred up he later had to keep a lid on, suppressing an African urge to get even for what many felt had been years of white exploitation. The new president was thus able to keep Malawi a tourist attraction for whites and a safe place for them to do business. But not far beneath the surface the resentments seethed, ready to burst through at any time.

A year passed following the meeting with Dr. Banda and the trouble on the hill outside Blantyre. And then I hit on a story that showed how the bitterness might boil through the restraint. The piece was written for the *Philadelphia Bulletin* and was picked up by the Associated Press and fairly widely used in the States, even prompting some editorial comment. The subject was Dr. Albert Schweitzer, but the malice reported was aimed at all whites. In part it went like this:

Marandellas, Southern Rhodesia (by airmail). Dr. Albert Schweitzer, long the preeminent purveyor of good works among the primitives at Lambaréné in French Equatorial Africa, is being attacked in the land of his labors.

He is generally "despised" by the Africans to whom he has given his life. So says the *Malawi News*, Nyasaland's fever-heat nationalist newspaper and vehicle for Dr. Hastings Banda's new African-controlled government.

Of "hundreds" of Africans talked to in "several countries," the report states, "not one had a good word for Dr. Schweitzer."

What these Africans did have, the *News* states, was "unvarnished contempt" for the doctor. He is not considered a genius and humanitarian, so the report insists, but "an inept old man" and a "sloven incompetent crackpot."

This is laying about among the idols with a vengeance.

It is obviously popular stuff in a land where discrediting the symbols of "white colonialism" is basic public relations. But to dismiss it as merely a cheap journalistic tilt at the great for political points in an anti-white community is to dodge the issues it raises.

For an impatient and self-conscious new Africa, Schweitzer represents both "white superiority" and a disruptive influence that has highlighted Africa's backwardness and converted it to degradation.

Few bush Africans know of his contributions to music or of his scientific and philosophic expertise and wisdom. They do know that while he has mended broken limbs, has treated untold thousands for such diseases as yaws, leprosy, and hookworm and has given the natives basic schooling, he has also been a stern "white" parent. He is accused of breaking up what has been termed "traditional leisure preferences" and has condemned the "grip of a savagery" that has kept the African, in Schweitzer's words, "pitiable creatures."

A statement attributed to him that Africa would be "beautiful without its savages" is calculated to spark screaming indignation from every nationalist who hears it. That Schweitzer's reference is to the stoneage human relics that have, largely, been his charges and not to Africans generically is purposely not read into his comment.

Here in the Federation of Rhodesia and Nyasaland, a pattern of near-hysterical charges, largely imaginary, is established nationalist practice. Banda refuses an $8 million grant for a vital water project because the money comes from a "white settler" government. Smallpox vaccination teams are stoned by tribesmen terrified by nationalist-spread rumors that the white man's medicine will make them sterile. In Northern Rhodesia, oral polio teams meet the same fate for the same reason.

To charge that this is biting the hand that has rescued them from disease, as in the case of Schweitzer, or dismiss it as the characteristic ingratitude of primitives is to misinterpret the fact. This antagonism is an essential element of African emergence.

Battering Schweitzer's image may seem no more than a frightening tantrum but it is more than that. It is symptomatic of the urge to utterly destroy the "white establishment" and the consequences be damned.

In June, 1970, almost a decade after my interview with Kumuzu and N'dege's timely intervention I returned to Nyasaland, now become black-ruled Malawi, and another set-to with the country's juvenile goon squads.

I reported it in the *Indianapolis News*:

> *Kutumbi, Malawi (by airmail)*. A confrontation with a gang of teenage toughs may be common enough these days, but in the deep of the African bush it is a special kind of trauma.
> There they were, dressed like Boy Scouts, howling around the Jeep at an improvised roadblock just outside this small village. They demanded passports and a search of the three of us, and of the heavily loaded vehicle, just like real, grown-up officials. Since long ago I had learned to guard my passport as my life, and, since my wife, Ria, was one of the passengers, I refused on all counts.
> Things turned a bit hairy when about twenty of them started chorusing assorted threats and pounding rhythmically on the fenders. One shouted that we were "dirty white spies," and another with peculiar restraint told my wife, "You white people are too cunning."
> All this suddenly struck me as essentially unconstructive, and I pushed the door open and dropped down into this pulsating mass. It may have been mock heroics, but it worked. The group fell suddenly silent, and one youth agreed to take me to his leader, a slovenly but quite pleasant youngster, laughingly ranked as "disciplinary officer." A bout with diarrhea, he explained in earthy detail, had kept him from closer supervision of his "troop."
> I produced an indignant harangue about press freedom and threatened "big trouble" on my return to the capital city, and, although not noticeably moved by these histrionics, he did agree to call off his carnivores.
> This sort of behavior among the young in Malawi was, I was assured back in Blantyre, most unusual. In the hands of Israeli instructors, military and agricultural, the former Youth League "heavies" of pre-independence days, I was told, had been hammered into units of the Malawi Pioneers. Some 2,000 of these are now in training, and 6,000 have already been returned to their villages as agricultural extension officers. They also serve, as we'd learned, in paramilitary companies, supplementing Dr. Banda's meager military establishment.
> Malawi has come a long way since its years as an "imperial slum." If it will occupy its young in the labors it takes to grow tea, tobacco, peanuts, rice, beans, corn, and cotton, all producing a potential $36 million in foreign exchange each year, it'll at least keep them off roadblocks like the one at Kutumbi.

In the eighteen years from 1957 to 1975, few of Africa's forty-five newly independent states were led by men the caliber of Balafredj and Banda. Of either the good or the bad, I met too few, although some I did confront professionally were an ample feast.

There was Balthazar Johannes Vorster, then prime minister of the Republic of South Africa, in an interview I likened to entering a duel with a rubber rapier, so handicapped was I by the old man's practiced cut and thrust. And the gentle, soft-spoken, often tearful Kenneth Kaunda, prime minister and president of Zambia, once northern Rhodesia, for whom I had great affection. Sir Seretse Khama and his red-haired English wife and new baby were refreshingly good humored, recently ensconced in their bungalow "palace" in the dusty Bamangwato capital of Serowe. And, of course, the Federation's Sir Roy Welensky, when he was still "Roy" and with whom I rode hundreds of miles on his pro-Federation campaign through the Rhodesias, a rough-and-tumble frolic during which he once threatened to knock the collective block off some hecklers. Sir Edgar Whitehead, soft-spoken English intellectual, I knew both as a neighbor in the country's eastern Vumba District and as Rhodesian prime minister.

I was present at many interviews with Rhodesia's last white prime minister, Ian Smith, and they were always unpredictable. At one of them I watched, in awe, at what the hostile overseas newsmen did to one of his basically innocent, if wildly impolitic, statements. Asked when he expected black government to take over the country (this was in 1975 at the height of the terrorist war) he snapped "never in a thousand years!" It was said without thought as an angry reply to what he felt was an antagonistic query and meant no more than an impulsive "not until Hell freezes over." Yet, added to his previous impatient rejoinder, that he wouldn't "see black government in my lifetime," this was grist for anti-Smith fulminations.

Smith was one of the most willfully misinterpreted politicians I have known, including Vorster and Botha in South Africa. I saw him purposefully misconstrued at every opportunity. I disagreed with his party's right-wing stand no less than the reporters who gleefully pounced on every malapropism and strangled phrase. But if Smith pressed his extreme white paternalism position with rather more vigor than was appropriate in Africa at the time, he did it with sincere conviction and greater flexibility than was ever credited to him.

CHAPTER XXIV

Success Story or Silly Season

Over a period of two decades I did write from the rarefied heights where politicians postured and sometimes labored, but not often. I felt my brush was a wide one and that I was producing a broad, clear picture of these exotic lands for what I liked to believe were my faithful readers. And then one of them who said she followed me "religiously" in the *Philadelphia Bulletin*, "hanging on every word for four years" said she hadn't really understood "a word" I'd written.

This was not flattering.

I did, I confess, try to educate readers, perhaps a mistake, even for a feature writer. Such pieces could get a bit ponderous. Yet, for the most part I tried to describe an "emerging" Africa by citing human examples. Mostly I wrote about those who survived an unfriendly setting and how they managed it. And about some who succeeded.

Some of those stories *had* to take.

Like this one.

In the category of "black opportunists," neither leading nor specifically following but plodding along, reaping the rewards, was one George Tawengwa. Setting the backdrop for the space this man occupied in life demands a bit of local history.

In the early sixties the Rotary Club in the small village of Marandellas, my Rhodesian home for close on nineteen years, published a costly, slick 120-page history of the town, touting its "Golden Jubilee, 1913–63." I headed the editorial committee. We put together sixty-five articles on a host of subjects, including discovering the bones of malaria-stricken New Zealand freebooters buried on the edge of town when they died on the trek to relieve Mafeking in 1900; thirty years of the Girl Guides; Ted Blackwell, the town's "ham" radio operator, who "talked" to Moscow and Chicago; "rare treasures" of the district, including pictures by van Dyck, Constable, Rembrandt, and Gainsborough, and one

Aubrey Berry's *Bellerephon Plaques*, decorative panels from a sailing ship of Nelson's fleet that fought at "The Nile" and "Trafalgar"; the boxing club; bird-watchers; and the Dolphin Club, an interracial political group, a daring concept for the times.

There was then a white population of 1,670, 10,000 Africans living in an adjacent native township, Nyameni, 15 Asians, and 2 coloreds (mixed race). The book carried an introduction by the Hon. Winston Joseph Field, C.M.G., M.B.E., Prime Minister of Southern Rhodesia.

Ten years later the Rotary Club repeated the effort, largely verbatim with, however, new figures (2,500 whites; the same 10,000 Africans—the limit accommodated in the townships—30 Asians and 10 coloreds), and its introduction consisted of a few words from the Hon. Roger Tancred Hawkins, M.P., Minister of Transport and Power, Roads and Road Traffic.

The town fathers might have done better with some pithy, if doubtless grossly ungrammatical, comment from Mr. Tawengwa, the richest man in town. But Marandellas, as the rest of Rhodesia, frightened by United States and British political pressure for what whites saw as too rapid "Africanization," had reacted by turning the clock back to the darker but more familiar days before the "partnership" experiment. Hence, recognizing the accomplishments of a black wasn't keeping the native in his place and would have sent tremors rippling through European settlements all over the country.

I'd met George Tawengwa before I decided to do a story on him. His trucks and buses hauled supplies to my farm on the Ruzawi Road six miles from town, and I knew him by reputation: he had the biggest house in Nyameni. By 1973, and the new Rotary "history," Nyameni was closing down in a mass move to Dombo Tombo, a new "location" the other side of the Rhodesia Railway lines. Tawengwa moved too, but not to Dombo Tombo with the 10,000 others. He took over the bungalow that had previously housed Nyameni's white superintendent.

George had come a long way, and I so reported to the *Tucson Daily Citizen*, among others, in this story:

> *Marandellas, Rhodesia (by airmail).* From goatherd in a poverty-stricken African reserve to millionaire company director is a reasonable improvement in status for anyone, anywhere.
>
> It is especially remarkable since the man who did it is black, and the place is Rhodesia.
>
> This southern African country is, popularly, rigid white supremacist. For it to produce a native black who could buy and sell an embarrassingly large number of whites has to be a contradiction.

Yet, in fact, it's not. Here, as in a rapidly decreasing number of other countries, success depends entirely on how much sweat is mixed with talent and opportunity.

At this moment, Rhodesia waits nervously for a settlement with Great Britain that will end the illegal international status that dates from its unilateral declaration of independence in November 1965. While it waits, there is endless behind-the-scenes maneuvering.

Yet, meanwhile, back on the farm (and at the bus company, real estate office, hotel, and liquor store) an African named George Tawengwa has been too busy to notice.

A crude estimate of his worth is $1,100,000. His first job paid him 70 cents a month.

Tawengwa is fifty-five, just under six feet, sports a bristling black moustache in as black a face, and carries some 200 pounds without noticeable effort. He speaks quickly but softly, in bad English and his native Shona, and what he says is worth listening to.

His mother died when George was three. With a younger brother he herded goats, scruffy sheep, and scruffier cattle and wandered the inhospitable, dusty bushland with his farmer father.

He worked as farm laborer for a European and as "mukokeri," a guide for a span of oxen. For this he got the 70 cents "and more hidings with the bullwhip than the animals." He was twenty-one when he was employed in his first real paying job as a carpenter's apprentice. It was no bonanza. It took him two years to save $122. But it was the beginning.

Tawengwa got married, three times; fathered nineteen children, some of whom work for him now. From three "kaffir truck" stores in the African reserve where he was born, his enterprises have grown in all directions.

The two stores were enlarged; he built a $50,000 shopping center and boarding hostel and bought a 5000-acre farm that sustains, among other things, 800 head of cattle—Sussex, Afrikander and Hereford—and $6,000 worth of breeding bulls.

Along the way he launched the "Hand-in-Hand-Cooperation Bus Service" now operating twenty large vehicles from two main centers and worth about half a million. He has opened the first three stories of what is planned as a seven-story African hotel complex worth, so far, another half-million.

Tawengwa Enterprises has a working staff of 115 employees not including white consultants and accountants.

No great shakes as conglomerates go, but not bad for a black in a "white supremacist" country.

"Perhaps," he says, "it's all just good fortune." It could, of course, be pure cussedness.

The name Tawengwa translates as "The unfavored one."

While George was busy amassing his million, other Africans loafed along or embraced the oddball fads afflicting the era, the period referred to as one of "rising expectations" (U.S. Assistant Secretary of State George Ball) buffeted by the "winds of change" (Britain's Harold MacMillan). To many of us it was simply the silly season, African brand. For example, to the *News*:

Salisbury, Southern Rhodesia (by airmail). The new Pan-African Nationalist technique of "wreck-the-economy-and-reap-the-dregs" is making itself felt in this one-time idyl.

To add to the country-wide rural unrest, where tribesmen have been burning cattle-dips (used to detick the animals and limit hoof-and-mouth disease) simply because the white man recommends them, the townsmen have organized their own peculiar protests.

First it was "no shoes," those symbols of white civilization. An estimated 12,000 in one African township went barefoot as instructed by the leaders of their African National Democratic Party.

Things got a bit out of hand when a "no skirts" edict was engineered by a rowdier element whose undiluted nationalist leanings are sometimes open to question. Some women disrobed in true, heartfelt protest. Others who wouldn't and couldn't run fast enough were forcibly assisted. In the end, as it were, it was hard to tell who was protesting what.

Or this:

Salisbury, Southern Rhodesia (by airmail). Not long ago in the country's Fort Victoria area, many of the 60,000 farmers were suddenly seized with panic if they saw a strange white man.

Reason: rumor had it that the stranger would blow a whistle and those blacks who heard it would be drawn, as if under Circe's spell, to a waiting truck. Loaded in, they would be carried away to a mysterious place and would end up as pork on the hook.

The victims of Homer's enchantress remained alive as hog on the hoof, it is true, but the similarity between the two myths suggests an educated black dissembler in the woodpile.

Or:

> *Salisbury (Ibid).* Recently Women's Brigade Members of the African United Nationalist Independence Party in Northern Rhodesia threatened that unless the British government "colonialists" granted all African nationalist demands, they would "go around naked" in the capital city of Lusaka and "stop having babies."
> Since, if the women pull off the first tactic, they may find it difficult to succeed in the second, this may well be one protest attempt hoisted by its own petard.
> But the African woman is no pushover, chattel or not. The British authorities could soon be confronted by hordes of nearly nude females supported by a rear guard of leering males. Acutely conscious of Britain's propensity for avoiding unpleasantness in Africa at whatever cost, including an assault by undressed womenfolk, I wager compromise will be reached, and the gals will not have peeled off in vain.

Nothing on the record indicates that this display of determination contributed to UNIP's ultimate victories. Yet, certainly it must be catalogued with other demonstrations of black solidarity.

At the same time as this incident I did a radio script that seemed appropriate. The subject was identified in the text as the "First Civil Rights Demonstration Worth the Name" and it went like this:

> I wonder just how many of you are aware of the libel that's gone round about Lady Godiva. You do *know* about it. I'm sure, but for the benefit of those who may be a bit short on the details, I'll expand a little.
> A short time ago some unchivalrous cad questioned her famous ride. He stated flatly that she never made it; that this business of cavorting about the English city of Coventry clad only in her birthday suit was poppycock. And, what's worse, he implied that even if it *did* happen it most likely was just absentmindedness: she was simply in a hurry one morning, he suggests, leaped on her horse and got halfway to the market square before she felt a chill—and then had no choice but to keep going, to put up a good front, as it were.
> Now, this makes a mockery of the lady's gesture, and since Godiva's ride is probably the First Civil Rights Demonstration worth the name, a rebuttal is demanded.
> There may be several versions of the ride itself, but the motive

behind this protest has long gone undisputed: she was pained by the injustice of crushing local taxes and the second-class citizenship status of those from whom it was squeezed, and she decided to do something about it.

She recognized that wandering about naked in public is a pretty foolproof method of catching one's husband's attention, and that, the story has it, is what she wanted. So she told the Earl of Mercia, her husband, that if he wouldn't lower taxes she'd go abroad with nothing on.

Something of a sport and fed up with her nagging, he told her to go ahead. He'd cut taxes if she did.

What actually happened in the streets of Coventry is variously described. Roger de Wendover in his *Chronica*, published in 1057, states this unseemly bargain stipulated she ride throught the crowded marketplace, completely starkers, as noted. And, de Wendover says, she did, at a snail's pace, accompanied by two soldiers and with only her long hair as covering.

Three hundred years later, Hidgon's *Polychronicum* takes some of the gilt off the gingerbread by insisting she made the trip before the break of day. This makes her welch on the spirit of the agreement, since few would be up and about so early, and I reject it.

Another version appears in Richard Crafton's *Chronical at Large* in the mid–fifteen hundreds. He states she arranged with the Mayor of Coventry to have its citizens remain indoors behind shuttered windows and, Crafton insists, she galloped the distance, flat out.

No one saw her, Crafton records, but a peeping tailor named Tom, who, as you know, was struck blind on the spot, pretty drastic punishment for a mere peek.

Anyway, whatever this spoilsport and others of his ilk have to say, I reckon she shamed herself for a righteous cause and won her case as, one way and another, the likes of Godiva have been doing ever since.

It's unlikely the women of Lusaka's protest committee ever heard of their eleventh-century predecessor, but no matter. In both instances the gesture seems to have worked.

Within the context of Africa's responses to the midcentury's upheaval, women measured their length upon the record by asserting their status as people. The male could have the kudos. The female reaped the wind that whirled around the tumult.

From Marandellas I commented on this for the *Philadelphia Bulletin:*

Almost the only time African women are heard from these days is in the crime statistics. Beaten up, starved or otherwise lashed into the headlines by gory circumstance.

Yet, even this may be better than it used to be, on the principle that, as George M. Cohan would have had it, it's recognition that counts.

Until recently, descriptions of the life of the African female concentrated on such items as finding one wearing a dress instead of a bramble bush. Normally women here have done little but "tote dat bale," file their front teeth to points, use mud-balls for a hairdo, plant saucers in their lower lips, and be swapped about as breeders or menial laborers. But changes are coming.

A decade ago Moslem women along some of the Mediterranean littoral seized the first vestiges of freedom. They dropped the veil; voted; became companions, socially and in business, to their husbands. To the south, the "mammy" of the then Gold Coast controlled almost all the colony's African-operated transport and black wholesale and retail trade. In South Africa's Transkei, women are no longer the family's only beast of burden.

Here in Central Africa women have emerged from limbo only lately, but they're making up for it.

One of the first institutions to be attacked by the girls, and in the urban areas especially, is that of plural wives. Polygamous marriages have not been simply a handy arrangement for lecherous males. On the contrary. They have provided a stable of workhorses, not a harem of Salomes.

Today there are recorded some 21,000 polygamous marriages in a population of about 4 million. The percentage used to be much higher. One African on a nearby farm boasts fifty brothers and sisters, those who survived of a total seventy-five. His father had eight wives.

This extravagance is falling away for two reasons. First, it's too expensive. Formerly a wife was bought for so many head of cattle, although this was not a true purchase price but a form of insurance: if she thrashed off into the underbrush with a lover, the husband could get his cows back. Today, however, a wife is "paid for" in currency, hard to come by and not subject to natural increase.

Second, it's not considered "civilized" to keep a coterie of women around the house. The white man doesn't (not in one house, anyway) and the white man still sets the example to be copied in spite of his increasing unpopularity. What's more, it's recognized that he's in power. Perhaps the African may now suspect that having fewer women to please has given the white man more time to develop his other talents.

All the men who worked for me when I homesteaded in Southern Rhodesia kept only one wife on the premises; usually the only one they had. Yet the one-wife system had its shortcomings, absence of competition for the male's attentions being the most obvious. Without fear of substitution or bettering, the sole mate often became lazy or, worse, cheeky.

We had a cook appropriately named "Dinner" who had a wife in whose large frame there resided all the latent defects of a one-wife custom. Dinner had to keep this amazon's nose to the grindstone by a method the *Philadelphia Bulletin* headlined over my story as "Simple Little System for Settling Family Spats."

Marandellas, Southern Rhodesia (by airmail). A simple system for settling disagreements between husband and wife is sometimes practiced by African families I've observed, and I think you should know about it.

After an argument has started a decent interval is permitted for preliminary noise-making in which the wife features at some length. Ultimately, however, victory nearly always goes to the male. This is sensible.

It shows a sophistication and good judgment the more "civilized" communities might emulate with profit. To have the outcome of any difference of opinion established in advance certainly simplifies the mechanics of togetherness.

Admittedly, sustaining this understanding does require an occasional muscular assist from father. Those females who may, however inadvertently, buck the system must be brought to their senses.

Subtlety may suffice, collecting large clubs and hanging them about the hut for example. The more direct approach, assorted forms of mayhem, is avoided whenever possible because of the effort involved.

Not infrequently, however, the wife of our cook can be seen streaking across the bottom of the garden hooting like a banshee, her clothing shredded out behind her. This usually is on a Saturday afternoon when there is no premium on spare time.

The cook, a nimble little powerhouse with a wavy moustache that whips in the wind, has learned he can cut her off just west of a clump of eucalyptus. There the argument, with tympanatic accompaniment, usually is settled in his favor.

Now and then this normally foolproof procedure for healing rents in connubial bliss fouls up. When it does, Dinner staggers homeward past the gum trees a battered loser but confirmed in the rightness of his techniques by the simple truism that "you can't win 'em all."

In any event the entire exercise has a sporting air about it, blood sport to be sure but a periodic event marked by challenge, excitement and good wholesome exercise. This cannot be said for the practice elsewhere.

A recent report from Lagos, Nigeria, indicates a preference for fulltime intimidation by the male, no quarter given.

An African columnist urges that insolent wives "should be beaten but not maimed." He justifies this by pointing out that "in England husbands box their wives about the head and sometimes give them an uppercut. In Java husbands use the tail of a crocodile. In Kenya husbands use hippopotamus-hide whips. In America," he reports, "husbands often use rubber canes."

For the American milquetoast husband accustomed to leaping to attention if his wife clears her throat, this bit of misinformation may tend to discredit the rest of the report, but our columnist, Antar, writing in the Lagos *Daily Telegraph*, restores his credibility by concluding on what he obviously considers a truism.

After explaining how he remonstrates with his wife by laying about with the "tail of a horse" until his arm is tired, he says, let's face it: it's necessary.

"A woman," he says, "is like a child; she must be disciplined to inject some sanity into her coconut head."

If some African women found the climb to respectability more difficult than sometimes seems fair, so did the male. He often discovered the advance into the professional ranks was so difficult he grew embittered and connived to catapult himself recklessly out of obscurity. Several of these, and not only in black Africa, thus abused my patronage.

As a newsman who could travel the globe repeatedly without once being recognized, I nonetheless somehow developed a degree of parochial fame wherever I settled for any length of time. This attracted hordes of neophytes with a yen for journalism who threw themselves at my feet, the better to snatch up whatever gems of trivia I let fall. Sadly, my success with some pupils was less than dazzling.

When I ran the news bureau in Frankfurt, Germany, for *Pathfinder*,

I accepted a measure of responsibility for a bright youngster who was eager, clever and certainly needed inculcation in the journalistic verities, not to say a few other whole truths as well.

It developed he was totally without those qualities of character differentiating decency from knavery. He stole (office supplies, money, food from the kitchen, booze, . . . anything); browbeat my hard-won news contacts in my name, demanding instant obedience; and was a thoroughgoing cad, with Nazi overtones. He was ablaze with indignatiion when I fired him and proceeded to broadcast that *I* was the Jew-baiting, Third Reich apologist and that he merely obeyed my commands.

Probably the most blatant rogue was Galahad Chisulu (not his real name, unfortunately). Indeed, I'd become so incensed by the behavior of these unprincipled ingrates that I put them together in one rotten collection as a radio script, the part about Chisulu going like this:

> When I maintained a news office in Salisbury, Rhodesia, I was subject now and then to visits by Africans in search of work: to make tea, sweep up or even learn the art itself.
>
> One of these I interviewed, Galahad Chisulu, brusquely made it known right off that he was above tea-making and wielding a broom and expected to very shortly be walking hand in hand with me through the intricacies of high-level reportage, bearding Prime Ministers and the like.
>
> Since this meant cultivating contacts who, at that time, were for the most part white and who treated nearly all blacks as if they were apprentice garbage collectors, this rousing expectation was doomed. Still, he remained optimistic and by the end of six months had mastered some of the rudiments.
>
> In his view, of course, he was Pulitzer-Prize caliber and I'm damned if he didn't take off with the weekly cash offering I gave him for expenses and set himself up as a one-man news bureau in Lusaka, capital of Zambia, Rhodesia's northern neighbor.
>
> I swallowed my annoyance and even employed him as a stringer covering activities of the new black government there. I accepted his freelance offerings and at one time requested a story about one Alice Lenshina.
>
> Alice was a religious fanatic who was then actively defying the Lusaka government from her tribal stronghold in the northeast provinces. This was to get her thousands of dead followers, briskly dispatched by heavily armed troops. It was a timely and important bit of news.
>
> All I got from Chisulu were his own opinions about a woman

he considered was a mad matriarchal miscreant, the stories totally without useful fact. I dropped him a note charging him with trying to peddle editorials and urged him to mend his ways. That ended his stringing for me from Lusaka.

Subsequently I followed his career through the wildly libelous world of African journalism but eventually lost interest in his empassioned fulminations. Then one early afternoon I was tuned in to Zambian radio and there he was.

"Take your bows, your axe, your spear," he was shouting, "and break the government of Ian Smith." (He'd made it to Prime-Minister level after all.)

"Even if blood is shed the government must be broken," he concluded.

After Rhodesia's unilateral declaration of independence, November 5, 1965, Zambia, then independent from Britain, began to beam slanderous radio fare at the black population of its southern neighbor. Chisulu had joined the "hit team" with obvious enthusiasm, mouthing bloodcurdling exhortations to "stab the whites with a kitchen knife and burn their farms," pretty strong stuff.

Here was my pupil, the product of my journalistic womb, not only biting the hand, mine, that had fed him but threatening to cut it off and stuff it down my throat.

CHAPTER XXV

Orthodoxy and Animism

Blocking true friendship with the Africans I met was my failure to learn their languages, an exercise for which I had neither the time nor the ability. This didn't prevent elementary daily communication. I knew enough for that. But unless he'd had a university education in South Africa, Britain, or America and used English almost as his native tongue, the African and I seldom sat down over a beer and exchanged ideas. There were a few with whom I did, of course, but the "man on the street," most often the subject of my stories, and I were in touch only crudely through third parties. And these interpreters were always suspect. Few could resist injecting their own views.

What's more, however readily we seemed to communicate, we are widely differing peoples, and an unbridgeable gap remained.

For example, it's difficult at best for me to accept the belief that hosts of active supernatural forces manipulate every event in our lives and can themselves be influenced by us, angered, placated, and so on. Just as it's nearly impossible for an animist to believe otherwise. As it would take more than a few generations immersed in such an alien world to convert the likes of me to such views, so exposure to my culture can hardly be expected to, ipso facto, disabuse the African of *his* convictions.

I did learn to accept that we were different and that there were, for me, unfathomable influences that exerted an iron grip on his will and behavior. Such as his dependence on the medicine man.

The only "witch doctor" I ever met was in a chance encounter in Rhodesia's native township of Harare, in Salisbury. He was dressed in a white open-neck shirt, gray flannels, and brown leather sandals. And his English was more exact in accent and grammar than my own. He so impressed me that I boned up on enough native medicine and practice to produce a few radio scripts on the subject:

> Recently the scientists have concluded that the majority of African "witch doctors" are first-rate psychiatrists with an advanced

clinical knowledge of nature's medicinal confection. And certainly they are substantially assisted in their cures by the deepseated religious convictions of their patients.

Yet, these same convictions, distorted in the context of modern life, have created problems for the "shamaan" unique in the history of his profession. For example:

In the northern Tonka tribal regions of Rhodesia along the Zambesi River escarpment, a prehistoric part of Africa, "supernatural lions" were reported at one time to have killed several hundred head of cattle and terrorized villagers for miles around. According to the reports of the headmen, the lions, not known in this riverine country, apparently materialized and faded away like wraiths in the wind leaving the mauled carcasses behind them. The suggestion it might have been a pack of hunting hyena was rejected. No spoor, no tracks at all, the headman said.

Someone, they opined, must have gone north from his country, crossed the river into the land where the lions came from and there murdered someone or stole a fetish. Vengeance for such deeds could be expected. The victims of the crime had obviously turned themselves into lions and come south, striking at the culprit's community.

The only answer, they said, had been to employ an Nganga. They'd sent for one, but, these days, there was often a long wait. Time was when there was a resident "shamaan" but no longer. He didn't even have "house-call" time from his clinic in a nearby town. His office was chock-a-block with out-patients, many of them seriously afflicted mental cases urgently requiring attention.

This rising flood of troubled souls has numerous causes. The most widely held explanation is that the African's sudden emergence from the primitive state has caught him off balance. Where once he was protected in the familiar, tribal bosom, he's now out in the strange, wide world beyond the village. At school, for example. Education promotes choice and with choice comes decision, uncertainty, tensions, and, often, emotional collapse.

Given time, the "medicine man" could manage to at least soften the effects of trauma. But he, as his white counterparts elsewhere, has too many patients. Some he simply sends to the white man's hospitals. More than one thousand paranoid blacks were admitted to one Rhodesian clinic in one year. A few years ago there were none, and not entirely, as some argue, because the ailment had previously gone unidentified.

All this pressure, this inability to cope, has harassed the "witch doctors" as well. One Ramadan Rodolo, head of South Africa's

Witch Doctors' Union, has said the membership's fees and "doctors' " charges would go up, the classic cure for upset physicians.

To drive the evil from a woman's heart will hit a high of six dollars, he said, double the former fee. The treatment will, however, be positively guaranteed. Which is miraculous.

Those lion-haunted villagers must hang on until the witch doctor comes. If he can drive the discontent from a woman's heart, sorting out "supernatural lions" will be child's play.

Admittedly, that closing comment was a bit flippant on a subject few Africans think is very funny. In fact, several generations of Britain's juridic community, its lawyers and judges assigned to the colonies, found the subject less than comic.

When the last British judge left the now-independent African colonies, I wrote in a radio script, he took with him an experience in the law few foreign jurists will have again. How, for example, does one rule, in a coroner's Inquest, on death from fright when a "murderer" can be named?

Such an instance can, of course, be related to the voodoo practice of sticking pins in effigies. That doesn't kill anyone, but the victim, convinced that such an act *could* kill him and knowing it has been done, may well die from it.

Here's a Central African case in point: Commissioned by a suspicious husband to do away with a worker on a nearby plantation, a native sorceress produced a murder weapon. The device was fashioned of a hollowed-out thigh bone taken from a "fresh" human grave. Wrapped in magical bark and herbs and bits of clothing filched from the target-to-be, this was boiled in a loathsome brew. Meanwhile warnings of doom, whispered along the grapevine, reduced the erstwhile Casanova to quivering jelly.

Armed with this disgusting contrivance, for which he'd paid the witch a tidy sum, the cuckolded husband stepped into the path of his rival one moonlit night, thrust the pointed end against the man's temple like a pistol to his head, and the deed was done.

Shrieking with terror the ill-starred swain thrashed off into the darkness, and his cold and stiffened body was found a few days later.

There'd been no "shot." There were no wounds of any kind. Only the man's pre-knowledge of the sorceress's determination to do him in was needed. So terrified was he that he literally died of fright.

Most certainly the husband murdered him. Or did he?

(In this instance he and his witch accomplice went to prison for an unspecified period, an uninspired but acceptable punishment.)

A vaguely similar case that never got as far as the courts is in my diary as having taken place in the home of one of my Rhodesian neighbors, where it began and ended in his kitchen.

George Pittock's African cook was a genius with comestibles, devoted to his "master and madam," cheerful and altogether a gem. The name appearing on his Nyasa passport was "Matches."

He was so highly prized he'd been provided with a house of his own near the Pittock's main dwelling. In this house he maintained a beautiful wife, Mary. She was coveted by a host of admirers but, being steadfastly faithful, routinely rebuffed their advances. This was bound to get Matches into trouble.

One morning his wife burst into the house sobbing that her husband was prostrate on his bed, agued, burning up with fever, semiconscious. At the village hospital out-patient clinic, the African doctor examined him, and then took George to one side.

"This is not for white medicine," he said matter-of-factly. "There is nothing we can do here. He says he is going to die. And he probably is." The medic shrugged his shoulders: "It's Tagati, a curse. I think he knows who bewitched him, but he won't say who it is. Just take him home and hope."

George, sympathetic and aware of the effect on the African of his animistic beliefs, took the man, gray and palsied, back to his own bed. In two days his breathing had become strangled, his pulse pounding. He could eat nothing. Death was imminent, and George was beside himself; he had tried everything from ignoring Matches to threatening him with a club. And then, at the last moment, the spirits relented.

Mary brought George a piece of cheap, lined, writing paper, neatly folded into a one-inch square. It had fallen from the pocket of the cook's white jacket as she packed his clothing to be taken, after his death, to his clan home in the native reserve. Inside this wrapping was a coin, an ordinary Rhodesian half-crown.

Looking at it closely, George saw that across the throat of the queen's profile image there was a deep scratch as if her throat had been cut. For Matches, this obviously was the sign that his own life was forfeit. And his wife admitted that it could be what was killing him.

George, who'd not seen murder in this guise before but wasn't surprised by it, decided on some improvised magic of his own.

"I got the poor man up," he told me, "and his wife and I dragged him into the kitchen where a roaring coal fire I'd built had the old Aga stove fairly jumping. We propped him up in a chair, and, while Mary bathed his face and shouted at him to keep him awake, I ritually prepared in front of him a fiendish brew of everything I could find in the liquor cabinet, mostly gin.

"By now," he went on, "the kitchen was literally as hot as hell, all of us in a running sweat. I forced a tumblerful of this magic drink down his throat and then dramatically produced the coin.

"With considerable flourish," George said, "I placed it on the butcher's block and, shouting cabalistic phrases like 'Honi soit qui mal y pense' and 'Quod Erat Demonstrandum,' I brandished the axe around my head and suddenly brought it down, luckily chopping the bloody coin into two pieces."

Gyrating round the room, one of the offending pieces in each hand, George finally made a dash for the stove, threw the bits into the roaring fire and slammed the lid.

At this moment, Matches, weakened unto near death to begin with, frightened by his master's frantic antics with the cursed coin and practically pickled by the gin, rose from the chair screaming and fell unconscious to the floor.

"It worked," George told me joyfully. "Allowing for a terrible hangover the next day, his recovery began forthwith."

Pittock later discovered it had been his old gardener, humiliated by the contemptuous treatment he got from Matches' virtuous wife, who had cursed the cook, willed his death, and concealed the tiny paper packet in his jacket pocket.

"I sent the old man packing," George said, "and Matches and his spouse lived happily thereafter."

H.L. Mencken once observed (*Smart Set* article, December 1921) that "civilization . . . is based upon order, decorum, restraint, formality, industry (and), regimentation . . . ," a set of irreproachable qualifications.

At the time, the early 1960s, that George Pittock was conjuring up his own brand of exorcism, there was a lot of feverish talk in the federation about the death of Mencken's enviable human state if black Africa's occultism was allowed to take over the reins of government.

In the process of defending "civilization as we know it," the federal community of white parliamentarians seriously bruised the very qualities Mencken listed and that they claimed to be protecting.

From the parliamentary press gallery in January 1963, I observed this unseemly performance and wrote a piece that later appeared in the *Indianapolis News* as:

Salisbury, Southern Rhodesia. The subject of today's lecture on Africa—and this is fair warning—is ghoulish.

Britian's Federation of Rhodesia and Nyasaland is coming apart at the seams. Complex political currents batter the sensibilities of 9 million citizens, black and white. Economies waver. A great human experiment in race relations falters.

Preoccupation with all this significance, it would seem, has simply been too much to bear. So, as relief, Parliamentarians this week took off down murky byways to debate a matter of no importance. Or so they imagined. The subject: the Human Tissues Bill.

The legislation enables the earthly remains of a deceased person to be donated for research at a planned new medical school here. The bill, modelled on similar statutes in other Commonwealth and western countries, scarcely breaks new ground. Yet hardly had the Minister finished his introductory outline than the matter became a *"cause celebre."*

"In a country such as ours," one speaker said, "where witchcraft is particularly prevalent and in which for the concoction of various remedies various parts of the body and bits and pieces come in handy," a clause should be introduced, he said, that would "prevent trafficking in human flesh, the sale of bodies, and so on."

This suggestion was applauded by a European member from Nyasaland who pointed out that "only last month in Nyasaland human tissue was used for witchcraft in one of the territorial by-elections."

The following day's debate involved standard Federal buck-passing (witchcraft is a territorial matter) and unflattering reference to the "morals or otherwise of medical students" who were considered to be, en bloc, lackadaisical concerning the "dignity of the human body."

The Minister of Health, by now nearly apoplectic, took the floor to state he didn't think bodies would be "loosely dealt with" and indicated he was "horrified" at the trend of the discussion.

This fastidious observation was brushed aside by a Member from Nyasaland who charged that the effect of the bill would be to promote plans for a witch-doctor's school, already on the drawing boards for Nyasaland, and hence would contribute to establishing an institution where human flesh would be used for "immoral purposes."

This ominous disclosure was related to the member's earlier charge that the "leader of the majority black party in my country is openly recognized as a witch-doctor." The implication could hardly be missed that Dr. Hastings Kumuzu Banda, now in London demanding independence for his homeland, would without hesitation foster the black arts as a political weapon.

In spite of all the frightening implications raised in this debate the bill was passed unchanged.

What the future holds for those whose posthumous contribution to science may be innocent of political implications remains, presumably, to be seen.

Witchcraft as a profession and the spirit world in general was to be officially recognized in Rhodesian life when, some years later, it was given special attention by a highly placed black government employee.

In the early eighties, when Rhodesia became the independent state of Zimbabwe, a young friend of mine, Joanna Pearson Emmett, then teaching in Bulawayo, wrote to her father in England. Among other observations she said that animism had been elevated to acceptable science.

"Witch-doctors and spirit mediums," she wrote, "are the new elite. An African," she continued, "who is rewriting the history of Zimbabwe is getting his facts straight from the horse's mouth; he reported in a highly enlightening TV interview recently that he was in close communion with the spirits of Muhate and Mutoto, two important kings from the tenth to fifteenth centuries.

"Now you will know," she went on, "why the African hasn't needed a written language. Whenever a useful fact is required, one simply gets through to an ancestor.

"Anyway," she concluded, "it is comforting to know that our history is coming from such an impeccable source."

Aside from a visceral conviction that spiritual power dictates the course in all matters temporal, the African reveres and depends upon tradition and familiar custom in everyday life. Of course, in this he's not alone. Tribal lore is rife the world over.

Indeed, in the same federal parliament that hosted the flippant discussions about witchcraft, European mythology markedly influenced formalities within the chamber. I made note of this, and, as the Human Tissues Bill was being discussed, I readied a radio script on that folklore that went, in part, like this:

The age-old ritual opening parliamentary sessions must include the parading of the speaker's mace, the ornamental staff that is the symbol of authority. Without the mace in place, no parliament's properly convened, and it is treated with ceremonial deference. For example, during the queen's Speech from the Throne the mace is mantled in black velvet, an indication that there is a suspension of the House's normal lawmaking business.

Now, great seals and scepters and other tokens of omnipotence are commonplace enough, but when they resemble a roccoco war club they invite investigation. So, I queried the origins of the mace and found, first, that it *was* a war club used, what's more, by medieval bishops.

The canons of the church inhibited the more excitable clerics from using swords. Flailing about with a claymore or the like could breach church strictures against shedding blood. So they used a mace instead, a club with a big end like a Zulu knobkerrie.

How they managed to hammer a nonbeliever into submission without making him bleed isn't clear. Still, since it was used mostly to pulverize protective armor, maybe the blood didn't show enough to be embarrassing.

The Turks were among the first to recognize this weapon as a symbol of authority. They decorated theirs with silver filigree and precious gems, and, later, Phillip II of France and Richard I of England followed suit. Sergeants-at-arms started carrying them as openers in parliamentary proceedings in the thirteenth century.

And here it was in the Rhodesian Parliament in the near-middle of Africa for no other reason than that it was traditional.

Will and Ariel Durant, philosopher historians, consecrate the traditional when, in their *Lessons of History*, they note that "no one, however brilliant or well informed, can come to such fullness of understanding as to safely judge and dismiss the customs or institutions of his society, for these are the wisdom of generations after centuries of experiment in the laboratory of history. The sanity of a group lies in the continuity of its traditions."

The Durants' observation isn't new, but it's authoritative, and it pertains especially to the African peoples I have written about, as I did in a story for the *Indianapolis News*, July 5, 1961:

Marandellas, Southern Rhodesia. On the upper slopes of a rocky hill towering over my farm near this country town I have built a study.

It is constructed of rough, gray granite and is covered with vines and a kind of lichen and it looks as if it had pulled the hill in around its shoulders and hunched down into the folds.

Cluttered with books and drifts of papers, it is a comfortable shambles, a bit tatty but peaceful. The view through the large picture window is Africa, hundreds of square miles of rolling, fawn-colored downs. The vista is broken here and there by stony hillocks like my own.

This sounds like an oasis of calm and splendid detachment. It isn't.

This hideout on the Kopje is home to a host of pains and apprehensions and exhilarating argument. And more than that.

A hand torn in a farm machine is patched. Paybooks are made out and wages dispensed along with family advice. Africans visit the place to unload their troubles, to talk about problems that go with political change, with the uncertainties suffered by a people that knows it is going somewhere, at top speed, but isn't sure of the direction and can't see the goal.

If this sounds very paternal of me, perhaps it is. But it's also part of the social mechanism here, for now at any rate.

The visitors and their problems are varied.

Walter is an African trucker. He has a fleet of six vehicles and a four-figure income and he talks contracts and about "arguments with my banker." He's moved too far too quickly and has gotten in over his head. Could the "baas" help him with a loan. (The "baas" couldn't.)

An ancient native, his wrinkled visage webbed with tribal cicatrices, in rags and supporting himself on two staves, wants to visit the graves of his ancestors. They are earthen mounds near a hill on what is now my land and he wants my permission to make the visit. He gets it and we feed him and give him an old overcoat.

An African builder, Cephas Shtabow, comes to ask about one-man–one-vote and wants to be told what a constitution is. And as he goes out the door at dusk in the cold and high winds that almost suck the fire up out of the grate, he passes a frightened Nyasaland migrant laborer who wants me to help him to go home because, he says, he is "bewitched" and he will die if he stays.

The "new" is certainly trampling out much of the "old," but the "old" still persists, tough and massive.

Not long ago I was present when a group of farm workers brought a man, half-dead, to a European contractor's temporary camp and dumped him at the office door. They had beaten him senseless. He was a stranger, they said; probably a witch-doctor's "messenger," one who is sent to steal small children who are spirited away to a secret place where they are smothered with magic smoke and their remains cut up to make charms.

If the old man died, it might be murder or manslaughter. For these men it was simple panic defense against criminal attack, and they were afraid, because the white man would say they'd done murder and would punish them and because the witch-doctor would curse them for tampering with his works. They were caught between cultures and harried within their own.

"Emerging Africa," inclined to strut and posture in the halls of the United Nations, doesn't like to be reminded that it fronts for a deeply mysterious and often deadly condition.

The tribesmen (never the women) came often to pass the time of day; to discuss their families, their days as hunters or, if they were old enough, the time of tribal warfare that banished boredom, replenished female bedmates, and, as one result, renewed the substance of the clan. And to dwell on their past as a people, on the fatalism that marks their religion.

Like most primitives without a written history, the African is a great storyteller. Much of his past came out as parables or rambling narratives and some of them, those having to do with the spirit world, were often chillingly macabre.

Two men who came most often and who had long since crossed over from mere acquaintance to friendship with me, were Shtabow and Paul Mandezera, my farm manager.

Cephas Shtabow was twentieth-century Africa at its best. Dark-skinned, handsome, he was tall and trim, dressed formally in slacks and jacket when not in the weeds he wore as a mason. His skill permitted him to be licensed by authorities whose standards were high and kept that way to preserve the field for the whites. But Cephas could read a plan and construct a building that readily met those standards, a competence acquired when he was a mission student in Old Umtali.

He invariably wore a gangsterish felt hat at a rakish angle, moved with a swinging grace, and possessed a faintly Gallic flair noticeable as soon as he came into view. He supported a comely schoolteacher wife, and he educated nine children on a varying wage that could reach £3,000 annually, phenomenal for an African in those days. Yet, maintaining a series of aged motor cars kept him constantly dead broke, and he was forever "moonlighting" at odd jobs I dreamed up, as much to keep him nearby for company as to provide him with the extra money.

Over the years we spent a lot of time together in the kopje house, and I'd picked his brain about African customs and superstitutions. At one time a rare white baboon had been seen in the hills north of Salisbury, and I'd asked him if he'd ever come across one in his wanderings.

He never had, he said, but he did know that they were the ghosts of tortured human souls assigned to remain on earth to pay for the wrongs of evil men.

Of course the master would know, he went on, that there were different kinds of "bobejaans" in Africa. He'd learned at the mission that the biggest and most clever, and the most dangerous, were in Rhodesia and that, for some reason he could not understand, the students of such things called them "yellow" baboons. To him they were brownish gray. Except for the white ones.

In a small kraal in the Zimunya Reserve to the east, he told me, a carpenter lived with his wife and children. He was a drunkard and often went mad, beating his wife and fighting with his neighbors.

One evening, full of some poisonous mixture, he stormed off into the bush and a short way from the village encountered a neighboring farmer tending his vegetable patch. A fight ensued, and the carpenter picked up a large stone and struck the farmer, crushing his skull. He dragged the body deep into the underbrush, buried it, and returned home, telling no one of the crime.

His hut was at the edge of the kraal, where the land rose steeply to a scrub-covered ridge topped by giant boulders. For as long as the villagers could remember, a troop of perhaps thirty "bobejaans" had spent the nighttime in the safety of this promontory, migrating away each day to hunt for food in the surrounding lowlands, coming back when the sun went down. On the evening of the day when the carpenter killed his neighbor, however, the troop did not return, and in the caves among the rocks, where they normally huddled together, barking and screeching, there was no sound.

In their place that first night there was an eerie, soft yellow light, and in the morning a huge white baboon could be seen on the hill above the carpenter's home. All day it sat there silently staring down at the hut. And so it was day after day.

The carpenter was filled with fear, but he told no one of the killing, and he even joined the others when they sent a search party out to look for the missing farmer. When no one was about, the carpenter shouted at the thing and threw stones, but the great white baboon never moved from its watch.

After a week, the other villagers, frightened by its presence and blaming the carpenter for a curse they believed had dried up the only community water well, met in council and decided to expel the man from the village. The blame for the dried-up well must be his, they reasoned, since the white baboon never took his gaze from the man's hut.

Before they could act, however, the carpenter came home from work in Umtali one evening, found his hut wrecked, the windows broken, all the family possessions strewn about, and his wife and children gone. And on the hill, but closer now to the hut, sat the great white bobejaan.

Terrified, the man ran from the village, stumbling through the darkness back to Umtali. There he scrambled aboard the Salisbury train, apparently hoping to stay with relatives in the capital's Harare Township.

At Inyazura, the first stop, the ticket collector found the carpenter, slumped over, dead, in a seat on the aisle.

Cephas grimaced and tossed his hands into the air. He'd heard, he said, that people sitting near the carpenter later testified the man had taken the seat without speaking, pulled his hat low over his eyes, and had gone off to sleep. But, Cephas said, doctors at the Rusape hospital where the police took the body, reported the man had been strangled and that his neck was broken.

That same night, Cephas said, the white bobejaan disappeared from the kopje above the carpenter's hut and was never seen again.

That the ghost baboon had killed the carpenter for trying to escape the consequences of the murder was foregone for Cephas. The story for him was not mysterious or about the supernatural. It was simply a straightforward account about the kind of things white bobejaans did.

This bland acceptance of the paranormal was characteristic of my visitors. My Nyasa native who claimed he was "bewitched," the cook who claimed his daughter had died not of dysentery as diagnosed at the hospital but of a curse on his house. And others. None declared any distinction between the material and the spiritual, since, for them, they were the same. Paul Mandezera, church-mission-educated and acutely intelligent with a wide range of employment in the white culture over his forty years, would relate to me as a matter of fact the weirdest tale told in all the years I held court in the Kopje house.

When he was younger, Paul said, he hunted, shooting for the pot and to collect skins and horns and other trophies to sell in the towns. Northeastern Rhodesia between the Mrewa district and the Mocambique pedicle, part of his tribal homeland, was good game country—rolling, desolate territory marked by deep ravines and rocky hills.

It was in a particularly inhospitable part of this area that Paul, hunting from a camp set up near his battered Land Rover, was caught in a sudden downpour. Struggling through the undergrowth, he came upon an opening at the base of a kopje he'd been using as a compass bearing.

Tearing away the mat of vines and brush laced across the entrance and rolling aside boulders blocking the way, he crept into a narrow passage that led into the depths of the hill. As he felt his way along in the gloom, the roar of the rain died away behind him and the silence was eerie, the air stale and musty. A torch he had made of dried roots illuminated the shaft and, after a few moments, groping forward in the wavering light, he stepped out into a large vaulted cavern.

The flames flickered off the walls towering upward into the blackness, and what he saw, he said, "made my heart burn in my throat."

Staring down at him from the shadowed heights were what he described as "the faces of the Mambos," tribal chieftains entombed long ago in this crumbling, natural mausoleum.

For as far back as tribal memory went, Paul explained, inhabitants of the area had preserved their dead for an afterlife. Embalming was perfunctory but a semblance of preservation was achieved by wrapping the remains in an oxhide, soaked in an herbal brew. With only the head showing, the corpse was then ceremoniously hung upright on the wall. As the hide dried, it shrank, forcing the body erect and, once hardened held it rigidly in place. For millennia. What Paul saw was a scattering of the white skulls grinning over the tops of these gruesome rawhide cocoons, broken open where decay had eaten them away to reveal other bits of gray bone.

Paul said he hastily lowered the torch, and the floor of the cave, thick with powdery debris and a sifting of the bat guano weighting the dead air with an acrid stench, seemed to shift beneath his feet in the fitful light. Near the base of the wall something flashed silver and crouching down Paul brushed away the rubbish from a narrow, foot-long spearhead, the surface deeply pitted, the cutting edge chipped but razor sharp and strangely polished and glistening.

Counting the skeletons, about a score, and viewing the decay inside the cave, Paul said he'd guessed the crypt dated back a hundred years and more. As an intuitive tracker, wise in the lore of the bush, he also said he'd swear no human being had been in the tomb for at least that long, far more than the time needed to rust the sheen off that venerable spearhead.

It was true of course, Paul conceded, that the spirits of the Mambos often went abroad to serve the living, avenging wrongs and remaining, he said, the guardians of the tribe even after death.

He admitted this was an unnerving thought at the time and he "got out of there very quickly." Once back out the entrance, he ran for the Jeep and slammed it over the rough veld to the main track. And he never returned, not even to the vicinity of the place.

But then, he looked at me, wide-eyed, and shook his head incredulously, he didn't need to. The Mambos came to him.

Some weeks later, hunting in the wild territory near the pedicle border but still many miles from the cave, he'd pulled over and camped for the night. In spite of efforts to stay awake and keep a fire going as some sort of protection against nighttime prowlers, he dropped off to sleep.

When he awoke, a pale mist oozed about in the gray dawn, and for a few fleeting moments he couldn't even see the Jeep, only a few feet away. When he could identify at least its outline it wasn't the vehicle that caught his attention.

What he saw, he said, not ten feet away from where he lay and sprawled out toward him was the bloody carcass of a large leopard. The blade that had been plunged into its heart just behind the right shoulder, ripping a great gash, still protruded from the wound. It had no handle. And the metal shaft was a "narrow spearhead about a foot long."

CHAPTER XXVI

Uproar, Mayhem and Genteel Spirits

For all their lingering grip on tradition the Africans I met, beginning in the Gold Coast, had been eager enough to espouse Western innovation. Especially if it proved to be a violent substitute for a practice or practices their colonial rulers had, for one obvious reason or another, forbidden, for example, raiding the neighborhood kraal for fun and females. There is nothing I know of that could really take the place of feminine booty at the end of a blood-warming barney with the locals. But an effort, however feeble, was made to replace some of this excitement, in part at least, by sporting contests such as boxing, soccer and even softball. This does, admittedly, harness some energies that might otherwise be devoted to less savory pursuits, but they're a very poor exchange for the real thing. The African reaction was to get them as close to legitimate bloodletting as possible.

Pursuing a story I'd undertaken about British imperialism at its basic best, I encountered, first-hand, this native enthusiasm for imported sports. When I recovered, I wrote about it for the *Indianapolis News*, and it went roughly like this, dated 27 January 1950:

> *Chito, the Gold Coast, British West Africa.* The African brand of softball is the original "bush league," with violence.
>
> The player's passion and great physical strength and endurance give the contest all the worst characteristics of lacross, gang warfare, and rugby. There is only the vaguest resemblance to the American game. I pitched, briefly, in a game among members of the Ewe tribe and I know.
>
> One hundred miles inland from the south Atlantic coast, Chito is a showpiece headquarters for the British Mass Education Team. I have spent several days observing something called "physical

training," an integral part, it turns out, of British academic planning. Softball comes under "P.T."

The field was laid out in a clearing made among the palm and banana trees. Players, barefoot and wearing shorts and nothing else, were divided, roughly, into teams of about a dozen on a side, a few more than normally allowed. Home plate was a plow disc and the bases were large orange medicine balls. A slide into home sent the player directly to the orthopedic section of the local infirmary, while an overly enthusiastic dive into second sent the runner rolling out into center field. The hazards of a successful hit were numerous.

The bat was a small wagon tongue narrowed at the handle end and weighing only slightly less than the catcher. Although I could hardly get it off the ground, the Africans handled it with ease. The force with which they hit the ball, when they did, and each other, which was often, passed belief.

As soon as bat met ball, all men on bases took off, the more fleet of foot overtaking the others, a chaotic contest to see who could reach "home" first. A fielder, retrieving a ball, never threw it in but sped like a deer after the runner, brushing aside basemen like tenpins, to deal the runner a paralyzing blow. Usually, onlookers, unable to restrain themselves, rushed onto the field to join in short, sharp karate sessions with members of both teams.

A "pop" fly belonged to the hardiest. Two or three players converging under a high fly was prelude to certain mayhem, and I closed my eyes and awaited the thud and sounds of tearing flesh.

Points were awarded for every few players crossing home plate. It depended on the speed with which an umpire could refocus his eyes after being trampled by the mob.

To be struck out was an insult, a personal assault by the pitcher on the character of the batter. I was invited to take the mound and to avoid angering enemy players on the sidelines I pitched as if tossing a ball of yarn to a baby. This compromising maneuver cost me the job and sent me out into right field where I retired far out among the banana trees and avoided the ball with professional cunning.

Admittedly, not all Western substitutes for a traditional African way of doing things got the same warm reception. Take the mundane matter of preserving law and order.

Presumption of innocence, rules of evidence, and the principle of rehabilitation were, for example, refinements in the white man's system the African sometimes thought were pretty silly. Letting a burglar off with a light jail sentence, after which he returned to his trade well fed and rested, struck the African as missing the point. Branding with a red-hot knife, on the other hand, labelled the criminal much as the skull and crossed bones does fluid in a bottle, and chopping off a hand could put at least a temporary crimp in his expertise.

Hence, although he was prepared to play by all the new rules when they were seen to be controlling the knaves and scoundrels, if he felt they weren't the African lapsed into his own forthright methods.

One such loss of patience produced an effective, if spectacularly vicious, response to a crime wave in the Ashanti province of the Gold Coast during my stay there in 1949.

I was in the provincial capital of Kumasi to follow up the story on the Asantehene, king of the Ashantis, when I'd learned that what was described as a "colorful" vigilante had taken over local law enforcement. The group was called the Zongo Volunteers and "colorful" was a modest description. They fought back at the lawbreakers with a garish terror that was chillingly versatile.

Not far from Kumasi's Aboabo ghetto I kept an appointment with one George Kwasi Adai, a thirty-eight-year-old druggist and organizer of the band. Very black, heavy set, soft-spoken, he hardly seemed the leader of a gang that had set the community a-quiver. Yet, apparently he had, and this was how it happened:

Before the white man occupied the province in the mid-1890s, there was very little outlawry. So Adai's father had told him. Swift and severe had been the justice meted out to wrongdoers, and few were tempted to return to crime even when physically able. Then the British came with their peculiar laws of evidence and lightweight punishments, and before long robbery and murder were rife.

Two world wars and the growth of Kumasi as a trading center brought the Moslem tribesmen in from the north, the Hausas, Grusis, Busengi, the Musi, the Grimas and the Fulani cattlemen, and a rough lot they were.

By 1936 three gangs of about 100 each, divided into groups called "Krafi Yakyi" (by strength we live) established a monopoly of murder and rapine. After World War Two, the Krafi Yakyi, running together, terrorized entire villages, even demanding "protection payments." If citizens resisted, their homes were pillaged when the men were in the fields; wives were raped and butchered. In one instance in Aboabo, Adai told me, a three-month-old baby, left in a crib at home, was stamped to death as a lesson to its uncooperative parents.

The gangs were made up of Zongos, those tribesmen from the north who crowded together in the ghetto. Their basic weapons were the bayonets brought home from the wars and a bow made of ejunue wood and strung with bamboo strips that could shoot a fifteen-inch reed arrow tipped with an iron barb clean through a buffalo, according to Adai. The ones the Zongos used often were poisoned in an adder-head brew.

By 1947 lawlessness got so out of hand that Adai, a member of the Kumasi Town Council, got permission to form a semiofficial vigilance committee. His first sixty recruits were from the Aboabo community, butchers, shopkeepers and tailors who financed their own purchases of weapons including a few aged flintlocks and bootleg Enfield rifles.

When I talked to Adai the number had grown to 780, the original sixty as cadre, and units were provided to patrol nearby villages, although the rabble I joined for one night exercise scarcely qualified as a "patrol."

Fifty-four of them crowded in deafening uproar into the hotel parking lot. Uniforms were a ragbag of outfits from Scots kilt and trews to a blue American air force jacket complete with captain's bars, British flat tin hats, glengarries and black crash helmets emblazoned with "Z.V." over a white half-moon. Arms included knobkerries, cavalry sabers and cap-ignition muzzle loaders. Filled with black powder, these aged relics lit up the night of an entire suburb with a thunderous roar.

It was little wonder the community observed a self-imposed curfew during the hours of darkness. The ten-man squad I accompanied caught two young men and ran them through such a mindnumbing interrogation that one of them fell to the ground insensible as we moved off.

From stories I'd heard, not denied by Adai, these two had been let off gently. In the few months before the night of my patrol an unspecified number had been "nailed," a torture technique that had done much to enhance the Zongo's dread reputation.

The first "nailing" on record took place in 1936 and had proved so effective as a method of terrorizing a neighborhood that it had been taken up by the volunteers.

"Nailing" was a delicate business. Yet, since the difference between a tidy operation and a clumsy one was only a variation in the time it took for the victim to drop dead, there was no premium on skill. Anyone could do it.

Field headquarters of the Zongo Volunteers was believed to be a huge, smoking city dump on the outskirts of Kumasi. Here, it was said, the Zongo's took the poor wretches caught in a crime or just out after curfew without an interesting excuse. They would be thrown to the ground, face down and a small wire nail would be tapped into the skull, piercing the scalp, the spongy dura matter or brain-case, and the meninges or plasticlike substance that bags the brain. The nail would then be pulled out. The man, his head aflame with pain, would then be carried into the empty marketplace during the wee hours of the morning and left to fend for himself.

Blinded with agony, too frightened or benumbed to consider going to the authorities, he would stagger about, his head slowly filling with blood. The internal pressure would increase until all brain function stopped and he keeled over dead.

By this time the market would be filling up with the day's crowds. Neither the merchants opening their shops nor the gathering patrons scarcely dared so much as a glance at the body. As for the authorities, little time would be spent on investigation. Autopsies were rare in the tropics of the fifties. The tiny puncture was almost invisible. The symptoms of a "nailing" were similar to malaria or spinal meningitis and that's what the death certificate would read. Case closed. But not for the townsmen. Chalk one up for the Zongo Volunteers.

As in the time of Adai's father, there soon was very little crime in Kumasi. The Zongos did wink at a bit of minor pilfering, and they "protected" the fences who paid for the loot, but, after all, the Zongos did have an establishment to support and routine contributions were insufficient to pay the bills. No one complained out loud.

Superstition, clinging to tradition, and brutalizing one's neighbors in the process, is hardly an African monopoly. Wherever man has fears to assuage or spare time to fill, he'll be beastly to his confrères and be ready with endless justification for the deeds—as, for example, in headhunting.

The Asantehene, it will be recalled, collected heads for display to frighten his minions and to intimidate nearby tribesmen. His demand that his showerbath be paved with the skulls of his enemies and the West African propensity generally for collecting these souvenirs aroused my interest, and resulted in a few radio scripts. Summed up, they went something like this:

> Recently a friend of mine, traveling in Malaya, noted in a letter that headhunting remains a problem there. A minor one, she said, but disturbing.
>
> Many of us have, of course, seen these mementoes, the shrunken ones at least. They are a bit grisly but nonetheless quite remarkable. Blackened by age and the mummifying process they're astonishing miniature samples complete with tribal scars and flowing hair. Some even bear tiny ear and nose ornaments.
>
> For parts of Africa this has been a popular hobby for years, as it has in Asia, the Pacific islands, and some parts of South America. It's no longer acceptable in Britain, by the way, but in

medieval times a head was produced by a hired assassin as proof that the person who'd lost it was out of circulation.

European demand for these unsightly oddments was considerable right up through the turn into the twentieth century. At one time, ships returning from exotic corners of the world carried so many of them that appropriate entries had to be made on the manifests. Yet Europeans might have picked them up in their own backyards, or at least something like them, and right up until a few decades ago.

The Montenegrins collected heads until the 1920s, when even Balkan authorities began to frown on the practice. Ears and noses were substituted for a time, but in the latter half of the 1900s the Continent has been officially free even of this drollery.

Actually it hasn't at any time been mere savage whim. Head-hunting has often had complex metaphysical significance.

In almost all such cases it has been believed that the head carried the soul. To obtain it added to the total soul matter belonging to a community. From this came human and agricultural fertility.

Heads also were collected as souvenirs of victory in battle, witness the Asantehene and, too, the Persians as far back as 700 B.C., although these ancients embraced the conviction that the head carried the courageous spirit of the warrior.

The shrinking of heads started in Melanesia, and similar practices took place in South America and west Africa. Initial reason for this dwarfing process is not known, although, as the number of heads picked up around the house, it could have been to save space.

Most convenient, of course, was the alternative collection of scalps, harvested also, in most cases, because of their religious connotations.

It's all been endowed with special purpose and ceremonial, and so it remains in many parts of the globe. The Nagas of India, for example, to this day bury the skulls *they* accumulate face down in planted lands so the spirit may watch over the beginnings of growing things.

One way and another the rite, and the recognition of the supernatural that attends it, has not been confined to Malaya or the backwaters of the globe.

It wasn't in the back bush that I first became seriously involved in the world of the occult. It happened within a few blocks of London's Fleet Street, a wilderness, perhaps, but not peopled by simple barbarians.

In June of 1949 a mild parliamentary fracas ensued on the subject of proscribing Britain's Spiritualist Church. In 1735 a Witchcraft Act had been passed that would have the effect, in the twentieth century, of labelling all members of the Spiritualist National Union as witches liable to be burned at the stake, and a Vagrancy Act of 1824 had filled in a legal gap in the 1735 legislation through which witches might have slipped, on grounds they were mere rootless drifters and might only be thrown into jail.

The acts had been ignored for more than half a century, and the issue in that June of forty-nine was not that the jails would suddenly be awash with condemned Spiritualists but that they *could* be. Psychics wanted the Act of 1735 repealed and statutes enacted that would remove them from the purview of the Act of 1824. Opponents of the movement urged that the acts be called into force not, obviously, to have adherents of psychic centers incinerated or flogged but to regulate its "church" activities and perquisites.

Neither got their way. The acts remained unchanged subject to some future attention and by tacit agreement would continue to be ignored. The dispute, so well mannered it went nearly unnoticed, fizzled out, a fortnight wonder as a news story. Yet, covering it had led me a chase around the city's seamier quarters into areas I won't forget.

At the Kings Cross Road Psychic Center, a Dickensian-era walk-up of shabby decor, a Mr. T.W. Ella, secretary, had answered my questions and walked me around his melancholy domain. On the gloomy ground floor, a "chapel" seated perhaps twenty on dilapidated wooden chairs; the walls were covered with a threadbare maroon material, and everywhere there was cheap, tinselled litter. The linoleum in the hallway was ravaged, the dusty boards showing through. I rarely have experienced such an un-self-conscious display of adversity and could hardly wait to escape the sour dreariness of the place. I dropped a pound note in a wooden collection plate in the hall and fled to my next appointment.

It might have been my mood, but at first blush this encounter promised to be even more saddening.

At 273 Grays Inn Road on a first floor reached by mounting worn wooden steps was the office of the *Archeological Newsletter*, a brochure with worldwide if esoteric circulation and covering matters of current interest about the culture of long-dead civilizations. I knocked on a door marked with the magazine's title, and another door with "Enquiries" on it was flung open.

In the doorway stood an entirely improbable woman, about five feet tall, with sharp features, sallow complexion, and wiry grayish hair pulled into an alarmingly tight bun at the back and secured with an elastic band. In response to my introduction, she grimaced, revealing two missing teeth, upper right, and beckoned me in. She wore a gray tweed skirt, stained on the seat, a jacket to match, scuffed brown sandals, brown cotton stockings, a whitish blouse under a rust-brown sleeveless sweater cinched in at the waist with a tweed belt of independent hue.

Her office looked like a furniture jumble sale doubling as an old-newspaper collection depot. When she sat down behind the junk-covered refectory table, she sank out of sight, her whereabouts betrayed by billowing clouds of smoke from the cigarettes she chain-smoked. And then she spoke. Her voice was breathy, softly husky, her speech precise and, in her, the English language received spectacularly respectful and imaginative treatment, an awesome example of the splendor to which the tongue may soar. And she was Charm itself.

She swept from a discussion of crime reporting, which she did for a number of London papers, to paleontology, anthropology, Dixieland music, and genealogy, without the slightest effort and never a drop in the level of excitement with which she imbued every topic.

The purpose of my visit had been to talk about the discovery of the *Sutton Ho* ship, a viking vessel recently dug up in Sussex. This we did, fulsomely, concluding when she showered me with documentation to take away for study. And then we talked about the Spiritualist Church, an issue that surfaced when she inquired politely about my other stories of the moment.

On this she was as knowing as on so many other things, and as opinionated, but here the matter was personal. She not only believed in contact with the dead, directly and through spirit mediums, but had had broad intimate experience with a whole host of ghosts.

"See them frequently," she said, "often several nights running."

"You see," she went on, "I live on the upper floor of an aged building in a section not far from here devastated by the Great Fire of the late sixteen hundreds. From the ashes buildings rose and fell over the years on the site where my dwelling house finally went up in eighteen forty, just over a hundred years ago.

"So, you see," she said, "many have lived and died there over a course of at least the last millennium, and they do rather have a claim to the place."

Her last encounter, she said, had been only two nights earlier.

It was her habit to read far into the night settled in a vast leather easy chair at one end of her library. The room was cluttered antiquity in itself, she said, oaken plank flooring, banks of boodcases, the electric light globes in the old gaslamp wall fittings casting a dim light over the heavy Jacobean furnishings. The far end of the room featured a large french door, permanently shut. Where once it had lead out onto a balcony, she explained, it now fronted for a blank brick wall, the end of the house.

She kept the door in place, she said, because of its beautiful teak construction, the old bubble-glass panes and the artistry of its wrought-iron hardware.

On the night she spoke of, she was immersed in her reading when movement at the far end of the room caused her to look up. Limping toward her and headed for a doorway leading into the hall where the clock had just struck one, was the stooped figure of a man. He wore a soiled, sleeveless leather jerkin, his long greasy black hair falling onto his shoulders. His head was bowed, concealing his face, and in his arms, clutched to his chest, he carried what appeared to be several pairs of boots. At the door, she said, he shifted the burden, freeing one hand to reach for the knob, and passed through closing it behind him. He made no sound.

"Obviously a servant off to polish his master's boots," she said. "I didn't take much notice since I've experienced him before, although I noticed this time," she added, "that he'd opened the door from the hinge side. Apparently there'd been a different arrangement in his day."

She explained that this sort of appearance was fairly frequent and included buxom servant girls in flowing garb and lace caps who flounced in and out of the room materializing through one of the far bookcases.

At one time long ago, possibly during the reign of the early Stuarts, this space, she supposed, had been occupied by a salon. Then the room may have catered in some vulgar manner to the needs of an aristocracy characterized as much by its cruelty and coarseness as by elegance and high rank. This she suspected because of one particular visitation that recurred, the only one that repeatedly frightened her.

The first incident took place, she said, several years before my meeting with her. It was so late at night as to be early morning, perhaps four o'clock. She'd closed her book atop the cluttered lyre table next to her chair and prepared to rise. Suddenly one of the french doors, held shut by wooden pegs for decades, swung violently inward. There was no sound. And the brick wall beyond it appeared to have dissolved in a fine mist, through which a man was backing into the room.

He was of medium height, wore a shoulder-length gray wig, pale-blue velvet waistcoat and matching breeches, white stockings, and buckled black shoes. There was lace around his throat and at his wrists.

"I recall every minute detail," she shuddered slightly, "and was frozen rigid watching this apparition, horrified by what he held in the hand nearest to me."

His left arm, she said, was held rigidly downward away from his side. Hanging from his fingers by its locks of long black hair was a severed head, blood dripping from the torn neck.

The figure staggered backward, holding up its right hand as if to ward off a pursuer's blow; stood just inside the door for a moment; and then spinning away in apparent panic dissappeared into the mist that now swirled about that end of the room.

"It would be simply another ghostly incident," she said, "were it not for the stain on the flooring."

The boarding beneath where the head had hung was blackened by a pool of what obviously was blood.

"Whatever it is," she said, "no amount of scrubbing will clean it away. It simply fades away—perhaps three days and it's gone—and stays away until the moment when the shade of this unhappy cavalier returns again."

CHAPTER XXVII

"Stay in Your Car!"

Journalists working in distant quarters of the globe after World War Two, especially those few assigned to cover an "emerging Africa," often found it very heavy going. Luckily, surfacing amid all these matters of importance were random topics that, if not always comic relief, were nonetheless refreshingly lightweight. Like elephants.

Elephants, I know, can be very human, running the gamut from tenderness to calculated cussedness. I've observed their gentleness in the herd and have learned of their intelligence. Yet, most of what I knew about them in the wild was scary. The beasts were dangerous and agressive. For example.

Out from England on holiday in the Gold Coast, where their son was a district officer, an elderly couple undertook a short upcountry motor trip in a tiny Mini Minor.

Early one morning, on the main road, they'd pulled off to the side for a "convenience" break and were just about to get out of the car when it was struck a mighty blow in the rear and catapulted down the dirt road. Possessed of more courage than sense the man calmly sorted out the chaos left by their flying luggage and turned to peer out through the cracked rear window.

About ten yards behind them was a huge beast, trunk raised, great ears flapping, rocking from side to side and obviously warming up for another go.

A piercing shriek as a signal for another attack was all the poor man needed as a suggestion for his next move and, very spry for his age, he spun around, slammed the vehicle into gear and didn't stop until the elephant was out of sight.

When they inspected the damage they found one of the animal's tusks had run through the trunk ("boot"), a piece of their luggage and the inside leather backrest, leaving a tangle of springs, cloth and tufts of horsehair on the seat.

Nonetheless, the old couple were luckier than the driver of a Dodge pickup truck, stalled in an open plain in neighboring Dahomey. A huge cow elephant hit this vehicle broadside, drove both tusks through the cab door, and narrowly missed impaling the terrified Frenchman. Without apparent difficulty, she then heaved the truck into the air and dropped it on its back, converting it to matchwood and thoroughly rupturing its mechanical innards. The driver, badly lacerated and suffering a few broken bones and a fright, barely got away with his life.

Although elephants in Africa were an entirely new experience for me, elephants as a species were not. I'd made the acquaintance of a few in the United States, specimens that were mostly mild-mannered and normally predictable.

On general assignment for the *Indianapolis News*, I'd managed to get the circus several times running. It was a plum, and old hands who'd savored the privilege in years past piled my desk high with backgrounder books on clowns and animals and showered me with old programs collected over the years. On one occasion when the Big Top ballooned up I'd found at least a half bushel of peanuts with a note to "Old Babe."

"Old Babe" was an Indian elephant. Except for the famous Ringling Brothers giant, Jumbo, an African said to measure eleven feet at the point of his shoulder, most of the animals came from the Asian subcontinent. They are more tractable, and, although Africans have been trained to work and perform, they are rarely as dependable as the likes of "Old Babe."

Stories about this famous elephant are legion. The time the infant crawled into the path of the big parade in San Francisco just as "Old Babe" loomed over the spot; she swayed to a stop, halting the entire show, raised one great foot, and gently nudged the child toward its frightened parents. How she'd once satisfied her appetite for watermelons when the circus was on the road by uprooting the peg to which one front foot was chained, tossing it over her neck, tiptoeing over sleeping mahouts and lumbering off for the nearest farmer's patch. Back on the line again she'd driven the stake into place with such force no one could tell she'd been away, until a keeper found watermelon on her whiskers.

The only recorded incident when "Old Babe" reverted to the wild involved an attack by a tiger on the little donkey with whom she worked an act in the center ring. The big cat escaped its cage, and the first thing it saw was the burro. "Old Babe" heard it honking in terror and exploding off the elephant lines, trumpeting encouragement, she swept through the grounds flattening anything in her way. She was too late to save her little colleague, the story goes, but wreaked a terrible vengeance on the tiger, seizing it in her trunk and smashing it to a pulp against the iron bars of the cage.

When I got around to introducing myself to her one balmy, spring afternoon she stood on the line, great head bowed, very old and boney—in her sixties—gray-bearded and superbly serene.

The animals I was meeting in the Gold Coast were a far cry from "Old Babe." I could expect very little of her kind of serenity from elephants that played jacks with motorcars. What's more I could also expect that, one day, if I remained on the continent, I must have my own private experience with one of them. Nor was it long before I narrowly missed it in the Nigerian town of Ilorin, about two hundred miles north of the coastal city of Lagos.

I was on a shakedown Jeep trip around the country prior to taking off overland for southern Africa and was booked to spend the night with the District Officer, Christopher Reynolds.*

A century earlier the migratory path the great elephant herds had used in the annual trek southward had gone through the Ilorin district. In recent years a growing human population had blocked the track with numerous settlements and the herds abandoned it in favor of feeling their way coastward through adjacent empty lands.

Now and then an old bull is driven from the herd by his younger, stronger colleagues and is left to wander alone. Painful wounds from the fighting often handicap the animal and getting enough to eat can be a major problem. (An African eats about 500 pounds of the landscape every day.) Lonely, wounded and hungry, it develops a ferocious temper.

One such bull, without the company and guidance of the rest of the herd but motivated by some strange instinct, had set off down the old track, untrodden for generations. Infuriated when he found it blocked, he had rampaged through villages, killing farmers and herdsmen and leaving the settlements a shambles. Eventually, he arrived in Ilorin, the same day I did, although happily for me the Reynoldses had seen him off the premises, literally, before I got there.

He'd hit the community on the run, converting huts to kindling and killing an African hunter. Snatching up a white district official who'd shot at him and missed, he kneaded the man on the ground with his trunk and then tossed him some forty feet, broken and barely alive. He was on his way through the rest of the town when, pausing for breath, he met his match: Chris Reynolds's irate wife.

Dallying momentarily in Mrs. Reynolds's garden was his mistake.

*Blackwoods Magazine, June 1964.

Inside the house she heard the commotion, thought cattle were loose among her beloved roses, and rushed out the back door to find the old bull stamping about in her flower beds.

An old "Africa hand" who knew better, she nevertheless lost all control at the sight of her mangled flowers, snatched up her straw gardening hat, and, waving it wildly, ran straight for him, screeching at the top of her lungs.

By her account, this rampaging predator eyed her speculatively for a moment and then, with a small squeal, spun away and shuffled off straight through a potting shed, a corner of the garage and forty feet of iron fencing.

Apparently he left town shortly after that. One more village on the old elephant trail suffered his rage before, far to the south, he was shot dead by a professional hunter.

Chapters have been written on the subject of the instinct that sent that lone bull inexplicably down the long-unused track toward cooler climes. Probably defining it as an inborn tendency to behave in a way peculiar to his natural family is as close as need be. Another strange elephant performance, one that certainly is covered by this obscure definition, I learned of years later when I was doing a story on Lake Kariba, the two-hundred-mile-long lake backing up behind a dam built in 1956 and forming part of the northern boundary of what was then southern Rhodesia.

I was in the region doing a piece on the use the Rhodesians were making of their new resource, and spent time on a fish-seeding expedition, sowing ten tons of tiny bream fingerlings from tanks in a government launch.

The warden in charge was Rex Adams, gangly and raw-boned and fascinated by his job. During one of the day's quiet moments I'd asked him if he'd had any unusual experiences in what seemed an often boring routine and he'd laughed ruefully and said, "Now and then."

A few weeks earlier, he said, returning from a fish-stocking trip in the western reaches of the lake, he saw what seemed to be a large log mostly submerged in the water off the port bow. Afraid it might do damage to boat traffic, he'd altered course to take it in tow and had almost reached it before he realized that what he was looking at was the high ridge of an elephant's backbone. It was ten miles to the nearest shore, a long haul for the big beast, so he pulled the forty-foot craft alongside with, he said, "visions of Adams roping an elephant to safety."

The elephant had other ideas. It had been resting, dozing in the warm waters, and frightened awake it wallowed instantly to the attack. Wrapping its trunk around an iron stanchion supporting the canvas roofing, it nearly capsized the boat before kicking off from the steel hull. It moved away, swimming easily for the distant shore, leaving Adams with a mangled canvas top and two large dents in the side of the launch. He said he watched the animal for a time and noted that, although it seemed to have no problems in the water, it did follow a peculiarly zig-zag course.

Back at the landing, Adams had described his run-in to a game warden familiar with the district and got this explanation for the presence of the beast in mid-lake and for the meandering course it swam.

Before the waters backed up behind the dam, this part of the Zambesi River escarpment had been the home of numerous elephant herds. For literally centuries the animals had moved about the area along tracks that snaked through the hilly country, keeping to a minimum gradient, since elephants avoid steep climbs. In fact, the government highway ultimately built to serve the area was surveyed along one of these old tracks, chosen as the easiest climb for motor traffic.

In the game warden's view, the submerging of the tracks hadn't concealed them from the elephant families which had always followed them by sense or intuition. The elephant sees but dimly. Those wanting to reach the far side of this new watery barrier entered the lake on the old trail still visible on the bank and, apparently unconsciously, followed it in its wandering route even though, in some places, it was 200 feet below them.

The Ilorin experience and other stories I'd heard of elephant attacks had made me a bit nervous about the trip I planned south down the middle of the continent through all that wild country. And then someone suggested I see Sandys George, a handy counselor in such matters and a chief inspector in the C.I.D. in Lagos.

Back in the capital I paid him a visit, and we discussed at length a frightening range of big game and safari problems and my own particular needs. In a radio script I produced, our meeting went something like this:

> I had occasion not long ago to deplore the fact that some hunting rifles have become so powerful that a good deal of the fun has gone out of the contests.
>
> This is presuming, of course, that you consider facing a charging rhinoceros to be fun. If you do and think you're skillful enough you choose a caliber that matches the challenge; you aim to hit a vital spot. If you miss and the beast grinds you into the thorn bushes, well, that's obviously one sporting event you weren't quite ready for, and you must be a good loser.
>
> Any professional hunter will insist that this risk is the test of

courage that sets the sportsman's blood to racing, sometimes all over the ground, admittedly, but in a decent and proper cause. There are those, however, who overdo this gambling spirit.

My plans for the African trip took me by Jeep through the Congo bush, where the buffalo and elephant dwell, and it occurred to me that, inept as I am with firearms, a gun of some sort could still come in handy. For advice I turned to Chief Inspector Sandys George, in the Lagos H.Q., Nigerian Constabulary. A great, bulky man pushing 250 pounds and who roared when he spoke, George turned briskly to be of help.

He'd recommend, he said, a twelve-gauge shotgun. When I protested this seemed a bit light, he said, no, it was a good all-around piece. I could shoot the odd buck or bird for the cooking pot, using say, SG shot, and if worse came to worst I could use the gun defensively. For this he prescribed a special technique.

"Take an elephant," he said. "Suppose you are away from your vehicle, and, suddenly, there he is. You have the shotgun with you. You load with double-O buckshot, that's like big ball bearings, and then you wait.

"When he charges you," and he did say *"when,"* "you stand firm until he's within about forty feet, and then shoot him in the knees."

I didn't say this out loud, but I wasn't at all certain that if I hadn't already fainted from fright I could pick out an elephant's knees, especially pounding up and down through the high grass in my direction.

"Shooting him in the knees," he went on, "won't hurt him much, but it'll trip him up, and if he doesn't land on top of you, you'll have time to buzz off, reload and do the same thing again.

"You repeat this tactic until either he tires of falling all over the shrubbery and goes away or you miss his knees." And he smiled.

I did get the gun, a second-hand 12-gauge, 32-inch–barrel Purdy, from the police lost property, a faulty spring on the left trigger having been repaired. I had a case made for it, packed it amid the heap of paraphernalia in the Land Rover, and took it out again for the first time 7,000 miles later at a South African Customs post on the banks of the great, green, greasy Limpopo River.

I'd walked the bush within feet of an elephant herd cats-cradling banana trees in the Congo and seen scores of them in Belgian and Rhodesian game parks. Nary a one evinced the slightest interest in me. This, I learned, was unusual.

Several years later, as I coasted along the dusty tracks of the Gorongoza Game Reserve in what was then Portuguese Mocambique, I had an escape from a mother pachyderm whose interest in me was extravagant. It was not the first time in my life I'd been scared witless, but it ranked so high among moments I can never forget that I opted for a radio script on the subject:

East Africa's Gorongoza National Park is so unspoiled it's primordial. Maintaining animal reserves in their natural state, unsullied by the hand of man, is all very well, but to run the place so casually that visitors are easy pickings for the indigenous carnivores is overdoing conservationist fervor.

One tourist had narrowly escaped being savaged by a hippopotamus, an Indian traveler lost an arm to a lioness and the elephant herds, numbering in the thousands, are reckoned by one African guide I met as "very, very rude."

When a friend, Dave McCombe, and I went there by Jeep a few years ago, park administration was loose at best. Visitors were permitted to travel throughout the reserve in or on anything during the daylight hours. Picnicking was limited only by the ferocity of the ants and mosquitos. Wandering about on foot was permitted if not encouraged. Park authorities simply assumed, wrongfully, that the mere presence of lion and other beasts of prey would automatically choke off such nonchalance.

In those early days, the park did provide an armed guard, but the poor man usually was stricken with bilharziasis and sleeping sickness and spent the day dozing fitfully in the back seat. It was generally accepted that his rifle, a vintage Mauser, would be used to sound the alarm rather than bring down a charging buffalo.

There were, however, several moments on our second day there when the wretched man was roused from his slumber to a state of undivided attention. This was entirely McCombe's fault.

Dave was at one time a paratroop major who'd dropped with the First Allied Airborne Army at Arnheim, a bloody debacle for the Allies, and now suffered his head to be held together with silver wire and metal plate. He was utterly fearless and a passionate photographer, and no risk was too great for a picture.

What this meant, however, is that all the Jeep superstructure had to be stripped away: no roof, the windscreen clamped down on the engine hood, doors removed and left in camp. Just a bare chassis. The result was that we jounced about in this open air zoo rather more unprotected from attack than I thought wise.

At one time we'd rounded a blind turn in heavy bush to confront a large male lion padding slowly our way, its great belly full and sagging from a recent meal—all that saved us. Still, no matter how sated, he was only fifteen feet away and, lethargic or not, could be in my lap in a single bound. In spite of McCombe's anguished protests, I reversed recklessly into a spectacular skidding half-circle and took off.

When a few moments later we spotted a large herd of buffalo, McCombe insisted on getting out with all his photographic gear draped around him, taking the guide along. I could go belting off if I wished, he said, but he was in the park to take pictures.

Very restive to begin with and faced with two human beings walking toward them, intent unknown, the herd began milling about alarmingly. One large bull, nose high in the air, stepped out purposefully in Dave's direction. I was parked parallel and close to a fallen trunk of a fever tree and had reasonable protection. McCombe, however, the guard hot on his heels, barely made it up the steep side of a large anthill as the animals in their hundreds suddenly stampeded his way.

For about three minutes they flowed round the hillock in a cloud of dust, a thundering torrent of brown bodies that, had it overwhelmed Dave and the guard, would have left them mere profiles in the sandy soil.

Back in the Jeep, rejoicing in what he was certain were splendid photographs and unimpressed by his narrow escape, he'd only just prepared his movie camera when we came upon our first elephant of the day.

For me this has always been an awesome experience, one that sends my blood pressure soaring and dampens the palms of my hands. The great beasts out in the open are a breathtaking sight.

I stopped the Jeep on firm ground, kept the engine running, the car in gear, feet hovering tentatively near clutch and accelerator. The wind, when we stopped, was blowing in our direction, carrying our scent and sound away from the group.

It did make a magnificent picture, two big cows and a young bull about thirty yards away, backsides to us, lazily stripping the bark from some msasa trees. The only tricky bit was the larking about between us and their mothers of two babies perhaps two years old. We knew that a female with young nearby functions on a hair-trigger and can go berserk in an instant, vicious beyond description.

McCombe, standing up on the front seat, was easily able to

grind away without fear of upsetting them. Elephants' eyesight is notoriously poor. So long as the breeze wafted in our favor we were safe.

Yet, thirty yards is a slim margin of safety; we were on open, sandy ground broken by groves of palm and msasa and littered with the rotting trunks of trees collapsed of old age and others pushed over by the elephants so they could get at the upper, more tender foliage. The motor tracks meandered through this debris on lines of least resistance, and the going was arduous and slow. Attempt at a quick getaway would be an interesting experience.

Oblivious to the risks, Dave was muttering about how perfect the light was, panning the whirring camera in a gentle sweep of the scene when, like eiderdown slowly settling to the ground, the wind dropped. In a second Dave's humming equipment sounded like a tin rattle. Without a pause in her feeding, the largest cow shrieked with alarm.

Exactly what happened in the next few moments I can't recall. In a flash the cow had spun around and, trumpeting, her trunk high, her great ears spread wide, was thundering straight for us. The ground shook.

I shot the Jeep forward with a lurch that dumped McCombe, tangled in photographic harness, on top of the terrified guard. Dead silent until the wind dropped, the African was now holding forth like a mezzo soprano. The gun was now forgotten on the floor of the Jeep and all his energies were devoted to holding on in the bucking vehicle and loudly exhorting me to greater speed.

Maneuvering masterfully I dodged fallen trees, boulders and whale-sized anthills, churned through deep sand and with a protesting roar from the bounding Jeep, somehow kept going. Yet I couldn't even get out of second gear. Meanwhile the bellowing cow picked up momentum in an almost straight line.

Most of the time elephants, the bulls at least, will make a great show of trumpeting, kicking up the earth, flapping their ears and often rushing forward threateningly. Even a charge can halt just short of the objective. It's all sound and fury, and it usually has the desired effect: sending a trespasser bowling away in panic.

Even as I concentrated on picking up speed, I toyed with the hope that this, too, would be no more than a mock performance. At full throttle, one of these huge animals can get up to thirty-five miles an hour. I'd never make that over the ground I had to cover.

Just as I ran into a patch of sticky going, Dave, flailing about in the back, shouted that she was barely a Jeep's length away. Didn't I think, he added, that I might "whip the horses into greater endeavor?"

More speed I couldn't produce, but, just as the elephant towered over the rear of the vehicle and Dave grabbed for the rifle, we entered a narrow draw tightly edged with thorn trees. The track's surface turned smooth and firm, and we shot forward, leaving her falling behind.

"She's gone," McCombe shouted, "swung off to the right, God bless her!" and, satisfied she'd really abandoned the chase, I coasted to a halt.

My hands were so palsied I couldn't feed a cigarette to my trembling lips, and even my legs quivered so I had to get out and walk about to give them something familiar to do.

When we did continue, Dave agreed, uncharacteristically, that a return to camp and tumbler of whisky was in order. On the way I drove past hippo at a great distance, widely circled two prides of lion and even kept totally harmless zebra well beyond focal range.

Not all my new experiences with African fauna was hair-raising. Most of it was pleasurable as with the family pets I met: deer, a cheetah, an eagle and even a small python (eight feet long). And a very special member of one family, Katacki, whom I didn't meet but fervently wished I had.

In March 1950, with most of the lowland Congo already traversed and only the high, forested mountains of the southeast, Lake Albert and the last of the country's cities, Elizabethville, separating me from the Northern Rhodesia border, I came across "Putnam's Camp." Sprawled beside the rapids of the Epulu River near the village of Boyo, the thatched mud and wattle huts blended into the surrounding jumble in perfect disguise, and, without having been clue'd up by the publican in the inn at Vicicongo, I'd have quite easily missed the place.

The proprietor and administrator of the "camp," by Belgian government fiat a wildlife conservatory, museum-collecting depot, and tropical-disease clinic, was an American, Patrick Putnam. Age forty-five and resembling a cadaverous young Lincoln, he'd been one of a team of anthropologists sent to the Congo in 1927. A fever outbreak on the West Coast had forced the Harvard University group to detour around through Alexandria, up the Nile Valley, and through the Sudan, an ordeal that obviously produced the beginnings of the lean and hungry look he wore when I met him.

His first wife had grown disenchanted with life in this moldy, insect-ridden bivouac, and, although they'd made several rejuvenating trips back to their native city, New York, she ultimately left him. When I met him, a second, hardier and less fastidious woman was calmly overseeing what she told me were his dying days. Emphysema in its latter stages demanded he be carried by natives in an open sedan chair, a "kipoy," whenever he left the main house and only this way could he supervise specimen-collecting for his overseas museums and study the unique wild life in this "lost world," including a community of about sixty pygmies. Pre-med at Harvard and six months in Brussels had qualified him to operate the clinic and to diagnose and treat some fifty cases a day. Most of the cases were yaws, a disfiguring spirochete infection faintly resembling leprosy but not related to it.

He knew he was dying, but Putnam nonetheless seemed a happy man, a free spirit fulfilled. During most of my stay he carried a tiny newborn squirrel in the breast pocket of his shirt ("for body warmth"), fed it by squeezing milk into its mouth from a pinch of cotton and quietly tolerated its wriggling and squeaking distractions during mealtime conversations.

The Putnams' home was in the shape of a dumbbell, two circular bedrooms connected by a large, oblong lounge. Dead center in the living room was an open fireplace raised about a foot from the floor on a brick plinth. Smoke eddied generally upward and out through a hole in the roof, an opening shielded from the rains by a small grass umbrella on the outside. It was an efficient system, warming the whole room evenly on cold nights and permitting occupants to sit around the fire and chat across the flickering flame.

Rough-hewn mahogany beams supported the framework on which the roof thatch was laid, and the walls of the main room were solid with bookshelves, a miscellany of faded pictures and racks of bird and animal cages.

In fact, the whole place appeared to pulsate. In addition to ranks of baboon, crocodile, gorilla, and other skulls, there were very lively pottos or rabbit-sized furry rodents and two psycopithicus ("putty nose") monkeys named Mr. Laff and Anna, whose baby squealed all round the room.

Unusual among the wild things cluttering up the area outside the building was an Okapi colt, one of nature's jokes, a mix of zebra and giraffe, to which it's related. A bit larger than a Shetland pony and slighter of build, it was tied to a veranda upright.

There were also cages of tufted forest guinea fowl, a 'possumlike, tree-climbing member of the elephant family Puntam identified as a hyrax with a nighttime cry like a woman being choked to death, and two giant fruit bats about the size of a chicken hawk. These competed with the hyrax at night, making deep gung-gunging sounds like a base viola.

Quite pathetic was a young female chimpanzee, Katolina, isolated and unloved, tied to a spindly tree near the front entrance. I asked Putnam why this so-human animal was treated this way, and, after a pause during which he stared vacantly out the window, he told me this story:

Years earlier the pygmies had brought him a baby chimp whose mother they'd killed. Putnam took him in, bottle-fed him, gave him the run of the house, and in time accepted him as a member of the family. He developed so explosive a temperament they named him Katacki, the Swahili word for the percussion cap on the old muzzle-loaders.

He ate at the table with the Putnams, and, although his manners were boisterous, he learned to use the right utensils and use them well. A scowl from Putnam was enough to prompt a quick, guilty change from a spoon to a fork during the meat course.

By the time Katacki was about six, he'd reached two-hundred pounds and five feet in height. He was good-natured, happy, and thoroughly accepted as a Putnam. The jungle well away from the house was his "Chic Sale," he washed himself on the banks of the Epulu, had a beer at "sundowner" time in the evening, and even joined Putnam relaxing into an easy chair with a cigar after a heavy meal. Twice he went to America as Putnam's companion.

Then all this began to change.

World War Two and Japanese hegemony over the Far East cut off normal rubber and some cotton supplies, and Putnam was assigned by the Belgians to help oversee the now-valuable northern Congo production. He took Katacki with him in his battered old Chevrolet, and all the police and country natives quickly grew to know the animal as Putnam's friend, an odd one perhaps, but then the white man generally speaking was a bit off.

The town-dwellers were different. Left in the car when Putnam had business to attend to, Katacki was prey to abuse by the gangs that gathered around, poking sticks through the window and laughing and shouting at the chimp's distress. It wasn't long before he hated all blacks excepting only those he knew at home in the camp.

On one trip to an administrative center Putnam left Katacki in the front seat of the car, as usual, confident that his many warnings to the locals about Katacki's temper would keep the tormenters away from the vehicle. Nonetheless, a crowd gathered, most of them keeping a respectful distance. One, however, took to thrusting a banana through the open window and snatching it back when the chimp reached for it.

This was asking for trouble. By now Katacki's strength was enormous. At an Air Force research station in the United States chimpanzees his size had been known to figuratively squeeze off the padlocks on the cages, and bending one-inch steel bars was recreation.

Infuriated at the teasing, Katacki waited his chance. As the man, overconfident now, moved close to the window, the chimp shot a long arm out around his shoulders and snapped his neck against the roof of the car, killing him instantly.

The case against the chimp was cut and dried, as was the verdict. The police regretfully demanded the animal be put to death but permitted Putnam to do it in any manner he chose.

They drove the endless miles back to Boyo, a trip Putnam will never forget, Katacki as usual chattering happily at returning home. The family had their evening meal and although Putnam was unable to eat, Katacki was in good appetite and afterward retired to his easy chair, surfeited and dozy. Putnam found some excuse to leave the room, asking his wife to go with him. When he returned, alone, he stepped behind his sleeping friend, pointed his big service revolver at the back of Katacki's head and pulled the trigger.

Since that night there'd never been another pet ape or monkey in the Putnam home. And there never would be.

CHAPTER XXVIII

"Shark!"

During the last six months I spent in Africa before leaving for a bureau assignment in Germany, most African news stories were in the heavyweight class.

Heading the list south of the equator was the remarkable postwar performance of a burgeoning economy in Southern Rhodesia, the country inclining toward enlightened conservative policies that created what was, for Africa, a radical multiracial experiment.

Next door, to the south, was Britain's Union of South Africa, the powerful, former colony resolutely marching toward independence as an uncompromising white supremacist republic.

Some light relief of sorts was supplied in the neighborhood by the return of Bechuanaland's chief-designate, Seretse Khama, bringing with him an attractive, red-haired white wife, Ruth. It was all very offbeat romantic, but it was complicated. Ruth was intelligent, personable, a credit to the eminent royal Khama family, but she was nonetheless white and, what's more, pregnant. There was a crescendo of tut-tutting about the implications in this pathologically race-conscious part of the world, but in the event the child, Jacqueline, was accepted calmly and later was a classmate of my daughters' at Arundel School in Rhodesia.

Within a few months of my arrival at the Transvaal border in the spring of 1950, there was the Indian and black African call for a "day of mourning" to commemorate the January 26, 1949, mass protest in Durban against the country's policy of "apartheid," or separate development of the races.

What had been planned that year as a passive strike with the workers "remaining in their homes to pray" had been converted by a bus station fight between an Indian and an African into a bloody three-day civil war, the whites caught in the middle and the army, navy and air force called out to aid the police.

Officially, 137 had died, 1,883 were reported injured, and millions of dollars of damage had been done to homes and shops and public facilities, a large part of the municipal market gutted. Hence, the commemorative "day of mourning" was receiving considerable advance attention, most of it designed to prevent recurrence of the riots. Both sides were uneasy.

Now, all this political pulsing, the subsurface rumbling with pent-up hostility, was portentous stuff, and I covered it. Yet, there were other events that absorbed my interest no less. One of them that scarcely qualified as of high-level significance but had its merits as a story was the shark scare along the Indian Ocean beaches of Natal.

I was in Durban, Natal's commercial center and one of the country's principal ports, readying for the possible repeat of the forty-nine rioting. I'd cultivated the military, civil officials, and news sources, made transport arrangements, and studied backgrounders, all preparing for chaos that in the event, didn't develop.

Massive military and police preparedness on January 26 and preliminary peace-pipe sessions between the South African Indian Congress and the black African National Congress resulted in a demonstration that was both successful and peaceful. Some 80 percent of the work force stayed home and more than 1,000 Indian and African businesses were silent behind steel shutters for the twenty-four hours.

For me, all this good news had overtaken the bad. And nothing kills a story more decisively. Nonetheless, it developed, as it does in most such cases, that my homework had been time well spent.

Part of that effort had taken me to the area around the Durban docks and some weeks after the non-riot I returned there one early morning. Interested in a whaling-industry story I'd gone to what was called the "south pier" or "south breakwater," a jetty flanking the entrance to the main harbor, and got into a rambling conversation with a group of fishermen. We talked about the racial troubles, on everyone's mind, and about how the "bloody Yanks" would do well to mind their own business and get off South Africa's back at the "bloody United Nations," a "blinking farce at best," and even about fishing. Especially fishing with a Scarborough reel, a heavy, "palm-braked" wooden wheel carrying as much as a thousand feet of flax or cotton line. In Durban, Scarboroughs were used only for shark and that morning I learned that the quest for the big fish had become a vengeful business.

A few days after my arrival to cover the expected troubles, a popular young lifeguard, Brian van Berg, had been dragged beneath the surface and never seen again. The youngster, just gone twenty, a big strapping lad and excellent swimmer, was the twenty-third Indian Ocean bather to be attacked and, the fisherman told me, the eleventh to die in shark attacks in the last "year or two."

"Horrible bloody things, they are," a big, ugly man spoke up. A sun-reddened blond in ragged khaki shorts and worn work shoes, he was fitting a reel to a seven-foot, wrist-thick malacca pole.

"Bloody eating machine. Eat all kinds of muck, they do," he kept working, head down over the reel. "Cut one open a while ago—last week it was—pulled a part of the stomach out, and there was a big bulge. Just for a lark I pulled the inner lining tight round the thing." He paused.

"Didn't half scare us," a companion interjected, "Ol' Jake, he says, 'looky here, this one's 'ad a monkey for scoff'!"

"But it bloody well wasn't," Ol' Jake broke in, looking up from his work. "No bloody fear. A man's head it was, eyes, nose, and ears gone. Them stomach enzymes; burn the skin off your bloody foot, they will."

Police collected the head and other parts for study.

"The bloke might've been one of your countrymen," Ol' Jake said to me. "They reckoned he was a white male, thirty-five to forty, medium height. Could've been a sailor, they said, fell off a Yank boat waiting out in the roads."

I checked with authorities and found they didn't know who it was. They'd prepared a dental record and filed it for reference. It was, after all, the third set of human remains pulled out of sharks in a week.

The *Natal Mercury* and other papers were following the van Berg story with charges of "shameful neglect" of bathers' safety in the face of mounting "shark infestation." Peter Benchley's horror story *Jaws*, about a Great White "maneater," was not to titillate perspiring readers and terror-numbed movie audiences for another twenty-five years or so. Yet at any time a tale told of shark attacks has quickly quieted all other conversation in a crowded room, and even random tidbits about the beast have a similar effect.

"Shark infestation" is scarcely "news." The menace has been around a long time, about 125 million years, and more than a million are killed in the world's waters every year—20,000 of them off the coast of East Africa alone.

The thing has no bones except its jaws, just cartilage. It has all-consuming digestive juices; tough abrasive hide ("only a shark can bite into a shark"); teeth that are not fixed but "float" in the jaw and if lost replace themselves, ready for the next biting opportunity.

Along the Natal coast where the warm Mocambique current eddies southward at a leisurely two-and-a-half miles an hour, the sea is a congenial environment for aquatic life, and food for the big fish including man, abounds.

Human beings abroad in boats in steadily increasing numbers over the centuries reached a peak in the Indian Ocean during World War Two, when hundreds of ships carrying fighting men and prisoners of war were sunk, many of them along the southern continental littoral. South African newspaper "morgues" carry reams of stories of beaches awash with torn human remains, most of it a kind of human chum left after wholesale shark attack.

In spite of its largely local interest, dealing as it did with a threat to South African bathers and to the local holiday economy, the story struck me as worth trying. The van Berg tragedy seemed a good beginning.

The month of March is late summer south of the equator, hot and muggy in Durban. It was early evening, about 7:00 P.M., of a cloudy day; the waters were murky and uninviting; and bathers were few in spite of the heat. The Durban Life Savers Club, taking advantage of the lull, readied for a practice drill, part of intense training sessions kept up by all the clubs along the coast. The surf at Durban can be mountainous, the currents are tricky, and a shark watch must be constantly kept.

Simulating a normal alert, the North Beach Club assigned young Neville Cook to don the rescue harness for the pretended emergency. This tackle was attached to a hundred-yard nylon line with the anchor end fixed to a windlass operated from up the beach by the team. The line would provide security and help the life saver and his charge in the long haul back to shore.

The "dummy" drowner for the day was van Berg, a bright, personable lad. Told to begin the drill, Brian pushed his way through the heavy surf and then struck out over the rollers. About seventy yards from the beach he turned and realistically acted out "bather in trouble," shouting, thrashing about, and holding one arm above his head. At this prescribed signal for help, young Cook scrambled into the harness and hit the water at a dead run.

A powerful swimmer, Cook quickly covered the distance and was within about six feet of van Berg when he saw him suddenly sink below the surface. The baffled rescuer was swimming in a circle around the spot when van Berg reappeared, floating motionless on his back, his eyes closed. As Cook reached out to grap his hair and continue the "rescue," the body was jerked beneath the surface and disappeared again.

Thinking Neville had a hold on Brian, the beach crew winched the rescuer back to within about forty yards of the shore before they saw Cook was alone and realized something was wrong.

No trace of van Berg ever was found.

Not long after that an African woman was taken in waist-deep water at the mouth of the nearby Umgeni River. When, two days later, South Pier fishermen landed a "lazy gray," a check of its stomach contents left no doubt about how the woman had died.

Her death increased the hue and cry raised by Brian's loss. Public demand was made for immediate protection at the beaches.

Teams of shark-catching fishermen proliferated, and hundreds of the fish were hooked from boats and along a twenty-mile stretch of shoreline.

The stomach contents of the fish were prodigious.

Dubbed the "garbage can of the sea" and the "Ocean Hyena," the shark will eat anything that has an odor or shines in the water. One 850-pound "lazy gray" caught off Durban contained the head and forepart of a large crocodile, the hind leg of a sheep, three seagulls, four two-pound cans of peas (American manufacture), a Craven A cigarette tin and fifteen feet of rope. The thing's digestive juices are so strong, that this beast had to have accumulated all this mass of rubbish recently and in a short period of feeding.

In another "lazy gray," an 800-pounder, fishermen found a large dog with collar, horses' hooves, chicken feet and beef bones, tortoise shells, a small pig, several lobsters, a six-inch shark hook with five feet of wire leader, numerous glass bottles, and a complete cowhide. This is a catholic diet. Nor was it all. One human head, a thigh, and other human bones were also found. Many more human beings, it became obvious, were being taken than ever were recorded in the statistical tables.

One lad who nearly became such a statistic I interviewed on the Country Club Beach one bright, sunny winter morning in mid-June. We'd retired to a quiet section, and the peaceful surroundings were in marked contrast to the chilling topic.

Gabriel Botha was twenty-five years old when we talked. He'd been a member of the Country Club's Pirate Surf Life Saving Club for eight years. A blond mountain of a man, he was placid and of a cheerful, easy disposition. He lay back on the sand propped up on his elbows, his bare legs stretched out toward the sea. His left foot was badly scarred and awkwardly twisted, but what was more immediately noticeable was his left thigh. There wasn't any. Or very little.

From hip to knee the top and outer side of the leg had been gouged away. The bulging muscular ham of his right leg, the typical rugby player's outsized thigh, made it seem even more pathetically deformed and fragile.

"Not as bad as it looks, that," Botha'd caught me glancing at his leg. "Anyway, I'm too lucky to be sorry for myself, for that or the foot," and he wiggled his toes.

"That happened first, the thigh," he went on. "Should have learned, but I didn't," he grimaced and told me this story.

He was working the afternoon shift at the country club beach and was off duty when, at ten o'clock one winter morning about thirty-five yards off North Beach twenty-five–year–old George Best, a London sailor, standing waist deep, was hit by a shark. The bite ripped out most of the thigh down to the femur, taking away the sciatic nerve. He was rushed to Addington Hospital, just off South Beach, and given twenty pints of blood and plasma. He never regained consciousness.

Following the morning attack on Best, Botha and the other Pirate Life Savers were told to "keep 'em out of the water the rest of the day."

About five in the evening, most of the bathers having left the area, Botha and Louis Johnson, bored with the inactivity charged down the beach and plunged out into the surf. In a matter of moments they had crossed the channel that runs parallel to the shore about thirty yards out and were swimming easily out to the large breakers beyond. Botha was "a bit nervous" and called to Johnson, "Let's stay together."

"Which is B.S. anyway," Botha snorted, "because there's no safety in numbers, not with shark."

He'd hardly cried out to Johnson when he felt a "sharp, quick tug at my left leg; that's all."

"I shouted 'shark!' then quickly felt down my left leg to a gaping hole in my thigh, kept feeling along trying to find the leg, convinced I couldn't be feeling in the right place."

Johnson shouted for help from the beach and then swam next to Botha, lifting him along. They went about twenty yards, and Botha said he just "quit; not out, mind you—just no more strength.

"Johnson dragged me in, and, as soon as we were on the beach, he grabbed a large vein and kept me from bleeding to death."

Botha was rushed to a hospital in a private car, sideswiping two other vehicles on the way, and was placed in the bed next to Best. The morphine they gave him "might as well have been water." He lay there, fully conscious, next to a bed holding Best that was so drenched with blood that it ran off onto the floor and "the nurses and doctors had to wear white cloth overshoes."

Best died at 1:00 A.M. the following morning.

"Me?" Botha laughed. "I'm too hard a case to go that easily."

The bite he suffered measured nine by twelve inches and took out what one doctor estimated was about nine pounds of flesh. The sciatic nerve was exposed but not severed, "so I kept the leg."

He later contributed fourteen pints of blood to the hospital bank, "and even that was far short, they said, of what they'd given me."

Determined to do his military service, he left the hospital after three months and did "every exercise imaginable" to get the leg back into working order. The workouts didn't get him accepted by the army, but he credits them with renewing his strength and leaving his leg as fit as it is today. Other muscles, he said, went into action to compensate, and, while he now has a deep pit in the thigh that "will never fill up again," he has fair use of the leg.

"The next time," he said, "I almost didn't make it out of the water."

"Next time" was almost exactly three years to the day, March 9, 1947, midafternoon.

He was "loafing about in the drink" off the country club beach when he sensed that the channel current was carrying him north toward the Umgeni River mouth. In a few moments he was taken well away from the beach proper, but, unworried, he rode the rollers that eased him up out of the pull of the tide and made slow but steady progress toward shore.

It was when he was still about seventy yards out that he felt something grab his left foot.

"Not at all like the other bite but a deliberate, crunching increase of pressure."

He kicked out in panic and screamed, a "cry no one heard," and struck out for shore.

He had taken only a few strokes when he felt the water swell up around him as the big fish rose from the depths to strike again. This time it sank its teeth into his lower back. Screaming hysterically he spun his body around, his right shoulder striking the shark's side, to find the thing "wallowing in the water inches from my face," the animal's huge dorsal fin level with Botha's eyes.

He struck out with both his fists, so hard his forearms were later covered with bruises, kicking and screaming in a frenzy, and then went blank for what he guessed was no more than a few seconds.

When he remembered anything again he was swimming hard and deliberately, measuring his strokes, numb with terror. He'd been pulled so far under by the second attack—he recalled the "redness all around me in the water and the sudden dead silence"—that he thought "ol' Botha's had his chips this time."

He was rolled up the beach in the breakers, a "chunk of bleeding meat." A passing motorist ran from his car and, fully clothed, rushed into the surf and dragged him out. Still conscious, Botha tried to walk but his left foot "just folded under like a flap, a fin, and I fell flat on my face." He and the motorist finally got the attention of the Pirate team, way down the beach, and, again, he was rushed to the hospital.

His left foot had nearly been bitten off at the instep and he had four useless toes to show for it. There were twelve deep tooth punctures across his lower back and more inside both thighs. If he hadn't twisted violently before the shark could close its jaws, Botha would have been literally bitten in half.

The Union Whaling Company station on the Bluff south of the harbor entrance had been active at the time I interviewed Botha. The blood and offal pouring down its slipways into the waters attracted shoals of ravenous shark, and I had visited this disgusting abattoir as part of the studies of shark feeding habits.

The fish attacked the huge carcasses as they were floated into the ramp, tearing chunks from the animals' flanks. Often they rushed at the meal with such a fever of excitement that, misjudging and hitting the slippery side of the whale, they'd shoot right over the top, some thirty feet through the air. It was an astonishing if sickening sight.

Some years later, but before the station was closed and out of a sense of perverted nostalgia, I revisited the place as one of a tourist group. A huge male sperm whale was sprawled in a shapeless mass on the slipway, and we watched the factory hands' efforts to extract a large shark, squirming about inside the great cadaver.

The thing had eaten its way into the whale, gotten itself trapped and couldn't get out. It had to be removed before the workmen could go to work, carving the blubber off with long, hooked knives. Winched out by the tail the shark, about 800 pounds, went berserk, clashing its great teeth at the men and soaking them with bloody foam as they clubbed it about the head until it was dead.

It had been a quite ghastly and incredibly smelly experience, and, relieved that it was over, the group was moving away when one of the number made a classic remark.

The business of pulling the shark loose had torn the whale's innards free to flow out over the concrete ramp. Prominent in this mass of entrails was the animal's astonishingly long and bulky "private member." One of the visitors behind me, a giggly young woman, whispered a question to her husband.

"Oh, I see!" she squealed. "That must be what they mean by having a whale of a time!"

The shark and whale stories, aimed at the old *Saturday Evening Post*, never got past my agent, Nannine Joseph, in New York. The query I sent her summarizing a month's work on "the menace" and including sample anecdotes was brushed off as involving the people in an area of the globe "too far away to be of interest in these parts."

This was neither the first nor the last such disappointment, but, since

I could use the material for news features and radio scripts, it had not been entirely dead time. What's more, as is usual, I had developed leads into other stories and had made professional contacts and lasting friends.

The year and a half spent in Germany from the autumn of 1950 to the spring of 1952 as *Pathfinder News Magazine* bureau chief was to net me much of the same. There was a rich harvest of varied subjects; I moved about from Oslo on the North Sea to Tunis on the Mediterranean; traveled through Portugal and the Low Countries and Switzerland and Italy and revisited Britain. It was a busy eighteen months.

The European assignment marked the end of the inning, as it were—the end of a strictly "foreign" commission. When I returned to Southern Rhodesia I was to settle on "home" ground. I was classified by the Rhodesians, optimistically as it turned out, as a "permanent resident"; I was to own my home; I edited a local newspaper, worked for Rhodesia Radio and Television, helped found a local school of aspiring amateur thespians, belonged to Rotary; presided over the convulsions of the Parent Teachers Association, and a lot more. In brief, I would "belong" and have a personal stake.

I remained "special correspondent" for the *Indianapolis News*, the *Philadelphia Bulletin* and others and considered Africa south of the Congo as my "beat." Yet, now my "beat" and my base would be synonymous. I moved about but I wasn't constantly on the move. It was a new beginning in many ways.

CHAPTER XXIX

Typewriter to Tractor

Generally speaking, it is accepted that a newspaperman who opts for a change of livelihood (barring only public relations and the priesthood) runs a serious risk of making an outright balls-up of the transition. I was no exception. The change of status was marked by two Aberrations and one Special Event, none of them minor.

I tried farming on a small scale, and I found myself in the earth-moving business, in command of a fleet of bulldozers, scrapers, graders, and trucks, all mine, and a staff I sometimes felt were akin to the hordes of the great khans in number, casual avarice and ruthlessness. And the "Special Event": I married for the third time.

Anyone can be unlucky enough to have a go at farming and earth-moving, circumstances such as money and poor judgment permitting, but it takes particular qualifications to qualify for this Special Event. Such as two previous marriages.

By that time, 1952, I had, altogether, three sons, the first two, John Huyler II, ten, and Donald Jameson, six, named for their paternal and maternal grandfathers respectively. Their mother was Patricia Jameson ("Trish"), a top-seeded nonpareil in the female rankings whose value I had recognized early in life, had lost sight of during a period of unaccountable obliquity, and rediscovered only when it was too late. Of striking good looks, confidently defiant by nature, and blessed with uncommon intelligence, she raised me from an untutored oaf who erred widely in the graces and didn't know Nijinsky from Kaminsky.

Matching patience and forbearance, she saw me through Georgetown School of Foreign Service, and stood behind me during my two years undistinguished army service in Europe. She'd seen her perseverance repaid when I was accepted as a cub reporter on the *Indianapolis News*.

I was determined to make a go of it, indeed so much so that Trish's reward for years of gentle attentiveness was to see me convert to a swaggering, macho, counterfeit copy of Joseph Pulitzer pretending he was Richard Harding Davis. Bereft of probity and elementary common sense, I set out on my own in all directions. Our divorce was an unhappy, out-of-court affair, made the sadder by the oft-stated determination of one of her uncles to "make that son-of-a-bitch pay if it's the last thing I do." My sons remained with their mother.

My second marriage to Norma Roslynn Dunn ("Peggy"), darkly pretty, vivacious and worldly, was far too soon after the end of the first one to be fair to either of us.

Among other follies I courted at the time was a determination to make a news photographer of her. Thus I felt, she would complement with pictures the stories with which I fully expected to dazzle my peers and prospective editors. That she viewed a part in newspaper work with the same enthusiasm she reserved for a career in female mud-wrestling was a sentiment I somehow overlooked.

Doggedly she completed a course at a New York photographic school, equipped herself with a Rolleiflex camera and several hundred pounds of related equipment, and we embarked on the journey through Britain and Africa that produced some of the stories I've told.

I have kept those stories solo for clarity and because I led the way, dragging her backward through the thorn bushes of discomfort and unfamiliar, and unwelcome, endeavor. She showed great courage and was remarkably long-suffering.

My third son, Jeffrey Duncan, was born in Germany, and by the time we arrived back in Southern Rhodesia he was age two.

Part of the change in the early Rhodesian days was deterioration in the association between his mother and me. We were going different ways in what was an Edwardian male-dominated society with a pervasive sense that things happened particular *for* men or because men did them. Women, depending on the woman, functioned in varying degrees in traditional roles as homemakers, mothers, and courtesans. The more skillful she was at this last, the less she drudged in the salt mines and the more she participated up front.

Whatever caused the collapse of the marriage, we'd effectively separated sometime before the crash. Jeffrey remained with his mother.

During the latter stages of the passage with Peggy, I met my present wife, at that time someone else's. Over the ensuing year and a big-dipper–like course from Umtali to Paris to London to Indianapolis and back to Salisbury, the sad details were resolved, and Maria Magdelena Elizabeth ("Ria") joined me at the beginning of what has stretched to twenty-eight years. We were married in July, 1956, in a magistrate's office in Johannesburg. Jean Fisher, a sparkling, warmhearted South

African I'd met when she was in America, was "family" witness.

Summing up my wife's qualities is bound to short-change her. Red-haired in fact and temperament, possessed of quick wit, a sense of humor both subtle and raucous, compassionate beyond description and, in time, of remarkably durable patience, she's gone about coping with my singular characteristics with spirit and determination.

In addition to my new wife, I acquired her three children, subsequently legally adopted as mine in the Rhodesian courts. At the time, Graham was six, Jacqueline, five, and Susan, one. Delite Maria was born to us at the Lady Chancellor Nursing Home in Salisbury July 29, 1959, her first name a gift from her paternal grandmother. Admittedly it was a speculative nomen. The hospital matron, a blunt sergeant-majorish type remarked, "What if, with a name like this, she grows up to look like the back end of a bus!" (She didn't.)

Of the two Aberrations, farming and earth-moving, and the Special Event that produced my ready-made family, only the Special Event can be said to have been anything like a success. Which, I suppose, makes me a winner whatever the losses. Especially, when looking back, it's obvious the defeats were preordained.

The year 1956 was a good year to strike out in any number of directions. The country was booming. The Federation of Rhodesia and Nyasaland was just three years old and with, apparently, a great economic future. Kariba Dam was nearing completion, the largest power project in Africa and soon to supply nearly 600 megawatts to a growing population bursting to create new agribusiness, commerce, and industry.

From my own farm a newly developed Katimbora Rhodes pasture grass high in protein and an ideal cattle and horse feed would, I felt confident, flow out to an eager market in a river of green bales.

Although I'd fallen into the heavy-equipment business by mistake, there really were roads and dams and housing developments to come that would assuredly require our machinery and our know-how.

Alas, there was the rub. Know-how.

When I bought my first farm tractor I had to ask the Ferguson agent if I plowed clockwise or right to left. As for the earthmoving, I got up from behind a typewriter to try and operate an International Harvester TD 9 bulldozer, and bigger things later; to have a go at managing company financing and personnel; submit complicated bids for construction work. . . .

As noted: defeat was built into both schemes from the start.

Meanwhile, other things began to slip, the federal political "experiment" not excluded. Steadily swelling black bitterness over what they rightly saw as indefinite postponement of their acceptance as a ruling majority tore the system apart.

Whatever else I toyed with, I still had a reporting job to do and had continued writing about federal developments. As the end drew near, I dropped concentration on my eccentric enterprises, no less doomed in any event, and focused my attention on the country's final political drama. While I was off in Victoria Falls where this tragicomedy would take place, my family, well established outside the village of Marandellas, would, as during my previous press junkets, get along until my return.

There were to be seven full years separating our settlement on the Marandellas farm from the federation's demise arranged at Victoria Falls in July of 1963.

Yet, the collapse of this Central African try at a solution to the mounting racial tensions didn't happen overnight. Failure was in the wind for most of those seven years. And those harbingers of its ultimate miscarriage, as much as the angry final event itself, would influence the nature and course of Southern Rhodesia's march of events.

Premonition of this human failure hung over us all and what happened there at the Falls unleashed hatreds that would lead to a bloody civil war within another decade.

From the small border town of Victoria Falls that July, I sent this dispatch to the *Philadelphia Bulletin*:

> *Victoria Falls, Southern Rhodesia.* The fragile remains of a once-robust experiment in nationhood was laid out on a conference table here this month and studiously picked to pieces by the politicians.
>
> The final dismemberment of the Federation of Rhodesia and Nyasaland has begun. It is a coldblooded business.
>
> Considering the proud beginning of a decade ago, this piteous demise lends testimony to the perplexities of the "indefatigable human spirit." The federation was created out of the self-delusion of its architects and supporters that what is "good for" a people must work. Indeed, it did deliver the promised material gain. But it also promised a quickening of spiritual values and produced only a universally troubled conscience.
>
> Because of this it failed, whatever or whoever else is publicly blamed. The idea of a black-white "partnership" that would light the way in an Africa torn by racial strife presupposed an enlightened humaneness and sense of common ends that proved to be unreal.
>
> Here at the Falls this month, there was no time for weary

phiolsophizing. No one dramatically cast the blame upon a humanity unfit to cope with such vast expectations.

This was a "business meeting," as one delegate put it, simple bankruptcy proceedings sending yet another well-meant enterprise out among the shades of a lot of other hopes. Certainly the dull mechanics of dissolution were a fact and had to be sorted out.

Logically the federation falls apart into its three components, Northern Rhodesia, Nyasaland, both now black ruled, and Southern Rhodesia, under a white minority regime determined to hold its own. It is more or less automatic and presents no new map-making problems. Not so easy is the severance of the ties that have bound these components together in the federal scheme.

A complicated system of controls has grown up—transport, communications, power, public health and education, defense, and others. More than 35,000 civil servants have conducted a federal business incurring some $800,000,000 in national and international indebtedness.

These functions, functionairies, and obligations are not reapportioned easily after years of booming development. If, it is estimated by one federal official, it took 100 civil servants six months to assemble this body politic, it is safe to assume it will take just as long to take it apart and create independent, viable entities.

In keeping with the "businesslike" approach to forestall emotional histrionics, the breakup conference was a sober affair. The shrill keening of African nationalists, long bitter opponents of the "White Man's Federation," was stilled.

Sir Roy Welensky, hulking federal premier, smarting under what he termed "British government betrayal" was an ominous, contemptuous presence unimpressed by the astuteness of R. A. Butler, Britain's canny minister for Central African Affairs and chairman of the conference. Butler deftly maneuvered controversial issues into ad hoc committees "for study" and smoothly paved the way for the Act of Dissolution he hopes to get through the British Parliament before its upcoming recess.

Winston Field, right-wing government leader in southern Rhodesia, was solemn, keenly alert to his country's position as the land of white supremacy in a blackening Central Africa, and stolidly cooperative.

Conference sessions were held in the seedy opulence of the Victoria Falls Hotel's "summer parlor," a vast windowed lounge antiqued to look vaguely Jacobean.

Over 120 delegates and staff, some housed in railroad sleeping cars near the hotel, bustled through lobbies jammed with vacationers or toyed with telex and duplicating machines, not a few installed in bathrooms for want of other space. Out of this pulsation of ritual and revelry fifty newsmen culled more than 100,000 words of copy in the seven days.

Looming over all this and symbolizing the federal failure was Sir Roy. Once during the session he had thundered to his feet threatening a walkout of his eight-man delegation "in one minute" if the subject of a commission to take over his dying government's dissolution functions was broached again. It wasn't and most of the time he remained broodingly watchful.

He refused a Butler cocktail invitation, went fishing alone when other delegates gathered at a peacepipe church service, and flew out early, leaving others behind to sort out a plethora of committees.

For the giant exrailroader and union man, it was a sorry end to 30 years in politics. He admitted mistakes and to being naive in a United Kingdom political scramble he insisted has lost any moral qualities. Resignedly, he said it was the end of an era, a retiring tide that swept back with it the hopes he'd held and the attitudes native to him.

He failed to place the blame where, in a large sense, it belonged: on himself and on the few blacks and most whites whose burning wish to make the system work disallowed the destructive forces of selfishness and fear in a context where they predominate.

Near the conference end he led his staff on a walk to the Devil's Cataract at the Falls, an awesome thing of roaring waters and towering sheets of spray. The big man was dwarfed on the lip of this natural holocaust and had to shout above the thunder. Perhaps this was too appropriate, even corny. I was touched by it.

"Of course it's galling," he frowned. "There's little of dignity in this for me, for many of us. Let's face it—it's failed. For Central Africa it's a disaster."

The new black states would not agree. For them it is a time of wonder and excitement. But it is a time not without the rumblings of Welensky's prophesied disaster. The pain in it all, paradoxically, stems from the ironies lurking in "rising expectations," in too much hopefulness.

Two independent countries were created: Zambia, or the former Northern Rhodesia, and Malawi from Nyasaland. Rhodesia, dropping the "Southern," remained bound to the Crown as a self-governing colony, denied independence from Britain because of its minority white rule.

For these three there would be plenty of trouble ahead and many would look back on the economic prosperity of the federal era, and in large measure a genuine coming-together of blacks and whites, as the most fruitful experience Central Africa would know in the twentieth century.

In the Southern Rhodesia of those federal days there had been rapid advance. The country, two-thirds the size of Texas with 250,000 whites and 7,500,000 blacks, was expanding in the public and private sectors with a vigor that altered the landscape from week to week.

Certainly for me the period had been pulsating with opportunities, at least two of them standouts, the enthusiasm of the efforts closely matched by the magnitude of the failure. My try at farming and my prodigal plunge into earthmoving.

Our farm, "Strafford,"* six miles from Marandellas, trapezium-shaped and 220 acres in extent, was 50 percent good granitic-contact soil, one quarter marshland, and the rest rocky hills. Two high stony ridges beginning close together and standing some fifty feet above the valley floor opened away from each other in a "V" as they sloped gently eastward toward an expanse of rolling veld.

The entrance to these lands was off the main country road into the narrow neck at the apex of the "V," so that, upon each entry to the lands, one had the remarkable sensation the world was suddenly opening out especially for you. The hush of a pine forest emphasized this strange illusion.

The dwelling, just inside the apex, was a brick oblong, single-story wearing a tattered thatch that sagged along its length with a tall chimney at either end. There was a guest cottage, a garage-cum-workshop, and two square-built huts in the backyard, one an "office," the other a sewing room.

Compass markings painted black on the front veranda pointed dead east from the center of the doorway.

When we left it nearly twenty years later, we had doubled the size of the main house, there was a three-box-stall stable with tack (or equipment) room, tractor, and miscellaneous sheds and a large "game room" with mukwa-wood sprung flooring and mirrors on the end walls for Ria's ballet classes—she is ex–Cape Town University Ballet, an accomplished dancer and a drill instructor of a teacher. One end of this structure housed a dressing room for a swimming bath. There was a Dutch barn for storing hay and, of course, on the hilltop above the main dwelling, the "Kopje House."

---

*For the Philadelphia suburban town where my family lived.

A native village crouched in a hollow portion of the south ridge and had six brick two-room cottages and one large four-room home for the farm "boss boy." It had an ablution block, vegetable and flower gardens, a few crude livestock pens, and, while it wasn't Windsor Great Park, it was comfortable for a staff population varying in size from three or four families to ten, depending on the season and the state of our finances.

The place was less a "farm," perhaps, than a smallholding, but for us it was a major undertaking, and we threw ourselves at it with a certain grim determination.

First came the repair and redecoration of the main house, for which we employed Max Weber, an old friend. Max dismantled parts of a house I had in the Vumba Mountains to the east on the Mocambique border and incorporated it into the renewal of the Marandellas dwelling. It was exacting, skillful work, laboriously and beautifully finished, and I was convinced I would die of old age before it was completed.

While talented cabinetmakers and artistic masons "created," Ria and I and three children huddled together in the guest cottage, a two-bedroom hovel infested with small wildlife so unique and cunning I prepared a radio script about one particular species:

> No doubt at one time or another someone's snapped at you, "Don't touch it!" and then continued in cooing tones to expand on how it eats flies and mosquitos and is, after all, a life. Meanwhile, crawling toward you along the back of the couch is a spider the size and appearance of a musician's wig.
>
> I find rhapsodizing about spiders very boring. This is because I have just been forced to accommodate my family in a dank and dismal concrete pillbox at the height of the worst tropical rains in decades and into which fetid cave came a host of creeping and crawling things.
>
> My wife was desperately ill with shingles, described in lurid detail in *Webster's International* as "an acute inflammatory skin disease of nervous origin in which vesicles occur in clusters causing extreme tenderness and usually spreading round the trunk like a girdle."
>
> As vivid as this is it falls far short of picturing her agony as she spent her days abed, staring miserably into the mist that eddied round her.
>
> One evening as the rest of us clustered in the darkness of the next room, we heard a piercing scream, and she catapulted out through the door, her face dead white.
>
> Behind her on the pillow was what we called a "hunting

spider," a great black hairy thing the size and appearance of an eight-legged hamburger with bristles. Having one drop on you from a mossy ceiling is bloodcurdling.

We'd fought off centipedes and scorpions and assorted large flying things that buzzed through the muggy household like wet prunes on the wing, but this crawler was the last straw.

Actually, our spider, although the sight of it made the flesh tighten on the back of my head, was nothing to speak of compared to some. My scalp would have constricted right off the top of my skull if I'd been confronted by one that inhabits parts of South America.

It's called Theraphose Blondi, is found principally in French Guiana and has a span of ten inches, larger than the average dinner plate. Similar to our "hunting spider" it's horrendous-looking but nonpoisonous. For the most part it's the appearance and the crawly feeling that's so upsetting, although perhaps it's really a matter of what one's accustomed to.

I lived for a time in West Africa, a hot humid climate that produces gigantic growth in the most ordinary bugs. The praying mantis we've discussed before that visited our drink table in the evening was one of these. It was a frightening sight and could nip sharply. Still you'll remember, we fed him gin in drops off a matchstick and he returned each night—to nip in a different way.

Nonetheless, I don't think I'd ever willingly play host to that hairy thing that dropped on my wife's pillow. Spiders, so far as I'm concerned, are doomed to drink alone.

Finally we moved into the main house and turned our attention to "farming." Ria and the cook, first a chap named "Dinner," and then his successor, Moffat, concentrated with Graciano, the gardener, on a large vegetable patch that produced softball-sized tomatoes, radishes as big as Idaho potatoes, tiny succulent strawberries, and tender stringbeans so large they looked like bunches of green bananas. There was celery and spinach and carrots and huge squash on vines the size of ship mooring hawsers and everything had that sweet earthy flavor that only your own lovingly tended plot can produce.

If Ria's vegetables were an instant success, my try at a crop was less masterly. My marshland melons were enjoyed by battalions of beetles from all over Rhodesia. If I sprayed them with enough insecticide to permanently poison generations of bugs, there was an immediate downpour that washed them clean and vulnerable again. I spent a fortune on seed, cotton netting, fertilizer and insect killer, and ultimately harvested for market five cantaloupe, two honeydew, and a watermelon. Mr. Petrikios at the Marandellas Milk Bar and grocery shop bought them from me out of pity. Two pounds sterling the lot. Loss of my investment was total.

Having decided that specialty items demanding a twenty-four–hour watch and scientific expertise were beyond my native aptitudes, I turned to planting on a massive scale. The principle I pursued was that so grand an effort couldn't all go bad.

Of 110 tillable acres I planted 80 in Katimbora Rhodes grass, a high protein cattle food developed in Rhodesian research stations. Before I could sow this feathery mash, however, I had to prepare the lands, a discouraging prospect.

They had been farmed before, more or less. Untold numbers of years earlier, the native Shona tribesmen had corrugated the marshy lowlands with three-foot–high ridging in which the women planted yams. The drier higher area supporting tussocks of sour veldt grass had been overgrazed by bush cattle and goats until reduced to a wasteland barely carrying cactus and thorny scrub. Actually, this was about par for most of the country's native settlements, traditionally no more than fugitive communities, prey to famine and marauding enemies.

The tribes had used the hills flanking the valley for lookout posts and crude fortifications, and we found a dozen caves still with the earthen bowls and amphora for storing grain and water during enemy raids. Arab slavers too had been a constant menace, sweeping through the district at frequent intervals. Proof of these gory forays were the rusted iron manacles and bits of chain that surfaced when we dug in the kopje ruins.

Anyway, for one reason or another the land had long been neglected and was in shocking shape for planting when I took over. It would have to be stumped out and cleared and this would require machinery.

For this speculative effort I was advised to buy a small Ferguson tractor, a "mouldboard plow" and a "rake harrow." An hour or so had to be spent by an irritated Phil Norris, the Marandellas dealer, teaching me to set the plow blade, avoiding the big bite into the soil that would jerk the machine over backward on top of me; showing me how to plow a straight furrow to save time and money, how to "bleed" a diesel engine if it got air in the fuel line. Altogether a baffling new world of endeavor.

Yet, perseverance in the face of a catalogue of numbing disappointments finally paid off. Acres of green fuzz grew into waving golden grain, a victory which called for the immediate purchase, also from Phil Norris, of a mowing attachment and a "side delivery rake." This rake scratched up the cut grass into lines for collection by a miracle of modern technology I also had to buy from Phil.

This monster straddled the windrows, picked up the grass, compacted it into bundles, and tied them into bales which marched for miles and had to be collected by wagon, another Norris purchase. It was little wonder that behind his ostensible irritation he was vastly amused, all the way to the bank.

Although soaking rains beat me to them and acres of grass rotted in the fields, I did manage to fill the Dutch barn with 600 bales twice a year for three years. This was plainly not enough. Hence, I wrote off staggering losses on what I insisted had been a gallant try and, with something like a sigh of relief, went back to my typewriter.

From then on, these now tailored lands were maintained as English meadows, appropriately fenced with pine post and eucalyptus rail.

CHAPTER XXX

Domestic Wildlife

Before the termites ate the farm's fencing off at ground level and some $3,000 worth of it crumpled to dust, we harbored three horses: Tomasan, a little gray mare; Ruksh, a bay gelding; and a Cape cart horse, Bokje.

Sadly, Ruksh developed what is called "broken wind." This is not what it sounds like but is a fatal lessening of the elasticity in the windpipe which prevents normal breathing and ultimately smothers the animal. He was a huge, goodnatured beast who licked the back of your neck or fondled your ear with his pendulous lips. Kids scrambled all over him, and he was greatly loved. When his hacking cough echoed from his stall far into the night and his flesh began to fall away, we could put it off no longer. A time had to be chosen on a holiday when the children were away from home. Tony Craig-Barr, our closest neighbor and a gentle Scot, undertook this unpleasant task and buried Ruksh on his land in a remote, unmarked spot. The children were told that Ruksh had died in some other way. A snake bite, perhaps. I don't remember what I invented. My mind has refused to retain a lie about so painful a subject.

Bokje, a docile, magnificently proportioned, high-stepping hackney who fairly lifted our four-wheeled trap off the roadway when he hit his trotting stride, fared no better. He succumbed to sunstroke, was crippled in his hindquarters, and swayed and staggered about the paddocks, alive and loved but never again in harness. He became a kind of lap-horse pet, useless for anything but giving and receiving affection and in time had to be destroyed. Tony performed this as well, a lethal injection, while the kids were away at school.

I concocted another trumped-up story and turned the children's attention to Tomasan, a goodnatured little pony of fine fettle and handsome confirmation. Lamentably, I made an African groom with the hands of a stonemason responsible for her exercise runs each morning. In only a month he had changed a mouth so tender Tomasan would respond to the slightest pressure to one so tough it took a rider with the arms of an Atlas to saw her to a halt. Sacking him didn't restore her gentle mouth, but she was clever and soon learned to respond to knee and body pressure. She was a near perfect little beast, and some years later she was bred and turned out fine colts.

We added another to our stables, Whisky, a name that should have tipped me off. Up from Umtali, he immediately went for everyone, teeth bared and hooves lashing out. I had to mount Tomasan and "drive" him to and from the paddock. In one ill-timed attempt at helpfulness Ria got too close and was sent sprawling through the post and rail. Although the wound to her ankle was less than to her ego, this was too much.

Joan Keene, a fine horsewoman who, with husband, Bill, will be ever loved by all Achesons, took him in tow for me and rode him—docile as a hamster, naturally—to Marandellas and the railhead for his return to Umtali.

I got my money back, and we bought rabbits, ducks, geese, and chickens. The geese were savage and attacked me repeatedly, but they were smaller than Whisky and I coped. The others left me alone.

Aside from this dwarfed wildlife, we had a donkey and, briefly, a deer. The donkey stayed with us as a pet for years, but the deer ate itself to an explosive death on dehydrated rabbit pellets which, imbibed while dry, swelled up inside the poor thing and literally inflated it to beyond its natural limits.

Our rural livestock ventures were not unqualifiedly successful, as may be seen, but we did manage to house myriad cats and a dog or two over the years, all of which survived.

The nasty brands of animal, potentially dangerous, were few. Lion and elephant had been driven from the district a few decades earlier and this left baboon, the odd leopard, bush pig, and snakes, which included the boomslang (tree snake), cobra, and puff adder.

As for the baboons, they stayed up in the kopjes and limited their depradations to pulling up seedling gum trees each time I planted them and raiding our garden and our African servants' mealie patches. They did overstep the bounds a bit and I once caught one sitting calmly in a chair on the veranda, but for the most part they kept their distance.

Leopard left pug marks about the place and kept the baboon, their favored food, in screeching hysteria far into the nights, but we never actually saw any on our lands. The pig, a member of the warthog family, could be very dangerous with long sharp tusks and the courage of a lion, but he too was nocturnal and rarely seen.

Attracted by the warmth, the snakes often slid into the main house on winter days and could be worrisome. One such encounter suggested a radio script for my "Information Plus" program that went something like this:

> I hope it's been a long time since I talked about snakes on this program. If it hasn't, forgive me but something strange happened on the way through our front hall the other day that's brought the subject up again.
>
> I do recall that, among other bits of useless information, we classified snakes according to deadliness and size. The deadliest, although this is not a view held everywhere as I'll show, is the Australian tiger snake. One fourteen-thousandth of an ounce of its venom can kill a man in a matter of minutes. Perhaps nearly as deadly, aggressive, and the largest poisonous snake in the world is the king cobra or hamadryad of Siam. One measured eighteen feet four inches in length.
>
> On the Rhodesian farm that is our home we've never really had much trouble with snakes: a few puff adder, banded cobra, some juvenile eight-foot python, and that's about it. But there have been several years of drought in the country, followed this year by torrential rains. And with the wetness have come a variety of crawling things, one of which was the something strange that happened in the front hall.
>
> I'd dropped the receiver back into the cradle of our old wallbox crank telephone and turned away, still preoccupied with the conversation. In the house that morning doing some electrical repair was Peter Taylor, local expert and friend of ours. As I moved away from the phone, he materialized from nowhere. I started to speak to him when I noticed he'd gone dead white and rigid, frozen in place. Staring fixedly over my left shoulder and speaking softly, he ordered me not to turn but to back slowly through the open door next to the telephone and out onto the veranda.
>
> Not fully understanding but sensing his fear, I inched backward until I'd cleared the opening. Then I raised my eyes to the top of the door.
>
> Six inches of green neck as thick as a garden hose with an agitating, tongue-flicking head at my end of it, wavered outward from the corner of the doorjamb. Behind it, draped along the top of the window curtain rod, was another five feet of green mamba.
>
> Now a herpetologist named Rose has dedicated a book on reptiles to "these much maligned and persecuted subjects." Obviously he favors them and scoffs at the "myths" grown up around

so many. But about the mamba he says: it is claimed that it is the most deadly and ferocious snake in the world, including the tiger snake and Hamadryad. Deadly he admits it is, front-fanged with highly toxic venom. For quickness it has no peers. Ferocious he insists it is not but since it's a tree snake that cannot feel warning footfalls, it's inclined to lash out at any unfamiliar movement. This one didn't lash out at me, my shoulder only a few inches away, probably because it couldn't get a good purchase on the curtain.

Peter and our African gardener knocked it down and with deftness born of panic severed its head with a hoe before it could collect itself on the slippery waxed floor.

That was the closest I came to venomous snakes on the farm, although I was sent skating out of my melon patch by a cobra described by Paul Mandizera as "big as my thigh and longer than the tree on an ox wagon." This description may do more for art than truth but it helps explain my retreat.

There was one other snake that wasn't, strictly speaking, "ours," but belonged to Dan and Muriel Wiley, farming neighbors. They had chickens, scores of them, who retired to a large, windowless coop near the house at night to sleep and lay small brown eggs.

One morning Muriel, a handsome blonde woman of many accomplishments, came shrieking into the kitchen from the barnyard announcing to Dan and anyone within two miles that a big cobra had just slithered into the chicken house.

Her husband grabbed his twelve-gauge repeater shotgun and plunged through the door into the semidarkness of the coop. Muriel was close behind him until, just short of making her own entrance, she saw the cobra's great flat head swing out into the doorway. Dan was out of sight, and, discounting the peril to him and not wanting the cobra to escape, she slammed the door, knocking the reptile back into the gloom of the hen house.

Dan later admitted he'd been a bit startled when she shut the door but was terrified when she screamed out she'd locked the thing in with him. On the understandable principle that killing a few chickens would involve less loss than letting this poisonous monster sink its fangs into his leg, Dan let fly at the slightest flurry. And flurries there were aplenty.

Outside, Muriel remembers it was as she'd always imagined a fire in an explosives plant might be.

At that close range Dan was blowing great chunks out of the walls and asbestos roofing, cursing and shouting in rage and fright in a thick Scots accent, selecting his pithier epithets with considerable imagination.

The chickens in concert produced a deafening squawking to which Muriel, understandably interested in her mate's fate, added a special screeching brand of her own.

All his shells discharged, Dan selected one of the new exits he'd blasted in the walls of the hut and stumbled out into the early dawn in a snowy fall of chicken feathers.

Muriel was to report that she saw the great snake, unperturbed, exit at speed but without panic to disappear up the garden path toward the quieter precincts and less apocalyptic picking of the pigeon roost.

As for the baboon that infested our farm and the leopard we never saw in person, I wrote about them for radio, and, since the scripts can't be much improved upon, here they are:

> In the rocky hills that hover over our Rhodesian home, there are, as I've mentioned before, a troop of baboons. Thirty or forty of them. They can be vicious, but it's not this that keeps us conscious of them. It's that they're such a ruddy nuisance.
>
> They can tear a large dog to bits, and our neighbors have lost a few, but mostly they make a shocking racket and periodically reduce our vegetable garden to garbage. I rush out and blaze away with a shotgun which makes a lot of noise and sends them packing for a few days but only back to their home above our house.
>
> On some of my impetuous and profitless pursuits into the bush I have run across porcupine quills and this has made it entirely worth my embarrassment. They are delicate, whiplike strands, ivory white and banded black and, although terrible weapons wielded by the porcupine, quiescent they are graceful souvenirs of the African veld.
>
> Where there are baboon and porcupine there should be leopard. They are his favorite dish. Yet until a short time ago none had been seen in this district for several decades.
>
> When the pioneers first arrived here some seventy years ago they shot out the leopard as vermin. The beast attacked the trek oxen in the dead of night and when farms were established he tore the life out of the cattle.
>
> But shooting him out upset the balance of nature. The baboon multiplied and, marauding through the farmer's corn fields, became as much a menace in his own way as the leopard had been. In response the authorities declared the big cat Royal Game, shot only under license, and slowly he's coming back into his own.
>
> This pleases the conservationists but has the ranchers worried.

Cattlemen near us have reported spoor and fleeting glimpses of the animal itself and they don't like it.

The weight of the common leopard isn't much, perhaps 110 pounds, and from nose to tip of tail it's rarely more than seven feet. Yet, they can reach 300 pounds, the older ones, and they're incredibly strong. One of them can haul an antelope carcass twice its own poundage twenty feet up into a tree for safekeeping. On the attack he's so quick he seems to explode out of the bush from all directions.

A baboon, out of the troop, makes an easy meal. The porcupine puts up a better fight, but in an argument with an adult leopard he's always the loser. Still, one weighing up to forty pounds can be a formidable opponent. He's known to go bristling into a pride of lion and drive them away from a kill. He can attack sideways as well as backward and forward, and only the leopard is fast enough to strike through his defenses.

The name "leopard," by the by, comes from an early belief that the animal was a cross between a lion and a panther, "leo" for lion and "pardus," the ancient Persian name for the smaller nocturnal cat. In some parts of Africa he's still called a "tiger."

Whatever he's called, he's bad news for the baboon, the porcupine *and* the farmer . . . and tomorrow I'll tell you just how bad.

After briefly reviewing the history of the leopard in our district and concluding by noting that after being declared "royal game," its numbers were on the increase, I went on:

Still the big cat's rare enough to cause a considerable stir when he does appear. For a neighbor of ours and more especially for one of his African workers, it certainly did.

The neighbor, John Morkle, is a farmer, grows tobacco, and, although he keeps a few chickens and a milk cow, he doesn't have much that would interest a leopard. Not compared to the ranchers. Yet assessing a leopard's tastes is a chancey business.

Early one morning, Morkle was walking a bush trail to check out a nighttime racket near the fowl run when he rounded a bend, and there it was—a big male crouched just off the path in front of him. John's a huge man, ex-Springbok rugby forward, ears cauliflowered by the head-bashing in the scrum, wise in the ways of the bush and coldly courageous. Without hesitating, he snatched up a stick and, bellowing like a mad bull, charged straight at the thing.

It worked, and in a flash of gold and black the leopard was

gone. In that split second Morkle saw that one of its front paws was badly swollen and bloodstained. He guessed it was porcupine quills, which can break off in the flesh and fester. An animal so painfully crippled can't hunt in the customary way and preys on easy game, young livestock, fowl and human beings.

About a week later, wading through waist-high rushes near a swamp where his men were making bricks, John heard one of them scream. Breaking into a run he burst into the open to see the man down, the leopard on top of him.

He's not certain what happened next, but apparently he threw himself off the streambank and landed on the animal's back. He recalls the thing twisting violently under him, throwing him clear, and then it was gone.

The African, his scalp torn away in a flap that hung forward over his eyes, his chest and thighs ripped open, incredibly struggled to his feet. Morkle rushed him to Marandellas Hospital, convinced the man wouldn't even arrive there alive, much less be saved if he did.

But, by the farmer's testimony, "this was the toughest, and the best boy who ever worked for me." Spurring the man's recovery, John said, was a consuming hatred he'd found in those few seconds of battle with the leopard.

Sewn back together and pumped full of new blood, the worker was back in his farm lodging the next afternoon. John was incredulous. The man was so swollen and torn he could scarcely see, not to mention walk.

A week later, still looking as if he'd swallowed an exploding hand grenade, he asked John for leave, to hunt down that leopard. His weapons were a spear and a long cane knife.

Morkle never saw him again. But, then, he hasn't seen the leopard either.

CHAPTER XXXI

Back to the Typewriter

"The only thing you'll ever grow on that farm,"—and Don Rattray, village chemist become close friend, smiled at me across his steaming retorts—"is older."

And evidence was piling up that he wasn't far off the mark. Failed pasture grass, hardluck livestock, infested melons, and baboon-wracked vegetables.

"And look at you." He flipped his spatula in my direction. "You don't even look like a farmer."

Except for the capital city, Salisbury, and for Bulawayo, the country's number-two town, where styles featured navels and nipples and male ballet dancer crotches in tight jeans, dress in most of Rhodesia was khaki and corduroy "bush." I wore the "bush" khaki shorts, useful safari jackets with huge pockets and broad-brimmed felt hats to ward off the searing sun. But not as a regular thing.

My costume during most of the African cross-continental strip had been, as noted, khaki shirt, lederhosen, or German leather shorts, held up with a wide leather belt, and canvas gaiters for stockings. Lace-up "high shoes" with hobnails completed the uniform. After years of wearing the lederhosen, wonderful protection for a soft journalist bottom, they had lost the grayish suede hue and texture and turned a hard shiny black. My son, Jeffrey, fell heir to them when I changed shape, losing most of my backside, and couldn't hold them up any longer. But during the time I wore them, which included several years on the farm, it *was* easy to pick me out in a crowd.

My other favorite garb made it even easier.

Since childhood days listening to my mother's brother, Douglas, tell tales of the Black Watch, the "little ladies from hell" in their swinging kilt, and since Jerusalem, too, and the giant pipe major, I'd determined to one day have my own Scottish "skirt." And wear it.

In fact, I had three. After a year on the farm I began suffering the pains of a congenitally bad back and finally was operated on in Johannesburg so I could keep going. The yards of heavy pleated material around the waist provided warmth and support. The tweed was excellent defense against bush and bramble and sudden rains and it was the most confortable garment I ever wore.

Mine was a "shepherd's kilt," no pretension to a tartan. It is speculated that the Achesons qualifty for a MacIntosh, but that's not yet been determined. Only the purist these days insists that one doesn't wear what one isn't authorized to (as a clansman) but I'm just stuffy enough to agree with this old tradition, and so I had three plain wool plaid.

Certainly there was a bit of play actin', if you will, in the wearin' o' the kilt, but it was practical as well. I wore it on the tractor, tree-planting, at pick-and-shovel work, and even on a horse. The canvas gaiters continued as substitute for the stockings, although I did have woolen pairs for "dress." Tony Craig-Barr had a pair he'd inherited from his father that were forty years old, if not more. So, they could stand the wear. But the gaiters and boots were tougher yet. A short-sleeved khaki shirt and, to shelter an inordinately large nose, I often topped all this with a peaked baseball cap.

A Zambian friend, visiting the farm for the first time, told me he'd found us because someone said his description of the place sounded "like the home of that eccentric American bod."

Anyway, so taken was I by the usefulness and comfort of the kilt that I told its history and touted its fine qualities whenever I could, including producing a radio script for "Information Plus":

> There's a question so worn and weary, asked the world over the centuries, that I wonder it persists: What's the Scotsman wear under his kilt?
>
> There are several replies to this query: It depends on the Scot and "it's nae yer bluidy business." Such answers probably explain why the question keeps coming. Since most of the answers I've recorded on the subject won't bear repeating in mixed company, I won't be much help either. But I will tell you something about the garment.
>
> The oldest form of highland dress was a long tartan blanket (the Scottish Saints presairve me) two yards wide and six long. It was tossed over the left shoulder, was belted round the waist, hung straight down in front, in overlapping folds, and was crudely pleated in back. It was also used as a ground sheet. This is a travesty of a description but the proper one is 200 words long, and this'll have to do.

This kilt (nothing under it) is rarely worn these days. The one most of us know is the "little kilt," the material thirty inches wide and seven yards long. It, too, hangs flat, overlapping, in front and is tightly pleated in the back.

Properly tailored—and it must be or the wearer resembles a dwarf wrapped in a rug—its fit is snug around the waist, fixed with leather straps and buckles on each hip and sometimes a wide belt. Its length is correctly to the middle of the knee, a measurement assured by kneeling down for the tailor.

The yards of material do keep the temperature high round the middle, but, as with other belly-band apparel, worn by the Himalayan Highlander and the desert Arab for example, this serves a purpose. It prevents stomach chill, long believed the cause of most intestinal disorders and still the cause of some.

Napoleon, dismayed by the fighting qualities of the kilted British regiments, praised the men but was confused by their dress. About the kilt he's reported to have said: "Pour l'amour c'est magnifique; mais pour la guerre ce n'est pas pratique."

One drawback is the lack of pockets. To make up for this, a sack, called a "sporran," made of leather, badger or sealskin, is hung in front from the waist.

Women, including the Queen, by the way, *never* wear the kilt. A pleated skirt of appropriate tartan perhaps but never the kilt. Certainly never a sporran. What they use in its place, what with all that junk they carry, is their own business just, in fact, as it is what they wear under their—er, uh—pleated tartan skirt.

Even as I floundered about as a comic opera farmer, I had begun editing the local newspaper and taking an increasingly active part in community affairs.

It was about this time that I discovered the torments suffered by a small-town editor: the brutal disharmonies in so ostensibly meek a medium as a parent-teachers association; the pain of covering the local magistrate's court when a popular town businessman is caught embezzling; the apoplectic rages produced in a milquetoast teacher when his amateur theater production in the Farmer's Hall gets a bad local review; the shock of finding the country's prime minister, Winston Field, standing in front of one's desk complaining because the paper never gave his party equal space with his opponents. And he a resident of the town, no less.

The *Marandellas* and *Watershed News* was started and financed by the owner of a liquor store, a chemist, a builder, a motorcar dealer, the manager of the Farmers' Co-op and me. It lasted four years, from 1958 through 1961, as a monthly and, latterly, as a biweekly, reaching a

Marandellas District circulation of 700 and a probable readership of three times that much.

It reported on everything of interest in a small town from garden club and church notes to council elections and a few matters a lot of its readers resented, such as United Nations debates about Rhodesia.

We covered this because the Rhodesian national press was so biased against the U.N. that it lifted from the wire services only the more egregious nonsequiturs and empty anti-colonial vaporings. What's more, we felt the readers might at least be benefited by some of Adlai Stevenson's delightful prose.

The paper was cosmopolitan and sometimes pretentious but it was not so sophisticated that it didn't make extraordinary personal demands on its editor as the community mentor. I enjoyed it hugely but found it often required judgments painfully made, such as for example, when news value had to be sacrificed in favor of local sensibilities. During a stay in the States I produced a radio piece on the subject:

> The small town may be what man was made for. His family, work and spare-time occupations are everybody's business. Nor is this just a nosy predilection for keeping abreast of the gossip; it's a natural sympathy for the condition of one's neighbors that's a reflection of the best in human nature.
>
> I live in a small Rhodesian village of some 3,000 people. There was a town veterinarian, a lanky Scotsman who worked himself into a lather for every kind of animal from Pomeranians to pedigreed cattle. He lived largely on credit. Few could pay when his bills arrived. One terrifying night his house burned down. He was way behind on his insurance payments.
>
> With his wife and children and crates of animals and the walking refugees he'd saved from the flames, he moved in with a more affluent neighbor.
>
> One day, anonymously, from a community that could ill afford it, he got a check for "about $2,500," a tidy sum in those days.
>
> I was editing the district newspaper, and this story was a natural, loaded with human-interest angles. But we ran it as a lean report, recapitulating the fire story, and approximated the value of the "gift."
>
> A few professional Samaritans suffered from this objectivity, but the villagers in the main were pleased to know the vet could make it, even get a new start. Few wasted much time congratulating themselves on what nice people they'd been.
>
> This is more often the case than you'd think.

I recall an incident involving a shattering story of murder and suicide.

On "the Green" there was a shoemaker, a retiring little man whose repairwork was indifferent at best but whose eagerness to please made up for it. Then, for reasons only intimately shared, he and his wife separated. She moved with the children to a friend's house, got a job, and began an independent life.

The shoemaker fell apart. One afternoon he drove out into the country, a bottle of brandy on the seat beside him. Careening back into town after dark he struck a tree and his car exploded in flames.

Somehow he got free of the wreck, and, as the police searched for him, he staggered to the home where his wife stayed, called her out and shot her to death with a twenty-two rifle. About an hour later the town constable, checking security, found the shoe shop door open and the shoemaker dead, the gun near his body.

By any standards this was a news story. The Salisbury papers and the wire services had a field day with gory coverage and sentimental excess that would squeeze tears from a turnip.

We reported it in some detail, admittedly, but without straining at it. The town was stunned, and we knew it didn't need all the slaughterhouse minutiae.

A few months later the Town Council decided to ask residents to contribute to a trust fund for the youngsters. Councilmen kept it quiet, visiting merchants and householders in person. In spite of this caution, the large papers got wind of it and produced a touching "small town" follow-up.

We reported it, too, "for the record," quite enough for a small town where a man sees himself too often not to be humble.

Certainly not all the duties were depressing or routine. The editor of a small-town journal has opportunities to toy with the most prosaic happenings in a way no city editor could think of doing.

The town had a race track with grandstands, viewing ring, a form of winner's circle, the lot. No self-respecting colonial community anywhere in the world could be without its horse track, and Marandellas was no exception. Punters came from all over the district and even jounced the fifty miles over a terrible "strip" road from Salisbury, or even the 120 miles of "strip" from Umtali.

The "strips" were two roughly parallel, eighteen-inch–wide ribbons of tar on which a motorist balanced at speeds of up to forty miles an hour. Newcomer drivers in Southern Rhodesia developed serious nervous disorders and were known to suffer heart attacks playing "chicken" with approaching cars.

A driver stayed on the hard surface as long as possible, naturally, and then at what often seemed the last minute swung off left,* running the inside set of his wheels on the outer strip, leaving the other strip free for the approaching car. If the wind was high this near-suicidal ploy took place in a cloud of blinding dust and a shower of gravel, some of which kept on coming through the windscreen.

Failure to check out the berm ahead could be fatal. The unwary, his vision limited in this gritty haze, risked writing off a goat or two, bashing in his front against a herd of donkeys or an ant hill, destroying the front suspension in an ant-bear hole, and more often than not sending a gaggle of terrified African pedestrians flying off into the bush.

Particularly at night a cow could loom suddenly out of the dense bush. Or a buck, attracted by the headlights, might leap gracefully in front of the car.

Contact with cattle was rather like hitting a giant leather bladder filled with kindling wood. Everything back to the dashboard crumpled. The car usually was a total wreck although occupants were seldom seriously damaged. A flying buck, however, often sailed through the windshield, handicapping the motorist by landing in his lap in a hail of tiny glass particles. Altogether, to undertake this ordeal over long distances for an afternoon's outing at the races took true devotion to the sport.

Turf tracks existed in many Rhodesian towns, the largest and grandest in Salisbury, and the most infamous in Inyazura in the eastern districts, where track trickery and management hanky-panky was developed to a fine art. Marandellas ran Inyazura a close second.

The *Marandellas News* covered the local events, a particularly keen follower providing us with highly colorful if not always accurate accounts. He understandably avoided any searching revelations of the seamy side of things and, anyway, the libel laws were strict, and we'd have spent most of our time in court if we'd taken ourselves too seriously. I could, however, report on the "goings-on" in the past tense and from a safe distance. And did. In the States for WILZ's "Information Plus" I wrote:

> For many years I have been a devotee of what's called in my Rhodesian hometown a "race meeting." Most of you'd recognize it. It's a bush league competitive horse event that takes place in rural areas the world over. Especially English rural areas.
>
> Of course compared to what it used to be, the English country

---

*British traffic.

"meet" is a pale and sissy reflection of the more robust past. No matter how hick the community, it's bound to have a covered stand, parade-ring, professional jockeys, and a royal circle (admission extra). The chances are also better today that none of the judges owns any of the competing horses, a marked step in the direction of impartiality. The bookmakers wear neckties, watch their language—and aren't permitted to bear arms. There's also a mutuel window where real accountants summon up odds and post them for all to see. They also pay off on a winning ticket without argument. These are improvements, no doubt, but much of the old zip is gone.

Wherever colonials have gathered to play, there were bound to be horses. Well—sort of horses. Some were calvary mounts, in India and northern Nigeria, for example. There were retired polo ponies, standard hacks, and in fact almost anything with "a leg at each corner."

Nor was there anything particularly genteel about the events, informal affairs that took place at distant outposts in the far reaches of the Empire. It took a tough type to get that far out and most of the gentlemanly polish had been bruised off along the way. Sir Geoffrey Whatnot entered his own nags, rode them himself, and was laughingly referred to as a "gentleman jockey."

The mayhem in the far turns, supposedly hidden from the judges' view, has seldom been matched for blood-lust. For example, Sir Geoffrey had the opportunity, the muscle and the inclination to produce a maiming backhander with his riding crop across a competitor's face. When it didn't knock the man to the ground, it left him bleeding profusely and temporarily sightless, a handicap on a crowded turn.

There was nothing so sophisticated as doping a horse—a nail wedged in the frog of a hoof, perhaps, but no pills or needles or enemas. Actually, it was the rider who suffered the "fix" one way or another.

There was one popular dirty trick I've had played on me, and it's difficult to prepare for. About to exit a turn into the homestretch, a jockey can be preoccupied with the finish line, forgetting for the moment his immediate danger. It's easy to crowd him, slip a toe under his stirrup, and flip him off. Since this is usually at top speed with a packed field pounding close behind, the results are discouraging.

In one Rhodesian country track, the slaughter became so general that the "gentlemen" drew lots in the milking shed dressing room before the race to select a winner. Anyone who broke ranks after that needed his head examined, literally.

The spectators knew "arrangements" were made and bet on the man, either because he was too independent to be intimidated or because it was his turn to win. No one ever deluded himself it was "good clean fun."

It was sometimes risky, but the public liability was limited. If a half-blinded rider who'd stuck to his mount rode through the rails near the finish, the damage might be no more than a few trampled grooms, broken beer crates, and a splintered judges' box occupied only by these worthies, busy working out their personal winnings.

It had dash and color, usually red, and the grounds weren't all cluttered up with well-dressed bookies, St. John's Ambulance Corps personnel, and a royal circle (admission extra).

CHAPTER XXXII

On the Air

At the same time that I walked the slack wire as editor of the *Marandellas News*, I traveled the federal area and South Africa for American papers and began work for the Rhodesian Broadcasting Corporation.

From 1963 to 1966 we'd sojourned as a family in the United States. During this time I'd held down a job at WILZ in St. Petersburg, Florida. Charles W. Mackey, a cousin so close he's been the blood brother I never had, owned the property, a daytime station he was trying to develop as having a "unique sound" in the area.

Part of this "sound" could be a lively news department, and I asked him to employ me to help establish one. He agreed, and his staff, principally Pat Chamburs and Jim Boynton, undertook to teach me broadcasting. With Bill South, a stock broker on temporary leave of his senses, I went "outside," and the two of us put together what was generally conceded to be a first-rate news team with Chamburs and Boynton, the real pros, on the "inside."

There were, of course, dead spots in our news work, and I began using them to put together commentary on foreign developments for our main noon and five o'clock programs. This slowly altered to include a series of general comment on almost anything. "The Dinosaur," "The Battle of Verdun (anniversary of)," "Alcohol," and "The Calendar," to mention a few. It found favor, and we sold it as a daily five-minute spot.

When I returned to Rhodesia, I took with me a file of 200 scripts and was preparing another 130 for the continuing St. Petersburg series. They constituted an asset that I felt might be of interest to the Rhodesian Broadcasting Corporation, Commercial Service. Winnowing out the stories of interest particularly to an American audience, for example, "Columbus Day," "The Two-Dollar Bill," and the like, I could still have enough of universal interest that, with minimal editing, might be saleable.

It was a tight market. For all its rapid advance and blooming new cultural pretensions, the Rhodesian professional class in the fifties and sixties, in radio and television, was thin on the ground. Although the country's amateur theater ranks could provide a score of retired West End veterans and local talent of high standard, these actors were not all that keen about the airways. The pay was terrible, and the studio facilities were primitive. With U.D.I. (Unilateral Declaration of Independence) in 1965 prompting a U.N. boycott of more or less worldwide reach, the country's foreign-exchange resources were limited. Funds for the purchase of up-to-date equipment from overseas couldn't be spared.

Resulting from this concourse of negatives was a small closed shop of good amateurs and professionals who bunched tightly together and hoped for better things to come. Trying to pierce this small but sturdy phalanx of regulars wasn't easy. Yet, with the help of Ian Mills, an old and good friend, quality newspaperman and a musician with radio experience and contacts, I prepared a demonstration tape. There were several interested buyers, and a candy company eventually took the five-minute spots for three thirteen-week periods.

In Durban on holiday, I subsequently approached the South African Broadcasting Corporation, did some trial tapes in the Natal studios, and sold the corporation some of the series for spot use.

Add to this a thirteen-week series for the R.B.C. of fifteen-minuters titled "Genesis in General, the Beginning of Almost Anything," and I was kept busy on radio as well as "print" journalism.

The "Information Plus" program was demanding. In all, I produced almost 400 scripts. Nonetheless, the labor was immensely rewarding. Not in cash. That was pathetic. But in the pleasure of researching, the writing and the studio production with the R.B.C.'s Leslie MacKenzie's gentle coaching and enthusiastic encouragement. Among the several hundred scripts produced, and in addition to those appearing throughout this personal account, there were a few I especially enjoyed. For example:

> Not long ago someone asked me if I knew where the necktie came from and quite by chance I had the answer. In fact, I'd had the answer for years, just waiting.
>
> I'd begun my research into the origin of the necktie not as a matter of spare-time whimsy but as a serious business.
>
> As an American I had grown tired of being accosted by angry Britons demanding to know by what right I presumed to wear such and such a bit of neckwear. Neckties, I was repeatedly and firmly told, are not mere adornment. They can be a badge, the striped ones and those with miniature escutcheons on them, and I was accused of displaying honors I hadn't earned.

This is the kind of thing that kept happening to me:

I was quietly leering at a show in a Paris nightclub when a bearded giant suddenly blocked my way. Now, blocking the view in a Paris nightclub is a misdemeanor and I rose to point this out.

As I got to my feet, this great oaf jerked out my necktie, a navy-blue–and–maroon-striped creation, and thundering "Sixtieth Rifles!" beamed at me and crushed all the knuckles of my right hand. It was actually "Abercrombie and Fitch," but I didn't dare correct him.

Again: the elevator man (liftman) in a London hotel caught me out wearing his Royal Engineers tie and had an attack of the vapors when I told him I'd chosen it because it went so well with my gray suit.

Probably the most painful accident of this kind took place on a sun-baked tropical street. A stranger panted up behind me, grabbed my shoulder, and spun me round and there it was again: that broad, happy grin of recognition, of brother meeting brother.

This time is was the Fifth Ghurkas I was impersonating. I wouldn't have knowingly masqueraded as a Ghurka for all the kukris in Katmandu, although this poor chap couldn't have known that, of course.

He was a big man—great craggy face and flourishing moustaches—and when I denied Ghurka affiliation he visibly deflated, muttered sadly, and turned away.

Quite by chance I met him later in the day over a drink. He was most apologetic. One does not, he said, often meet Ghurka officers ("other ranks" are only four feet six inches tall) which had upped his surprise and enthusiasm when he saw me flying the green and black stripes.

This made me feel an outright cad and, what with both of us so distraught, we swapped drinks until we couldn't have distinguished one necktie from another.

After that I gave away all my stripes to those qualified to wear them and have studiously avoided sporting false colors, which is just what they could be—as I'll explain when next we discuss the origins of the necktie.

Which we did the following day:

I recently saw advertised in an American shop window "Imported Regimental Ties." To those who've served with distinction in these regiments this sort of merchandising is culling profit from the rankest sort of impersonation.

The following paragraph taken from the British magazine, the

Field will underscore the importance attached to this sort of felonious sales gambit:

"It has come to the notice of Senior Engineers," it reads, "that besides the official Royal Engineer tie, an unofficial crested one is being offered for sale and, indeed, being bought and worn.

"The practice," the article continues, sputtering with outrage, "is, of course, viewed with disapproval. There are rumors, too, of attempts to tamper with the Brigade tie, the most sacrosanct of all neckwear, by splattering gilt thistles or leeks on it to suggest the wearer had the honor of serving with the Scots or Welsh Guards."

The magazine, now thoroughly aroused, goes on to note that the "wearers of a modified Brigade tie deserve the fate of a man saved from drowning who was found to be wearing braces (suspenders) of Regimental design. His rescuer threw him back."

Now, these fulminations from the *Field* are not so mindlessly stuffy as, at first, they may seem.

Originally the necktie was part of a battle flag. In the sweating, bloody scramble of armored knights in battle, this standard was held high. If it fell, the battle might be lost. Unless it was quickly raised again the men, seeing it downed might bolt from the field. It was not unusual for the officer commanding to wear a replica of this flag round his neck as identification during close-in fighting and to show the troops that their banner still flew.

Quite obviously for him and his men, its design and insignia had a practical use and a special significance; and it still has for those who earn it.

There are, confusingly, about twenty thousand authorized patterns of necktie, not only Regimental and Old School for example, but, latterly, those identifying pioneers in the oil industry and even zoologists.

And no amount of money will buy them, unless accompanied by authorized credentials.

From this esoteric review of the sanctity of assorted types of cravat, I shifted gears to produce a horror story:

How many know what the word "Bedlam" means? By definition it means uproar, pandemonium. But whence the word itself?

Actually there is no such word as "Bedlam." That is, it has no classic derivation. It's a cockney corruption of the word Bethlehem, as in Bethlehem Royal Hospital, London, and this is its history:

In the year 1247 a rambling stone house on the outskirts of

London was refurbished and extended as a priory, a religious house. And so it remained for 150 years, a Christian refuge and a place for scholarly study and worship. In the year 1400, however, it was converted to a house of horror: the Bethlehem Royal Hospital for the Insane.

For those days it was a progressive innovation, the first asylum of its kind in Europe. At that time the insane weren't considered ill. They were thought to be cursed and either were killed by mobs or driven away like wild animals.

Into this institution went the most violent and dangerous cases, to be buried alive, not to be cured. There was no cure, just isolation in a great stone cage. For squalor and beastliness it's rarely been surpassed.

If chroniclers of the age can be believed, the shrieking and babbling of the inmates could be heard for blocks; the prisoners were clothed in rags, fed on swill, and beaten, often in battles that saw the guards fighting for their lives against human animals frenzied by the loathesome surroundings.

It wasn't until as recently as 1930, after more than 500 years, that the hospital location was changed from Lambeth Borough to Croydon, and it became a true home for the mentally ill. The name remains the Bethlehem Royal Hospital. For the cockney just "Bedlam."

Yet, real "Bedlams" of the old kind still exist. Every now and then one is found that paralyzes a community with shock. Not long ago I played a part in such a discovery.

As a new reporter on the city desk of a Midwest newspaper, I'd answered the phone. The voice at the other end was muted and tremulous, a woman's voice. She whispered that she and others were held prisoner in a private mental home on the north side of town. The police, she said, wouldn't believe her. Would we help? And as she was giving me the address she gasped and the phone went dead.

I was ordered to turn over what I'd learned to a more experienced man and with only a partial address and an unlikely story he went to work.

Two weeks later the police raided the place, our reporter with them. Inside it was the Bethlehem Royal Hospital all over again: patients chained to beds, stumbling about in straight jackets; ill-fed and filthy. Twelve of them.

Soundproofed and barred, the building stood alone on a large tree-shaded lot in the better part of town—and straight out of the year 1400.

I would like to continue with examples from "Information Plus" indefinitely, but since perhaps that could pall, just one more, albeit in two parts, will do.

Having, on a previous broadcast, promoted "The Return of the Duel" as a "cheap, speedy and conclusive" substitute for tiresome and costly courtroom confrontations in matters personal, I stepped back a bit in the piece that followed and reviewed the history of the art:

> Traditionally, the duel served two functions: to determine guilt in judicial proceedings and to obtain "satisfaction" in a matter of honor.
>
> Judicial duels were first reported by Caesar as practiced among the Germanic tribes. It seems that the litigants told such appalling lies that even primitive judges were affronted. As a remedy they demanded that fighting skills dictate a verdict. The gods would be on the side of the innocent.
>
> The rules were exacting. The contest was fought on a prescribed list and observed by court officials. Strict silence was enforced on spectators, and anyone in the congregation who so much as expressed enthusiasm, impartial or not, was liable to have an arm or even his head severed when the main event was over.
>
> Before the battle, contestants swore their testimony had been true and that they carried no concealed weapon or charms that could give them the edge.
>
> The duels were fought between men, and sometimes women, with swords and hatchets. This could be rather messy, so eventually guilt was determined by first blood drawn rather than awaiting wholesale dismemberment. The one unlucky enough to bleed first was dragged from the field by his heels and hanged or burned at the stake, nasty but final.
>
> In later years the English were more circumspect. Duelists, on foot or horseback, were suitably encumbered by a few hundredweight of armor, and, while swords and great iron clubs with spikes on them inflicted noticeable contusions, death was rare. The **French**, however, with typical Gallic fervor, overran reasonable bounds. So numerous, in fact, and fatal, were these judicial duels that they were outlawed as early as the late 1500s.
>
> As for duels of honor, the French again led the field. The maiming and slaughter occasioned by the merest pretext was classic. In one fifteen-year period, more than 8,000 rapier-wielding Frenchmen died on the field of honor. In at least one instance four men including the hapless seconds were killed and even a few spectators were seriously lacerated.

Today, dueling almost everywhere is outlawed, and penalties for it are humiliating—jail sentences and the like. Yet, there is one country where lawful dueling of sorts still takes place, and we'll talk about that when next we're together.

After reviewing the history of dueling I recalled that judicial duels had first been seen in Germany:

Allowing for a brief nondueling period after World War One, it returned in Germany and was only labeled a criminal exercise in 1953. And, it should be noted, these strictures applied only to the Banker and Baker and Bratwurst producer. The embryo citizens in the universities were exempt.

Now, this exception didn't grant students the right to hack one another about at will. For them it was an extremely formal sporting event.

What's called the "mensur" is a tradition in such ivied hills as Gottingen, Wurzburg, and Erlangen, and it has been for more than 100 years. It's a duel conducted under rigid rulings and is purported to engender physical and mental agility and a sense of fair play. And perhaps it does.

What it definitely does is to produce "membership badges" worn by mature associates of the fraternities: the disfiguring facial scars. To earn them takes guts and a rather distorted sense of values, but they're easy enough to come by.

A "schläger" or saber is the weapon. Combatants face one another standing well within the length of the blade. The sword arm and neck are padded, the eyes protected by steel masklike glasses. The object is to break through the opponent's guard and deal him a slashing cut somewhere between hairline and chin. The rounds are timed, and, when a contestant appears to be losing more blood than he can spare, the duel is ended.

Normally it's not fatal, but it can be. During the days of Nazi enlightenment, when all manner of dueling was legal, one fencer thrust with an epée, piercing his opponent's face through the roof of the mouth and killing him instantly. The court ruled the death a "sporting accident."

After the last war, when the occupying authorities declared the "mensur" illegal as a fascist hangover, the fraternities simply went underground and carried on.

I heard about it and in a Gottingen pub over hot buttered rum cultivated a former U-boat captain, Gunther Jurst, still young, in years at least, and finishing university studies the war'd interrupted.

A hard-eyed youth, blond and square-built, he was well mannered in a brittle, precise way and calmly self-confident. Publicizing his fraternity's illegal activities worried him not a jot. On the contrary. He took me along to watch the action.

The youngsters wore leather face masks, metal helmets, chest-padding and other sissy refinements, but they considered all this to be a form of conditioning rehearsal for the real thing that would come. They slashed and hacked with vigor, feet planted squarely—none of the ballet turns featured in dueling with the epée. Each one took a sound beating from the blunt edge of his opponent's schläger and, padded or not, finished the romp with more than one painful contusion.

Still, this wasn't the incision that produced the badge of honor. That would come later when the "mensur" would be official again and they'd be ready.

CHAPTER XXXIII

Led Astray by a Machine

Notwithstanding that journalism drew me away more and more from my ventures in farming and other erratic rural speculation, I still had time to tote up an impressive catalogue of gaffes and misjudgments. Probably the gaudiest of these was an accumulation of hamhanded faux pas and downright botchery that also took place out of doors. It was highly technical on a huge scale, although, ironically, its beginnings were quite modest.

Several years before my try at growing things, I had steadfastly stuck to my lathe and ground out reams of copy about the wonders of a new Africa a-borning.

In spite of the fact that initally my editors hadn't the faintest idea where Rhodesia was located on the map, and had easily contained their curiosity, my earnestness was intimidating. They consistently found me space—sometimes on page thirty-two, second section. But space. The old *New York Herald-Tribune*, in March of 1961, even ran one of my stories on the editorial page.

The piece was about a production of Shakespeare's Macbeth in an eighteenth-century African tribal setting. The show had been performed in Rhodesia's open-air Salisbury showgrounds by a cast of hundreds of blacks, most of them plucked off the streets, and was a howling success, literally. With this sort of product I may not have been scaling the heights of journalistic elegance but it was different. And if the likes of the *Herald-Tribune* were pleased, I was satisfied to keep trying to do what I knew best.

Then one day in Umtali, and I won't dwell on the preliminaries, I lent Harry Went £1,500 to build a mobile stone crusher. Went was a local entrepreneur possessed of energy and an impressive array of irons in the fire. This Heath-Robinson invention he proposed to construct was to be drawn about the district on four rubber-tired wheels to a plethora of new construction sites. Once there it could, by crushing stone *in situ* for concrete slabs and driveway gravel, undercut the competition by eliminating expensive haulage.

In the granite-rock-strewn community, where blasting often was part of clearing a building location anyway, the idea seemed a natural. And building of all kinds was booming. I liked Harry, had the money to invest, and made a mistake the consequences of which were to badger me for almost a decade.

Several months after this magnanimous move, Harry, having repeatedly failed in his contests with the larger contractors, decided to put the stone-crusher up for grabs and told me I was out the £1,500. He was all apologies but in his sickly financial state all he could repay me with was the contraption my funds had fathered. And so saying he had parked it in my driveway.

I can't say how long I pretended it wasn't there. It seems, in retrospect, a long time. I did finally tire of neighbor's complaints about the area's growing resemblance to the light-industrial sites and of being forced to park my car in the street. I might have been more patient and long-suffering. As it was, I rashly stepped out into a civil-engineering adventure.

I was building a home in the reaches of the Vumba Mountains out near the Mocambique border. Although the mountains were not very mountainous, they were rocky, and it was wild country. One eight-mile roadway strung together about a dozen homes, a farm, one quite imposing estate, a school, and two small hotels. After this, it plunged off, demoted to a stony track, down into what was called Burma Valley. In the valley it passed two farms and then faded into the wasteland of Mocambique's Manica e Sofala District. The place I was building was atop a bluff overlooking this last bit.

My property consisted of a bush-covered ridge with the house site laid out round a giant Cape fig tree at one end, a saddleback in the center, and a granite kopje at the other, Mocambique, end. My entrance driveway was a crude track which snaked through this wilderness, climbing and plunging downward over breathtaking slopes, from the main Vumba Road to the center of the saddleback. It terminated at the house site where the hardier transport vehicles, and the certifiable lunatics willing to drive them, dumped off supplies for the building work.

These "lorries" frequently slid off into ravines, stuck in the mud, and broke axles over boulders or gashed tires on the razor-sharp granite outcrops. It was a nightmare of a trip.

If one turned east along the ridge away from the house site, there was nothing but untrod veld. It was at that location I was to set up my quarry, supplying the contractors working on my house, and store up enough stone to lay a "strip" road as replacement for the existing track.

The topheavy two-ton crusher blew three tires and cracked the frame supporting the engine but finally made it to the edge of a mass of stone roughly the size of Moby Dick, and we were ready.

"We" was John Hill, a local boy who knew something about such things, and me. Hill was six feet two inches tall, built like a diesel compressor and needed the work. Together we founded the Achilles (Acheson and Hill) Construction Company (Proprietary) (Ltd.). With his brawn and experience and my money and reckless disregard for the odds, we went to work.

Suffice it to say that we did actually construct a quarry, creating small terraces in the classic manner, provided the stone for customers as planned, and accumulated gravel supplies that prompted us to take the next fateful move in this saddening saga.

I won't give details of the activities of ensuing months. The recollection is hazy. But there are a few particulars that do stand out.

The procedure for blasting out the rock went something like this: the holes were made in the granite by pounding a hand-held, tungsten-tipped "jumper" some twelve inches long into the stone with a four-pound hammer. It took about a half hour to drill one hole eight inches deep, and we needed sixteen holes before it was worth setting the explosive charges.

Normally such holes are bored by pneumatic drill in something like two minutes.

Each explosive charge, which can obliterate a grand piano, came in three separate pieces, a do-it-yourself destruction kit. The dynamite stick, often melted with age to a soggy blob of almost pure nitroglycerine; the detonator, ignited by a spark and independently combustible; and ten inches of time fuse. I had to learn to assemble this lethal device and tamp it gently into a hole without setting anything off prematurely. And then do it hundreds of times in upcoming months.

The first afternoon I tried priming the sticks, I settled in the hot sun on a flat rock out in the open, isolating my three African comrades at ten-yard intervals. There was no point in blowing up the entire quartet at once.

Within half an hour I had such a headache I thought my ears would burst into flame. Handling the glycerine with sweaty palms had, I learned, leaked the chemical into my bloodstream and a headache is what happens. The Africans routinely treated this by rubbing the glycerine-soaked pulp on their heads, creating a burning sensation so severe it counterirritated what was going on inside.

If priming is dangerous for a new boy, our method of setting off the charges was a dance of death. The fuses were cut to a length that let them burn for two minutes before ignition. With, say, sixteen sticks to light, this allowed about six seconds for each fuse with twenty-four seconds left over to make it to safety. A "cheesa stick" (a hot stick, or Chinese punk) with hot ashen tip was used. Matches would blow out in the wind or inadvertently light the fuse too far down its length, with obvious consequences.

Either John Hill or I, with puck, scrambled across the rubble from fuse to fuse. All of them had to be lit. Sticks that weren't, frequently, were left unexploded by the general concussion and had to be found and retrieved for reuse and to make certain a faulty fuse wasn't still slowly working its way toward the detonator. It was a tricky business.

Refuge for the man lighting the fuses was a large boulder on the fringe of the blast area. As the last fuse sputtered into life, the man with the puck scuttled for the shelter. Twenty-odd seconds is time to cover two hundred yards, on the flat. Over the debris of the quarry it took uncommon agility to cover fifteen. And we had to have time to settle down behind the rock and make ready to count the explosions.

When the charges went off, it was like a mortar barrage. The ground shook, bits of trees joined the hail of stone chips and larger "bombs" showering around the huddled workers. The mountains echoed the "shots," birds flew up in sheets from roosts all round the area, buck were sent wheeling, and troops of jabbering monkeys lifted out of nowhere. Life in the Vumba was hell for 120 seconds every few days. And my nervous system suffered permanent dislocation.

Often, in the panic to get from fuse to fuse, one of them would refuse to catch. The end had to be frayed to get to the powder. This meant holding the "cheesa stick" between your teeth and frantically picking at the end of the cord with your fingernails. Seconds ticked away as surrounding fuses, already lit, hissed toward the detonators. Why I, a self-taught neophyte, wasn't splattered over a large area of the eastern districts, I'll never know. It was altogether a painfully amateur performance. We blew the trommel, or sifter, off the crusher (hidden behind banks of corrugated iron), blasted the tires, picked vital pieces off the engine with flying chips, and often had as much down-time as useful operation.

Yet we made it and had so much gravel in surplus, we decided to go into road-building to dispose of it. To launch this gamble we bought an International Harvester TD9 bulldozer, the smallest, and cheapest, machine capable of the work.

A shiny red monster bristling with mysterious levers and holding a menacing blade across its front like a shield, the thing thoroughly intimidated me. Its arrival also inaugurated my fateful career as a civil-engineering contractor.

Hill taught me the rudiments of operating, and, electing humble beginnings, we contracted initially for simple jobs: rough tracks through the bush, cut-and-fill excavation for building foundations, leveling driveways, tennis courts and bowling greens. In the event, it didn't turn out to be all that humble.

I had quit the quarry to sell the earthmoving work. John labored at the crushing site and was expected to handle the 'dozing on a planned schedule. And so he did. But not always. In fact, in the early days of our new enterprise, there was much trouble with the quarry, and he was tied to the rockpile trying to make little ones our of big ones with faulty equipment. So, I drove the 'dozer.

The Vumba is a tangle of vines and tropical undergrowth, an almost impenetrable mass as resilient as steel mesh. Much of the time the machine simply rode high on a springy mat of creepers. As a result I had limited control of the equipment, which consistently plunged headlong down unseen "dongas" or wadis and had to be pulled out by my irate employers. Most of them were farmers and had better use for their tractors and, in any event, were paying me by the hour.

Tentaclelike vines literally tore me out of the driver's seat, and the whiplash of saplings, slashing back after the moving blade passed on, thumped and clawed me until I dreaded the arrival of each new day. The tennis courts and driveway excavations were more civilized but no less fraught with complications.

The TD9 brakes, one for the right tank-track, one for the left, were activated by spring-loaded levers operated by hand. Released, they shot forward to disengage instantly. This action also sent the lever recoiling back again against whatever was in the way, a kneecap, shin, or a hand. Until I learned to jerk out of the way, I was battered black and blue. The recoil snapped back against my fingers so often that the first month I operated my cracked and swollen knuckles looked like peach pits.

The first try at a driveway was not a success. I caught a lever on the tender knuckles of my right hand just as I approached the corner of the house. I flinched violently, and the reflex swung half a ton of steel blade in a sweep that slashed off a good four feet of veranda.

Subsequently, I gouged out underground power lines and telephone cables and uprooted yards of drainpipe. These are accidents that happen to the best of operators, but that argument did not impress my clients, and John repeatedly had to set his tools down at the quarry and come bail me out.

After a few months we abandoned the quarry, sold the Harry Went Mobile Stone Crusher, or what was left of it, and concentrated on work with the TD9. Inevitably it proved to be too small for jobs we wanted to bid on, and, without anything like sufficient capital, the company expanded at breakneck speed.

Once again, I won't detail the follies of ensuing months, and years. John Hill's departure to greener personal pastures and a move to close down the operation were Achilles' only steps in the right direction. In the event, dissolution was waived in favor of mass expansion.

By the time I began dabbling in agriculture on the Marandellas acreage, Achilles had grown to two Caterpillar D6's, twice the TD9 in size, performance and cost; a D8, twice the D6; a road-grader; excavation-scrapers; rippers; a low-loader transporter to carry the tracked vehicles; trucks; a compressor; a workshop the size of a basketball court; three white employees, one of whom collected snakes and four-foot-long lizards in the service pits; a dozen Africans; and a mountain of debt.

We built hundreds of miles of rough track and national highway in the eastern districts of Rhodesia, excavated for a score of buildings and sports fields, opened up a thousand acres of new farm and grazing land, built dams, the last of which held 60 million gallons, and went broke.

I sold everything at auction, much of it going to the Mocambique government, still Portuguese, and paid off all our creditors. We didn't owe a bean, as the saying goes. I wrote off $50,000 in bad debts, and the entire experience as no more than I deserved. It took many years of astute planning to recoup the losses, a fiasco born the day I reached into my pocket to finance the infamous Harry Went Mobile Stone Crusher.

CHAPTER XXXIV

Back on the Air

As Achilles Construction Company (Proprietary) (Ltd.) went down for the last time, I was able to turn to a new journalistic effort in Salisbury: a series of documentary films for the Rhodesian government. A squad of photographers, sound men, editors, and scriptwriters, including me, formed ranks at the studio workrooms of the Rhodesian Information Department and put together a thirteen-week series titled "This Is Rhodesia."

Although the title fell short of inspirational, the production didn't.

What appeared on the screen *was* Rhodesia: its mines and industry and African master farming; its dams and water conservation schemes; its tourist amenities; the game parks, home of the rare black rhinoceros on which we did a special program, the national airline, Air Rhodesia, and the Natural History Museum for starters.

This was not my first television try. The year before I'd been quiz master on a show aired live from the studios of the Rhodesian Television Corporation in Salisbury. The production, "Baffle the Panel," was aimed at what few viewers there were on Sunday evenings at seven o'clock, not a prime time. What was supposed to "baffle" the panel was an assortment of uncommon articles, mostly antiques, which had been in general use in the past—not a challenge with wide appeal.

Laid out on the table where viewers and panel could study them, the items, a chatelaine's silver belt, a lady's derringer disguised to resemble a prayer book, fifteenth-century bullet-ball molds—that sort of thing—were selected singly and passed among the experts who play-acted a guessing game with appropriate comedy to keep it active. The owner of an object that stumped the panel received voluminous praise for his recherché tastes and got his object back. The RTV gave away nothing. Each member of the panel and I received the munificent sum of $8.25 for an appearance.

I had as panelists regulars from the ranks of the city's arty set, its actors and painters, musicians and university teachers and even journalists. They could be counted on to put on a good show, and I leaned on them heavily. On one occasion this almost cost me my sanity.

It was my first live television, and, since I was more or less in charge, I felt keenly the responsibility for its success. One television critic unkindly suggested that I must suffer from a severe scalp irritation since my nervous response to the pressures was to scratch my head rather a lot, but most comment was favorable.

I stopped scratching, odd gadgets poured into the studio from interested viewers, and we finally made it a hit performance. Certainly the panel did.

As noted, I counted heavily on their professionalism. My personal appearances before the public had been limited to speeches to Rotary and other civic organizations for which I had ample time for preparation. On "Baffle the Panel" I had to extemporize, playing it by ear. I do this badly and had to rely on the practiced wit of my colleagues to fill those deathly hushes that can afflict amateur efforts.

The sprightliest member of the panel was Brian Durdin, experienced actor, cool and unruffled and ever-ready with a meaty quip or weighty observation. He was my mainstay.

Each Sunday evening before the show, we met in the studio coffee shop to discuss the upcoming half-hour. These were anxious moments for me. My nervousness obviously showed and the producer, Marilyn Thyne, and some of the others pitied me. Not so Brian Durdin.

We normally foregathered at 6:30 P.M. and moved into the studio at 6:55 to settle in for last-minute instructions and make ready to face the camera.

One Sunday evening, the hands of the clock reached nine minutes to the hour and no Durdin. At precisely 6:53 P.M., with two minutes to go before we were expected in our studio spots, Durdin's Mini Minor screeched to a halt outside the coffee shop window. After what seemed an interminable time struggling with the door, he got it open and fell out, flat on his face on the parking lot surface.

With great difficulty he got to his feet and staggering backwards off balance fell down again, this time dropping a bottle, which shattered, splashing the contents all over his trousers. For a moment he sat there absentmindedly flicking at the mess with little fluttery motions of his hands. Brian was obviously the worse for half a bottle of something.

I was paralyzed. I could see the show going on with only two "judges," not enough to sustain it, or with Brian in no fit shape to sit up straight, much less talk coherently about some bizarre memento that was the pride and joy of one of our eager viewers. What he might say could destroy the show, and us, forever.

Marilyn left the coffee shop and returned with a thoroughly disheveled Durdin and set about buttoning his shirt, adjusting his tie, and creating some order out of his mop of blond hair. The table in front of the panel would conceal his soaking trousers.

I was later told I'd gone dead white. He must have noticed my plight because he kept drunkenly assuring me he'd be fine, as he fell over coffee shop chairs and giggled inanely. I was speechless.

It was two minutes to seven when we began getting frantic calls from the studio. Marilyn assured me that Brian was "too professional not to be able to carry it off." He would be "okay." I nodded and numbly led the way down the hall and onto the firing line.

In the studio Brian jerked his chair from under the table, overbalanced, promptly fell down again and had to be helped into his seat.

With less than thirty seconds to go before the green light signalled the beginning of the performance, Brian suddenly sat up straight, checked status of his tie and jacket, ran his fingers through his tousled hair, and smiled broadly.

"Twenty seconds to go, chaps," he spoke crisply, all business. And obviously cold sober.

We opened the show that night with members of the panel obviously suffering from hysterics and with a Master of Ceremonies stricken with a sickly grin, a quavering voice, and palsied hands.

Brian and Marilyn had staged the entire affair, feeling perhaps that I, a TV novice, a "new boy" in the ranks, and in charge for all that, needed initiation in the true pressures of theater.

Never after that have I been anxious about a public appearance. Hence, when the opportunity to try "This is Rhodesia" came to me, I took it on without a qualm.

To economize, the government photographers working on "Rhodesia" often returned the film they took out on location to headquarters and we put the stories together in the sound and editing rooms of the studios. I did most of the scripting and was "presenter," or the narrator, frequently appearing on camera.

We had unusual technical problems, most of them tied to the U.N. boycott against the country. Film was costly, new equipment and spares were hard to come by, and innovative techniques requiring imports had to be waived.

A "Teleprompter," a device that rolls an enlarged transcript at speaking speed on a screen situated off camera, had been bought just before the U.N. embargo and replaced the old "boob cards" used to assist actors, including "presenters," with a tendency to fluff their lines. The machine was a godsend for those of us who had to jump from one script to another without time to memorize the copy. Then, halfway through the series, it broke down. There were no spare parts, and it certainly couldn't be replaced.

Inventiveness never failed the team. With scarcely a pause in production, we'd put together a contraption consisting of twin rollers, one above the other. Having hand-printed the entire script in crayon on a roll of wall paper, we wound the text by hand from spool to spool at reading speed, as before.

Multiple reflectors were used to enhance lighting in the absence of unobtainable high-powered globes and tape recorders substituted for the voice and picture synchronization normally provided by a sound track. In spite of the problems we produced footage that was excellent by any standards.

My first experience "in the movies," it was exciting, exacting and unpredictable. Some of the "presenter's" shots were taken on location, and this was often a disorderly process.

One Air Rhodesia sequence opened with me as a passenger disembarking through the door of a small Piper Comanche. According to script I was to turn to the pilot, thank him, get halfway out, pause and, facing the camera, explain that this little plane had been a "main liner" for the airline in the beginning, some thirty years earlier, a midget that grew into the DC-10s and 727s now in service.

We must have done five "takes;" a sudden gust of wind slammed the cabin door on my fingers, and my language ended up on the cutting-room floor. Trying suddenly to avoid a spot on the wing I hadn't noticed before marked "NO STEP!" I sprawled onto the runway. I blew my lines. Altogether a shambles.

We filmed my opening for the National Museum story on the premises during open hours. In fact we filmed it four times in spite of the fact that, for a change, I had all my moves down pat and the memorized introduction was letter perfect.

During the first shot, a workman carrying a mop and bucket walked in front of the camera; a group of chattering visitors milled round through the set as the camera rolled for the second try; and the third had just started when a man walked deliberately up to me and asked the way to the "gent's." All this with "FILMING IN PROGRESS" and other signs and barricades ringing the scene.

The series ran at 8:00 P.M., on Saturday night, the worst viewing time of the week. We reckoned fewer people watched the first run of "This Is Rhodesia" than saw each TV night's closing prayer.

Luckily the series later was broken up into single "feature" documentaries and run at various times. This spread the viewership more widely. A native-born garage owner in Salisbury, fitting extra leaf springs to my Wagoneer, identified me and was enthusiastic.

"I've watched 'em all," he told me. "Some of 'em twice. I was born in this country and I kept askin' myself: 'How the hell can this bloody Yank know so much more about my own country than I do.' "

CHAPTER XXXV

The Devil's Work

Near the end of our residence in Rhodesia we built a house in Umhlanga Rocks, on South Africa's Natal coast near Durban, and commuted from Marandellas. This had given me the opportunity to do the South African Broadcasting work and a home base there from which to cover Republic stories.

One such story took me to upcountry Natal, searching out the facts about a man who was said to have flown a heavier-than-air craft off a mountainside in the region decades before the feat was accomplished in Germany and officially recognized as the first flight of its kind. If the Natal story was true, and proof could be found, aviation history would have to be rewritten.

I spend three months rattling around the hill country collecting yards of taped interviews and a bale of documents, wrote volumes of letters to those who might help me, visited twoscore friends and kinsmen of the "flyer," and nosed about in acres of dusty attics and family archives. Newspaper editors, long fascinated by rumors of the flight, went out of their way to be helpful.

Indeed, seldom have I spent as much time or had as much gratuitous assistance trying to pin down the facts in as elusive a tale. Here is the story:

> Hang-gliding may be a latter-day wrinkle in this era of playful self-destruction, but it's not new. A "madman" charged with "tampering with the Powers of Darkness" may have invented it more than one hundred years ago and flown over the hill country of remote colonial Africa trying it out.
>
> Admittedly, no one has insisted that leaping off a cliff to keep company with the birds is a novel idea. Leonardo da Vinci, 470-odd years back, sketched out a machine for flapping about in the

air. Early in the last century, four Britons, one of whom died in the process, designed, built, and vainly tested the first fixed-wing, man-operated flying thing. Otto Lilienthal, the German named "Father of Flight," piloted his hang-glider in 1891, and in the United States Gustave Chanute perfected the craft beginning in 1896, the year Lilienthal killed himself in a crash landing.

Yet, although it's acknowledged that the idea has been around for years, it's probably not known that in the period between the efforts of those early Britons and the flights of the 1890s, an English colonial farmer could have outdone them all. Documents recently collected suggest that during the period October to May, 1871, John Goodman Household built and flew the first hang-glider of the type plunging off promontories all over the place today.

The man was born somewhere in England, December 9, 1845, the second son in a brood of five boys and a girl. When the lad was six his father, William John, occupation unknown, emigrated to Britain's new-found South African colony of Natal, prudently leaving his family to follow later.

The sailing ship *Minerva* climaxed the three-month voyage by foundering on Fountain Rocks off Durban Harbor, dumping the cargo and William John onto the colony's Indian Ocean beaches.

It was to be thirteen years before the family decided to join him, probably one good reason for the delay being the tenor of father's letters home describing his arrival and the place in general.

Roughly the size of the state of Maine with a population, when Household hit the beach, of just under 8,000, Natal was no tropical paradise. The towns were jerry-built out-stations, and the life was rugged. From the hot, wet jungles along the coast, the landscape deteriorated suddenly into the gouged-out valleys and jagged moonscapes of the interior. The native Zulus were so hostile that the colonists spent the last half of the nineteenth century fighting them off.

The Household family, together at last in 1864, settled at Magtenburg Farm in the desolate highlands some seventy miles inland from Durban. In the forbidding, tangled scrub of the Karkloof Valley, they worked hard and successfully. Especially Jack.

Tall with jet-black hair and a close-trimmed beard, the youth was to be described in later years as "a bit mad." Certainly he seems to have been withdrawn and pensive, absorbed in subjects such as astronomy, the Devil's pastime in those days. Yet he was resourceful and keenly inventive.

He mechanized ore-crushing at a gold mine, produced a complex contrivance for logging up steep slopes and engineered a water-powered saw that converted the family mill from a part-time, muscle-operated hobby to mass production of the colony's much-needed building materials. And the evidence indicated that he also dreamed up, built, and flew the first hang-glider.

According to ample testimony this took several years and some hazardous experiments. He slid off a flat-topped thorn tree on an oxhide, careened down precipitous hillsides and flapped off towering pinnacles. The inevitable injuries could scarcely go unnoticed. His father threatened to beat him senseless if he kept it up, and his Victorian mother, fearful of God's wrath and, on an earthier note, aware her son might easily break his neck, scolded him as she patched him up.

But it was no use. Committed by now, Jack swore his brother Archer, a willing collaborator, to secrecy and "went underground." His continuing cuts and bruises he blamed on falls during berry-picking and egg-hunting on surrounding granite bluffs.

As Lilienthal and others would also do, Household studied birds, and was awed by their long pauses on the winds. He shot vultures and the huge Marchall and Crown eagles (he was a trophy-winning rifle shot) and dissected and measured the remains. Eventually, he concocted a mathematical table of weight proportionate to surface, hoping to reach a wing shape and size producing buoyancy and lift. Once he had completed them, sometime in 1871, when he was in his midtwenties, he sent the calculations to Natal's Anglican bishop, John Colenso, an outstanding mathematician and considered "a bit mad" himself. Energetic and combative as well as brilliant, the bishop was a happy choice as mentor. It's recorded that he couldn't fault the maths and that, characteristically, he encouraged Household.

The materials Household used to build his glider probably were whatever he could lay his hands on. Some say he "imported silk from Switzerland and steel tubing from England," but this is unlikely. He was conducting his experiments in secret. Such exotic imports would have set the yeoman community by its ears. What's more, transported across 7,000 sea miles in the 1800s, they would have cost more than a farm boy could manage.

Rather, he seems to have conned his sister, Mary, into, as she wrote, "sewing long lengths of calico," a pioneer staple, to provide the fabric. For the framework, he tried flexible, lightweight strips of wood. Dr. J. W. Cronje, a family friend, wrote that the skeletons of the various contraptions were made of "umhlanga," a whiplike river reed, and bamboo.

The early attempts involved strap-on wings, batlike in shape and varied in size.

The first set he tried were of "enormous span" according to Dr. Cronje, and were carried to the launching site by Zulu farm laborers. His brother Archer harnessed him up and pushed him off the edge of a thirty-foot drop.

The warm updraft of air he needed wasn't there at the crucial moment, and the results were harrowing. He exploded in a fountain of dust and flying debris at the base of the cliff. One wing somehow remained intact; the other was a write-off; and a lesser man than Household would have been hospitalized for a month.

Sam Hartman, manager of the Karkloof Timber Estates when I saw him, is a believer who says the boy learned from doing.

"This lad was no fool," Hartman said. "He hurt himself jumpin' off that krantz (cliff) and the next time he took off from a riverbank no higher'n this room."

No hard evidence supports Hartman's view, but it's clear on aerial maps used to plot Household's attempts that he chose a softer landing place for the next try.

When the wing and the pilot had been repaired and the apparatus reduced in size, Jack tried a new technique. Holding the wings rigidly out at his sides, he stood on a flattened oxhide and was pulled downhill at scorching speed by the long-suffering Zulus. A strong gust of wind actually snatched him upward and threw him into an erratic glide that carried him perhaps one hundred feet. Then the wind dropped. His feet, too heavy for the tail, dragged him down, and he hit the hillside in a welter of flapping calico and snapping struts.

For the third and final try, Household had designed his first sailplane: wings arching outward at right angles from a fuselage consisting of a light wood frame and fitted with airfoils at the tail.

The local *Weekend Advertiser*, October 8, 1927, in an article recalling the Household experiments, confirms this description and adds: "To carry the passenger (sic) he constructed a seat swung on four ropes from the wing and maneuvered by tipping this seat."

On a moonlit night he pursuaded his reluctant Zulus and the faithful Archer to haul the plane to the crest of a hill not far from the darkened farmhouse. Peering out across the narrow valley, the ribbon of the river picked out in the pale, eerie light, Household could see the black-iron profile of the distant ridge. Selecting a naked patch of white as a target, he ordered the helpers to ready for takeoff.

The front of the glider frame protruded out over a humpback of earth, permitting the swing seat, pilot aboard, to hang free below it. At a prearranged signal from Household, the helpers heaved the sailplane off the hump, Jack swung forward tightening the rear ropes to lift the wings' leading edges, and he was airborne.

Conditions were ideal, and in moments, Archer wrote, he could see the plane's lacy outline as it skimmed the tops of eucalyptus trees towering above the banks of the river.

With considerable speed but not nearly enough height, Household headed for the bluff half a mile away. Struggling frantically to gain altitude, he found the thermals had deserted him once again.

Unable to obtain enough lift, he would have crashed into the stone face but for a desperate tipping of the seat to lift the wing's leading edges. This pulled him up sharply but also spilled the air from under the wing surfaces, stalled his forward progress and tumbled him backwards out of control.

The craft thrashed into the top of a yellowood tree, and Household was catapulted out of the "cockpit" through the thorny tangle of branches and into a millpond twenty feet below.

According to written evidence the flight covered approximately thirteen hundred yards at an altitude of at least two hundred feet, the first hang-glide flight in history.

Household broke a leg on the way through the yellowood, and, for his tormented mother, that did it. She extracted a promise from him that he never fly again, and he never did.

Packing the glider remains away in the loft of the family home, he remained earthbound, and on March 13, 1906, he died of malaria, aged sixty. He was buried in St. Mark's Churchyard, Shafton Grange, the village serving the Karkloof Valley.

He left no drawings, and the tables he allegedly sent to Bishop Colenso are missing. Fearing public ridicule (they called him "un-Christian") and his father's disapproval, he'd kept all the figures in his head. The old family farmhouse burned down, and the world's first hang-glider was consumed along with it.

So what of the evidence?

The story of Household's flights comes from the testimony, written and oral, of some thirty persons, five of them relatives. The facts often are contradictory, and jaded memories sometimes invent unlikely situations. Nevertheless, from all the information a credible essence emerges. Some of the "evidence" is well nigh irrefutable.

Margaret Roach (Killie) Campbell, founder of the world's largest library of South Africana (30,000 volumes, stacks of documents and pictures) was convinced the flights were made. Quoted in a letter from Dr. Cronje, she said: "Howevermuch traditional accounts of the flight may differ, the flight in the early seventies by Goodman Household in a glider constructed by himself did definitely take place."

Papers giving details of the flights molder in the William Campbell Museum, Durban, the Howell Wright Collection of South Africana at Yale University Library, New Haven, Connecticut, and at the Natal Archives depot in the provincial capital at Pietermaritzburg.

Moreover, on September 21, 1966, the Natal Branch of the South African Commission for the Preservation of National and Historic Monuments, Relics and Antiques determined to erect a plaque on the site where the Englishman took off on his last flight, with wording to read:

THE FIRST GLIDER FLIGHT IN SOUTH AFRICA

> During the period 1871 to 1873, Goodman Household, son of the farm owner, undertook two flights in a self-constructed glider from the ridge on the opposite side of the river. The most successful flight carried him about 500 yards across the Valley.

Aside from being overly cautious, the proposed inscription (the plaque has never been placed at Magtenburg Farm by a dilatory bureaucracy) hardly does Household justice. The estimate of the distance measures a beeline from monument site (actually selected and marked by the commission) to the opposite bank. In fact, Household started much higher and farther up the valley and flew, as we've seen, an erratic course. Still, the commission's formal decision to make and locate the plaque gives the flight official recognition.

Convincing evidence too is the survival of the Household exploits in the district's native folklore traditionally based on fact if often improved in the telling. One excellent example is the tale told me by an aged Zulu, Msekaan, a retainer on a farm near Shafton Grange.

By his own account he was, in the 1920s, the time of his

experience, quite a boy. He lived in Shafton Grange, he said, and had a job loading freight cars in Crammond, a town some ten miles east of his kraal. What with suffering blinding hangovers from "Barberton," a native brew spiked with wood alcohol, and his running dalliance with the indigenous belles, he was invariably late for work. For this, he said, "they beat me and took away money," adding, quite reasonably, that he didn't like this treatment and had tossed about for a remedy for his tardiness that wouldn't deny him his pleasures.

One day, he said, he was inspired by the sight of an aircraft overhead and decided to make a plane of his own, fly it down to Crammond in the morning and ship the machine back each evening on the daily logging wagon.

His contrivance, he explained, consisted of bamboo and canvas wings, a tail and three cones "opening backward to catch the wind." A complicated webbing of leather reins enabled him to flap like a bird and control the movement of the tail. As a final touch, small Zulu warshields were attached to his wrists beneath the wings to act as airfoils.

A spot was chosen at the top of a craggy ridge, near where we sat as we talked, and he was ready for takeoff.

The plan, like Household's, was to ride the thermals rising from the valley floor and use what he called the "terrible north wind" for his forward push, the thrust concentrated in the cones.

Like Household's, his first attempt proved catastrophic. Decked out in his equipment and wearing magic necklaces of leopard's teeth and strings of monkey tails, Msekaan mounted the crag, took an appropriate stance, and promptly was blown off headfirst.

He landed in a heap twenty feet down on a rocky ledge and, in a classic understatement, said he was "very sore and my eyes and mouth were filled with dirt."

His second, and final, attempt was nearly fatal. Judging both the updraft and the tailwind correctly, he soared off the ridge, but "just beyond the top of those gum trees," he said, he ran into trouble.

The competition between the thermals and the "terrible north wind" began to "twist me around," he said, and, although he "used the shields to correct one accident, the wind changed again," and he was whipped into a spin.

Flapping wildly from about sixty feet up, he plunged head down through a stand of stunted thorn trees onto a heap of brush-covered boulders near "a small dam used for watering the cattle."

If Household's falls would have hospitalized a lesser man, Msekaan's should have killed him instantly. But he admitted only that his "chest, liver, and head were painful for a long time" and that even "rubbing on Mrs. Fife's embrocation didn't help."

The similarities between Msekaan's experience and the Household flights are too obvious to be ignored. The Zulu's try might have been pieced together from native legend stemming from tales of the Household flights. Possibly it was Msekaan's very own.

Either way, it's an extraordinary distillation of all the reports of the Household attempts, those experiments that ended with what I am convinced was the first hang-glider flight deep in the moonlit African bush more than a century ago.

CHAPTER XXXVI

Twilight of an Empire

My news and feature coverage of the southern African scene underwent a bout of accelerated confusion during the nineteen sixties and early seventies. Our commuting between Marandellas and Umhlanga Rocks homes caused some of the disorder, as did a two-year stint testing Texas as a possible future home in the event the situation in Rhodesia became untenable.

The precipitate independence of, first, Mocambique in April, 1974, and then Angola in February, 1976, unbalanced the delicate political equilibrium of the area and added to the gathering concern about our future. It also placed further emphasis on my peculiar position as an American inhabiting a region where the lives of expatriates and "colonials" was becoming increasingly unstable, even dangerous. Particularly was this so since, as a "permanent resident" I'd undertaken specific commitments in my adopted country.

Almost from the time I took up residence in Southern Rhodesia in 1952 through the federal era and into the seventies, I had been a member of the British South African Police Reserve. In the early fifties, reserve membership required the civilian rankers to appear once or twice a year at a specified target range and fire government weapons, listen to desultory lectures by bored police regulars on such subjects as the "law of arrest," and drink lots of beer. Approached about membership, I thought it sounded like an attractive hobby, and I learned that if I could vault a few bureaucratic hurdles I'd be in.

My United States passport No. 185093, issued April 6, 1948, in Washington, ominously declared on its last page that "American nationality may be lost through . . . taking an oath or making a declaration of allegiance to (or) serving in military forces of . . . a foreign state." From the date of its inception as the British South Africa Company's police force in October 1889, the B.S.A.P. had been considered at least paramilitary. This would include it in my passport prohibitions. Since its duties as a fighting unit had, however, given way long before the nineteen-fifties to routine police functions along the lines of Canada's "Mounties," I decided to give it a try.

With my passport in hand I'd visited the American Consulate in Salisbury and explained my intention, as a "permanent resident" of Rhodesia, to join the reserve on the grounds that it was my duty. Protected as a resident by the laws of the country, I argued I could do no less than make myself available, on call, to assist the civil authorities.

Off the record and chuckling in a "just-between-us-boys" manner, one of the consuls, whose name conveniently escapes me, told me that there was no official U.S. objection to my joining. However, he added solemnly, that should I be injured or involved in some contretemps inimical to United States interests, I could rest assured that "this conversation has never taken place" and that I could face the consequences as outlined in the back of my passport.

Thus comforted by my parent government, I formally joined the B.S.A.P. as a reservist in Umtali in 1953. And went on beer picnics for the next four years.

This quite popular languor ended in 1957, when, then living in Marandellas, I was instructed to report to the local post, whence I would proceed to Salisbury to collect a uniform from the main police depot. There was no urgency to the order, but a new businesslike tone had crept into the normally chatty communiqués.

By now, the federation was four years old, and the earlier rampant optimism about its future had given way to glum reassessment of its chances for survival. In any event, many felt that whatever unease there was went with the territory, as it were, and was to be expected. Yet, racial barriers were coming down politically and in the professions. Socially the changes were hesitant, but they were real enough. The very fact of this fitfulness, it was argued, must lead to restless demands for "more," more quickly than the system could handle it.

There were those of us who felt that events were moving in the right direction, that we should do our best to speed up the change, and that, in the meantime, we'd just have to manage the problems as they arose. It was a carefully calculated and sanguine view. That we were in the minority became apparent later on but in the interim we were buoyed up by the ferment around us.

Part of this excitement was the revivifying of the moribund Police Reserve.

When I collected my uniform, the sergeant behind the counter took my claim documents and specifications, eyed me pityingly and heaped in front of me heavy, black, hobnailed boots, blue canvas anklets, denim trousers, a pair of gray suspenders (braces), a short (Eisenhower-type) blue-denim jacket, khaki web belt and flat British army style "tin" hat painted white with "POLICE" in blue lettering across the brow.

The hat, with an adjustable liner, was the only item that fit. I could almost turn around before the trousers moved, and the jacket hung on me like a shroud. These shortcomings Ria could remedy by boiling the uniform to shrink it and by tailoring the remains. The size-ten boots had to be returned for eights. After a week of frantic readjustments, including two-hundred miles of back-and-forthing to Salisbury, I was reasonably presentable. And just in time. The national corps of reserves was called to Salisbury in July to parade before Queen Elizabeth, the Queen Mother, on an official royal visit to the colony.

About forty of us were available from Marandellas. I was the only American. Hence, only thirty-nine of us knew what to expect. There was not a man among them who hadn't seen military service with the British forces in World War Two. Foot drill, crisply performed by the numbers as an age-old disciplinary tradition, had become second nature to them during their service, and it remained so. Not so the practice in the United States Army, which, compared to the lowliest British Commonwealth unit on parade, merely ambled along in a group. Add to this the fact that Commonwealth military commands were different from the American, and my plight is obvious. Only "To the rear, March!" was common to both.

We gathered on the Salisbury Police Grounds midday of an unusually hot July. Acres of dusty field were acrawl with thousands of men in blue, the khaki-clad regular B.S.A.P. behaving in a military manner about the edges of this civilian hoi-polloi.

As a wry and unfunny joke, a young regular officer, with the playful connivance of my colleagues, ordered me to take charge, form up the unit, and lead them in marching drill. This would accustom the men, he said, to moving together and would ready them for a smart appearance before the "Queen Mum."

How I had the gall to accept and not rather plead a sudden attack of the glanders, I do not know to this day. I managed to form three ranks, dress off the lines, face the columns to the right, and march off. The men, New Zealanders, Scots, and Australians, Irish and South Africans and native-born Rhodesians, exercising considerable imagination and improvising good humoredly, responded like good soldiers as if I really knew what I was doing.

Even my "Forward March!" fairly simple, caught them unawares. The Commonwealth command is "By the Right Flank, Quick-March!"

which does provide a preparatory hint of what's to come. After fifteen minutes of good hearted effort, my "Column Left!" instead of some more particular form of "Left Wheel!" threw them into a disorderly crowd milling aimlessly about shrieking with laughter. The regular police C.O., appearing inappropriately, took a dim view of this girlish giggling, demoted me to rear rank, and put a former Guards officer in charge.

After that, I was the sole clown in the ranks, fouling a series of otherwise-precise drill maneuvers.

I did manage to slam to attention facing the right way for the Queen Mother, who stood in a glittering Land Rover fitted with chromium handrails and eyed us with uncommon tenderness as she glided slowly past our unit.

Ria sat in the stands with hundreds of other wives, watched her husband march past, and said she was proud of him . . . which was kind of her.

The "Queen Mum's" parade had been a rare event. Our reserve activities in the months after that were to be more to the point. "Classroom" blackboard sessions, marksmanship with the latest government weapons, combat organization of squads, practice of area alert procedures, and establishing locations to "laager" women and children. And riot drill with tear gas.

Our riot kit, in those early days, consisted of regular uniform with tin hat, gas mask, wicker shield and a three-foot-six-inch hardwood baton, a nasty weapon close in. We were taught stabbing and striking techniques with this club and practiced attacks on riotous mobs by moving in line across an open space holding up our shields and flailing at imaginary hoodlums. Our expected adversaries were presumed to be armed with bottles, rocks, and half-bricks. Tear-gas bombs were tossed indiscriminately into our midst by sadistic police instructors.

I quickly discovered that, as in the '39/'45 War, my readiness for sudden gas attack was faulty. My regular spectacles wouldn't fit inside the mask, and I carried a special steel-rimmed pair in a breastpocket case. When the shout "Gas!" chilled us all, I had to halt, drop my shield, put my club between my knees where I could get at it, remove my horn-rimmed glasses, replace them with the steel-rimmed pair, put my everyday ones into the case, and return it to my pocket. Only then could I rip out my mask and fit it on.

By that time I had invariably trapped my own private supply of benzyl bromide inside the face piece. The mask did keep out the clouds of gas in the area, but, small as my own special supply had been, it had me gagging and weeping copiously. This interfered with my vision as first cause, but even when, by some miracle of dexterity, I managed to mask up before the gas arrived, I could see through my glasses only dimly. The authorized clip-in frames I'd been provided during the war had rarely positioned the lenses in front of my eyeballs, it is true, but this Rhodesian extra-small set I used as a police reservist was a cruel joke. The tight rubber mask squeezed the temples against my head so firmly that the glasses were lifted off my nose and forward into the eyepieces. Nothing I could prearrange would alter it. I almost had to follow my glasses wherever they showed the way, regardless of where the action was outside in the real world.

As it was, unsuspecting, I repeatedly walked into someone's swinging baton with excruciating results or fell blindly into holes where the stinging mist had settled, suffering burns through my wide-open sweat glands. Indeed, I might well have staggered, alone, my baton flashing, off into the silent and empty bush but for the compassion of my sighted compatriots.

Over the next few years, these contortions, as is normally the case with military training everywhere, produced in us orderly and automatic reflexes, a subtle sense of joint purpose and an espirit de corps. We were scarcely a "crack" outfit, but we had acquired some common skills. And not too soon.

A national referendum on a new constitution for Southern Rhodesia was scheduled for late July, 1962. When it was over I filed the following story on its worrisome aspects with the *Indianapolis News*:

Marandellas, Southern Rhodesia (by airmail). "If I come to work on Monday," the old man said, "they say they will cut off my hands."

"We will work, but you must take us around the town, not through it," was the word from laborers on road construction.

"There may not be trouble, but if there is I will send my children to your house," the African builder said, "and I thank you."

There was no trouble. The old cook came to work and left and kept his hands. The road gangs went unmolested, and the builder did not bring his children to my house. Yet the threats had been real enough, and there'd been cause for worry.

For months this country has suffered bitter controversy over proposals drawn up by Britain and the Southern Rhodesian government for a new constitution. A national referendum to decide the issue had been scheduled for July 26.

The proposals would give some 3 million Africans the first

direct parliamentary representation in the country's history: fifteen seats in a new sixty-five-member house. It would provide for a declaration of rights and a constitutional council to watchdog it. It was a forward step for the African.

African nationalists didn't agree. They claimed it denied them one-man one-vote and continued, even entrenched, "white supremacy," and they were against it.

Also against it was the right-wing, white Dominion Party, which labelled it a "sellout" to African extremism and charged it raised the issue of integration of the black and white schools and would massively lower standards.

Hence, these two parties were on the "no" camp for rather different reasons.

Then the African National Democratic Party announced that its own referendum would be held three days before the official ballot, and it called for general protest strikes. The referendum and the strikes are illegal.

A few days before the African vote 17,000 European and African police reservists and half as many regulars blanketed the country with foot and Jeep patrols. Army units stood by.

The "illegal" referendum was held. By African party count there were 370,000 "nays" and 471 "yeas." Violence exploded in one suburb during that day; one African was shot dead. A handful were arrested. Elsewhere it was quiet.

The "secret" referendum ballot had been a joke. Intimidation by party thugs at the filmy grass polling "booths," multiple voting by party members, and widespread ignorance of what the vote was all about nullified its usefulness as a test of sentiment.

The strike call failed as 90 percent of the labor force turned up for work. The African leaders cried "Police State," charging that there was employer intimidation. Its leader, Joshua Nkomo, who had at first approved the new proposals and then repudiated them, flew off to London with the referendum "proof" of African rejection of the new constitution.

Of the 63,000 Europeans voting, the "yes" ballots were double the number of the "nos," and the new constitution is scheduled to go into effect next year sometime.

The police reserve units faded back into the scenery and a calm, of sorts, returned. For now.

I had participated as a reservist in this call-up, and, although the grim report I sent the *News* certainly portrayed the countrywide situation, the local reserve action was scarcely ominous, as a WILZ radio script I did sometime after the event suggests:

> Police brutality is a charge levied at almost any police unit that manages to maintain a modicum of order in a riot.
>
> In Rhodesia this charge has been heard a great deal, although the British South Africa Police had not fired a shot in anger for more than sixty years as a national police force until this year, an incredible record for police anywhere.
>
> Still, let me describe to you just how this alleged brutalizing of the African natives by the white cops works out in practice.

I explained the referendum troubles as set out in my story to the *News*, noting that, since trouble had been expected between rival groups of African nationalists, we police reservists would be called up.

> I was in a country district outfit, a field unit; got my orders at dawn one day and piled into a truck along with half a dozen others. Our job was to patrol a "voting booth" in a bush location called the Soshwe Native Reserve, not unlike an American Indian reservation.
>
> Armed with wooden batons, assorted personal firearms, government-issue World War One Enfield rifles and suited up to the nines in blue denim, we must have been an imposing, if not threatening, group.
>
> No doubt we were also quite capable of sickening brutality.
>
> On the way we stopped several times to go through what was called a "de-bussing drill." Practiced on training days, this exercise is to insure that, if we had to act in a trouble spot, we got out of the vehicle in good order. We might otherwise have fallen out of the back all at once in a welter of flying picnic baskets, army blankets, and assorted personal effects to end up a tangled heap on the ground.
>
> I personally was convinced such a clownish performance would touch the African's combustible sense of humor and break up a riot much more effectively than a baton charge. Unfortunately, police brass didn't agree. So we practiced.
>
> There was a lot of nervous laughter among squad members as we approached the reserve entrance, a break in the cattle fencing, and we lapsed into a tense silence near the polling booth.
>
> It seemed a peaceful setting for an event that had been billed as a show of fervent anti-white feeling. The "booth," an oblong,

roofless, grass hut with openings at either end, stood in the center of a shallow vale surrounded by craggy kopjes. The winter "burn" had converted the fertile surroundings into a barren heath dotted with thorn bush and Mopani tree. There was a natural hush about the place, and clumps of voters sat in the hot sun muttering softly together, although one did cry out "Halo! Boss Ackison" as we rolled past.

Our job was simply to maintain order. Yet, as any television viewer knows, keeping order can be rough and tumble, and we were uneasy. Obviously, we would know many of these people, and the last thing we wanted was to hurt anyone. As it turned out, we needn't have worried.

After an hour of watching what was more a social occasion than a political demonstration, some of us left our weapons in the truck and wandered over to the "booth." I went inside, where there were two metal boxes on a table, a slot in the top of each into which the ballot went. The red box was a "no" vote against the constitutional proposals; the blue box was a "yes." While I stood there, four Africans I knew voted "no" three times each, going out and reentering in a solemn parody of correct procedure. But they were very orderly, and that was my sole concern.

By midday, things were palling a bit, and some of us went to sleep in the Land Rover. Others stood around the hand-clapping songfest developing under a large, spreading Msasa tree, occasionally accepting a drink of the thick, gray Chibuku native beer from the cartons passed round the circle.

We went home when darkness fell. Behind us the singing, although "howling" would be more like it, carried on far into the night.

Meanwhile in one big town there'd been rioting; an African was killed.

In the country districts, where most of the natives lived, the police reserve presence, brutality held in check, had been enough to maintain the peace.

By the time the late sixties arrived, this happy state would have become a memory, and bitter hatreds would take over.

Nkomo, considered by the whites an irresponsible and essentially insignificant black politician, became leader of a newly formed party, the Zimbabwe African People's Union (ZAPU). After a Rhodesian rightist white government unilaterally declared its independence from Britain in November, 1965, Nkomo would take his followers north to Zambia, where, as terrorists forces, they would be equipped and trained by the Russians, many blacks being sent to Moscow for indoctrination.

The dirty terror war that was to make Kenya's Mau Mau horrors of the fifties seem like a neighborhood "rumble," would spread. The reservists in my old field unit would join regular police and army units and go into a vicious bush combat from which too many failed to return.

Meanwhile, the July, 1962, referendum had passed, but the discontent it had revealed broke through the surface calm repeatedly during August and September. Finally the essentially "liberal" government of Sir Edgar Whitehead reluctantly took action. The story I wrote about the reserve went like this:

> *Salisbury, Southern Rhodesia (by airmail).* More than 25,000 civilian police reservists were among security forces recently mobilized following a month-long wave of arson and sabotage throughout this troubled colony.
>
> The butcher, the baker, and the banker took common cause with others from the factories and farms, blacks and whites. Into navy-blue denim uniform and out on patrol went 20,000 whites and 5,000 Africans in the largest "home guard" action in the country's history. With them were regular police, army and territorial (reserve) army units, the air force and air force reservists.
>
> The move was made simultaneous with the outlawing of Joshua Nkomo's Zimbabwe African People's Union, charged by the government with responsibility for the violence. In the first three days 800 persons were caught in the dragnet thrown over 150,000 square miles of farming, mining, and cattle country.
>
> It came as no surprise. Security laws were tightened last month. A business recession, blamed on political unrest fanned by running condemnation from the United Nations in New York and from Pan African movements, had turned the ruling whites edgy.
>
> The Africans, outnumbering the whites 11 to 1, increasingly vocal about real and imagined grievances, had fired up to a boil of revolt. There have been a rash of "Molotov cocktail" attacks on homes, African and European, the stoning of vehicles, and intimidation involving at least one African murder.
>
> The police reservists, probably the toughest and best organized civilian security body anywhere, snapped into action within two hours of the midnight banning of ZAPU and arrest of its leader.
>
> It is claimed by African nationalists and white "liberals" that the police reserve is a "stormtrooper" organization of "white su-

premacists." This is hysterical rhetoric, but there is no question that the reserve, trained by regular police officers tested in Kenya's Mau Mau outbreak, employs techniques tried in terror. I went along as a reservist on the latest action.

The farmhouse living room where we gathered was too small for the fifteen blue-uniformed men. They sat on the floor or stood in groups. Some of their wives, faces swollen with sleep, hair tousled and wearing dressing gowns, served coffee. Small children, brought along when the alert was sounded, slept in adjoining rooms. Scattered about the room were bandoleers of ammunition and armaments ranging from .22 rifles to elephant guns.

The section leader, Ray Pratt, a thin, wiry cockney farmer, told us ZAPU had been banned and then assigned patrol duties. Collecting arms and canteens of coffee, we moved off in three groups of five men each and in radio-equipped Land Rovers fanned out over the dusty roads. Banning notices were nailed up on African shops, at bus stops, and wherever Africans or Europeans gathered. We set up gasoline-drum roadblocks; cars were stopped, papers checked, Africans found with ZAPU membership cards were held for routine questioning by the regular police. African reservists helped with interrogations at the roadblock.

As days and long nights wore on, reservists grew tired and worried about how their wives were coping in the shop or managing on the farm. Most of us worried about "what next?"

Sir Edgar had deplored the need for the ZAPU banning, had declared it was "scarcely an answer" in attempts to manage the spinoffs of mounting African aspirations.

How often he'd have to push the button calling out the home guard was a question nagging reservists. Certainly the police action had restored order. For now.

But "what next?"

CHAPTER XXXVII

Bloody Ending

From that time on Rhodesia's race relations grew steadily worse. The pervasive uneasiness created a poor climate for the economy and the country slid into recession. The *Marandellas News* was doomed. Advertisers pulled out, and the paper's board of directors could do no more than stand by and watch it die on the vine in 1962.

I lowered the masthead from our storefront window opposite the post office but kept my own nameplate on the front door and converted the premises to my private office. I'd also clung, as if my professional life depended on it, which it did, to the services of Lilian Close, a frail, white-haired secretary extraordinary.

For eight years in four different Marandellas offices, two of them grotesque substitutes for chambers, Mrs. Arthur Close and I battled with the problems of the *News*, with Achilles Construction Company, with a medley of Marandellas duties from the parent-teachers association and the coordinating committee (to coordinate all other local committees into one, great, big, impossible conglomerate) to the Players Guild and the International Horse Show, to say nothing of my own American affairs made more complicated than ever by being conducted over a distance of 8,000 miles and three weeks postal turnaround. We also had the WILZ program deadlines to meet, my news work for the *Indianapolis News* and the *Philadelphia Bulletin* and as many others as we could interest (the *New York Herald-Tribune*, the *Christian Science Monitor,* and the *Tucson Daily Citizen*, breathtaking catholicity) I also tried marketing my shark and other stories to any magazine we thought might be receptive.

One success I had with Scotland's prestigious *Blackwoods Magazine* was not really my own but Mrs. Close's. Her faith in my talents were boundless. After receiving a torrent of exhortations by post from Mrs. Close (we ever remained "Mr." and "Mrs.") the magazine accepted a story I'd done about my West Africa and Congo trips titled "Elephants I Have Known."

I never knew her age, only that she was born rather a long time ago in Graaf Reinet, a small town in South Africa's Karroo region, and that she treasured the memory of her birthplace all her life. I suppose she was in her fifties in 1962, and she was so wispy of body she'd have wafted away in a stiff breeze.

Strength of will was matched by her sense of the honorable, in turn matched for quality by her sense of humor, never brought low. She played the piano beautifully and the church organ passably, was a gourmet cook, and loved The Arts with the intensity of the deeply talented. She wept as readily as she laughed, and life for her was full to overflowing.

Mrs. Close died in a Salisbury hospital in December 1978, a few months after the death of her husband, Arthur, who was ninety-seven years old. I don't know to this day the cause of her death. I had been back in the States two years by then, the terrorist war was tearing the heart out of "her" Rhodesia, and, of course, Arthur was gone. I suspect Mrs. Close died because she decided it was time.

Back in 1962, however, she'd led her life, and a good part of mine, with vigor and wit and uncommon good sense. A paragon of a woman. Only once did her foresight fail us, and even then we were able to capitalize on the frightening results.

She'd urged me to take time off after the death of the *News* and other personally felt debacles and go on a fishing trip into the wilds of Mocambique. And I'd agreed.

Max Weber, the builder who'd refurbished our shoebox-shaped Marandellas house, and Bill Hayne, quantity surveyor in the construction trade, had initially invited me to accompany them deep into Portuguese East Africa along the jungle reaches of the Pungwe River. They could get official licenses, they said, to shoot one elephant, several buffalo, and one leopard along with a variety of small buck. I'd refused point blank on the perfectly reasonable grounds that, half-blind as I am, with a heavy-caliber rifle, I'd be more of a menace to the hunters than to the hunted.

As my luck would have it, they were in a compromising mood and instantly agreed to downgrade the adventure to a fishing trip, a casual safari, they said, a three-day picnic on the banks of a peaceful stream. Since I couldn't argue successfully I might kill someone with a fishing rod, I was trapped, and, with Mrs. Close pushing as Max and Bill pulled, I had no choice.

I am not terribly keen on camping out. I've done a fair amount of it in a score of countries, but I have never gotten used to bugs and dirt and things that roar and shriek in the night. Yet I knew Max and Bill were good at this sort of thing, and it did promise to be better than an average outing. It certainly proved to be different.

We loaded an old pickup truck with gear, food, and two African experts, George and Tickey. They'd cared for Max for years and would do the donkey work and show us how to fish. After a bone-shattering two hundred fifty miles, we rattled to a halt at dusk beneath a huge spreading acacia about a hundred feet from the Pungwe.

At this point the river was deep but boiled over hidden boulders, the main, black body of the stream coiling past like some great python just beyond the quiet pools that edged the sandy banks. Thick groves of reeds flanked the beach, and downstream, where the old track we'd taken stopped at the river's edge, were the remains of an aged wooden bridge, now only a sagging wreckage that reached halfway to the opposite bank some sixty feet away.

With George and Tickey in charge, we settled in quickly. The moon was soon high, hidden now and then by lazy clouds. A crackling fire quickly dispelled the chill and with tents up and whisky flowing we lounged blissfully on sleeping bags dragged near to the flames, the waters thundering through the darkness behind us.

We slept inside the tents, securely zipped up against most of the bugs and the hyenas, and at an early hour Max referred to as "sparrow fart" they were off to the river with fishing gear, Tickey with them.

They caught a few bream, and Max hooked, and lost, a ferocious, fanged tiger fish, but for the most part the three of them spent the day nodding over the rods. I wandered the bush, taking arty pictures of some old stone ruins or shamelessly napped in camp.

That night, in the sickly moonlight oozing intermittently through the clouds, Max and Tickey settled in near the reeds near one end of the beach for another try. Bill and I lay on our backs near the fire and listened to the African night, a cacaphony of shrieks and whistles and barking noises muffled in the hum of a million insects. Balm for the soul.

And then, just as the moon slid behind a cloud, there was a blood-curdling scream from the beach. Bill and I, reasonably familiar by now with the terrain, stumbled through the blackness and started down the slope to the sand just as the moon came out again. There was no sign of Max or Tickey, but the beach wasn't empty.

Lumbering along not ten feet away across our line of march was a huge crocodile. I recall dimly that it swung toward us, opened its cavernous maw with a revolting sucking and hissing sound, and, for some reason, started doing pushups. Bill skidded hard left abaft the beast's tail and was gone from the picture. As for me I had no place to go but up. And that's where I went in a classic leap.

I hit the beach on the offside of the croc still running and, unable to do anything else, surfed out into the stream. As I came up gasping, now neck deep in the beast's natural habitat, I saw the thing glide swiftly toward the water's edge.

My endurance as a swimmer is limited, but I can almost leave the water in short sprints. And a short sprint might get me to the old bridge. I had the current with me. So did the croc but he wouldn't need it as much as I would. The water was deep and black and narrowed to a fast moving, coiling flow between the sandbank and a wall of weeds and scattered boulders. The old planking leaned down into this, backing it into an eddy about thirty feet away.

My first few, panic strokes did, literally, lift me forward on the surface, but, as I settled in again, the bridge only a few strokes away, I could feel the water thicken around my legs as the thing surged forward through the depths. Expecting momentarily to feel the crunching pressure of those scabrous teeth, I threw myself over the eddying bow wave and thrashed up on the old planking, totally indifferent to splinters, nails, and other old iron.

As I rolled up the timbers from the water, the croc heaved itself up on the platform not five feet behind me, the rotten reek of its breath clotting the air around us, its front claws scrabbling for purchase on the slippery boarding. It would have kept coming, too, had the old beams not collapsed under its great weight.

Bill was there and, lifting me up under the arms, dragged my quivering remains to the shore. Back in camp, as he bathed my wounds in whisky and pulled mahogany splinters out of my chest and shoulders, Max and Tickey appeared. Out of breath and covered with mud, they told us their story.

He and Tickey, Max said, had been dozing in the warmth on the edge of the stream, their bobbins rocking on the ripples not far from shore, when Tickey "did the screaming Diva bit and ran right up my frame and off up the beach."

Max said he could smell the stink of the croc and clambered to his feet just as the reeds to his left suddenly flattened. After that, he remembered only that he was halfway up the bank before he realized he was moving at all. By the time they'd headed back for the beach, Bill was pulling me off the bridge.

We stacked wood on the fire, drank a lot of whisky and, after much unseemly laughter at my expense and endless rehash of the incident, fell into a drugged sleep with George on watch.

The next day, Max, determined to "blow its bloody brains out," took his .303 and prowled the riverbank and adjacent swamp. Tickey and I warily beat the rushes for the reptile, but we had no luck, and that evening we left for home.

Mrs. Close went rigid when I told her the story and stayed partially paralyzed for several days, confident she'd been responsible for nearly sending me to my death. Still, she wasn't above suggesting we capitalize on it and we ground out a radio script and a story or two on the subject. Ever the "pro," Mrs. Close.

The Pungwe trip was the last outdoor expedition I undertook in Africa. There were other opportunities, all of which I was able to avoid without prejudice. Anyway, when terrorism in Rhodesia became a nationwide vogue, "le Camping" was restricted to troops in the field. Crocodiles, for them, were a minor problem.

Unlike my work during the Palestinian terrorist conflict, my reporting in Rhodesia was, of necessity, cursory. In and around Jerusalem it had been possible to do a story about any battle taking place if one could just get there without bleeding too much. In Rhodesia security was so tight that newsmen were kept away from the action except on rare occasions. I never had that luck.

Occasionally we were shepherded about in groups to "protected villages" guarded by government forces against hit-and-run terrorist raids; were permitted to observe "body counts" and the instruction in antiterrorist tactics given rural tribesmen by Rhodesian troops. Other times we attended military briefings in Salisbury or outlying headquarters. Otherwise we were treated as an affliction by Prime Minister Smith at formal press conferences, seldom held.

Hence, I left the "fighting front" to the wire services and concentrated on stories most of which featured the steady disintegration of recognizable daily life. Even this type of reporting in country districts soon became impossible for me.

As an American citizen I could visit Rhodesia professionally or "on holiday" but was not allowed to continue living there on pain of losing my United States passport. This prescription had been laid down by presidential executive order in 1968 and could be conveniently ignored only so long as terrorist activity was sporadic and without serious effect.

By the early seventies, however, this was no longer the case. The country was on a war footing. A clampdown by the U.S. Consulate General in Johannesburg was expected momentarily. The Salisbury office had been closed.

As a result, my privileges as a "permanent resident" with easy access to newsworthy areas of the country unknown to, or forbidden, the visiting newsmen fell away. What's more if my family was to continue living in our Marandellas home, I'd have to leave the country and accept the role as a member of the "foreign press" corps.

Therefore, when we returned as a family from a Stateside stay in

1974, I went to an address in Johannesburg, and Ria and daughter Delite, then age seventeen, went back to Strafford. I set up my "office" in Johannesburg's Union Club building and established my South African "home" with Len and Jean Fisher in the city's Savoy Estates. From there I regularly made the 1,200-mile round trip by road to Rhodesia.

Once there I stayed in Marandellas but used the Salisbury Club on the town's Cecil Square as my official address. All my mail left from and arrived there. Most galling was the long, dreary drive to my Johannesburg "bureau," usually alone, every four weeks.

This state of affairs, added to an escalating war, did eventually pall, and I began to consider emigration from Rhodesia.

As a family in a "war zone" we were luckier than most. My son, Graham, had long since completed his stint in the Rhodesian Army Independent Companies and had married and settled in South Africa. Indeed, he insists the only frightening incidents during his service were a disciplining for cutting his hair in a "Mohawk ridge" and being treed for three hours by a rhinoceros. Two daughters were in the United States, Susan in college and Jacqueline married to a Texan. Delite left the farm and was concluding her horsemastership schooling in the relative safety of Salisbury's Ascot Equitation Centre.

The last years on the farm increasingly were conditioned by the terrorism around us. And although the overseas press preferred the less emotive term "guerrilla," for us and those around us—black and white—it was "terrorism," plain as a pike staff.

I used the term in my stories and, to their credit, my editors never once altered it to the more palatable, if incorrect term. The words are not interchangeable, and only the one applied in Rhodesia.

Webster's New World Dictionary defines a "guerrilla" as "any member of a small defensive force of irregular soldiers, usually volunteers, making surprise raids, especially behind the lines of an invading enemy army."

"Terrorism," *Webster's* defines as the "use of force or threats to demoralize, intimidate and subjugate, especially such use as a political weapon or policy."

It wasn't a difficult distinction to make.

It was terrorists who, ambushing a white farmer walking to his tobacco barns not far from where we lived, shot him repeatedly in the stomach, gathered his laborers to watch and methodically broke the bones in his arms and legs and, the man still alive, stripped him and mutilated him in the classic manner, warning the terrified workers that his was what they could expect if they continued to work for "the white man."

It was terrorists who chopped off the lips and cheeks of an African

Headman they considered a government employee and made his wife cook and eat the flesh. Not guerrillas.

Sensing that the end of the best years of our lives was nearing, in December, 1975, Ria called the family together from wherever they were, as far away as Houston and Dallas. Including Graham's children, there were ten of us altogether. John, Donald and Jeffrey were unable to join us. At least for the "immediate" family, it was a happy Christmas and the last we would have together in the home where we'd grown up.

Within three months of the children's departure we'd started carrying a gun in the car, disciplining ourselves to be in before dark, accepting that trips by motorcar between towns had to be made in armed convoy. The pressures of these and other requirements made up our minds for us.

In March we determined to leave, and on the sixth of August, 1976, having packed and shipped a houseful of belongings and twenty years of memories, we flew out of Salisbury's Kentucky Airport for the last time.

Behind us, the Rhodesians, black and white, anguished and unbelieving, staggered bloody and battered out of the remains of the Colonial Era.

Epilogue

In the mid–nineteen-eighties, not many American newspapers can boast of "our man in Cairo" . . . or Johannesburg, Oslo, or wherever. From well over two thousand foreign correspondents post World War Two, the number of reporters on overseas duty has dropped to perhaps four-hundred.

And, because television coverage whips the cream off "hot" news stories, these few seldom enjoy the jousting for "exclusives" that once enlivened that foreign beat.

Electronic innovation and mounting costs have wrought the change. Indeed, the print journalism that hosted the likes of me is doomed.

And the storied era of the "foreign correspondent" is dying along with it.

Index

Acheson, Dr. Edward Goodrich, 32
Acheson, Jeffrey Duncan, 274
Acheson, John Huyler, 32, 43, 99
Acheson, Maria Magdelena ("Ria"), 274
Adai, George Kwasi, 241
Adams, Rex, 252
Amin, Idi, 158
Anotchi, 184
Arafat, Yasir, 52, 53
Armattoe, Dr. R. E. G., 186, 188
Ashanti, 186

Balafredj, Ahmed, 199–200, 212
Ball, George, 216
Banda, Dr. Hastings Kumuzu, 201, 203–205, 207–212, 231
Bargasch, Ali, 197–198
Basmadjian, Tony, 161
Begin, Menachem, 28, 100–101
Ben-Gurion, 100–101
Benchley, Peter, 265
Bernadotte, Count Folke, 100–102
Berry, Aubrey, 214
Best, George, 268
Bey, Fawzi, 51
Bilbey, Ken, 39, 49, 51, 66
Blackwell, Ted, 213
Botha, Gabriel, 267–270
Boyd, Max, 11, 13, 16, 21, 23–25, 32, 71
Boynton, Jim, 301
Buchwald, Art, 109
Burns, George J., 59
Butler, R. A., 277

Calder, Jock, 39–40, 54–55

Campbell, Margaret Roach, 326
Cassidy, Morley, 70, 103, 105, 136–137, 140, 142, 144, 146
Cassidy, Phyllis, 103, 105, 140
Ceuesnon, Jacques, 189–191, 195–196
Chamburs, Pat, 301
Chanute, Gustave, 322
Chisimongana, 179, 181
Chisulu, Galahad, 222
Close, Lilian, 339–340, 343
Colenso, John, 323, 325
Constantos, Connie, 124–125
Cook, Neville, 266
Cooper, 161–162
Courvoisier, Jean, 48
Crafton, Richard, 218
Craig-Barr, Tony, 285, 294
Cronje, Dr. J. W., 324
Cunningham, Lt. Gen. Sir Alan, 61

da Vinci, Leonardo, 321
Danso, 185
Davidson, Carter, 19, 31–32, 38–41, 43, 45, 47, 49–51, 60, 96
Davis, Richard Harding, 274
Davison, Arthur "Ginger," 167–169, 175
de Wendover, Roger, 218
Devonshire, Duke of, 74
Dinner, 281
Dokman, Amer Ben Said Ben, 81
Dunn, Norma Roslynn, 274
Durant, Ariel, 232
Durant, Will, 232
Durdin, Brian, 316–317

Edward VII (King), 188
Elizabeth II (Queen), 76, 331
Ella, T. W., 245
Ellerie, Nora, 71–72
Emmett, Joanna Pearson, 231

Farouk, King, 14, 17
Fassi, Allal El, 197
Ferguson, Harry, 74
Field, Hon. Winston Joseph, 214, 277, 295
Fisher, Jean, 274, 344
Fisher, Len, 344
Fitzsimmons, 66
Fitzwilliam, Earl, 76
Fowle, Farnie, 39
Fox, Henry Clay, Jr., 33
Francombe, Reg, 111, 113, 115–117, 119–120

Gannon, Thomas J., 59
George V (King), 76
George, Sandys, 253–254
Girard, Paul, 81
Godiva, Lady, 217–218
Gossett, Carl, 39–40, 48, 54
Graciano, 281
Guthrie, Wayne, 69–71

Hanika, Bob, 69
Hartman, Sam, 324
Hassan II, 200
Hawkins, Hon. Roger Tancred, 214
Hayne, Bill, 340–342
Hecox, Bob, 39–40, 42–44, 66
Henriques, Carlos Abel, 114
Herzl, Theodor, 27
Hill, Herb, 3
Hill, John, 311–314
Hodgson, Sir Frederick, 185
Hollingworth, Clare, 64, 66, 103
Household, John Goodman, 322–323, 325–328
Huyler, John, 33
Huyler, John II, 34, 273

Jameson, Donald, 1, 273
Jameson, Patricia, 33, 273
John, William, 322
Johnson, Louise, 268
Jones, Francis Emilius Fletcher, 176

Jones, Sir Glyn, 205
Juin, Gen. Alphonse, 196, 199
Jurst, Gunther, 307

Keene, Bill, 286
Keene, Joan, 286
Kenyatta, 29
Khama, Sir Seretse, 212, 263

Labonne, Erik, 196, 199
Lenshina, Alice, 222
Lide, Jimmy, 59
Lilienthal, Otto, 322–323
Littlewood, Lothian Alfred, 160–162, 168
Lyautey, Marshal L. H. G., 196

Machel, Samora, 121
MacKenzie, Leslie, 302
Mackey, Charles W., 301
MacMillan, Harold, 216
MacMillan, Kirkpatrick, 73
Maher, Margaret, 32
Mandezera, Paul, 236–237, 288
Martin, Bob (Pepper), 39–40, 61–62, 66
McCarty, Mickey, 1
McClure, Jim, 39
McCombe, Dave, 255–258
Meikle Family, 165, 167, 176
Meikle, Tom, 169
Mencken, H. L., 229
Mercia, Earl of, 218
Middleton, Drew, 103
Miller, Glenn, 14
Mohammed V, 196
Morkle, John, 290–291
Murchison, William, 157
Muzorewa, Bishop, 158

Nannette, Delite Cornelia, 32, 33
Nasser, Gamal Abdul, 17
Nkomo, Joshua, 334, 336
Nkrumah, Kwame, 29, 201–203
Noderer, Al, 39–40, 96, 107–109
Norris, Phil, 282

Pasha, Nashas, 15
Passaportis, Paul, 91–92
Pentzopoulos, Brig. Gen. Thos., 146
Petrikios, 282
Phillip II (King of France), 232

Phillippi, Wendell, 71
Pittock, George, 228–229
Pratt, Ray, 338
Prempeh, King Osai Agyemon II, 187–188
Pringle, Jim, 19, 21, 23–24, 31–32, 38–40, 42–44, 49, 52
Pulitzer, Joseph, 274
Pulliam, Eugene S., Jr., 71
Putnam, Patrick, 171–172, 258–261

Rattray, Don, 293
Renders, Adam, 113
Reynolds, Christopher, 251
Richard I (King), 232
Rodolo, Ramadan, 226
Rukavina, Kathleen Stevens, 176

Saad, Zaki, 14–16
Sagesse, 150–152
Sargent, John Singer, 75
Scherschel, Frank, 40, 103–104, 106–109, 111, 135
Schmidt, Dana Adams, 39, 47
Schofield, Anna, 129
Schofield, Ivor, 129
Schweitzer, Dr. Albert, 209–210
Scott, Sir Francis, 185
Seniagya, 185
Serrot, Col. Andre Pierre, 102
Seymour, Bert, 175
Shakespeare, 309
Sharpe, 178
Sherif, 150
Shtabow, Cephas, 233–234, 236
Smith, Ian, 158, 212
Smith, Prime Minister, 343
Smuts, Jan, 176

South, Bill, 301
Spencer, Eric, 76
Sperry, Gordon Taylor, 72
Stephenson, John Edward (Chirupula), 167, 169, 175–176, 178–180, 188
Stern, Isaac, 28
Stevenson, Adlai, 296

Tawengwa, George, 213–216
Taylor, Peter, 287–288
Thompson, 178
Thyne, Marilyn, 316–317
Tickey, 341–342
Truman, Harry S., 58
Tucker, Dick, 71
Tutu, Osai, 184

Underwood, Don, 71

vanBerg, Brian, 264–266
Victoria (Queen), 76
von Sauerbronn, Baron Drais, 73
Vorster, Balthazar Johannes, 212

Walker, Herbert N., 57–58
Wasson, Thomas, 12, 58–61
Weber, Max, 280, 340–342
Welensky, Sir Roy, 212, 277–278
Went, Harry, 309–310
Wentzel, 167
White, Theodore H., 29
Whitehead, Sir Edgar, 212, 337
Wiley, Dan, 288–289
Wiley, Muriel, 288–289
Woolley, Cornell, 33

Yogo, 185

PN 4874 .A26 A37 1984